Beyond Cyberpunk

Routledge Studies in Contemporary Literature

Beyond Cyberpunk

New Critical Perspectives

**Edited by
Graham J. Murphy and Sherryl Vint**

Routledge
Taylor & Francis Group

NEW YORK AND LONDON

First published 2010
by Routledge
270 Madison Avenue, New York, NY 10016

Simultaneously published in the UK
by Routledge
2 Park Square, Milton Park, Abingdon, Oxon OX14 4RN

*Routledge is an imprint of the Taylor & Francis Group, an informa
business*

© 2010 Taylor & Francis

Typeset in Sabon by Taylor & Francis Books

Library of Congress Cataloging-in-Publication Data
Beyond cyberpunk : new critical perspectives / edited by Graham
J. Murphy and Sherryl Vint.
 p. cm. – (Routledge studies in contemporary literature ; 3)
Includes bibliographical references and index.
1. Science fiction–History and criticism. 2. Cyberpunk culture.
3. Technology in literature. 4. Postmodernism (Literature) 5. Literature
and technology. I. Murphy, Graham J., 1970- II. Vint, Sherryl, 1969–
PN3433.6.B49 2010
809.3'8762–dc22
                    2009045559

ISBN10: 0-415-87687-7 (hbk)
ISBN10: 0-203-85196-X (ebk)

ISBN13: 978-0-415-87687-2 (hbk)
ISBN13: 978-0-203-85196-8 (ebk)

For Douglas Barbour, our supervisor, mentor, and friend

Contents

Acknowledgments

The editors would like to thank Trent University's Office of Research and CUPE Local 3908–1 for their financial assistance on this project.

Permission to quote from or reprint the following material is gratefully acknowledged:

Altered Carbon by Richard Morgan. Copyright© 2002 by Victor Gollancz, an imprint of The Orion Publishing Group, London. (UK)

Altered Carbon by Richard K. Morgan, copyright© 2002 by Richard Morgan. Used by permission of Del Rey Books, a division of Random House, Inc. (US)

Dialectic of Enlightenment by Max Horkheimer and Theodor Adorono. Copyright© 1944 by Stanford University Press. Quotations in excess of Fair Use reproduced by kind permission of Stanford University Press.

"Feminist Cyberpunk" from *Science Fiction Studies* 22.3 (November 1995): 357–72. Copyright© 1995 by *Science Fiction Studies*. Reproduced by kind permission of the author and *Science Fiction Studies*.

"Global Economy, Local Texts: Utopian/Dystopian Tension in William Gibson's Cyberpunk Trilogy" from *The Minnesota Review* 43/44 (1995): 182–97· Copyright© 1995 by Tom Moylan. Reproduced by kind permission of Tom Moylan.

Red Spider, White Web by Misha. Copyright© 1999 by Misha. Quotations in excess of Fair Use reproduced by kind permission of Misha Noghe.

Escape Plans by Gwyneth Jones. Copyright© 1986 by Gwyneth Jones. Quotations in excess of Fair Use reproduced by kind permission of Gwyneth Jones.

Signs of Life by M. John Harrison. Copyright© 1998 by Victor Gollancz, an imprint of The Orion Publishing Group, London (UK) and Mic Cheetham Agency (US). Quotations in excess of Fair Use reproduced by kind permission of the author, Orion Publishing Group, and Mic Cheetham Agency.

"Towards a poetics of cyberpunk" from *Constructing Postmodernism* by Brian McHale. Copyright© 1992 by Routledge. Reproduced by kind permission of the author and Taylor & Francis Books UK.

Introduction

The Sea Change(s) of Cyberpunk

Graham J. Murphy and Sherryl Vint

Literary cyberpunk has had a tumultuous, conflicted, at times contradictory history. Scholars and fans acknowledge its birth in the fictions of, chiefly, William Gibson and Bruce Sterling, only to carbon-date cyberpunk's origins in such predecessors as J. G. Ballard, James Tiptree, Jr., Joanna Russ, John Brunner, Vernor Vinge, or Philip K. Dick. Almost before the Movement—as it was known in the early-1980s, with a core membership usually argued to include William Gibson, Bruce Sterling, Lewis Shiner, Rudy Rucker, John Shirley and, at times, Pat Cadigan—was firmly established, eulogies quickly followed the subgenre's meteoric success. Shiner writes in his *New York Times* editorial "Confessions of an Ex-Cyberpunk" (1991) that "[o]ther writers had turned the form into formula: implant wetware (biological computer chips), government by multinational corporations, street-wise, leather-jacketed, amphetamine-loving protagonists and decayed orbital colonies." Arthur Kroker and Marilouise Kroker proclaim in *Hacking the Future: Stories for the Flesh-Eating 90s* (1996) that "*Johnny Mnemonic* [1995], the movie, is the day when cyberpunk died" (51). Claire Sponsler went so far as to argue that if "cyberpunk has finally arrived, then it has come in crucial ways DOA—dead on arrival—powerless to sustain the socio-political radicalism and representational innovation its champions claim for it" (47). She cites Veronica Hollinger who, in spite of her enthusiasm for cyberpunk, writes in "Cybernetic Deconstructions: Cyberpunk and Postmodernism" (1991) that

> cyberpunk—like the punk ethic with which it was identified—was a response to postmodern reality that could go only so far before self-destructing under the weight of its own deconstructive activities (not to mention its appropriation by more conventional and more commercial writers).

(217)

Even Bruce Sterling, who grabbed cyberpunk's promotional reins with *Mirrorshades: The Cyberpunk Anthology* (1986) and perhaps thereby contributed to cyberpunk's perceived terminal condition, declared in "Cyberpunk in the Nineties" (1998):

[T]oday, it must be admitted that the cyberpunks—SF veterans in or near their forties, patiently refining their craft and cashing their royalty checks—are no longer a Bohemian underground. This too is an old story in Bohemia; it is the standard punishment for success. An underground in the light of day is a contradiction in terms. Respectability does not merely beckon; it actively envelops. And in this sense, "cyberpunk" is even deader than Shiner admits.

Thus, cyberpunk is dead.

R.I.P.

And yet ... cyberpunk has "shown remarkable resilience" (Easterbrook, *Fifty* 86) that belies its oft-repeated, perhaps premature, termination. A few recent examples will suffice to highlight this resilience: David Soyka asserts that Geoff Ryman's *Air* "reclaims the literary ambition of cyberpunk by inverting its landscape" through the combining of "mythology and neuroscience, the cyberpunks' wet dream of achieving Nirvana via electronic interface"; Jillana Enteen argues Nalo Hopkinson builds on "Gibson's and other cyberpunk authors' flair for forecasting digital futures" by revising "cyberpunk to render visible current socioeconomic inequities, suggest[ing] alternative formulations of the relationships between humans and technology" (263); Jason W. Ellis describes Ian McDonald's *Brasyl* (2007) as "postcolonial cyberpunk" (36); Stacy Gillis proposes the emergence of a third-wave cyberpunk "with Gibson and Bruce Sterling at the forefront of the first generation, Neal Stephenson at the forefront of the second and the post-dotcom writers forming the third" ("Introduction" 3); British SF author Charles Stross declares that he and others like him seek "'to distill ... cyberpunk into something that works again, from the point of view of someone who has actually gone through a dotcom start-up, worked on the 'Net, worked as a programmer" ("Exploring Distortions" 86) (Foster xv). In our digital age of CGI-driven entertainment, the information economy and globalized capital, Movement-era cyberpunk's vision of a radical underground hacking the power centres of dominant culture seems quaintly naïve, perhaps even nostalgic. And yet we have never more been in need of a fiction capable of engaging with the world as shaped by information technology, which perhaps explains the sub-genre's persistent afterlife.

Beyond Cyberpunk: New Critical Perspectives is a collection of essays—original submissions and a handful of reprints—organized around what Thomas Foster calls cyberpunk's "sea change into a more generalized cultural formation" (xiv), a multi-facted anthology that takes into account changing historical, social, political, economic, and philosophical conditions. Cyberpunk is no longer an emergent phenomenon and, as Vint argues in the Afterword, we live in a cyberpunk future, albeit one different from that imagined in most Movement-era fiction. *Beyond Cyberpunk* offers less hyperbolic reflections on cyberpunk that emerge from cultural climates that have significantly changed. These essays explore our cyberpunk realities to soberly reconsider Movement-era cyberpunk while also mapping those post-Movement currents of the past two decades. *Beyond Cyberpunk* seeks to move beyond the narrow strictures of cyberpunk and contribute to an ongoing discussion of how to negotiate exchanges among information technologies, global capitalism, and human social existence.[1] *Beyond Cyberpunk* therefore does not look to define a field that was "influential if never quite coherent" (Easterbrook, *Fifty* 86) but rather to offer a variety of perspectives on cyberpunk's diversity and how this sub-genre remains relevant amidst its transformations into a more generalized set of practices. It is not surprising that many of our contributions return to the work of William Gibson. Just as Movement-era demogogues positioned it as a touchstone which gave shape to the emerging sub-genre, so too do recent critics position the cultural moment beyond cyberpunk in references to reassessments of and reactions to Gibson's seminal (in more ways than one) fiction. We aim to pose, to engage, maybe even answer the question of what it is that Movement and post-Movement cyberpunk narratives *continue to offer* us in those intersections of literary, cultural, theoretical, academic, and technocultural environs.

This collection is divided into three Parts that collect 12 essays showcasing the complexities of cyberpunk's cultural formations. Reprints by Brian McHale, Tom Moylan, and Karen Cadora organize the collection around three critiques that followed once cyberpunk's hyperbolic energy began to wane. The original contributions build upon these foundations, demonsrating the diverse ways that these positions have evolved in both criticism and new fiction.

Part I: Situating Cyberpunk opens with McHale's "Towards a Poetics of Cyberpunk." McHale's linking of cyberpunk and postmodernism in *Constructing Postmodernism* (1992), the book from which this chapter is reprinted, was one of the most influential academic discussions of cyberpunk in the 1990s. It demonstrates that, even as early as 1992, critics were already struggling to define cyberpunk, a subgenre whose definition requires "several answers, all different, none of them necessarily reducible to any of the others" (3). It is an excellent survey of the authors and motifs that informed the academic understanding of cyberpunk, and it reveals a number of trends that would become points of controversy in ongoing assessments of the genre.

Rob Latham follows in Chapter 2 with "'A Rare State of Ferment': SF Controversies from the New Wave to Cyberpunk." Latham's essay is an invaluable reassessment of the place of cyberpunk in SF's history, examining the continuities as well as ruptures that informed cyberpunk's rise, rule, and eventual dispersal. Latham focuses on "ideological stakes of aesthetic legitimation" (59) and compares them to similar struggles attendant on the rise of the New Wave, helping us to situate cyberpunk within a pattern of boom-and-bust cycles that have shaped the ongoing history of print SF. This chapter enables us to see more clearly what truly was innovative about cyberpunk's ascendancy.

Movement-era cyberpunk crystallized around Gibson's *Neuromancer*, and his more recent work proves diagnostic of new cultural preoccupations and anxieties as cyberspace has become a material reality. In Chapter 3, "Recognizing Patterns: Gibson's Hermeneutics from the Bridge Trilogy to *Pattern Recognition*," Neil Easterbrook offers an important recontextualization of Gibson's fiction, considering how Gibson continues to explore the interpenetration of technology, subjectivity, and ontology. Easterbrook begins with an extensive comparison of the Sprawl novels with Gibson's next interlinked series of books, the Bridge triptych of *Virtual Light* (1993), *Idoru* (1996), and *All Tomorrow's Parties* (1999), and then argues that *Pattern Recognition* (2003) represents a culmination, of sorts, of Gibson's aesthetics. The greater change wrought by cyberculture in Gibson's work, Easterbrook concludes, is "how *homo sapiens* has become *homo significans*, the hyperbolic posthuman of the Sprawl books recuperated to a more humanist, humane task" (60).

Part I concludes with Chapter 4 by Andrew M. Butler's "Journeys Beyond Being: The Cyberpunk-Flavored Novels of Jeff Noon." Butler demonstrates Noon's novels—*Vurt* (1993); *Pollen* (1995); *Automated Alice* (1996); *Nymphomation* (1997)—reside at the margins of cyberpunk and might be better qualified "cyberpunk-flavoured" than cyberpunk-proper. Yet they too use virtual realities as a literary device, chiefly, according to Butler, to explore "cyberpunk's attitudes to the body and death" (65). The *cyber* of cyberpunk has been replaced with the *bio* that is biopunk and we find Noon "appropriating cyberpunk materials for his own ends" (66), including the undercutting of the escapist and naïve fantasies of earlier cyberpunk.

Part II: The Political Economy of Cyberpunk opens with Chapter 5, Tom Moylan's "Global Economy, Local Texts: Utopian/Dystopian Tension in William Gibson's Cyberpunk Trilogy," originally published in *The Minnesota Review* (1995). Moylan unpacks Gibson's trilogy (*Neuromancer* (1984), *Count Zero* (1986), *Mona Lisa Overdrive* (1988)) to locate the novels in the Utopia tradition and reveals that this ever-popular sequence is actually an extremely *dark* series of novels, perhaps even darker than most recognizable dystopias. In spite of Gibson's dizzying narrative style and increasingly well-crafted tonalities, there really is not much to commend living in Gibson's anti-utopian future, a particularly nightmarish world made all that more distressing if it is truly a metaphor for contemporary late capitalism.

In Chapter 6, Sherryl Vint extends cyberpunk's relationship to capital by examining marketing, both within and outside of fiction in "'The Mainstream Finds its Own Uses for Things': Cyberpunk and Commodification." She considers the relationship between cyberpunk and postmodernism in terms of the "social function of art" (95), using the little-known text *Red Spider, White Web* (1990), written by a Native American woman, Misha, to provide a cognitive map of the information-technology saturated and commodity-driven society that is cyberpunk's world. Vint's reading of Misha's avant-gardist and modernist aesthetics suggests that although her work differs in significant ways from Movement-era cyberpunk, her desire for authentic art outside or beyond the commodity system leads her to a conclusion that reinforces individual transcendence over social transformation, a position not that different from that of texts considered central to cyberpunk.

Chapter 7, Mark Bould's "Why Neo Flies, and Why He Shouldn't: The Critique of Cyberpunk in Gwyneth Jones's *Escape Plans* and M. John Harrison's *Signs of Life*" provides two important recontextualizations of cyberpunk: within a longer history of images of transcendence and escape from bodily limits, and in comparison to fiction published contemporary to Movement-era cyberpunk which responds in another way to the social and economic conditions which gave rise to cyberpunk. Bould finds in Jones's and Harrison's novels an alternative response to the changes consequent on the rise of neoliberalism in the 1980s and beyond. Both Jones and Harrison demonstrate a more dialectical understanding of life under late capitalism, emphasizing equally the allure of the fantasy of transcendence and its inevitable failure as it comes up against the limits of materiality.

Part II ends with Jonathan Boulter's "Posthuman Melancholy: Digital Gaming and Cyberpunk," an essay that looks ahead to digital games that may well become the dominant mode of cyberpunk narrative in the twenty-first century, and back to Gibson's first moments of inspiration, watching people play video games and wondering at the integration of human and machine the activity implied. Thus, Boulter argues, it is important "to recognize the degree to which the discourse of cyberpunk has been woven into—and perhaps out of—what I am calling the visual imaginary of digital games" (137). Boulter makes an important intervention in current cyberpunk scholarship, requiring us to focus on both narrative and media in future work.

The final part, *The Politics of Embodiment in Cyberpunk*, opens with Karen Cadora's *Science Fiction Studies* essay "Feminist Cyberpunk" (1995). Much like Nicola Nixon's influential "Cyberpunk: Preparing the Ground for Revolution or Keeping the Boys Satisfied?" (1992), Cadora positions feminist cyberpunk as imbuing "the conventions of cyberpunk with the political savvy of feminist sf" (157) and (re)situating cyberpunk as a medium better suited to addressing contemporary social realities where the body has always already been political and politicized. Cadora sees in feminist cyberpunk ways of both surviving and thriving within cyberpunk futures while also challenging masculinist cyberpunk's perceived heteronormativity.

Next, in Chapter 10, Pawel Frelik probes contemporary British author Richard K. Morgan, a relative newcomer who has most explicitly deployed cyberpunk motifs for a post-millennial audience, notably in the Takeshi Kovacs trilogy: *Altered Carbon* (2002), *Broken Angels* (2003), and *Woken Furies* (2005). Frelik posits, in "Woken Carbon: The Return of the Human in Richard K. Morgan's Takeshi Kovacs Trilogy," that what makes Morgan unique is his fusion of cyberpunk's *noir* and *cyber* motifs into a trilogy that departs "from and undermines not only the Cartesian paradigm [of mind/

body dualism] but cyberpunk aesthetics at large" (173). In addition, Frelik argues Morgan appears to be embracing the utopian potential of SF: Takeshi Kovacs's attitude by the end of *Woken Furies* makes "it very clear that, unlike in the two previous installments which excluded hope of a better tomorrow, Morgan does not reject the possibility of an alternative" (180) and in so doing distances "the trilogy from the political indifference of classic cyberpunk narratives" (183).

In Chapter 11, Veronica Hollinger, in "Retrofitting *Frankenstein,*" examines cyberpunk's relationship to *Frankenstein* as part of a broader technocultural dialogue that has (re)stitched Mary Shelley's classic novel into "a precursor text" of a cyberpunk ethos that permeates "both SF in particular and technoculture in general" (195). Victor Frankenstein's classic creation is an ideal form to leap from the nineteenth century and (re)appear "in technoculture in a newly complex role, both promising and abhorrent, at once our double and our technological other" (192). She concludes that cyberpunk "is one narrative shape of our deeply unnatural nature as human beings who are also technological beings, for whom technology has become a second nature" (207).

Beyond Cyberpunk concludes with Graham J. Murphy's "Angel(LINK) of Harlem: Techno-Spirituality in the Cyberpunk Tradition." Murphy demonstrates that cyberpunk's immense popularity ironically came at a time when religious revivalism and fundamentalism were on significant upswings. Thus, the visceral thrills of digitally transcending the material world by uploading into alternate, cyber-mediated dimensions not only hearken to SF's earliest roots but also to the long history of religious iconography that posits a higher spiritual realm for the faithful. Murphy draws our attention to the "spiritual iconography" (212) in both Movement-era and post-Movement cyberpunk, providing a close reading of Lyda Morehouse's AngelLINK series, *Archangel Protocol* (2001), *Fallen Host* (2002), *Messiah Node* (2003), and *Apocalypse Array* (2004). The Angel(LINK) tetrad blends Movement-era cyberpunk motifs, cyberpunk's feminist/queer potential, and the social critique of utopia to highlight "the importance of transcendence, (spiritual) faith, political commitment, and social action in a narrative arc whose political critique addresses post-millennial concerns regarding identity, religious revivalism, and techno-spirituality" (220).

Our assessments of cyberpunk in the twenty-first century are inevitably informed by our experience of a material reality that is both unlike the future projected by cyberpunk, yet shaped by the unfolding of those 1980s social and economic forces that gave birth to both cyberpunk and the world in which we live.

The essays of *Beyond Cyberpunk: New Critical Perspectives* offer a number of rubrics through which to understand the influence and scope of cyberpunk and to explore its continuing relevance into the twenty-first century: the cycle of SF movements (Latham); postmodern or slipstream aesthetics (McHale); a moment in Gibson's ongoing engagement with humanity as *homo significans* (Easterbrook); and posthumanism discourse on embodied subjectivity (Hollinger). As Moylan so ably points out, the one consistent element in cyberpunk texts is their portrayal of the "triumph of planetary capital" (82). In important ways, the continued relevance of cyberpunk tropes for understanding our current material reality is best summed up by this expression. The fact that we live in a cyberpunk world is in large part due to the dominance of neoliberalist globalization in our day-to-day lives, the heritage of Reagonomics which reshaped U.S. society contemporary with the birth of the Movement (which was, of course, paralleled in important ways by Thatcher's restructuring of Britain). Perhaps one of the reasons cyberpunk seems both so dated and yet paradoxically so relevant is that the ideological assumptions of neoliberalism have become as ubiquitous as information technology. If the technological cutting-edge of cyberpunk, in Bould's phrase, "turn[s] out to be eight-track" (130), perhaps more concerning is the degree to which cyberpunk's resistance to neoliberalism now seems similarly antiquated. In Jameson's phrase, people are "convinced" by the "permanence" (*Archaeologies* 229) of global capitalism: perhaps to such a degree that stories about its planetary triumph no longer strike us as futuristic.

Another important trend addressed in this anthology is the debate regarding the potential cyberpunk offers to help us rethink the politics of embodiment. As Karen Cadora points out, Movement-era cyberpunk emerged near contemporaneously with Donna Haraway's influential "A Cyborg Manifesto" (1985), an essay that urged feminists to rethink their characterization of technology as masculine and instead explore what the myth/metaphor of the cyborg might enable for liberatory politics. For Haraway, the cyborg was a potent image as it resists "seductions to organic wholeness" (150) and escapes from the constraints of both Oedipal and Creationist narratives. Similarly, Cadora sees in feminist cyberpunk a use of the cyberpunk tropes of disembodiment, split subjectivity, and human fusion with machines as an opportunity to escape the ideals of a gender ideology that biology is destiny. Yet cyberpunk and responses to it have always been rife with contradictions, the tension between its radical potential and its reactionary manifestation. New essays assessing more recent forays into cyberpunk imagery, such as Graham J. Murphy's reading of Lyda Morehouse and Veronica Hollinger's discussion of "A Real Girl," prove the continued relevance of these debates. As we continue to think about the persistence of cyberpunk in our cultural imaginary, we would do well to keep in mind Hollinger's dual focus on its "retrospective as well as its prospective influences" (192).

NOTE

1 Our title is also partially inspired by Larry McCaffery's groundbreaking *Storming the Reality Studio: A Casebook of Cyberpunk and Postmodern Fiction* (1991), an edited collection that provided the most detailed map of cyberpunk's territories

when it was the new (and rambunctious) kid on the block. Although there have been a handful of books focussing on William Gibson—Dani Cavallaro's *Cyberpunk and Cyberculture: Science Fiction and the Work of William Gibson* (2000); Carl B. Yoke and Carol L. Robinson's *The Cultural Influences of William Gibson, The "Father" of Cyberpunk Science Fiction* (2007)—there has been no significant anthology on cyberpunk in general since *Storming the Reality Studio*. *Beyond Cyberpunk: New Critical Perspectives* seeks to fill this void with its diverse critical methodologies that focus on a broad range of both common and uncommon authors.

Part I
Situating Cyberpunk

1 Towards a Poetics of Cyberpunk

Brian McHale

"CYBER WHATSIS"

> [T]hat old chestnut *cyberwhatsis*, or whatever it was, he couldn't remember.
>
> (Pat Cadigan, *Synners* 87)

What is cyberpunk, anyway? The question itself is wrong-headed, pre-supposing as it does that cyberpunk "is" some one thing or other, that it is some kind of "object" about which demonstrably true or false statements could be made. Nevertheless, wrong-headed though it may be, the question "What is cyberpunk?" does admit of an answer—or rather several answers, all different, none of them necessarily reducible to any of the others.

No doubt cyberpunk is, as its critics within the science-fiction (SF) community insist, a barefaced marketing device of SF publishers. But, if it is anything more than that (as I believe it is), then cyberpunk SF must, first of all, be a generational and "school" phenomenon. It has its own "school" institutions—manifestoes and literary polemics, group anthologies, fan magazines, panels at SF conventions, etc.—and its forms of "school" solidarity; e.g. cyberpunks write jacket blurbs for one another's books and otherwise promote the careers and reputations of fellow members of the school.[1] There does exist (as I shall undertake to demonstrate below) a shared cyberpunk poetics, but this is to some extent a consequence of membership in the cyberpunk group rather than the other way around. That is, the initial question to be asked about cyberpunk SF is not so much "*What* is it?" as "*Who* are the cyberpunks?" As with other school phenomena, we can identify an inner circle of "hard-core" cyberpunks—including Bruce Sterling, its leading propagandist, William Gibson, John Shirley, Rudy Rucker, and Lewis Shiner—and a more fluid outer circle of writers who have at some point or to some degree affiliated themselves with the cyberpunk group, or have had such an affiliation thrust upon them by others. This outer circle might include, among others, Greg Bear, Pat Cadigan, Richard Kadrey, Marc Laidlaw, Tom Maddox, Lucius Shepard, Michael Swanwick, and Walter Jon Williams.

A CHILD'S HISTORY OF SCIENCE FICTION[2]

Second, cyberpunk is the latest in the succession of phases or "waves" constituting the modern history of the SF genre. The SF genre, Jameson ("Progress" 149) reminds us, has "a complex and interesting formal history of its own ... with its own dynamic, which is not that of high culture, but which stands in a complementary and dialectical relationship to high culture or modernism as such." Malmgren ("Worlds" 30–34) has usefully suggested that an account of the genre's history in the twentieth century might be structured around the oscillation between two modes or types of science-fiction world-building, which, adapting familiar terminology of SF criticism, he calls "extrapolation" and "speculation." Extrapolative SF begins with the current state of the empirical world, in particular the current state of scientific knowledge, and proceeds, in logical and linear fashion, to construct a world which might be a future extension or consequence of the current state of affairs. Speculative world-building, by contrast, involves an imaginative leap, positing one or more disjunctions with the empirical world which cannot be linearly extrapolated from the current state of affairs. Worlds constructed by extrapolation, one might say, stand in a metonymic relation to the current empirical world, while worlds constructed by speculation stand in a metaphorical or analogical relation to it. These categories partly (but only partly) coincide with the distinction which has often been drawn in SF criticism between "hard" and "soft" SF (i.e. between SF based on the "hard" or physical sciences and SF based on the "soft" or human sciences); "hard" SF, says Malmgren, has certain "affinities" with extrapolation, "soft" SF with speculation.[3]

Naturally, these two modes of SF world-building are not mutually exclusive, either in historical periods or in individual texts. That is, extrapolation and speculation can coexist in the same text, and certainly in the same period of SF history, though in every case one of the two modes is likely to be relatively more salient or more central than the other. In other words, to label a text or period "extrapolative" or "speculative" is not to identify the presence of one mode and the corresponding absence of the other, but rather to specify the structural-functional *dominant* of the text or period (see Jakobson). Consequently, an internal history of the SF genre which utilizes these categories will be a history of the successive shifts of dominance between extrapolation and speculation.

According to one widely-accepted version, the history of modern SF commences (or recommences, if one counts H.G. Wells as its founding father) with the pulp-magazine fiction edited by Hugo Gernsback in the 1920s and 1930s. Gernsback's so-called "scientifiction" had extrapolative world-building as its dominant, and thereafter each successive phase or wave of SF has reacted against the dominant of the preceding phase, swinging toward the opposite pole of the extrapolation/speculation polarity. Thus, Gernsback's extrapolative "scientifiction" provoked, by way of reaction, a swing to speculative "space opera" and space fantasy (K.E. Smith; Edgar Rice Burroughs), which in turn provoked a counter-reaction against speculation and back to extrapolation in the so-called "Golden Age" magazine SF of the 1940s and 1950s. The "New Wave" SF of the 1960s clearly marks a return to the speculative dominant, in reaction against the extrapolative dominant of the preceding phase. This speculative phase has prolonged itself into the 1970s and 1980s, partly through the rise, in the aftermath of Tolkien's neo-fantasy trilogy *Lord of the Rings*, of hybrid "science fantasy" writing, a new sub-genre which seems likely to secede from SF altogether (if it has not already done so (see Malmgren, "Towards").

These successive shifts of dominance do not entail any simple return to or recovery of the poetics of the phase before the last; rather, some part of the poetics of the preceding phase is preserved and integrated in the new phase, even while other parts are rejected and replaced by elements retrieved from an earlier phase. Thus, the latest wave of SF writing rejects the speculative dominant of 1960s New Wave SF, and swings back to extrapolative world-building, while at the same time retaining certain elements of New Wave poetics. "When I was starting out," the cyberpunk novelist William Gibson explains, "I simply tried to go in the opposite direction from most of the stuff I was reading" (McCaffery, *Across* 228): this might be taken as a typical (though atypically frank) expression of the relation between successive generations of SF writing in general, and between the generation of the 1980s and its predecessors in particular. This newest phase includes neo-extrapolative "hard" SF writers (e.g. Gregory Benford, David Brin) as well as, problematically, cyberpunk SF—problematically because, while the cyberpunks themselves describe their own world-building practice as extra-polative, other extrapolative SF writers tend to regard them as continuators of the New Wave, more preoccupied with style and "texture" than with extrapolation.[4]

REPERTOIRES

Finally, whatever else cyberpunk may be, it is also, as I sought to demonstrate in the preceding chapter [editor's note: see McHale, 1992, *Constructing Postmodernism*: Ch. 10, "POSTcyberMODERNpunkISM"], a convenient name for the kind of writing that springs up where the converging trajectories of SF poetics and postmodernist poetics finally cross. It arises, in other words, from the interaction and mutual interference of SF and mainstream postmodernist writing. Consequently, no attempt to describe the repertoire of cyberpunk motifs would be adequate that failed to take into account cyberpunk's relations with both the SF repertoire and the postmodernist repertoire.

From the point of view of the SF repertoire, there are few, if any, absolute novelties in cyberpunk SF. Most cyberpunk motifs have precedents in earlier SF; some, indeed (e.g. the renegade robot motif), are among the hoariest of

SF clichés. Cyberpunk's critics within the SF community have sometimes adduced this fact as counter-evidence to cyberpunk propagandists' excessive claims for the novelty and "breakthrough" character of cyberpunk. There is, nevertheless, an important sense in which cyberpunk is innovative despite the familiarity or formulaic character of its SF motifs. What is new in cyberpunk is, first of all, the conspicuousness of certain selected motifs rather than others, their foregrounding relative to other motifs from the SF repertoire; and, secondly, the co-occurrence of certain motifs in the same texts, the solidarity among these motifs, the way they mutually corroborate and reinforce each other to create a motif complex which is distinctive of the cyberpunk wave of SF, even if every one of the individual items making up the complex can be traced back to earlier SF phases. The novelty of cyberpunk, in other words, lies not in the absolute newness of any particular component or components, but in a shift of dominance or center of gravity reflected in the combination of components and their relative conspicuousness in cyberpunk texts.

Cyberpunk's relation to "elite" postmodernist poetics is rather different. In what follows I undertake to demonstrate and substantiate the overlap between the postmodernist poetics of fiction and cyberpunk poetics. It is worth noting right at the outset, however, that the shared motifs I identify typically occur at different levels of textual organization in postmodernism and cyberpunk. That is, what typically occurs as a configuration of narrative structure or a pattern of language in postmodernist fiction tends to occur as an element of the fictional world in cyberpunk. Cyberpunk, one might say, translates or trans codes postmodernist motifs from the level of form (the verbal continuum, narrative strategies) to the level of content or "world."[5] To put it differently, cyberpunk tends to "literalize" or "actualize" what in postmodernist fiction occurs as metaphor—metaphor not so much in the narrow sense of a verbal trope (though that is also a possibility), but in the extended sense in which a narrative strategy or a particular pattern of language use may be understood as a figurative reflection of an "idea" or theme. In this respect, too, cyberpunk practice is clearly a continuation or extension of SF practice generally, for SF often generates elements of its worlds by literalizing metaphors from everyday discourse or mainstream fiction and poetry (see Todorov 76–77; Delany "Shadows"; Lem).

There are three large bundles or complexes of motifs which cyberpunk SF shares with mainsteam postmodernist fiction: motifs of what might be called "worldness"; motifs of the centrifugal self; and motifs of death, both individual and collective.

COWBOYS AND SUNDOGS

> Isn't this an "interface" here? a meeting surface for two worlds, sure, but which two?
>
> (Thomas Pynchon, *Gravity's Rainbow* 668)

Both science fiction and mainstream postmodernist fiction possess reper-
toires of strategies and motifs designed to raise and explore ontological
issues. Here is the ultimate basis for the overlap between the poetics of
postmodernist fiction and SF poetics in general, including cyberpunk poetics
in particular. SF, that is, like postmodernist fiction, is governed by an
ontological dominant, by contrast with modernist fiction or, among the
genres of "genre" fiction, detective fiction, both of which raise and explore
issues of epistemology and thus are governed by an epistemological dominant. Thus, while epistemologically-oriented fiction (modernism, detective
fiction) is preoccupied with questions such as: what is there to know about
the world? Who knows it, and how reliably? How is knowledge trans-
mitted, to whom, and how reliably? etc., ontologically-oriented fiction
(postmodernism, SF) is preoccupied with questions such as: what is a
world? How is a world constituted? Are there alternative worlds, and if so
how are they constituted? How do different worlds, and different kinds of
world, differ, and what happens when one passes from one world to
another? etc.[6]

To explore such ontological issues, both SF and postmodernist fiction
naturally use and adapt the resources common to all varieties of fiction, in
particular the universal fictional resource of presentation of virtual space.
If all fictional texts project virtual spaces, not many of them foreground
and exploit the spatial dimension to the degree that SF and postmodernist texts do.[7] This shared poetics of space is partly to be explained
by the common historical origins of both SF and postmodernist fiction in
romance. In medieval romance the category of "world," normally the unre-
presentable, absolute horizon of all experience and perception, is itself
made an object of representation through a particular metaphorical use
of enclosed spaces *within* the romance world: castles, enchanted forests,
walled gardens and bowers, etc. Such symbolic enclosures, functioning as
scale-models or miniature analogues of worlds, bring into view the normally invisible horizons of world, the very "worldness" of world (see
Jameson's "Magical Narratives" and *The Political Unconscious* 103–50; cf.
Harvey's *The Condition of Postmodernity* 240–41). Space, in other words,
becomes in medieval romance an all-purpose tool for "doing" ontology—a
means of exploring ontology *in* fiction, as well as (potentially at least)
the ontology *of* fiction. And this is true not only of medieval romance
itself, but of its "heirs" as well, including both SF and postmodernist fiction.
SF in particular has developed in the course of its history as a genre an
entire repertoire of "microworlds," scale-model worlds designed to bring
into view the "worldness" of the category "world" itself. Ultimately
derived from the castles, forests and bowers of medieval romance, these SF
microworlds—domed space colonies, orbiting space-stations, subterranean
cities, "cities in flight," and the like—recur throughout the genre's history.
They recur yet again in cyberpunk SF, but with a new intensity of
emphasis, sharpness of focus, and functional centrality.

MICROWORLDS

The typical cyberpunk microworld uses the familiar motifs of outer-space fiction as building-blocks: orbiting space-stations or platforms, domed space colonies and the like. However, if the basic construction materials are SF clichés, the treatment of these materials in the cyberpunk context is typically revisionist or parodic. Where space-stations and space-colonies of traditional SF are glamorous showcases of high technology (think of Kubrick's *2001*), those of cyberpunk SF are likely to be orbiting slums—shabby, neglected, unsuccessful, technologically outdated, as in Gibson and Sterling's "Red Star, Winter Orbit," Shiner's *Frontera* (1984), or Shirley's *Eclipse* (1985). Alternatively, for the miniature liberal-egalitarian democracies of traditional SF (think of *Star Trek*), cyberpunk substitutes off-world havens of privilege, orbiting penthouses to which the wealthy and powerful withdraw to escape the poverty and danger of the planet surface, as in Gibson's *Neuromancer* (1984) and *Count Zero* (1986), or Williams's *Hardwired* (1986).

Moreover, the cyberpunk adaptations of these familiar motifs heighten precisely the "worldness" of outer-space microworlds. This tendency is particularly conspicuous in Sterling's *Schismatrix* (1985), Swanwick's *Vacuum Flowers* (1987) and Williams's *Voice of the Whirlwind* (1987). These texts extrapolate a future in which the human race, having evacuated planet Earth (partially in Williams, totally in Sterling and Swanwick), lives dispersed throughout the solar system in artificial planets and space-colonies (on asteroids, the moons of other planets, etc.). Not only do these orbiting city-states differ from one another in the ways that nations differ in our world—in language, culture, political systems, etc.—but they also differ in much more basic, indeed ontological, ways—in light, gravity, temperature, strains of bacteria, etc. They differ, in other words, as worlds differ, and their differences heighten the world-modeling function of these enclosures.

Another cyberpunk variant brings these microworlds down out of orbit to the terrestrial surface and superimposes them on the current map of the world. In Marc Laidlaw's *Dad's Nuke* (1985) and Williams's *Hardwired*, for example, the United States of the near future has been balkanized (or, I suppose, "lebanonized"), that is, it has disintegrated into self-contained, warring enclaves sustained (in Laidlaw, less so in Williams) by disparate and competing ideologies and epistemologies. In Lucius Shepard's *Life During Wartime* (1987) and Lewis Shiner's *Deserted Cities of the Heart* (1988), it is Mexico and Central America that have disintegrated in this way; in Shirley's *Eclipse* it is Europe. These extrapolated near-futures literalize a familiar metaphor in the sociology of knowledge (see, e.g., Berger and Luckmann), that of the multiple, competing "subuniverses" or "enclaves" of meaning into which complex (post)modern societies have diversified. Here the diversification of knowledge is literal and geographical, and Berger and Luckmann's epistemological enclaves have erected barbed-wire perimeter fences and armed themselves with the latest military hardware against their epistemological competitors.

Alternatively, microworlds appear as islands: the artificial island of Freezone in Shirley's *Eclipse* (symmetrically mirroring and balancing the orbiting space-station FirStep in the same text), or the islands of Sterling's "Green Days in Brunei" (1985) and *Islands in the Net* (1988). Some of Sterling's islands are fully integrated "in the net" of global communications and information, while other island enclaves, some of them literally islands (Grenada, Singapore, Brunei), others only figuratively so (renegade guerrilla bands, African pocket dictatorships) remain defiantly outside the net. It is these latter islands—disparate, marginalized, renegade, resisting integration into the homogenizing world-system—that most strongly foreground the "worldness" of island microworlds.

It is especially with these enclaves and island microworlds that cyberpunk SF returns to its distant historical roots in the kinds of romance worldspaces that Jameson has described. Cyberpunk also returns to its romance roots through its use of wandering adventurer-heroes as a device for foregrounding its microworlds. "Worldness" in medieval romance (and in later sub-literary derivatives, such as the Western) was heightened by the narrative device of the conventional knight-errant's itinerary, which took him from microworld to microworld—from castle to enchanted forest to cave to bower to another castle, and so on. Freely crossing world-boundaries, the knight-errant thus served to expose the differences among (micro)worlds.

How conscious cyberpunk is of the adventurer-hero tradition is suggested by the nickname of Williams's hero in *Hardwired*, who smuggles contraband across the internal frontiers of what used to be the United States: he is (what else?) Cowboy. Space-traveling versions of the knight-errant or cowboy abound in cyberpunk; Swanwick's Rebel Mudlark (*Vacuum Flowers*) is one, Sterling's Abelard Lindsay (*Schismatrix*) another, Williams's Etienne Steward (*Voice of the Whirlwind*) yet another. Sterling even coins a name for them: they are "sundogs" (by analogy, I suppose, with seadogs, another adventurer-hero model), and the interplanetary spaces they traverse on their itineraries from microworld to microworld are "sundog zones."

IN THE ZONE

When Sterling calls these interplanetary spaces "sundog zones," he alludes to similar multiple-world spaces projected by postmodernist texts, in particular the "Zone" of Pynchon's *Gravity's Rainbow* and William Burroughs's "interzone." All these spaces, cyberpunk and postmodernist alike, are instances of what Michel Foucault called "heterotopia," the impossible space in which fragments of disparate discursive orders (actualized in cyberpunk as disparate microworlds) are merely juxtaposed, without any attempt to reduce them to a common order.

In its terrestrial versions, this cyberpunk Zone typically takes one of two forms. One form is that of the War Zone, the familiar spaces of our world fragmented and "reconfigured" (Pynchon, *Gravity* 520), sometimes literally, by the impact of war—whether guerrilla war, as in Shepard's *Life During Wartime* and Shiner's *Deserted Cities*, tactical nuclear war, as in Shirley's *Eclipse*, or unconventional forms of so-called "conventional" warfare, as in Williams's *Hardwired*. The model of Pynchon's Zone of postwar occupied Germany is a strong presence in some of these texts (e.g. *Eclipse*); in others, especially those involving tropical jungle warfare (*Life During Wartime*, *Deserted Cities*), the model is rather Michael Herr's Vietnam War journalism in *Dispatches* (1978), or the fictionalized version in his screenplay for Coppola's *Apocalypse Now*.

The other typical cyberpunk Zone, and the source of what is perhaps the most characteristic cyberpunk imagery, is the Urban Zone. This is, so to speak, an "imploded" Zone: instead of microworlds spaced out along a narrative itinerary, here they have been collapsed together in the heterotopian space of a future megalopolis where "fragments of a large number of possible orders glitter separately in the dimension, without law or geometry, of the *heteroclite*" (Foucault xviii). The most characteristic and most influential example of this cyberpunk Zone is the "Sprawl," the near-future cityscape of Gibson's stories ("Johnny Mnemonic," "New Rose Hotel," "Burning Chrome") and novels (*Neuromancer, Count Zero, Mona Lisa Overdrive*). Similar Urban Zones occupy the backgrounds and sometimes the foregrounds (e.g. L.A. in Richard Kadrey's *Metrophage*, 1988, and Cadigan's *Synners*, 1991) of many other cyberpunk novels. They have even been projected into outer space to become the slummy asteroid-belt "tank towns" and the "cislunar sprawl" of "orbital hongkongs" in Swanwick's *Vacuum Flowers*.

The compositional principle of the Sprawl and its cognates, terrestrial and extraterrestrial, is maximally intimate juxtaposition of maximally diverse and heterogeneous cultural materials (Japanese, Western, and Third World, high-tech and low-tech, elite and popular, mainstream "official" culture and youth or criminal subcultures, etc.). The Sprawl is an image of the carnivalized city, the city as permanent carnival. Kadrey makes this explicit when, in *Metrophage*, he introduces in the background of his narrative a literal carnival, that of the Día de los Muertos, which serves to mirror *en abyme* the carnivalesque structure of the "reconfigured" Los Angeles of his near-future world.

At the center of this imploded multiple-world space—though "center" is a rather infelicitous term for a space whose organizational principle is precisely centerlessness—one typically finds an even more compact zone of cultural heterogeneity and juxtaposition, a kind of dense node of collapsed microworlds. This zone-within-the-Zone—red-light district, ghetto or barrio, sometimes a single building—can be read as a synecdoche (*pars pro toto*) or *mise-en-abyme* of the broader Zone that surrounds it.

Examples include the multi-storey flea-market, the Hypermart, of Gibson's *Count Zero;* OmeGaity, the homosexual cruising warren on Shirley's island-city Freezone, with its "strange vibe of stratification: claustrophobia layered under agoraphobia" (Shirley, *Eclipse* 129); the Iron Barrio prison-camp of Shepard's *Life During Wartime;* and the Golden Age of Hollywood Pavilion of Kadrey's *Metrophage*, an "enormous tented structure" housing reconstructions of classic Hollywood movie sets, left over from a world's fair and now home to a floating population of vagrants and squatters.

CYBERSPACE

All the strategies of "worldness" described so far have involved juxtapositions among microworlds occupying the same ontological plane and arranged along the same horizontal axis. It is also possible, however, to foreground the "worldness" of world by juxtaposing worlds not, as in all these cases, in series, on a horizontal axis, but rather *in parallel*, on a *vertical* axis; that is, it is possible to juxtapose worlds occupying *different* ontological planes—worlds and meta-worlds, or worlds and inset worlds (worlds-within-worlds).

The characteristic cyberpunk form of inset world is "cyberspace" (Gibson's coinage), the computer-generated space mentally experienced by computer operators whose nervous systems are directly interfaced with the computer system. According to the fictitious history developed in cyberpunk novels, cyberspace evolved from the "virtual worlds" of military simulations, but its real origin (as Gibson has cheerfully admitted in an interview) is less glamorous, namely, contemporary video-arcade games and computer-graphics programs (McCaffery, *Across* 138). More generally, the cyberspace motif arises from the potent illusion, experienced (I suppose) by all computer-users, sophisticated and unsophisticated alike, of gazing into (or even moving around inside) some space lying somehow "within" or "behind" the flat screen of the computer monitor.[8] And of course, apart from its immediate experiential source in illusions of this kind, cyberspace also has a long SF pedigree, including all the many variations on the SF motif of "paraspace": parallel worlds, other "dimensions," worlds of unactualized historical possibility, etc.

Gibson's cyberspace, also called the "matrix," is a three-dimensional grid ("a 3-D chessboard, infinite and perfectly transparent" (Gibson, *Count Zero* 168)) in which concentrations of data (those stored by corporations, government agencies, the military, etc.) are represented by color-coded geometrical shapes: "the stepped scarlet pyramid of the Eastern Seaboard Fission Authority burning beyond the green cubes of Mitsubishi Bank of America, and high and very far away, the spiral arms of military systems" (Gibson, *Neuromancer* 52). The user of this system has the illusion of moving among these representations as through a landscape, but a landscape entirely mental and virtual. The matrix is a "consensual hallucination," that is, exactly the same hallucinatory landscape is experienced by everyone who "jacks into" anyone of the system's terminals.

Apart from this second plane of shared cyberspace reality, parallel to the primary reality plane, Gibson's fictional world also incorporates a number of "private" paraspaces, limited-access worlds-within-the-world. The billionaire Virek, for instance (*Count Zero*), whose sickly body is kept alive in a vat, has had a private mental reality constructed for himself, one that simulates the city of Barcelona, while Bobby Newmark (*Mona Lisa Overdrive*) is permanently jacked into a unit that contains its own separate cyberspace world-construct ("an *approximation of every-thing*"(Gibson, *Mona* 128)). These private paraspaces are not, however, hermetically sealed, but may be entered not only from the primary reality plane but even, in extraordinary circumstances, from other inset worlds: Bobby Newmark, for instance, penetrates Virek's world-construct from the cyberspace matrix at the climax of *Count Zero*. It is possible, in other words, to adventure from parallel world to parallel world on the vertical axis, just as one can from microworld to microworld on the horizontal axis of the primary reality plane.

Where texts such as *Neuromancer*, Cadigan's *Mindplayers* (1987) and Laidlaw's *Dad's Nuke* construct a two-tier ontology (see Pavel) by juxtaposing a primary reality plane with an inset cyberspace world, other cyberpunk texts do so by juxtaposing the primary reality plane with a parallel realm of mythic archetypes. Examples include Shiner's *Frontera*, whose protagonist, Kane, acts out the hero "monomyth" simultaneously in the real world and the myth-world, to which he has access in dreams and hallucinations; Shiner's *Deserted Cities of the Heart*, where the myth being re-enacted is the Mesoamerican one of Kukulcan/Quetzlcoatl; and Shepard's *Green Eyes* (1984), where the parallel myth-world is that of voodoo divinities. In other words, these texts literalize or actualize the kinds of mythological materials that function metaphorically in modernist texts such as *Ulysses* and *Doktor Faustus*. While Joyce's Leopold Bloom "is" Odysseus only figuratively, in a kind of extended metaphor, Shiner's Kane *really* is the Hero with a Thousand Faces on a different but parallel plane of reality.[9]

The paraspace motif, including cyberspace and its functional equivalent, the myth-world, not only serves to bring into view the "worldness" of world; it also offers opportunities for reflecting concretely on world-making itself, and on science fiction world-making in particular. For paraspace is, at least potentially, a scale-model of the fictional world itself, a fictional-world-within-the-fictional-world or *mise-en-abyme* of the text's world. The paraspace motif makes possible, in other words, metafictional reflection *by* the text on its own ontological procedures.

Cyberpunk texts often foreground this metafictional potential of paraspace. For instance, they develop an analogy between the author of the text who has written the fictional world into being, and the "author" of the cyberspace or paraspace world. In Gibson's *Mona Lisa Overdrive*, this subsidiary "author," the real author's fictional double, is evidently the artificial intelligence Continuity, who intervenes in and manipulates the cyberspace world. Continuity is described as "writing a book ... *always* writing it" (Gibson, *Mona* 42); is this "book" cyberspace, one wonders queasily, or *Mona Lisa Overdrive* itself? Similarly, in Shepard's *Green Eyes*, it is the protagonist Donnell who seems to be the "author" of paraspace, for the paraspace myth-world first manifests itself in stories (fictions-within-the-fiction) he has written. Later this myth-world will acquire independent ontological status, so that Donnell's role comes to be that of a subsidiary world-builder in his own right, uncannily doubling his own author.

SIMSTIM

> Which world is this? What is to be done in it? Which of my selves is to do it?
>
> (Dick Higgins 101)

Postmodernism's shift of focus to ontological issues and themes has radical consequences for literary models of the self. A poetics in which the category "world" is plural, unstable and problematic would seem to entail a model of the self which is correspondingly plural, unstable, and problematic. If we posit a plurality of worlds, then conceivably "my" self exists in more than one of them; if the world is onto logically unstable) self-contradictory, hypothetical or fictional, infiltrated by other realities) then so perhaps am "I." Dick Higgins's first question would seem to entail his last: if we can ask, "Which world is this?", then it follows that eventually, we must also get around to asking, "Which of my selves ... ?"

Modernist perspectivism (e.g. *Ulysses*, *The Sound and the Fury*, *To the Lighthouse*, *Les Faux-monnayeurs*) multiplied points of view on the world, but without, for the most part, undermining the underlying unity of the self. Though in modernist fiction the perspectives on the world are many, and each differs from all the others, nevertheless each perspective is lodged in a subjectivity, which is itself relatively coherent, relatively centered and stable; and this is true even of those modernist texts (e.g. *A la recherche du temps perdu*, *La coscienza di Zeno*, *Die Mann ohne Eigenschaften*) in which the unity and continuity of the self is problematized. Still, perspectivism does exert considerable centrifugal pressure on the self and there are tendencies in modernism toward fragmentation and decentering. Never brought to full fruition during the modernist period, these centrifugal tendencies could not be fully realized until the emergence of a postmodernist poetics exploring and problematizing the ontologies of worlds and texts (see Thomas Docherty; Uri Margolin).

For the most part, fragmentation and dispersal of the self occur in postmodernist fiction at the levels of language, narrative structure, and the material medium (the printed book), or between these levels rather than at the level of the fictional world. In other words, postmodernist fiction prefers to represent the disintegration of the self figuratively, through linguistic, structural, or visual metaphors, rather than literally, in the persons of characters who undergo some kind of literal disintegrative experience. There are exceptions. Pynchon and Sukenick, for instance, have both produced characters who fracture or disintegrate not at all metaphorically (psychologically), but ontologically. In *Gravity's Rainbow*, for instance, Pirate Prentice is literally a medium, a "fantasist-surrogate" possessed by alternative selves, while the novel's supposed hero, Tyrone Slothrop, undergoes disassembly and "scattering," entirely disappearing from the world by the closing episodes. Similarly, there are characters in Sukenick's texts who, before our eyes so to speak, "peel off" from other characters (Roland Sycamore in *Out*), "split" into two (Boris Ccrab in *Blown Away*), infiltrate and take possession of other characters by "a kind of psychic osmosis" (*Blown Away*), and so on.

Ontologically oriented like postmodernist fiction, science fiction has also developed a repertoire of strategies for asking, "Which world is this?", yet it has for the most part managed to avoid asking the corollary question "Which of my selves?" It has, in other words, appeared to evade the consequences of its ontological pluralism and experimentalism for its model of the self. Or rather, SF has tended to neutralize the issue of the (re)presentation of self by keeping characterization generally "thin," "shallow," and impoverished, strictly subordinated to the foreground category of "world." In this respect we might even say, paradoxically, that traditional SF, otherwise so "pre-modernist" in its orientation, has always been postmodernist. "The disappearance of character (in the traditional sense) from contemporary ('postmodern') fiction," writes Christine Brooke-Rose (102), "is one of the ways in which SF and the more 'serious,' experimental fiction have come close together"; character, newly absent from "serious" fiction, has always been absent from SF!

Cyberpunk practice, here as elsewhere, is to actualize or literalize what in postmodernist poetics normally appears as a metaphor at the level of language, structure, or the material medium. Where postmodernism has figurative representations of disintegration, cyberpunk texts typically project fictional worlds which include (fictional) objects and (fictional) phenomena embodying and illustrating the problematics of selfhood: human-machine symbiosis, artificial intelligences, biologically-engineered alter egos, and so on.

Since cyberpunk handles the centrifugal self at the level of fictional world rather than, as postmodernist fiction prefers to do, at one or more of the formal levels of the text, its motifs of dispersion and decentering fall naturally into categories based on the types of fictional objects and phenomena represented. Here we can turn to Sterling's fiction for a convenient taxonomy. In a series of five stories published between 1982 and 1984 (and now reprinted in *Crystal Express*, 1989), culminating in his 1985 novel

Schismatrix, Sterling projects a future history in which humankind divides into two "posthuman" species in competition with one another, each species employing a different range of technologies to enhance and transform itself so as to improve its own chances for success. The "Mechanists," or "Mechs," use electronic and biomechanical means to augment themselves: prostheses to enhance the body, but with the side-effect of violating its integrity; brain–computer interfacing to extend the mind, but with the side-effect of attenuating and dispersing it. Their rivals, the "Shapers," use bio-engineering techniques—cloning, genetic engineering—to achieve the same ends, and with similar side-effects: who am "I" if I am a member of a "congenetic clan" of identical cloned individuals? These two technological options—the Mech option and the Shaper option[10]—define alternative ranges of representational motifs of the centrifugal self. We might call the first set, corresponding to the Mech option, cyberpunk proper, and the second set, corresponding to the Shaper option, "biopunk."

RIDING THE EYE-FACE

The traditional SF iconography of the humanoid robot, as developed by Čapek, Binder, Asimov and others, is relatively rare in cyberpunk; only Rudy Rucker (*Software*, 1982; *Wetware*, 1988) has exploited it in any very ambitious way. More typical of cyberpunk are its artificial intelligences (AIs), software surrogate humans, i.e. programs, rather than the hardware robots (or "wetware" androids) of traditional SF. Examples include Cadigan's AI "character" Artie Fish (*Synners*) and Gibson's Wintermute and Neuromancer, AIs who merge at the end of *Neuromancer* but by the time of its sequel, *Count Zero*, have already broken up into multiple software "selves." All of these variants on the robot motif serve to raise the classic SF question, who (or what) is human? At what point does a machine cease being a "mere" machine and begin to count as a human being?

This same question is also raised, but in inverted form, by the cyberpunk motif of prosthesis: at what point does a human being cease to be a human being and begin to count as a machine? The Mechanists of Sterling's Shaper/Mechanist cycle present an entire range of prosthetic possibilities, from biomechanical arms and legs, through remote-control "waldos" that enable human beings to extend their presence into unlivably hostile environments (deep space, ocean abysses), to "wireheads" who, abandoning their organic bodies entirely, survive as software ghosts in electronic machines. Less total prostheses are recurrent motifs in Gibson, Kadrey (*Metrophage*) and Williams (*Hardwired*, *Voice of the Whirlwind*), especially artificial eyes and surgically-implanted weapons, and even, in Kadrey, prosthetic genitalia!

Prosthetic augmentation is possible for mental capacities as well as for the body's physical capacities. There are minimal forms of this mental-augmentation motif, in which units ("microsofts," "augs") introduced permanently or temporarily into the nervous system supply specialized knowledge of preprogrammed technical skills when needed. Maximally, as in Swanwick's *Vacuum Flowers* and Cadigan's *Mindplayers*, mental augmentation takes the form of temporary programming of individuals with any of a whole range of useful or desirable personality constructs ("personas"), either for the sake of the specialized skills which these latter possess (doctor, police, skilled worker, weapons operator), or simply for reasons of entertainment and fashion.

At some hard-to-define point prosthetic augmentation shades off into a complete human–machine symbiosis or fusion, and the borders of the self blur and erode. The image of a human being coupled with a machine—"jacked-in," "riding the eye-face" (i.e. the "I-face," or human–machine interface)—recurs in many variations throughout cyberpunk; it is, indeed, the most characteristic piece of cyberpunk iconography. In these postures of fusion, the human partner in the symbiosis may experience an exhilarating expansion of self, as Williams's protagonist Cowboy does when he plugs into his armored vehicle, or, alternatively, an identity-threatening dilution or attenuation, as does, for instance, Williams's part-human, part-prosthetic character, Reno, or the "wirehead" Ryumin in *Schismatrix*. In extreme cases, the human self may be entirely absorbed into the machine. Williams's Reno, for instance, who begins as part prosthetic, ends by being a literally centrifugal self, diffused throughout the worldwide information network; similarly, Cadigan's Visual Mark (*Synners*), interfaced with the electronic network through skull-sockets, finally abandons his ravaged body ("the meat," as he contemptuously calls it) and "spreads" into the system. Rucker's Cobb Anderson persists as disembodied, taped "software" capable of being booted up in a variety of "hardware" vehicles, custom-made bodies as well as machines. Both in Rucker's two cyberpunk novels and in Swanwick's *Vacuum Flowers*, renegade cybernetic systems aspire to absorb the entire human race into a collective group-mind incorporating human and machine intelligences alike—the ultimate form of human–machine symbiosis.

ZOMBIES

The "bio-punk" sub-variety of cyberpunk SF makes available an entirely different, though complementary, range of motifs of the centrifugal self. Where machine-oriented cyberpunk produces electronic and mechanical surrogates of human beings (robots, AIs), the bio-punk variety "grows" new human individuals in vats, or clones identical multiples of the "same" individual, literally pluralizing the self. Where the machine-oriented variety augments and extends human capacities through mechanical means (prostheses, "waldos"), bio-punk accomplishes the same thing through bio-techniques, engineering new, reconfigured human types: "angels" (*Schismatrix*, *Wetware*), or mermaids and mermen (Shiner's "Till Human Voices Wake Us").

Finally, where the machine-oriented variety threatens the individual human self with diffusion throughout an electronic network, bio-punk threatens bodily fusion with other individuals (the effect of the drug "merge" in *Wetware*) and, ultimately, physical diffusion and loss of differentiation (the woman grotesquely reconfigured as a wall of undifferentiated tissue, the "Wallmother," in *Schismatrix*, the planet-wide biomass in Greg Bear's *Blood Music*).

It is not hard to see that these bio-punk motifs revise, update and rationalize classic Gothic-horror motifs of bodily invasion and disruption. This is especially the case with the bio-punk variations on the classic B-movie Gothic-horror motif of the zombie. The traditional zombie, of course, is a corpse reanimated by powerful voodoo magic to do the magician's will. In its various bio-punk adaptations, the zombie is rarely a corpse, more often a living human being "possessed" by some alien, or under the irresistible control of some other human being. The technologies of possession and control vary.

One variant, for instance, extrapolates from the familiar capacity of present-day drugs to induce in the drug-user temporary personality changes of a regular and to some extent predictable kind, changes in effect "coded" in the chemical structure of the drug. These extrapolated "designer drugs" of the future temporarily efface the "real" self and induce, for instance, a prostitute-self (Gibson's "meat puppets"), or a soldier-self (Shepard's "samurai," the name both of the drug and the personality it induces; Williams's "hardfire"). In one sophisticated version, found in Sterling's *Islands in the Net*, the capacity for transformation into an assassin personality is chemically pre-programmed into the individual, requiring only an enzyme trigger to activate it: merely eating a carton of yoghurt turns a personable Rastafarian into a "killing machine." Clearly, this military use of drugs to induce a soldier personality is functionally equivalent to the motif of human–machine symbiosis in which the pilot directly interfaces with his weapons system, as in Swanwick and Gibson's "Dogfight," Williams's *Hardwired*, and many other cyberpunk texts.

A second bio-punk variant on the zombie motif extrapolates from a classic paranoid theme, what Pynchon (*Gravity* 542) calls "the old Radio-Control-Implanted-In-the-Head-At-Birth problem." In other words, this variant involves biotechnological devices, such as surgically-implanted radio receivers, by means of which the individual self is subjected to some irresistible remote control by others. Shiner's hero Kane, in *Frontera*, for instance, is subjected to just this sort of biotechnological control, while the "spook" (i.e. secret agent) of Sterling's story by that name (1983) has been transformed into a human weapon, a "psychopath in harness" (Sterling, "Green" 177), by the introduction of a "Veil" over his cerebral cortex that, disrupting his personality, leaves him vulnerable to manipulation by his masters and handlers. Shepard (*Life During Wartime*) even has an entire radio-controlled zombie army. Rucker, in *Wetware*, elaborates a range of horrible baroque variations on this control motif, including a "zombie box" which, affixed to the spine, turns a human being into a remote-controlled zombie; a miniaturized "robot rat" which replaces the right half of the human brain, transforming a human being into a puppet-like "meatie"; and a robot "Happy Cloak" which, draped around a vatgrown, mindless cloned body, is capable of animating it and inducing in it a semblance of sentience. Here, obviously, the distinction between machine-oriented cyberpunk motifs and bio-punk motifs has become a purely notional one, and biotechnological control devices such as those found in *Wetware* shade imperceptibly into the range of techniques for superimposing personalities which we have already mentioned in connection with *Vacuum Flowers* and *Mindplayers*.[11]

Finally, closest of all in some ways to the traditional zombie of horror fiction and movies, is what might be called the motif of the cellular-level self. In *Green Eyes*, Lucius Shepard's self-conscious revision of the zombie myth, a particular strain of bacteria introduced into the brain of a fresh corpse generates there a short-lived ersatz personality (a "Bacterially Induced Artificial Personality"). Under these bizarre circumstances, the self is literally plural and decentered, literally "a disease in a borrowed brain" (Shepard, *Green* 89).[12] The ultimate elaboration of this variant of the centrifugal self is to be found in Greg Bear's *Blood Music* (1985), in which the cells of the human body acquire their own collective intelligence, like that of an ant hill, wholly independent of the intelligence of their human "host." Seizing control of their "environment"—in the first instance, the bodies of their hosts, ultimately the entire planet—and reshaping it to their needs, they transform Earth into a vast, constantly metamorphosing biomass, possessing a single collective selfhood. Simultaneously the one and the many, centripetal and centrifugal, Bear's cellular-level intelligence mirrors the world-spanning symbiotic human–machine intelligences of Rucker and Swanwick.[13]

SIMSTIM

The theme of the centrifugal self, and the representational motifs through which it is manifested in cyberpunk SF, are essentially incompatible with the perspectivist narrative strategies of modernist fiction. Such modernist strategies (multiple limited points of view, "parallax" of perspectives, etc.) rest, as I have already suggested, on the assumption of relatively centered, relatively stable subjectivities. Recognizing this, postmodernist writers have either sought to "background" these strategies, relegating them to a subordinate and ancillary role, or have, like Pynchon in *Gravity's Rainbow*, deployed them in ways that undermine the modernist assumptions upon which they rest, in effect parodying modernist perspectivism. But Pynchon's is a difficult precedent to emulate, and cyberpunk writers have all too often ended up falling back on perspectivist structural clichés inherited from modernist poetics (either directly, or indirectly by way of SF's own modernist generation, the so-called "New Wave" SF of the 1960s).

This is true, for instance, of Shiner's *Frontera*, Shirley's *Eclipse*, Gibson's *Count Zero* and *Mona Lisa Overdrive*, Cadigan's *Synners*, and other cyberpunk novels composed on the modernist model of multiple, shifting points of view.

But the modernist assumptions underlying perspectivism can be countered, and in ways that are distinctively cyberpunk rather than weak imitations of Pynchon's postmodernism. How this can be achieved is best demonstrated by Gibson's *Neuromancer*.[14] Gibson's world includes an extrapolated communications and entertainment medium called "simulated stimulus," or "simstim," involving not only audio and visual sensory channels, as television presently does, but the entire range of senses, the full human sensorium. As an entertainment medium, Gibson's simstim is a cross between the "feelies" of Huxley's *Brave New World* and American commercial television's egregious *Lifestyles of the Rich and Famous*: simstim stars travel, interview celebrities and enjoy the good life while wearing equipment that records the full range of their sensory experience for broadcast (appropriately edited, of course) to consumers who re-experience vicariously through simstim receivers at home what the stars have directly experienced in real life. Typical SF extrapolated technology, in other words— but with interesting implications for literary perspectivism.

Twice in the course of *Neuromancer*—once when she breaks into the Sense/Net corporate headquarters, and again during her raid on the TessierAshpool refuge of Villa Straylight—Molly, the female ninja, wears a simstim broadcast rig, enabling her partner Case to accompany her on the raid vicariously, as it were. Using simstim technology, Case can occupy Molly's point of view at will, literally at the flip of a switch. The action in these episodes unfolds simultaneously on two "planes," three if one counts cyberspace, for Case shifts back and forth among his own point of view on the primary reality plane, Molly's point of view, and the secondary, cyberspace reality plane. The effect is that of "split-screen" cinema or television— or indeed, that of multiple-point-of-view fiction.[15]

This is, in one sense, a purely formal solution ingeniously motivated by a representational motif at the level of the fictional world. The text of *Neuromancer* is consistently focalized through Case, but in these episodes Case is not at the center of the action, or rather he does not occupy its only center; the action involving Molly is at least as important and engaging. The simstim motif allows Gibson to introduce Molly's experience without violating the basic point of view convention of the text.

Ingenious though it may be, this is not, however, only a characteristically cyberpunk solution to a formal problem. It is also a subversive gesture, implicitly undermining the model of the centered, centripetal self upon which modernist perspectivism rests. For with the flip of a switch Case is able to experience another's body, "other flesh," *from within*. He experiences another's physical pain when he shifts into Molly's sensorium a moment after she has had her leg broken (Gibson, *Neuromancer* 64).

He even has the opportunity to see himself from another point of view, literally *through another's eyes* (or eye, in fact):

> [He] found himself staring down, through Molly's one good eye, at a white-faced, wasted figure, afloat in a loose fetal crouch, a cyberspace deck between its thighs, a band of silver [elec]trodes above closed, shadowed eyes. The man's cheeks were hollowed with a day's growth of dark beard, his face slick with sweat.
>   He was looking at himself.
>
> (Gibson, *Neuromancer* 256)

And of course finally, and perhaps most radically of all, when Case flips the switch that displaces him into Molly's point of view, he literally *changes gender:* he inhabits, if only temporarily, a woman's body. "So now you get to find out just how tight those jeans really are, huh?" wisecracks the Finn after he finishes explaining the simstim hook-up to Case (Gibson, *Neuromancer* 53), and this witty, subversive literalization of male clichés of sexual conquest ("I wouldn't mind getting into *her* pants!") suggests just how disorienting this motif can be, at least potentially. As a vehicle for imagining what it would be like to *be* a centrifugal self—to be in two places at once, to occupy two different points of view and two different bodies simultaneously, to change genders at the flip of a switch—the characteristic cyberpunk motif of simstim gives fresh, concrete, and radical meaning to Dick Higgins's question, "Which of my selves is to do it?"

THE FINAL FRONTIER

> His whole psychology, his point of orientation, is to dabble with death and yet somehow surmount it.
>
> (Philip K. Dick)

The ultimate ontological boundary, the one that no one can help but cross, is of course the boundary between life and death, between being and not-being. It is only to be expected, then, that an ontologically-oriented poetics such as that of postmodernist fiction should be preoccupied with death. Perhaps, though, it would be more accurate to put this the other way around, and say rather that the ontologically-oriented poetics of postmodernism is the latest, renewed manifestation of our culture's protracted struggle to represent, and thus symbolically to master, death. Either way, postmodernist fiction might somewhat reductively be characterized as one long, resourceful, highly diversified, obsessive meditation on the intolerable fact of personal extinction—your death, my death, our collective death (see McHale, *Postmodernist Fiction* 227–35).

Pynchon (1984: 5) has remarked that in science fiction "mortality is ... seldom an issue," and that this mark of the genre's immaturity helps to explain its appeal for immature readers. This is unfair; there are a number of SF writers (Philip K. Dick and Thomas Disch, among others) who have been as seriously preoccupied with mortality as any "mainstream" writer, and who have used SF conventions and formulas to explore death in ways not open to writers outside the SF genre. Nevertheless, it could be argued that no generation or group of SF writers has made the exploration of death its special province until the emergence of the cyberpunk "wave" in the 1980s.

There is one important exception to this generalization, and this has to do with a particular variant of the theme of death which has been a special province of SF writing in general since 1945 (and in fact before), namely (Sterling, "Slipstream" 79–80) the theme of nuclear holocaust. If late-twentieth-century literature in general, including postmodernist fiction, has turned with renewed attention to the perennial human preoccupation with death, no doubt this is in part because for the first time in history human beings feel threatened with "double" death: inevitable personal extinction, as always, but also the probable global self-destruction of the race and its posterity through nuclear war (or, alternatively, some ecological disaster). To SF writing in particular has fallen the task of feeding our imaginations with images and scenarios of our impending global extinction.[16] This task has been inherited in due course by the cyberpunk generation of SF writers, who have stamped their own distinctive mark and emphases on the nuclear-war theme.

DAD'S NUKE

A distinguishing mark of cyberpunk SF, writes Bruce Sterling, is its "boredom with Apocalypse" (in Gibson, *Burning* xi; Sterling, "Get"), which does not mean that cyberpunk disregards the nuclear war theme but rather that, like its SF and postmodernist precursors, it seeks ways of renewing and de-familiarizing it.

Thus, for instance, John Shirley prefaces his *Eclipse* (1985) with an alarming and enigmatic "note from the author":

> This is not a post-holocaust novel.
> Nor is this a novel about nuclear war.
> It may well be that this is a *pre*-holocaust novel.

Distancing himself in this way from familiar SF nuclear war motifs (those of the "post-holocaust novel"), Shirley prepares us for his revisionist treatment of nuclear war, for what follows is a representation of the nuclear apocalypse as a long drawn-out agony, a tactical nuclear war of attrition in Europe. In other words, Shirley challenges the image of apocalypse as a punctual, transformative, irreversible event, substituting for it an image of "slow-motion" apocalypse, an endlessly protracted "pre-holocaust" from which the world never emerges into a transformed, post-holocaust future.

Bruce Sterling's *Islands in the Net* (1988) de-familiarizes the nuclear threat in a particularly powerful and subtle way. Projecting a near-future world from which nuclear weapons have supposedly been abolished, Sterling, has his heroine Laura, the quintessentially normal citizen of this world, uncover a cabal of renegades armed with atomic weapons and intent on nuclear blackmail. Before our eyes, as it were, her nuclear-free world is shockingly transformed into our own brink-of-apocalypse world. The effect is that of a double de-familiarization: Laura's nuclear-free world, alien to us but familiar to her, is abruptly transformed into a state of affairs utterly alien to her but only too familiar to us, yet, since it is through Laura's eyes and from her alien perspective that we view this familiar state of affairs, it jolts us with a shock of de-familiarized recognition.

Another powerful de-familiarizing strategy of cyberpunk nuclear war fiction is what might be called the motif of "backyard apocalypse." The nuclear threat is literally reduced to backyard dimensions in Marc Laidlaw's satirical *Dad's Nuke* (1985), where suburban neighbors in an embattled Neighborhood enclave compete over who possesses the most advanced family arsenal: when the neighbor across the street acquires his own backyard tactical nuclear missile system, Dad responds by installing a miniature nuclear reactor in the garage! Sterling exploits a version of this same motif in *Schismatrix* (1985), where he de-familiarizes nuclear war by reducing its dimensions and making it a universally available option. In a future in which "world" has been reduced to the dimensions of orbiting "micro-worlds," the threat of annihilation becomes correspondingly small-scale: every orbital microworld is vulnerable to instant micro-apocalypse through the simple puncturing of its airtight outer shell. Furthermore, anyone, even a crew of pirates, can possess technology sufficient to destroy such a world:

> *Worlds could burst.* The walls held life itself, and outside those locks and bulkheads loomed utterly pitiless darkness, the lethal nothingness of naked space ... There was no true safety. There had never been any. There were a hundred ways to kill a world: fire, explosion, poison, sabotage ... The power of destruction was in the hands of anyone and everyone. Anyone and everyone shared the burden of responsibility. The specter of destruction had shaped the moral paradigm of every world and every ideology.
>
> (Sterling, *Schismatrix* 79–80)

Scaling it down to microworld proportions in this way restores to the motif of nuclear apocalypse its power to shock and haunt: Sterling's microworlds are transparently scale-models of our world, his microapocalypses displaced versions of the collective death we face.

Certain critics (e.g. Sontag 223–25; Wagar's *Terminal Visions* 70) have suggested that the literary representation of nuclear war is itself a displacement, that, in fact, every image of collective death is only a kind of metaphor for personal death. Perhaps so; in any case, it is striking that in cyberpunk SF motifs of apocalypse and motifs of personal extinction co-occur, mutually corroborating and reinforcing each other. If anything, though, it is at the level of personal extinction, rather than that of collective disaster, that the cyberpunk meditation on death is most innovative, most resource-ful, and most persistent. "The spectre haunting all c[yber]-p[unk]," as McCaffery ("Introduction" 15) has observed, is *the* Spectre, the spectre of death.

EXCLUDED MIDDLES

Life and death form a binary opposition, of course. As Pynchon reminds us in *Vineland* (1990), returning to a metaphor from his earlier *The Crying of Lot 49* (1966), ours is "a world based on the one and zero of life and death" (72). Between life and death there is no third option, no middle state; the law of the excluded middle applies. But, as we know from *The Crying of Lot 49*, excluded middles are "bad shit, to be avoided" (Pynchon 136), so in *Vineland* Pynchon tries to imagine a middle state of "mediated death" (218) occupied by beings called Thanatoids who, because of some "karmic imbalance" (173), are not permitted fully to die but must linger on in an ambiguous condition "like death, only different" (170).[17] Pynchon's is one version of the postmodernist modeling of the ontological frontier between life and death. Other, parallel versions are to be found in SF, for instance, the "half-life" state upon which Dick's *Ubik* (1969) is premised, and the many other SF variations on the theme of "suspended animation."

Fusing the SF and postmodernist strategies for modeling death, cyber-punk, too, seeks to imagine some middle state beyond or outside biological life yet not a state of non-being, not death itself. Here, as in the case of other cyberpunk motifs, the range of motifs for exploring this middle or half-life state divides along the lines laid down in Sterling's future history of the "posthuman" race: on one side, the Mechanist options, or cyberpunk proper, that is, electronic means of "resurrection" and persistence beyond death; on the other side, the Shaper or "bio-punk" options, that is, bio-engineered means of "posthumous" survival.

We might take as the paradigm of cyberpunk motifs of death and machine-mediated resurrection a cinematic rather than literary example: the death of the policeman Murphy and his "resurrection" as the hybrid Robo-Cop in Paul Verhoeven's film of that name (1987). In this extraordinary sequence, Murphy's death on the operating table is represented from his subjective point of view. Emergency procedures fail to save him, the doctors declare him dead, the screen goes black; then, after a moment of darkness, the subjective "camera-eye" perspective returns, this time framed as in a camera viewfinder, and with LED numbers flashing in one corner of the screen: Murphy has been "revived" as RoboCop, part human being, part machine. This same interior perspective on the experience of dying and being posthumously "booted up" in a machine, so graphically represented in the *RoboCop* sequence, is persistently explored by Rudy Rucker in *Software* and its sequel *Wetware*. Throughout Rucker's texts, intelligences both human and machine face death and experience the disorienting transition to a new mechanical or biological body and the limbo state between existing in one body and existing in another. This is, in a sense, the focus or dominant of Rucker's poetics, and he is relentless in his experimentation with means of representing the subjective experience of death and resurrection.

If Rucker seems particularly obsessive in his exploration of this theme, his preoccupation with death is by no means unique in cyberpunk writing. For instance, Cadigan (in *Synners*) has one character who dies and revives not once but twice—once when he leaves his body to enter the electronic network, a second time *within* the network—and another character, literally a death addict, who wills himself to die over and over, having acquired implants that allow him to shut down his metabolism temporarily (to "flat-line") and then restart it again to return to life. Plural deaths is also a leit-motif of Swanwick's *Vacuum Flowers*. His heroine Rebel Mudlark survives her first death thanks to her personality having been taped, and "dies" a second time when that taped personality is superimposed over another personality—or was it the other who died? The former personality (called Eucrasia) has not, in any case, been wholly obliterated but persists "under" the Rebel-personality as a kind of "ghost" self, "haunting" Rebel from within. Similar variations on the motif of the "ghost" self and "haunting" from within recur throughout Cadigan's *Mindplayers*, where residues of the personalities of the dead persist within the minds of the living, thanks to mind-to-mind contact mediated by machines.

In fact, "ghosts" of various kinds, both in and out of machines, abound in cyberpunk. There are, for instance, the "wireheads" of Sterling's *Schismatrix*, Williams's *Hardwired*, and Cadigan's *Synners*, human selves persisting outside their natural bodies as configurations of information in computer and communication networks; and the "personality constructs" of Gibson's trilogy, ROM units preserving the selves of deceased characters. In both these variants, the dead manifest themselves to the living as uncanny posthumous voices like those of certain postmodernist texts (e.g. Flann O'Brien's *The Third Policeman*, 1940/1967; Russell Hoban's *Pilgermann*, 1983; Thomas Disch's *The Businessman*, 1984); this effect is exploited particularly powerfully by Williams in *Hardwired*. Gibson actually calls certain beings in his *Mona Lisa Overdrive* "ghosts." These, however, are not posthumous selves but constructs, computer-simulated selves who have never existed as biological organisms in the first place, but spring full-grown from artificial-intelligence programs—ghosts *from* the machine. Another version of the ghost from the machine appears in Swanwick's *Vacuum Flowers*, in the form of "interactive ALIs," or Artificial Limited Intelligences, short-lived computer simulations of human beings. In one of its formats, the ALI is agonizingly aware of its brief life-span and imminent death; in another, however, its memories are recorded and made available to a successor ALI, ensuring "a kind of serial immortality" (Swanwick, *Vacuum* 242).

At the end of his trilogy, in the closing pages of *Mona Lisa Overdrive*, Gibson assembles representatives of all his posthumous or out-of-body types on the cyberspace plane: a computer-simulated "ghost," a posthumous ROM personality construct, three human beings who have "died into" the cyberspace matrix. We had already, as early as the end of *Neuromancer*, had intimations of the possibility of posthumous survival in cyberspace, but here the association is confirmed: cyberspace is the machine-mediated version of the World to Come, and in this function bears a certain resemblance to some of the postmodernist variations on the World-to-Come top as (e.g. Christine Brooke-Rose's *Such*, 1966; Alasdair Gray's *Lanark*, 1981; and especially the double-agents' Hell of *Gravity's Rainbow* (Pynchon, *Gravity* 537–48)). "There's dying, then there's dying," as one of Gibson's characters somewhat unhelpfully explains (Gibson, *Mona* 252); there's dying the death of the organic body, then there's dying into the half-life of cyberspace.

The "bio-punk" versions of the death and half-life motif do not figure so conspicuously in cyberpunk writing as do the machine-mediated versions. Nevertheless, it is striking that several of the essentially machine-oriented treatments of this theme have a strong body-oriented component, a strain or undercurrent of Gothic-horror imagery of the disrupted, exploded, or dis-membered body. This is the case, for instance, with Cadigan's *Mindplayers*, where, in one episode, the heroine must make contact with the mind of a deceased poetess whose brain has been extracted and preserved in "stay-juice"—a typical Gothic-horror image. It is also true of Kadrey's *Metroph-age*, where the crime-boss Conover maintains, in an off-limits precinct of his house, a grisly "farm" of multiple clones of his own body, alter egos from whom he "harvests" transplant organs in order to keep himself alive: a case of "suicide and murder all rolled into one package" (215). Rucker's two cyberpunk novels, too, abound in Gothic-horror imagery of dismember-ment, cannibalism, necrophilia, and so on; *Wetware* in particular alludes explicitly, and appositely, to Edgar Allan Poe.

Specifically bio-punk equivalents of the various machine-oriented motifs include cloning, which serves the same function that booting up a software self in a new body does in the machine-mediated variants: it ensures "serial immortality." Thus Steward, at the beginning of Williams's *Voice of the Whirlwind*, is already a "Beta," i.e., the clone of his dead "Alpha" self; later he will die and "return" yet again as his own "Gamma," the clone of his cloned self! Similarly, a character who dies in the first pages of *Schismatrix* "returns" near its close, many decades later, as a cloned *Doppelgänger* of herself. Sterling also exploits the familiar SF motifs of suspended animation and extreme longevity, especially the latter. In the course of *Schismatrix*, only one natural death is recorded; otherwise, characters live on and on, either dying by violence or, in extreme old age, "fading" into an ambiguous half-life state.

The bio-punk equivalent of "wirehead" survival, i.e., posthumous existence as a configuration of information in a cybernetic system, occurs in Bear's *Blood Music*. Here human selves are encoded as information at the level of the component cells of their own bodies; thus, when the body is dissolved and its component cells dispersed, the original self can nevertheless be posthumously reconstituted from the information encoded at the cellular level. This, eerily, is what happens late in *Blood Music* to an entire family who are physically dissolved into undifferentiated tissue and then reconstituted as "themselves," returning to "haunt" (benignly) the surviving family member.

If Bear thus gives a distinctively bio-punk twist to the ghost motif, Shepard does the same with the zombie motif. In his *Green Eyes*, posthumous life is induced in corpses through the introduction of a strain of bacteria. The life-span of these "Bacterially Induced Artificial Personalities" ranges from a norm of a few minutes or hours, to several months in extraordinary cases, so-called "slow-burners." Shepard, especially in the early parts of the novel, explores the subjective experience of posthumous life in "slow-burners": their struggles to gain control of their new bodies, their growing awareness of the imminence and inevitability of their own second deaths. He gives us, in other words, the bio-punk version of the death and half-life of Verhoeven's RoboCop.

In its preoccupation with the representation of death, both in its machine-oriented and its bio-punk forms, cyberpunk shows to what degree it has converged with mainstream postmodernist fiction, and how far it has outstripped all the earlier "waves" of science fiction, where the representation of death, even in the boldest and most sophisticated New Wave examples (e.g. Dick's *Ubik*, Disch's *On Wings of Song*), seems somewhat primitive and flatfooted by comparison. The cyberpunk writers (and film-makers) demonstrate that conventional "old-wave" science fiction of the *Star Trek* type has it all wrong: death, not space, is the final frontier of the imagination, beyond which only the most innovative adventurers boldly go.

ACKNOWLEDGEMENTS

Reprinted from *Constructing Postmodernism*, Brian McHale (Routledge 1992) © by kind permission of the author and Taylor & Francis Books UK.

NOTES

1 On cyberpunk "school" institutions, see Bruce Sterling's introductions to *Mirrorshades* and Gibson's *Burning Chrome*; and McCaffery's interviews with Gibson and Sterling in *Across the Wounded Galaxies* 211–32.

2 The joke is Dick Higgins's; see his "A Child's History of Fluxus."

3 Malmgren's proposal of alternating phases of extrapolative and speculative dominance in the history of twentieth-century SF seems to echo David Lodge's (1977) account of alternating phases of metaphorical and metonymic dominance in the history of "mainstream" fiction in our century. But if the rhythm of

historical change in SF parallels that of mainstream fiction, it does so only in principle. For the pendulum swings in the history of SF are not synchronized with those of mainstream fiction: SF does not shift from an extrapolative to a speculative dominant when mainstream fiction swings from its metonymic to its metaphorical pole, or from speculation back to extrapolation when mainstream fiction swings from metaphor to metonymy. Nor, for that matter, is SF history simply mainstream fiction's inverse, speculative when the latter is metonymic, extrapolative when it is metaphoric. Out of synch with each other, the two cycles do interact, but in a more complex rhythm of influence, counter-influence, and feedback (see above, "POSTcyberMODERNpunkISM").

4 For cyberpunk claims to extrapolation, again see Sterling's introductions to Sterling's *Mirrorshades* and to Gibson's *Burning Chrome*). For expressions of skepticism from "hard" SF writers, see Benford's and Brin's contributions to McCaffery (1988b: 18–27). It is perhaps paradoxical that one of Gibson's earliest stories, "The Gernsback Continuum" (reprinted in both Sterling's *Mirrorshades* and Gibson's *Burning Chrome*), involves a parody and explicit critique of Gernsback-style extrapolative "scientifiction." On the one hand, this might be read as an unconcealed manifestation of "anxiety of influence," Gibson's attempt to get the SF "Great Tradition" off his back. On the other hand, it aptly demonstrates the principle of no simple "return" to an earlier phase; rather, each return, e.g. of 1930s-style extrapolation in the 1980s, is inevitably a return with a difference.

5 Underlying my rather casual use of "levels" here is Harshav's (1979) three-dimensional model of the text.

6 See Calinescu's "From the One to Many" and McHale's *Postmodernist Fiction*; and see above, "The (post)modernism of *The Name of the Rose*."

7 On space in postmodernist fiction, see Malmgren; on the "spatial turn" of postmodernism in general, see Harvey, Soja, and Jameson's *Postmodernism* (16, 154–57, 364–76 and *passim*).

8 Computer technology is rapidly outstripping science fiction, for actual, functioning versions of computer-simulated "virtual reality" closely resembling Gibson's fictional "cyberspace" are currently under development (see, e.g. Stewart).

9 Literalization of modernist-style mythic archetypes is also a motif of postmodernist writing; see, e.g., Donald Barthelme's *Snow White* (1967), *The Dead Father* (1974), and *The King* (1990), Robert Coover's *Pricksongs and Descants* (1969), Italo Calvino's *The Castle of Crossed Destinies* (1969/1973), Gunter Grass's *The Flounder* (1977), Angela Carter's *The Bloody Chamber* (1979), John Fowles's *Mantissa* (1982), and especially the fiction of John Barth, including *Giles Goat-Boy* (1966), *Lost in the Funhouse* (1968), *Chimera* (1972), and *The Tidewater Tales* (1987). Barth puts the case for literalizing mythic archetypes in quite explicit terms: "to write realistic fictions which point always to mythic archetypes is in my opinion to take the wrong end of the mythopoeic stick, however meritorious such fiction may be in other respects. Better to address the archetypes directly" (Barth 1973: 207–8).

10 See Maddox in McCaffery's *Storming the Reality Studio*; and Bukatman's "Postcards." Swanwick, in *Vacuum Flowers*, offers a parallel future history and an alternative pair of categories; in his version, the division is between the "wettechnic civilization" (roughly, the Mech option) of the solar system proper and the bioprogramming technologies (roughly, the Shaper option) of the comet worlds.

11 Also related is the motif of telepathic mind-control, a much more conventional SF motif, to be found in Shepard's *Life During Wartime* alongside the more distinctively cyberpunk variants of the drug-induced personality and the radio-controlled zombie.

12 It seems likely that Shepard's motif of bacterially-induced personality owes something to Thomas Disch's New Wave SF novel *Camp Concentration* (1968), in which, in a medical experiment on prison inmates, a strain of syphilis is introduced which produces a temporary heightening of intelligence.

13 Another bio-punk version of the motif of collective selfhood is Sterling's "Swarm" (1982), the first of the Shaper/Mechanist stories, featuring an anthill-like collective organism (the Swarm of the title) that horribly absorbs one human interloper and establishes a symbiotic relation with another.

14 Other striking examples of the use of extrapolated technologies to motivate modernist-style perspectivism can be found in Sterling's *Islands in the Net* and Kadrey's *Metrophage*. In the former, agents of a multinational corporation wear broadcast rigs which allow their colleagues throughout the world to occupy their points of view electronically. In the latter, the modernist techniques of flashback and involuntary memory are technologically literalized through prosthetic eyes which enable the user to record and play back past scenes.

15 See above, "POSTcyberMODERNpunkISM," on Kathy Acker's rewriting of one of these simstim episodes from *Neuromancer*.

16 See Wagar and Dowling; and see above, "The (post)modernism of *The Name of the Rose*."

17 See above, "Zapping, the art of switching channels."

18 Compare the premise of the *Max Headroom* television series (in the United States, ABC, spring 1987), in which a television journalist named Edison Carter, the victim of foul play, is "resurrected" as his manic alter ego, the computer simulation Max Headroom. It transpires that Carter isn't really dead after all, so that Max doesn't replace but merely mirrors (however distortedly) his human "original." A postmodernist analogue is McElroy's *Plus* (1976), in which the supposedly deceased human protagonist, who has allowed his brain to be reused as the control system for an orbiting satellite, feeds on cosmic radiation and gradually regenerates "himself," recovering piece by piece his supposedly "lost" memories and identity.

2 "A Rare State of Ferment"

SF Controversies from the New Wave to Cyberpunk

Rob Latham

Science fiction today is in a rare state of ferment. This happy situation had been created only with great effort and must now be prolonged and intensified.

(Bruce Sterling, *Cheap Truth* #15)

In his celebrated essay "The Many Deaths of Science Fiction," Roger Luckhurst argues that science fiction is obsessed with its own imagined death, whether envisioned as an ecstatic fusion with the literary "mainstream" (the heady goal of SF's various avant-gardes) or as a corruption of generic purity via the contagion of foreign elements (the perennial fear of SF's irascible Old Guard). According to Luckhurst, the history of SF is marked by a series of crises in which emergent movements—"the New Wave, feminist SF, cyberpunk"—announce themselves as "transcendent death-as-births, finally demolishing the 'ghetto' walls," while at the same time being denounced as "degenerescent birth-as-deaths, perverting the specificity of the genre" (43). This dialectic exposes the ideological stakes of aesthetic legitimation: the avant-gardists bemoan SF's segregated "low-art" status and yearn for acceptance by the standards of "serious" literature, while the Old Guard decries such arty pretension and cherishes SF's characteristic values and practices. In the eyes of the former, SF needs to be radically transformed, must die to be reborn as Art, while for the latter it is being cruelly slain by this very process of creative emancipation. According to Luckhurst, this "panic narrative" is theoretically misguided, and critical analyses of the field might move "into more constructive areas" if it were finally dispelled (47–48).

Another way of grasping this dynamic, however, is as a practical problem having to do with the way SF (or any) history is narrated: should historical development be understood as a continuous process, a teleological unfolding, or as a sporadic sequence of ruptures and deviations?[1] This is a particularly potent question in the context of a genre that tends, on the one hand, to see itself in terms of the ongoing elaboration of a set of durable themes (space travel, alien life, future societies, etc.), but which is, on the other hand, notoriously marked by a boom-and-bust publishing cycle that can lay waste to whole traditions virtually overnight (the collapse of the pulp market in the mid-1950s, for example), making for abrupt turnovers in the readership that sustains the field. Whether the history of SF is perceived as a steady development based on cumulative growth or as a succession of disruptions ushering in phases of radical overhaul depends to a large extent on the relative stress one places on conservation versus innovation: clearly, the genre could not survive as a cohesive corpus without some significant continuity of content, yet at the same time it could hardly remain a vital literature without an openness to new ideas and methods of treatment. Indeed, it is entirely possible to argue that a recurring cycle of messianic avant-gardism and old-school intransigence is the very motor of SF as an historical genre; its true death might thus lie in the potential remission of this energizing and revivifying agonism.

Rather than exorcizing this cycle of crisis, as Luckhurst demands, what SF criticism ought to be doing, in my opinion, is charting more carefully and in greater material detail its basic structure and mode of operation. What are the intra- and extra-generic stakes, during particular historical periods, of the avant-garde critique of traditional SF? By what rhetorical strategies and through which specific sites do the activists for change construct and diffuse their manifestoes? How does the Old Guard respond to these provocations, and how sorely tested is SF's subcultural network in coping with the spreading controversy? Is the conflict facilitated or hampered by the emergence and consolidation of new institutions within the field (e.g., publication venues, convention meetings) or by the ramifications of a boom-and-bust economy? What impact does the struggle have on the careers of established authors and magazines, and how do new writers and editors negotiate the resultant fallout? Is the ideological clash manifested or thematized within SF stories released during its height? Finally, what lingering effects (if any) does the dispute have on the further evolution of the genre? Which aspects of the avant-garde incursion are accommodated, in whole or in part, and which are cast off? How does conventional wisdom about what SF essentially *is* shift, whether comfortably or uneasily, in response to this assimilation?

Obviously, these are complicated—and intricately intermeshing—questions, and I hardly have the space here adequately to address, much less try to answer, them all. But I would like to make a start by analyzing, in a comparative way, two of the most prominent and influential debates of the past several decades in SF: the New Wave controversy of the 1960s and the quarrels over cyberpunk in the 1980s. Such a comparison should permit widescale judgments about the structure of SF's legitimation crises during the postwar era, as well as providing insight into the relationship between two of the most strident and confrontational activist movements the genre has known. In what follows, I will pursue three broad, dovetailing tracks of analysis. First, I will trace the emergence of these major avant-gardes within the context of the genre during their respective periods, seeking to specify the local conditions that paved the way for their interventions; the focus will thus be on the *immanent* history of SF, its evolution as a discrete institutional formation. Second, I will examine how the New Wave and cyberpunk controversies were connected to encompassing trends in the general culture; the focus here will be on the *extra-generic* phenomena combatants in the debates drew upon for their polemical inspiration. Finally, I will explore ideological connections between the movements themselves; specifically, I will show how cyberpunk's champions sought to distinguish their aesthetic and political objectives from the New Wave's important but now-dated innovations and how the surviving partisans of the latter faction responded to the militant swagger of this fresh cohort of genre rebels. In conclusion, I will offer some meditations on how these controversies have reverberated down to the present day.

1. While acknowledging the many significant differences between the genre of the mid-1960s, when the New Wave appeared on the scene, and the mid-1980s, when cyberpunk surfaced, it is nonetheless possible to identify three common trends prevailing in the field immediately prior to the advent of each movement. Briefly stated, these were: (1) a widespread sense of malaise among writers and fans owing to economic developments impacting the publication and dissemination of SF, combined with a dawning sense of possibility linked to the arrival of new markets; (2) the retirement or obvious decline in productivity of a number of major authors whose output had dominated the previous decade; and (3) the inchoate but growingly palpable influx of fresh thematic material, partly inhibited by prevailing orthodoxies and thus awaiting mobilization by talents less beholden to SF traditions. None of these tendencies by itself would be sufficient to explain the emergence of either avant-garde, but taken together they contributed to a climate that was favorable to calls for a radical refurbishment of SF; indeed, the manifestoes that emerged to herald the two movements made much of the purportedly baleful situation of the field and the urgent need for fresh voices and perspectives.

The boom-and-bust cycle characteristic of the genre was never more in evidence than during the late 1950s and early 1960s. In the summer of 1957, 23 SF magazines were published in the United States (Ashley 179), representing a broad range of styles, from classic space opera (e.g., *Science Fiction Adventures*) to futuristic satire (e.g., *Galaxy*); three years later, the total had dwindled to six, controlled by only four editors. The pulps, which had survived since Hugo Gernsback's *Amazing Stories* debuted in 1926, had vanished utterly, replaced by the more sober-looking digests—which also were suffering financially due not only to a competition with paperback books but also to the abrupt collapse of their biggest national distributor. The result was a momentous contraction of the market, from 142 separate issues released in 1957 to a mere 60 four years later; between 1958 and 1963, only one magazine debuted—*Vanguard*, edited by James Blish—and it lasted a single issue (Ashley 189).

At the dawn of the new decade, the genre was widely perceived to be in crisis. A contemporaneous index to the parlous state of the field may be found in Earl Kemp's Hugo Award-winning fanzine from 1961, *Who Killed Science Fiction?* A one-shot symposium featuring some six dozen contributions by major SF authors, editors, and fans, it addressed the topic of whether SF magazines, heretofore the field's dominant market, were now moribund. According to Kemp's prefatory tabulation, eleven respondents answered "yes" while 55 said "no," though a large fraction of the latter cadre pessimistically indicated that "the death struggle was already in sight."[2] The general tone of the assessments was somber, ranging from Blish's judgment that SF had become "a cramped and unrewarding genre" to Jack Williamson's contention that it had been "hurt in a triple squeeze between television, the comics, and the paperbacks." Interestingly, according to Kemp, 24 contributors, in response to a corollary question, affirmed that the growing paperback market could potentially be seen as "a point of salvation" (while 16 said it could not); though at the time only a handful of publishing houses—most notably, Ace, Ballantine, and Doubleday—had initiated SF lines, these were thriving (by contrast with the magazines) and seemed to hold out hope for an imminent revitalization of the field. Unfortunately, despite the apparent promise of the SF book market, the field was hemorraghing talent at an alarming rate: as magazines folded in rapid succession, a number of major authors whose careers had defined 1950s SF packed up and fled. Many stopped writing altogether, either returning intermittently in later decades or falling silent forever: Alfred Bester, Algis Budrys, Katherine MacLean, Walter M. Miller, Jr., Ward Moore, Theodore Sturgeon, William Tenn. "The fifties ended dismally for most science fiction writers," Barry N. Malzberg glumly asserts. "There is no other way to put this" (46).

This pessimistic portrait of SF at the cusp of the 1960s is not quite fair, of course, since it stresses rupture at the expense of continuity, depicting an epochal calamity rather than focusing on emerging trends that would eventually repair and regenerate the field. One of these, already mentioned, was the burgeoning book market, which would basically supplant the magazines as the main venue for SF by the end of the new decade. This diverse publishing scene spurred a host of new writers who would lay claim to the terrain in the name of competing traditions—of Old Style versus New Wave. The late 1950s and early 1960s also laid down institutional structures and began to explore fictional themes upon which the New Wave would vigorously capitalize. The Milford Conferences, established in 1956 by Blish, Damon Knight, and Judith Merril, had become an annual fixture by the end of the decade, fostering a higher consciousness not only of narrative style but also of the sort of professional standards prevailing in the literary mainstream. One may perceive, in the inauguration of this ambitious series of workshops and in the casual grousings against their alumni as a "Milford mafia" by an older generation of writers, the first glimmerings of the harsher controversies that would roil SF in the mid-1960s, and Knight and especially Merril would find themselves at the center of them. Certainly, the Milford Conferences were seedbeds for apprentice talent that would come to full bloom during the New Wave wars.

Commencing also in 1956, Merril had edited an annual book series, *The Year's Best S-F*, whose capping "summations" increasingly pushed a proto-New Wave agenda of ambitious experimentation that would, so she contended, eventually win SF the embrace of literary critics and non-genre readers. Indeed, she boldly surmised—in the seventh annual volume, covering 1961—that the "specialized cult of science fiction (for which many of us still ... feel a lingering nostalgia) is rapidly disappearing, as [its] essential quality is absorbed into the main body of literature" (391). Her preferred term for the resultant mixture was "speculative fiction," which referred to a more aesthetically ambitious and socially critical form of writing than the pulps had generally favored. The foremost practitioner of "spec-fic" within the genre, in Merril's view, was J.G. Ballard, whose early work had appeared exclusively in John Carnell's magazines *New Worlds* and *Science Fantasy* in the UK (though sometimes being reprinted in Merril's annuals). In 1962, Ballard began to place stories in the US magazines, and his first four books were released by Berkley Press (where Knight was developing an SF line). While American readers were beguiled by his dreamlike imagery and the offbeat lyricism of his prose, they were probably not cognizant of the agenda driving them, which Ballard had outlined in a 1962 guest editorial for *New Worlds* entitled "Which Way to Inner Space?"

One of the first volleys in the battle that would consume the genre, on both sides of the Atlantic, later in the decade, Ballard's essay sweepingly decreed that pulp SF's fascination with interplanetary travel had been rendered obsolete by the advent of the Space Age, and that the genre's future lay in the disciplined exploration of "inner space": mind control, psychobiology, altered states of consciousness. Ballard's line of reasoning essentially raised the stock of 1950s talents such as Bester and Philip K. Dick, whose work (e.g., *The Demolished Man* [1953], *Eye in the Sky* [1957]) had already begun the transition from outer to inner space that he demanded. Thus, the characteristic themes of the New Wave lurked, in embryo, on the margins of a genre widely perceived to be moribund, and could thus be activated by inventive writers willing to take risks in order to push SF in fresh directions. When Michael Moorcock took over the editorship of *New Worlds* in the summer of 1964, the risk-takers would acquire a highly visible platform from which to agitate and transform the field.

I have written elsewhere about the origins of the New Wave in Britain, the ideological program evolved in *New Worlds*'s pages, and the contours of the spreading controversy on both sides of the Atlantic[3] and I will not rehearse that story at length here—the basic outline of which is, in any case, familiar from existing histories. What I would like to focus on, following Luckhurst's analysis in his "Many Deaths" essay, is the way that the movement's defenders sought to legitimize SF by expanding its borders to include perspectives culled from the experimental arts and the youth counterculture, while its enemies struggled to preserve the field's imagined purity against these incursions. My purpose in this discussion, however, is not, *à la* Luckhurst, to expose the phantasmal character of the debate, but rather to illuminate ideological strategies and rhetorical tactics at a specific moment of genre crisis, showing how all the feverish jockeying for position played out against the backdrop of the institutional ruptures and continuities that characterized 1960s SF.

Ballard's militant brief for inner space, and his dismissal of the familiar pulp megatext of starships and interplanetary adventure, was essentially a call for a new speculative tradition that would be responsive to the host of "soft" technologies—from the pharmaceutical to the communicational—that had come to pervade the postwar landscape. According to Ballard, a writer like William S. Burroughs, with his cut-up novels anatomizing sinister invisible systems of addiction and control, had already moved into this postindustrial terrain, while the genre imaginary remained bound to industrial-era high-tech gadgetry. Deploying classic SF imagery but in no way beholden to genre constraints on plot or narrative technique, Burroughs had shown the way towards "a new set of conventions" that could reinvigorate the field ("Myth-Maker" 127)—a judgment with which Moorcock agreed, going even further in claiming that "a *popular* literary renaissance is around the corner," with Burroughs its figurehead and *New Worlds* its standard-bearer ("New Literature" 3; emphasis in original). In short, SF needed to absorb from the experimental arts, as well as from cutting-edge theorists of mass-media society (most centrally Marshall McLuhan), a mode of responding to postwar techoculture that would have relevance to contemporary readers, for whom pulp-era SF existed at best as a nostalgic memory and at worst as a campy embarrassment. "SF is growing up," Moorcock asserted, and must thus "use images apt for today": "It is up to the young writer to find terms and symbols which make sense in the sixties" ("Symbols" 2–3).

What this demand that SF be "relevant to the world of Now" ("Symbols" 25) came to mean in practice, as a host of new writers and fans took up the crusade, was that inner space became, as Thomas Disch flippantly observes, "shorthand for sex, drugs, and rock 'n' roll" (*Dreams* 108). The stolid rocket jockeys of the pulp tradition suddenly seemed boringly square, and were readily satirized in *New Worlds*' pages; more disturbingly, they were perceived as dutiful agents of a faceless technocracy increasingly under assault from leftwing quarters—"human robots inhabit[ing] landscapes that mirrored their own alienation," as Disch himself put it at the time ("Introduction" 5).[4] The inner space agenda converged neatly with the counterculture critique of what Theodore Roszak called "the myth of objective consciousness"—the notion that scientific expertise, "cleansed of all subjective distortion" (208), was the highest possible wisdom. This orientation, "remote from the rewards of warm engagement with life," tended, according to Roszak, to repress the body and its pleasures, favoring instead a mechanistic regimentation and an attitude of "cool curiosity untouched by love, tenderness, or passionate wonder" (219).[5] Given this critical context, it is perhaps not surprising that the New Wave was experienced, by many of its advocates and not a few of enemies, as an explosive desublimation, a release of libidinal energies that seemed to threaten SF's core commitment to the technoscientific world-view.

According to one of the most vigorous opponents of the movement, Donald A. Wollheim, the New Wave had, like the feverish artists who inspired it ("the William Burroughs and Allen Ginsberg schools" [103]), effectively abandoned all reason and restraint: "sensual pleasures come to the fore as the only immediate real values left. Hence a great deal of the New Wave writing concerns itself with shock words and shock scenes, hallucinatory fantasies, and sex" (105). This perspective, which converged with mainstream anxieties about contemporary youth as a horde of hedonistic barbarians, points to the emergence of a "generation gap" within the field, dividing Old Guardists like Wollheim from avant-gardists like Moorcock and Disch, whose respective fan followers translated the struggle into their own hip lingo of sedition and reaction. Old Guard stalwart Lester Del Rey, for example, found himself elevated to the role of "First Speaker" of the "Second Foundation," an organization modeled on the secret society in Isaac Asimov's *Foundation Trilogy*, whose task it was to preserve human learning amid an encroaching Dark Age.[6] According to Del Rey, the New Wave was precisely such a barbarian incursion into SF's holy citadel, spearheaded by a cabal of decadent aesthetes who sought "to cajole by new art the attention of mainstream critics [and] ... seduce the approval of the academic world" (3).

What is most interesting about Del Rey's polemic, aside from its hysterical tone, is the fact that the movement's ultimate vacuity emerges not in its counterculture values or its anti-science themes, but in its tendency towards incestuous self-promotion—"the uses of publicity and controversy as publicity; the wooing of publishers; the sympathetic critics and what they can do for a writer; the prestige that can be gained from college appearances" (3), and so on. This sort of complaint suggests that the stakes of the struggle were, at some basic level, perceived as economic, a matter of successful positioning within a rapidly evolving marketplace. As the magazines were shouldered aside by the paperbacks, and as an older cohort of fans weaned on the pulps gave way to a fresh generation of readers with different interests and lifestyles, a quickening competition for hearts and minds was only to be expected, and such a contest could hardly help but take on harsh tonalities given the growing split between establishment and counterculture in the general society.

Indeed, the New Wave deeply impacted the packaging and promotion of SF, its influence ranging from the pervasion of psychedelic imagery on paperback covers to the use of adjectives like "subversive" and "taboo-breaking" as terms of praise in reviews and on book-jacket copy. Major works of the period—e.g., Harlan Ellison's *Dangerous Visions* (1967), Norman Spinrad's *Bug Jack Barron* (1969)—came equipped with an apparatus of storm and hullaballoo that likely only boosted sales figures; and Merril's attempt at an agenda-setting volume, *England Swings SF* (1968), featured an editorial blurb talking up "the revolution of new thinking and the mind-tingling innovations" of the movement and ending with the provocative query: "Is it indeed time for new forms and new approaches to imaginative speculative fiction? Has science fiction as we have known it really become moribund?" The power of this promotional discourse of controversy-mongering is indicated by the fact that the blurb in question was penned by none other than Wollheim, then chief editor at Ace Books, who, though a stern enemy of the New Wave, was shrewd enough to know which side his bread was buttered on. The New Wave was, in short, a creature of the boom years of the mid-1960s, its rise coeval with the consolidation of an SF book market that favored a greater diversity and spoke to a larger audience than the magazines could ever have hoped to do.

2. Turning now to an assessment of the condition of the field prior to the dawn of cyberpunk—roughly, from 1978 to 1982—the first thing that needs to be acknowledged is the extraordinary commercial explosion of the genre following the early 1960s. Writers who had abandoned SF due to the seismic contraction of the late 1950s could hardly have imagined the transformation in the market two decades later: in 1978, for the first time ever, more than 1000 SF titles—including original and reprinted material—were published (Brown, "1978 Book Summary"). The book market grew steadily to a peak in 1979 of 1288 titles, at which point the genre succumbed to a recession in the publishing industry, losing some of its gains and bottoming out at 1047 titles in 1982 (Brown, "1982 *Locus* book Summary": 12). Of course, this "bottom" was an unimaginable ceiling for those who could remember the 1950s crash, but it is important to recognize that a drop of some 19% in the market was still significant for authors struggling to make a living at the time; the fact that these losses seem modest by historical standards does not mean that SF had shed its boom-and-bust habits or the corrosive effect this cycle tended to have on the psyches of practicing professionals.

Moreover, these gross numbers do not give an adequate sense of the evolving ecology of the SF marketplace during the period. On the one hand, a small cohort of writers began to command unprecedented financial rewards based on their proven ability to deliver blockbusters. The first book packaged as SF that managed to place on the *New York Times* best-seller list in both hardcover and paperback editions was Frank Herbert's *Children of Dune* (1976): the Berkley softcover "had an initial print run of 800,000 copies but went back to press even before publication" (Brown, "Third *Dune* Book": 1). Within a few years, other authors had scaled these dizzying heights; as Charles Brown commented in his *Locus* year-end summary for 1983, "[i]t would be more surprising now if a new book by Herbert,

Heinlein, Clarke, Asimov, etc., did *not* make the bestseller list" ("1983": 1; emphasis in original). This sort of success led to record paydays as publishers battled to corner the next smash hit: Joe Haldeman, fresh off the multiple-award-winning triumph of *The Forever War* (1974), was handed an advance of $100,000 by Avon to produce *Mindbridge* (1976), while Robert Silverberg was lured out of a brief retirement by a $127,500 advance from Harper & Row for *Lord Valentine's Castle* (1980), the first volume in what became his "Majipoor Trilogy" (Brown, "New Silverberg Novel": 1–2). Indeed, trilogies or even open-ended series—Herbert's "Dune" sequels, Asimov's later "Foundation" and "Robot" books, McCaffrey's "Pern" novels— became the norm as major names, seeking reliable income, established themselves on the charts as stable brands.

On the other hand, mid-list writers unable to trademark themselves in this way, or uninterested in generating steady product of a recognizable type, were increasingly squeezed between the best-sellers, which commanded large promotional budgets and ample space at the chain bookstores, and the proliferating presence of film novelizations and other media tie-ins, which grew speedily following the box-office success of George Lucas's *Star Wars* in 1977 and the rebirth of *Star Trek* as a movie franchise in 1979. By the early 1980s, SF had become a potentially quite lucrative field, and the publishers, undergoing a period of monopolistic consolidation,[7] were committed to squeezing as much profit out of it as possible. To this end, wheeler-dealer packagers like Byron Preiss developed high-concept properties such as shared-world anthologies (which united various writers under pre-fabricated narrative umbrellas) and sharecropper novels (which hired aspiring talents to churn out works set in the best-selling worlds of Asimov, Clarke, and company). Working in such a system was economically as well as aesthetically exploitative, since it provided considerably smaller royalties than otherwise prevailed (Disch, *The Dreams Our Stuff Is Made Of*: 211–12).

This ongoing commodification of SF tempers somewhat the startling statistical portrait of exponential growth. Of the 581 new books published in 1983 (that is, excluding reprint titles), only 186 (32%) were original SF novels, while at least 50 (9%) were media tie-ins or other mass-market products.[8] 146 of the total (25%) were original fantasy novels, the SF field (and *Locus*'s year-end summaries) having expanded to include this turf in the wake of the runaway success of the Del Rey fantasy line beginning in 1977; this number also includes works of occult or supernatural horror, a subgenre then enjoying a massive takeoff thanks to Stephen King's and Peter Straub's wildly popular books. In response to this mounting rivalry, SF of the period began to adopt textures and tones borrowed from these affiliated genres: Silverberg's "Majipoor Trilogy" (1980–83), Gene Wolfe's *Book of the New Sun* tetralogy (1980–83), Brian Aldiss's "Helliconia" series (1982–85), Joan Vinge's *Snow Queen* (1980) and its sequels were works of science fantasy with crossover appeal to diverse audiences. Some dyed-in-the-wool purists—especially hard-SF writers with a commitment to technoscientific rationalism—stoutly condemned this hybridization, which threatened (so they felt) to submerge SF's legacy of disciplined extrapolation in an ocean of dreamy pap, an indictment with which many cyberpunk polemicists concurred. Whatever one may think of these claims, the fact is that the genre, especially during the recessionary trough of the early 1980s, was experiencing all manner of aesthetic distortions under the pressure of a competition for resources that, however expanded since the 1960s, were still quite clearly finite.

Finding a niche in this complexly ramifying ecosystem was particularly difficult for authors not interested in churning out trilogies or doing literary piecework for some corporate brand-name. Unlike the early 1960s, when a well-established market (the SF magazine) was palpably decaying and a new one (the SF paperback) swiftly opening up with a sense of frontier promise that lured a host of young writers, the late 1970s and early 1980s were characterized instead by a well-entrenched system with clearly defined parameters for success that newcomers ignored at their peril. Perhaps unsurprisingly, a substantial fraction of the New Wave cohort—whose careers, as the nascent book market expanded, had followed idiosyncratic paths driven largely by their own artistic visions—found the new situation uncongenial enough to bow gracefully out of it: Disch, Malzberg, Samuel R. Delany, Joanna Russ, R.A. Lafferty, and other leading lights of the 1960s and 1970s either produced scant work in the following decade or else disappeared into the marginal (and relatively unremunerative) terrain of the specialty presses.[9] This was a die-off of talent quite as remarkable as the one that capped the 1950s, again driven by a spreading sense of general malaise: for all its vast commercial appeal, SF seemed, to many contemporary observers, to have hit an aesthetic wall. The 1983 Hugo ballot for best novel (which honored work published in the previous year) provides a stark measure of the enveloping crisis: scanning it, one would think that the field had regressed to the 1950s, given the presence of Heinlein's *Friday*, Clarke's *2010: Odyssey Two*, and Asimov's *Foundation's Edge* (the eventual winner).

This was the basic institutional framework within which the major cyberpunk writers—William Gibson, Bruce Sterling, John Shirley, Pat Cadigan, Lewis Shiner, and Rudy Rucker—kicked off their careers. Most of them broke into print in the late 1970s, after the New Wave had clearly ebbed and in the midst of the new corporate culture that devalued individual style in favor of slick marketable properties. Until Sterling and Shiner began issuing polemical edicts in defense of the new movement, in the pages of their fanzine *Cheap Truth* in 1983, the group's work tended to fly "well below the genre's radar"—as William Gibson put it in his foreword to a 1996 reprint of Shirley's *City Come A-Walkin'* (2), originally released in 1980 as a Dell mid-list original. Shirley's other SF novels—*Transmaniacon* (1979), *Three-Ring Psychus* (1980)—appeared as Zebra paperbacks and quickly sank without a trace, as did his occasional forays into supernatural horror (e.g., *Cellars* (Avon, 1980)). Rucker followed a similar trajectory with his early books: *White Light* (1980), *Spacetime Doughnuts* (1981), and *Software* (1982) all emerged as disposable Ace softcovers, jostling for attention on the bookstore shelves alongside dozens of similarly packaged efforts. Sterling's first novel, *Involution Ocean* (1978), was released in a short-lived "Harlan Ellison Discoveries" series sponsored by Jove Books, and while his second effort, *The Artificial Kid* (1980), managed to score a hardback edition from Harper & Row, it did not make a substantial impact.

The first real breakthrough by a cyberpunk writer were the so-called "Sprawl" stories—"Johnny Mnemonic," "Burning Chrome," "New Rose Hotel"—that William Gibson began publishing in *Omni* magazine in 1981. A New-Agey science fiction/fact publication funded out of the deep pockets of *Penthouse* editor Bob Guiccione, *Omni* was itself a prominent example of the corporate takeover of SF during the period; debuting in 1978 to cash in on a genre that *Star Wars* had put on the commercial map, it would provide the cyberpunks with their highest-profile—and best-paying—market prior to 1984, when *Neuromancer* exploded on the scene (as a paperback original, in Terry Carr's Ace Specials line) and utterly changed the stakes of the game. That the cyberpunks were aware of the prospective disaster of a mismanaged career is indicated by Sterling's tongue-in-cheek analysis, in *Cheap Truth* #11, of the predicament of Russell M. Griffin, an intensely original talent whose "succession of poorly-marketed novels, each from a less successful publisher than the one before," compelled him "last week [to] devour ... his own foot in order to stay alive."[10] Indeed, the creepy corporate-dominated future depicted in so many cyberpunk texts was perhaps a projection of the bleak publishing landscape in which the writers felt themselves immured. Gibson's triumph was important to the cadre because it enabled affiliated figures to be picked out against the backdrop of a glutted market—a development that readily led cyberpunk's enemies to dismiss the movement as mere marketing hype (an attack, as we have seen, that had been leveled against the New Wave as well).

Just as the New Wave had capitalized on emergent inner-space themes in the early 1960s, so the cyberpunks drew out threads submerged in the tapestry of 1980s science fantasy, in the process helping to refurbish the genre's thematic repertoire. While Sterling's preface to *Mirrorshades: The Cyberpunk Anthology*, one of the most prominent manifestoes of the movement, claims that an "allegiance to Eighties culture has marked ... [the] group" (ix), in fact the key themes he highlights—the increasing cyborgization of experience, the fusion of high-tech and subculture, rampant globalization—had been explored in the previous decade by writers as diverse as Ballard (e.g., *The Atrocity Exhibition* [1970]), D.G. Compton (e.g., *The Steel Crocodile* [1970]), and John Brunner (e.g., *The Shockwave Rider* [1975]). Indeed, cyberpunk inherited from the New Wave a fascination with corporate mass-mediatization and "global integration" (Sterling, Preface xiv) derived from the critical and creative work of Burroughs, McLuhan, and Alvin Toffler, mixing in an ambivalent posthumanism that tended to view these processes as ethically neutral if not politically neutralizing. Most significantly, cyberpunk reverted to the hard-edged near-future orientation of much 1970s SF, marking a sharp contrast with the dreamy landscapes of contemporary science fantasy. As Sterling commented in praising Gibson's "Burning Chrome" in *Cheap Truth* #2:

> THIS is the shape for science fiction in the 1980s: fast-moving, sharply extrapolated, technologically literate, and as brilliant and coherent as a laser. Gibson's focused and powerful attack is our best chance yet to awaken a genre that has been half-asleep since the early 1970s.

Attracting attention by drawing invidious distinctions was a major tactic of the cyberpunk polemicists, though unlike the New Wave's partisans they were hampered by never gaining control of a major platform such as *New Worlds* (though they found sympathetic editorial ears at *Omni* and *Isaac Asimov's Science Fiction Magazine*). *Cheap Truth* was, however, widely read within the community of fans and authors, and its broadsides against the "reptilian torpor" of contemporary SF (as Sterling put it in the first sentence of issue #1) had the intended incendiary effect. Aggressively demanding that SF "reform itself, re-think itself, and re-establish itself as a moving cultural force instead of a backwater anarchronism" (*CT* #2), Sterling, under the pseudonym Vincent Omniaveritas, and his sometime collaborater Shiner (a.k.a. Sue Denim) sprayed rhetorical buckshot at all and sundry: Asimov's recent best-sellers were "the decaying flesh of ideas, plots, and characters dead thirty years now" (*CT* #4), the *Analog* hard-SF school "exude[d] the stale, mummylike odor of attitudes preserved too long" (*CT* #7), Kim Stanley Robinson's near-future utopias were "overwrought, reactionary, and anti-visionary," full of a cloying "moist-eyed urgency" (*CT* #10). By contrast with a vibrant 1980s art-form such as music video, "a blazingly vigorous new medium that exploits a host of new technologies to dazzling effect," SF was a dusty museum of dead gadgets and dull ideas "sleepwalking its way into the middle-aged pipe-and-slippers comfort of the *New York Times* Bestseller List" (*CT* #5).[11] John Shirley's "Make It Scream" column in the fanzine *Thrust* was, if anything, even more confrontational, goading the genre establishment as a bunch of scared "old ladies ... peeking past the curtains ... as they shake their jowls at the parade of ideas passing them by" (15).

As these insolent gibes suggest, the generation-gap logic of the New Wave was re-emerging twenty years later as a fresh cohort of genre rebels struggled to shake off the shackles of a stale tradition. 1960s figures suddenly found themselves on the opposite end of the hip-square dichotomy, with Shirley's self-important posturing particularly enraging since it basically repeated familiar counterculture attitudes in "punk" guise. The cyberpunks, attuned to "futures infused with the wave of cultural and social revelation swelling in the present," were, claimed Shirley, "operating according to the rules of a relational system you [Old Guardists] haven't yet allowed yourself to perceive" ("Make" 16). Suitably provoked, Silverberg and Gregory Benford—both singled out by Shirley for contumely—responded in a subsequent issue of *Thrust* with letters bemoaning his "chip-on-the-shoulder adolescent condescension" (Silverberg 31) and all the "hype and over-reaching" (Benford 31), while Shirley blasted back that "cyberpunk is simply written for a younger crowd—or at least a hipper one" ("Letter" 32).[12] Meanwhile, in a recapitulation of the dynamics of the New Wave controversy, every major SF convention or seriously-minded fanzine was compelled to confront the combustible issue, mounting countless squabbling panels and symposia throughout the remainder of the decade.

A key problem in grasping the contours of the schism was the sheer diversity of SF output during the 1980s, which made it difficult to grasp precisely what the cyberpunks were reacting against—a very different story from the 1960s, when the New Wave essentially colonized a genre vacuum while blasting away at the moribund "outer space" tradition. As suggested by the list of enemies detailed above, which ranges from ancient survivors like Asimov to younger talents like Robinson, the cyberpunk critique of current SF was fairly scattershot, and its occasional acknowledgement of debts to previous writers was equally haphazard, if not grudging. In his *Mirrorshades* introduction, Sterling credited a handful of precursors—e.g., Delany, Norman Spinrad, John Varley—with having helped form the cyberpunk ethos, leading one almost to suspect that the new movement might be an extension of 1970s themes, while at the same time conducting a shadowy argument with unnamed others offstage. Sometime cyberpunk Michael Swanwick, in an essay published in the August 1986 issue of *Asimov's*, gave a name to these mysterious others: "humanists," a loose-knit cadre—including Robinson, Connie Willis, and John Kessel—who "produce[d] literate, often consciously literary fiction," heavily character-driven and given to philosophical or religious speculation, by contrast with the cyberpunk emphasis on "high-tech future[s], 'crammed' prose, punk attitudes ... , and bright inventive details" ("User's Guide" 24). What is most telling about this division is that it separates writers within the same generational cohort—broadly identified by Swanwick as the "postmoderns"—and sets them in contention for plum publishing slots and major awards against the backdrop of an economically flush, but complacent and perhaps even slightly corrupt genre. The purported ideological struggle between these groups thus devolved, in Swanwick's treatment, into a competition for financial and promotional resources, with cyberpunk celebrating a major triumph when *Neuromancer* bested Robinson's *The Wild Shore* for the 1985 Nebula Award for Best Novel.

Despite the *intra*-generational nature of the contest, the humanists were, in Swanwick's tortured genealogy, the ultimate heirs of the New Wave tradition, so some vague form of *inter*-generational strife was implied as well. Like their 1960s progenitors, the humanists "bring a strong interest in outside literature, the high art 'mainsteam' stuff that outrages the pulp

traditionalists" ("User's Guide" 27)—but which also irritated the cyberpunks, who, for all their frequent citations of Burroughs and Pynchon, had
little sympathy for "the self-satisfied pretension of would-be literateurs" (as
Sterling put it in *Cheap Truth* #7). The attitude of New Wave survivors
towards these upstarts could sometimes be equally prickly, with Silverberg,
for instance, dismissing their work as "a bunch of stylistic mannerisms ...
and a cluster of already overfamiliar high-tech images" ("Letter" 31); but
many who had lived though the genre wars of the 1960s looked upon
cyberpunk rather fondly, if a bit patronizingly, and with a defensive resentment that many of its key themes had been plucked, without attribution,
from the New Wave corpus. Spinrad's lengthy anatomy of the "Neuromantics" (his preferred term for the movement) in the May 1986 issue of
Asimov's was a case in point, praising the techno-intensive cyborgian
fictions of Gibson, Shirley, and Sterling, while pointing out their unreckoned
debts to Moorcock, Ellison, and himself. Even more precisely, Delany traced
Gibson's lyrical evocations of cyberspace to Zelazny's early short stories
and his depiction of female characters to the 1970s work of Joanna Russ and
James Tiptree, Jr., commenting that perhaps Gibson was constitutionally
"blind to any mention" of such correspondences (quoted in Tatsumi 6).[13]

Some of the academic champions of cyberpunk have been equally blind to
these connections, contrasting the movement's subcultural energy, its vision
of posthuman possibility, and its hard technological edge with the 1960s
New Wave, dismissively characterized as formalist, humanistic, and tech-
nophobic. Fred Pfeil, for example, defines the New Wave as a narrowly
aesthetic phenomenon, obsessed with "autotelic language practices, experimental forms, and ... inadequately motivated but luxuriant image play," by
contrast with 1980s SF, which shifted "from formal and aesthetic experimentation back to experiments in social thought" and thus re-engaged with
the utopian/dystopian dialectic of technological innovation ("Disintegrations" 85–86). Explicitly building on this argument, Scott Bukatman has
claimed that cyberpunk "returned the experimental wing of the genre to its
technocratic roots," rejecting the New Wave's defense of inner space—"the
alternate-reality experiences of a somewhat solipsistic youth subculture," in
Bukatman's acerbic view—in favor of an exploration of "the transformation
of quotidian existence by a proliferating set of global electronic technologies" ("Terminal" 140). Yet this pat opposition tends not only to distort the
New Wave's achievement, ignoring the serious socio-political engagement of
its major writers, but also exaggerates the path-breaking qualities of cyberpunk, which were, as noted above, often extrapolated from New Wave
precursors: the media-based obsessions of Ballard and Spinrad, the wise-
cracking hipness of Ellison, Delany's wild explorations of the underground, the cynical anti-technocratic posture of Disch and John Sladek, and
numberless other influences.

What works like Pfiel's and Bukatman's do show, especially when considered alongside the 1988 special issue of *Mississippi Review* edited by

Larry McCaffery (which eventually became *Storming the Reality Studio: A Casebook of Cyberpunk and Postmodern Fiction*), is that the movement's polemicists managed to raise sufficient clamor to attract the attention of academic critics, who swiftly canonized the cyberpunks as, in the words of Fredric Jameson, "the supreme *literary* expression if not of postmodernism, then of late capitalism itself" (*Postmodernism* 419). At the same moment, however, cyberpunk was being declared dead within the genre, sometimes even by its former champions who, disillusioned by the rapid influx of trendy imitators in the wake of Gibson's triumph, saw the movement being reduced (in Shiner's words) to "a very restricted formula: to wit, novels about monolithic corporations opposed by violent, leather-clad drug users with wetware implants" ("Inside the Movement" 17). Swanwick had foreseen this fate in 1986, feeling that the cyberpunks "had created a subgenre that was easy to imitate" ("User's Guide" 46)—as evidenced, perhaps, by his own *Vacuum Flowers* (1987) or Walter Jon Williams's *Hardwired* (1986). The premiere issue (Winter 1987) of the cyberpunk-inspired fanzine *Science Fiction Eye* opened with an editorial entitled "Requiem for the Cyberpunks," which looked forward to the day when all the "clouds of hype and imitation" (Brown and Steffan 5) would have dissipated, the controversy waned, and the true achievements of the major cyberpunk authors could be meaningfully descried.

Now that we are as distant in time from the cyberpunks as they were from their New Wave forebears, it is possible to make some general observations about the impact of the two controversies on the development of the genre as a whole. As with the debates of the 1960s, the furor over cyberpunk was eventually resolved by the movement's unqualified success in gaining markets, awards, and readers, as it became, in essence, yet another historical avant-garde assimilated as a distinct subgenre of SF. This is not to say that the polemical posturing was ultimately insignificant or meaningless since it was precisely by means of the manifestoes, and the reactions they summoned, that both the New Wave and cyberpunk managed to highlight—and capitalize upon—crises in the genre's development, and to carve out spaces for their own creative interventions to be recognized. For New Wave authors, the challenge was to blaze the frontier of a burgeoning SF book market; for the cyberpunks, it was to find and exploit a niche in an already densely settled field. Given the relative scope of these challenges, I think it is fair to say that the New Wave's impact on the field was more sweeping and influential, but also more readily accomplished (despite the shrieks of the Old Guard); for the cyberpunks, as for every upstart movement since the commercial expansion of the genre in the late 1970s, it has become increasingly difficult to mount a credible campaign for the thoroughgoing transformation of SF simply because of the diversity and complex segmentation of the marketplace.

Both movements show that, despite their partisans' aspirations to transcend genre boundaries, the fate of SF avant-gardes is ultimately to be defused and assimilated into a field they temporarily disrupt but, in the long run, help to refit and sustain. Given their final destiny of generic incorporation, it is easy enough to see why Luckhurst would want to argue that the struggles were somehow bogus or illusory, and from his theoretical vantage-point perhaps they were. Certainly, neither movement managed to lift SF wholesale into the mainstream, and in fact both accomplished rather the opposite: to further strengthen SF as a literary institution by infusing it with fresh substance and energy. But that is exactly the point: such a boom-and-bust genre cannot help but suffer periodic doldrums and, in response, generate activist incursions whose final effect, whatever their revolutionary purpose, is to reform and reinvigorate the field. Thus, a focus on rupture at the expense of continuity—or vice versa—tells only half the story, since SF is a form of literature in which phases of perturbation and stability overlap in an unfolding sequence whose end is not as yet in sight.

NOTES

1 This is perhaps the place to note that the current essay is adapted from an article that appeared in *The New York Review of Science Fiction* in June 2007 entitled "Cyberpunk and the New Wave: Ruptures and Continuities." I would like to thank Kevin Maroney for his invaluable feedback as I prepared the original draft, and Sherryl Vint and Graham J. Murphy for their help in assembling this streamlined version.

2 *Who Killed Science Fiction?* Has been re-published online (with a 1980 update, featuring about a dozen contributors, plus some recent musings and contextualizations by Kemp) at: http://efanzines.com/EK/eI29/. All the quotations given below are from this source.

3 See my "New Wave," "*New Worlds* and the New Wave in Fandom," "'The Job of Dissevering Joy from Glop," "Sextrapolation," and "A Young Man's Journey to Ladbroke Grove."

4 In the Introduction to an anthology of stories on ecological themes, *The Ruins of Earth* (Disch 1971), the general purpose of which was to promote a more holistic, less aggressively technophilic approach to the representation of nature within SF. For a discussion of the New Wave's eco-consciousness, see my "Biotic Invasions."

5 Roszak's book was one of many popular studies—e.g., Herbert Marcuse's *One-Dimensional Man* (1964), Lewis Mumford's *The Myth of the Machine* (1966)—that offered wide-ranging critiques of the underlying world-view of postwar technocracy and its psychological ramifications; these works exerted a subterranean influence on the New Wave's vision of the possibilities and limitations of technoscience.

6 For more on the anti-New Wave credo of the second Foundation, see John J. Pierce's "Prospectus" in the first issue of his fanzine *Renaissance: A Semi-Official Organ of the Second Foundation*.

7 Charles Brown's annual summations in *Locus* give a sense of the fallout in the SF world specifically, e.g., "Ballantine (5.3% of the total paperback market) swallowed Fawcett (7.5% of the market); Berkley (3.9%) took over Ace (2.6%) and Playboy (1.6%); Warner got Popular Library [and] the remains of CBS/Fawcett," etc. (Brown "1982 *Locus* Book Summary": 1).

8 See Brown, "1982 *Locus* Book Summary" (18), from which the above data have been culled. Brown's method of distinguishing categories of titles in his annual

Locus summations doesn't permit particularly fine discriminations between types of SF commodities: the category of "Anthologies," for example, includes shared-world enterprises alongside more aesthetically autonomous products.

9 Some of these writers tendered, along with their resignations, angry and/or despairing critiques of the corporatization and mass-mediatization of SF literature: see, for example, Disch (*The Dreams Our Stuff is Made of* 208–26) and Malzberg (165–66).

10 The back issues of *Cheap Truth* are available online at various sources, having been released sans copyright with an encouragement to piracy; all quotes from the fanzine given below are taken from the archive link at The Fanac Fan History Project website: http://www.csdl.tamu.edu:80/~erich/cheaptruth/. Specific issues are undated, but #11 was probably released in 1985 since it discusses Griffin's novels published through that year but does not mention the author's untimely death in 1986 (not, apparently, from side effects caused by eating his own foot).

11 This specific comparison was readily turned against the cyberpunks by critics such as George Slusser, who dismissed their fiction as "Literary MTV" – a "matrix of images that is more a glitterspace" than a coherent world of "mythos or story" (334). Indeed, a number of academic critics have attacked cyberpunk as little more than a self-consciously slick new SF commodity, part and parcel of the cynical hyper-consumerism of the Age of Reagan: see, for example, Huntington, Moylan, and Whalen.

12 In an even later issue of *Thrust*, Lawrence Watt-Evans published an anti-cyberpunk manifesto that drew explicit connections with the New Wave: both movements were driven by a self-important tribalism that traded on a facile "counterculture/establishment conflict" (6). The fallout extended over several subsequent letter columns.

13 Delany was perhaps too modest to mention the obvious debts of Gibson's early work to his own mid-1960s stories, especially "Time Considered as a Helix of Semi-Precious Stones" (1968); in many ways, *Neuromancer* is a retelling of Delany's *Babel-17* (1966), with its skittish caper plot, its motley crew of counterculture oddballs, and its pointed contrast between "straight" and "street" incarnations of technology.

3   Recognizing Patterns

Gibson's Hermeneutics from the Bridge Trilogy to *Pattern Recognition*

Neil Easterbrook

[T]o build a bridge—a most hermeneutical task and virtue in itself.

(Jean Grondin 986)

Everyone's had a chance to view it repeatedly, and brainstorm, and now the more personal, more deeply felt interpretations are emerging.

(*Pattern Recognition* 142)

A considerable amount of scholarship—perhaps too much—has been devoted to William Gibson's first three novels, *Neuromancer*, *Count Zero*, and *Mona Lisa Overdrive*, sometimes referred to as his Sprawl trilogy, since much of the action winds through BAMA, the Boston-Atlanta metroplex, also called The Sprawl. It is particularly *Neuromancer* that continues to attract critical interest, especially from academics who have no deep concern with SF; generally, they treat the novel as a kind of slipstream,[1] with Gibson's text more an instance of postmodernism or of cyberculture than of SF.[2] I would put real money on the wager that *Neuromancer* is the singularly most discussed SF text since 1984, the year it was published. While the book has been indisputably important and influential, the almost exclusive critical focus on *Neuromancer* is a shame, and for several reasons. One results from my reluctance to festishize individual novels, especially given the very elaborate and remarkably nuanced intertextual relationship between *Neuromancer* and other works of literature, within and without SF.

A second, more significant reason is that during the 1990s Gibson published a second suite, usually called *The Bridge trilogy* (Leaver calls it "the Interstitial trilogy"), for the first and the last books center around a San Francisco–Oakland Bay bridge, one now (because of economics and politics and natural disaster) abandoned by automobiles and transformed by squatters into a rich, alternative community, something John Clute has called "a Rube Goldberg banyan barrio" (*Scores* 243). (There is a bridge analog in the second book—a virtual community and proto-cyberspace called "Walled City.") These three novels—*Virtual Light* (1993), *Idoru* (1996), and *All*

Tomorrow's Parties (1999)—set in an undated[3] near-future, constitute a remarkable series, certainly one as arresting as the Sprawl novels.[4] Like *Neuromancer*, it operates according to "an intricate protocol" (*Neuromancer* 7), providing a concise reflection on the Sprawl books, on the nature of post-cyberpunk SF, and on hermeneutic practice. Similarly, Gibson's 2003 *Pattern Recognition* extends and continues the model of the Bridge books, though this newer novel has appealed to many readers otherwise allergic to the narrative protocols and paratextual branding of SF.

More triptychs than trilogies, these two series toggle back-and-forth in a "binary flicker" (*Idoru* 216)—the central pattern we should recognize, and the hermeneutic that should be traced. This development culminates with *Pattern Recognition*, which while entirely separate from the Bridge series, etiolates that model, something Gibson himself repeatedly mentioned in interviews promoting *Pattern Recognition*: "In the three previous books, each was in their own little way an anti-*Neuromancer*" (Interview with Dorsey 11a). Or as Gibson told *Locus*:

> The previous three books seem to me to play with genre, and particularly to play a fairly complicated game with the conceit of 'the future.' If you look at my interviews over those three books, I think you'll find that I've been threatening to write a book like *Pattern Recognition* for a long time: a novel that makes what I've *always been doing* overt.
>
> (63b)

Despite the fact that "there is a considerable degree of overlap, of contradiction" (*Mona Lisa Overdrive* 238), we can understand the second set of books as *Neuromancer*'s palinode.

Indeed, the post-Sprawl titles openly recant or revise much of the earlier technological imagery, human interaction, and cognitive tone. By *Pattern Recognition*, this tightly patterned revision crystallizes as the "mirror-world" (2, 25, 194) trope. *Mirrorshades*, the central emblem of early cyberpunk, marked nothing if not diffident self-enclosure. The mirror-world operates differently, opening rather than foreclosing reading. More than a simple metaphor for the uncannily "sideways" inversions Cayce feels in a London where cars drive in the left lane and oddly-shaped electrical plugs pull in an alternative current (2–3), the trope names a general liminality, the threshold of transition that enables or blocks transformation. Globalization and its erasure of borders provide the prime example (106), and others include the emergence of internet markets (such as eBay) that uniformly level values (230–31); this is the central threat represented by Hubertus Bigend (106). Cayce prefers "different stuff" (105), alterities persistently resisting homogenization: the regional, the local, the "authentic," something best represented by the Curta calculator (252). Even more suggestive is that the trope of mirroring reversal exteriorizes the crisis of interiority that marks the implicit armature of Sprawl novels.[5]

Rather than a devolution or regression from the more adventurous conditions and speculative conceits of the Sprawl books, the Bridge sequence confronts rather than evades questions of individual agency and human responsibility, which in my view was the signal characteristic of the earlier titles.[6] In this sense, the newer books are far less "posthuman" than classically humanist: in these books the technology and the SF topoi are *entirely* secondary, entirely *subordinated* to the human. Think, for instance, of the way that the two series end. *Mona Lisa Overdrive* concludes with Bobby's total and willing absorption of his conscious self into the Aleph (240, 257–60), a cybernetic nodule whose name signals both the notion of an initial act and a vaguely theological sense of transcendence; rather than configuring cyberspace as a prosthetic extension of self, Bobby leaves his human body behind, the culmination of what had been Case's deepest desire in *Neuromancer*. *All Tomorrow's Parties* reverses this *telos* in every pertinent respect: Rei Toei materializes from the nanofax (268–69) "naked and alone," to quote Hamlet, a rebirth that privileges human corporeality above all else. All readers ought recognize the heavy irony of the fact that, while the Bridge series evokes some of the Y2K paranoia common at the end of the last millennium, the singularity or spike accomplished by Rei Toei constitutes a return to human corporeality and agency.

In this respect, the second series emerges as remarkably more interesting than the first, though most of the difference might better be described as a *lateral* move, a paralogical gesture that violently reorients the books' hermeneutic codes—they provide parallel constellations, mirror inversions. And the lateral arrangement makes for what *Idoru* names "a neat rectilinearity" (150). Here's one example: the early mockery of a "dated, nameless style of the previous century" (*Neuromancer* 9) now becomes an ideal of "semiotic neutrality: *styles without names, without logos, without dates*" (*Pattern Recognition* 90, 355). In the late 1980s, "cyberpunk" itself became a commodified brand, producing in the 1990s both laments and celebrations of its death. Gibson now notes that he does not hear the word "used by anyone under 40" (Interview with Dorsey 11a). Here's another case in point: the agonist of both *Neuromancer* and *Pattern Recognition* is dubbed "case": though named after Edgar Cayce, Cayce pronounces "Cayce" as "Case" (31).

Let me present a crude, but I hope stimulating scheme[7] of some of the relevant conceptual dichotomies, that "binary flicker."

Each of these differences could be separately detailed and argued. There might also be many alternatives to an index of cardinal binarisms. We could chart the differences through the primary functions of the main characters:

Case—spatial relations
Laney—hermeneutic relations
Cayce—temporal relations

Table 3.1 Comparison of the Sprawl Triptych and the Bridge Triptych and *Pattern Recognition*

The Sprawl Triptych	*The Bridge Triptych and* Pattern Recognition
Finding and using information	Interpreting information
blissfully unconcerned with meaning	seeks meaning
Homo faber	*Homo significans*
Exteriorized	Interiorized
focused on plot	focused on motive
architectural surfaces, façades	human psyche
simulacra	authenticity
logophilia	*logophobia*
Object	Event
"things are things"	motives, causes, feeling
modernist	postmodernist[8]
avant-garde collage	performative fragment
implicitly nostalgic	belatedly nostalgic
Binary Trope: cyberspace	Dialectical Trope: the bridge
virtuality	immediacy
rejects the physical	accepts the physical
Case/Bobby escape the meat	Cayce/Rei seek corporeality
mirrorshades	mirror-world
Writerly	Readerly
readers as consumers	readers as participants
Wintermute as authorial metonym	Laney/Cayce as synecdoche
melodrama	satire
"hard-boiled" closure	ironic collapse
"emblematic" reading	"symptomatic" reading
Ethical displacement	Ethical confrontation
deferral, denial	answerability
prosthetics/hard-wired	no alibis
escape/transcendence	problematization
Style[9]	Style
manic hyperbole	increasingly plain, litotes
visual	verbal
iconic	indexical
oxymoronic	ironic

(an analysis that would associate Case with *epic* and Cayce with *Bildungsroman*), or perhaps the characters' ends:

Molly/Case (can't cry N 183)
Cayce cries (*PR* 355)
Case "loses" Molly
Cayce "gets" Parkaboy

We could even chart this as a series of jokes: where the first series speaks melodramatically with unvariegated sophomoric *gravitas*, the second frequently invokes a middle-aged slapstick: the "terminal overdrive" of *Neuromancer* (7) becomes the "terminal priapism" of *Pattern Recognition* (222).

Following the fundamental oppositions I have sketched out above, the remainder of this chapter will explore the nuances and implications of the different hermeneutic structures of these triptychs.

Virtual Light initiates both the mood and the mode of the second series. More sedate and understated than the oxymoronic overdrive that characterizes the Sprawl books, it also sets the stage for a more explicit interrogation of the present that provides a joy ride though the future. Chevette Washington is a San Francisco bike messenger who, in a rash and intemperate moment, steals a pair of sunglasses from an obnoxious drunk who had accosted her at a party. These glasses, it transpires, are a technological marvel, and they contain secrets about the pending transformation of the city that their true owners, mysterious movers and shakers of international capital (Sunflower Corporation), would prefer not be made public (251). They hire a skip-tracer, Lucius Warbaby, to recover their lost property; Warbaby uses Berry Rydell, bumbling former cop and former armed guard of the private security company IntenSecure, primarily because he is unknown on the transformed Bridge, where Chevette lives. The movers also employ an assassin, a Mr. Loveless, to secure the glasses by more ruthless methods. A pair of corrupt San Francisco cops complicate matters. Most of the book intercuts a chase sequence with backstory;[10] Chevette and Berry find themselves thrown together, running from Loveless until, with the help of Berry's ex-partner Sublett they contact "The Republic of Desire," mysterious and anarchist hackers vaguely reminiscent of *Neuromancer*'s Panther Moderns, who help them contrive a sting to contain Warbaby, Loveless, and the SFPD cops without themselves being killed.

In most respects, the book seems an erratically conventional thriller, and the least compelling of the series. But all of Gibson's writing has been less about plot than immersing readers in the richly imagined worlds he builds from nuanced minutiae. From the small details—naming the décor of a television lawyer's apartment as "Aggressive Retro Seventies" (26), employing a minor character in a "wind-surfing boutique called Just Blow Me" (47), or describing a bicycle's "paper-cored, carbon wrapped frame" (45)—to the larger cultural modes: the very anachronism of Chevette's profession, "at the archaic intersection of information and geography" (93), bike messenger in a cosmopolitan city wherein every desk already links electronically with all others. *Virtual Light* contains one figure of the writer/reader, a character whose business it is to stand aside, observing and capturing those details. The only character to appear in all three novels, Shinya Yamazaki, is a doctoral candidate (230) from Osaka University, an ethnographer studying the Bridge culture (62–66), especially Skinner, its senior resident. A student of "existential sociology" (*Idoru* 8),[11] Yamazaki reads and records the cultural around him; portions of this empirical record appear directly in the novel—two chapters (§33 and §36) drop the convention of a third-person focalizer and allow readers direct access to his electronic notepad. In this sense, Yamazaki's deceptively passive distance from plot provides the core motif of the novel, something also represented in the "virtual light" glasses (122), which introduce the notion of seeing through obscure or quotidian surfaces to uncover something secret or interpret something otherwise occulted (131, 144). Revising the mirrorshades trope, a figure of enclosure, the VL glasses suggest a hermeneutics of suspicion, an opening of containment that explicitly reverses the codes of the Sprawl sequence.

In the Sprawl novels, the culture is "pre-read," its meaning understood and explained by the narrative. In *Virtual Light*, Yamazaki actively *reads* the deep structure of the culture, caught most explicitly at the anachronistic intersection of top-down global capital and bottom-up local resistance: the Bridge, the node around which the novel revolves (62–66, 94–95). Damaged by a major earthquake, made obsolete by new tunnel construction technology, and subsequently "occupied" by the city's homeless underclass, the hybrid Bridge has become a counter-hegemonic, heterotopian space, a cultural condition captured comically in the name of one of its bars—"Cognitive Dissidents" (136). Yamazaki catalogs that heterogeneous intricacy: aleatory accretions (64) producing "something amorphous, startlingly organic ... as viewed through some cracked kaleidoscope of vernacular style" (62). Skinner insists that in the emerging Bridge culture, there's "no agenda here whatever, no underlying structure" (126). Like Yamazaki, Gibson too operates as an ethnographic bricoleur, his own cracked kaleidoscope focused on interpreting the disjecta of apparently random cultural accretions.

An ordered architectonic emerges with the second book of the series. Only then does Colin Laney, the "net runner" or internet "researcher" in *Idoru* and *All Tomorrow's Parties*, provide the key to the books' "*relational*" (*Idoru* 194) figures. Just as the Bridge books comprise the hinge between Gibson's early and present work,[12] Laney bridges the relation between Case and Cayce, the "console cowboy" of *Neuromancer* who inverts data and the "coolhunter" (2) of *Pattern Recognition* who everts data, recognizes designs that have not yet emerged. Laney's individual "intuitive" (31) genius has "something to do with pattern recognition" (*Idoru* 193), an inexplicable ability to penetrate the obfuscations created by what one social critic has named "infoglut." The patterns that coalesce Laney calls "nodal points" (31).

Nodal points constitute the central thematic node and hermeneutic model of the Bridge triptych, implicit from first to last. Their strongest articulation comes in Laney's two books. In *Idoru*, we learn that, while a child in a Florida orphanage, Laney served as a test-subject in trials of the drug 5-SB; somehow this exposure, combined with some limited experience gained training in another experiment run by a group of French scientists, has gifted him with the ability to see "things in clouds" (193) of data; while others struggle "in the messy, constantly proliferating interface with the ordinary yet endlessly multiplex world" (150–01), Laney's "parallax" (330) combines "image and reality" (216), much in the manner that the way a creative, literary reading coalesces for us all.[13] Laney's skill is openly, explicitly hermeneutic, that is, interpretive. Laney enables the rock celebrity Rez (from the U2ish band called Lo/Rez) to attempt a physical union with Rei Toei, an entirely virtual being, who "induced the nodal vision in some unprecedented way; she induced it as narrative" (233). I will return to this point at the end of the chapter, but at the moment let me underscore that as the series continues the books become increasingly self-reflexive and self-ironizing in an unmistakably postmodern fashion.[14]

In *All Tomorrow's Parties*, Laney, still in Tokyo but now homeless, living in a cardboard city where each citizen inhabits a coffin-sized carton linked contiguously, rhizomatically—reminiscent of the legendary convoluted labyrinths of Kowloon Walled City, that peasant suburb of Hong Kong that the British ignored, and which by 1930 became the most densely populated region of the planet, unregulated in just the manner of the Bridge. (Another analogy might evoke the arcades of Walter Benjamin's Paris.) In *Idoru*, cyberspace's Walled City provides the virtual analog of the Bridge—the emerging local reply to global capital's control of information and its attempt to mediate or "pre-read" meaning. Laney engages several characters from *Virtual Light* to assist him assist Rei Toei and to hoist a pretentious, meddling capitalist on his own petard. As in the earlier book, in *All Tomorrow's Parties* Laney's talent "perceive[s] change emerging from vast flows of data" (56), sees through the static that surrounds us (the ambient, the aleatory, the ambivalent), something best represented by that stochastic color of the sky that defines the landscape of *Neuromancer*. Laney's interpretive ability proves both cause and catalyst, presages and performs the requisite actions, assembling the conditions that allow humanity to exploit the right technology, not (as in the case in the Sprawl books) to permit the technology to exploit us.[15]

In the Sprawl books, the technology involved was cybernetics. Here the novum is nanotech—variously sinister, promising, and miraculous. In *Virtual Light*, a mysterious company plots to transform the entirety of San Francisco for their own profit, no matter the cost to its inhabitants; in *Idoru*, a nano-assembler, similar to the ones that have rebuilt Tokyo after "The Big One," suddenly appears as the means through which a virtual being might consummate a marriage with a human being; and in *All Tomorrow's Parties*, our still-virtual girl hijacks the "nanofax" machines in a thousand "Lucky Dragon" convenience stores around the globe, creating a thousand corporeal copies, each a simulacrum of her cybernetic self. This new cycle replicates the Sprawl books' romantic fascination/revulsion with new technology, but with a significant difference: here, the technology metonymically represents human behavior; both Yamazaki and Laney, and later Cayce, function as "nano-assemblers," compiling obscure bits of data into larger narratives, transforming the world's background "static" into a dynamic, lived interpretation (in this way, they are now fully synecdochic of readers).

Pattern Recognition simply simplifies and extends this now recognizable hermeneutic pattern, though explicitly transforms it toward the human dimension. For all his individual sensitivity, Laney remains a reified being, like the Bridge itself "a medium of transport become a destination" (*ATP* 273). As a kind of technology, he serves finally only as a propaedeutic, a catalyst, an allegory—for the onion-like node of his own interiority is null: "The Hole is absence at his fundamental core" (*ATP* 40). If unlike Laney, Rei Toei is a metaphor—"the posthuman coded as information topology" (Farnell 480)—then *Pattern Recognition* everts this pattern: turning the hole inside-out metonymically returns the human to, one might say, its proper place.

Set in the summer of 2002, primarily in London, *Pattern Recognition* is both utterly like and unlike the two preceding sets. A semiotic "sensitive" (2), Cayce Pollard identifies new cultural trends even before they emerge as recognizable patterns; she then sells this prescience to various industries, calling herself "freelance." One established company's mogul, Hubertus Bigend, asks Cayce to deploy "your talents, your allergies, your tame pathologies" (65) to track the source of some 135 film clips that have been circulating the Internet and have become the obsession of diverse but dedicated connoisseurs who share their interpretations on listservs and blogs; Cayce is one such "footagehead." Before she really knows it, she finds herself hunting for "the maker."

Concerning the maker two "schools" of analysis emerge—the "Progressives" and the "Completists" (46). While the latter group "is convinced" that the 135 segments are from some whole of which we have yet discovered only fragments, the former "assume that the footage consists of fragments of a work in progress." Mama Anarchia leads the Completists while the Progressives' most vocal advocacy comes from Parkaboy. While some footageheads think some established international director circulates the cinematic fragments as a publicity stunt (20):

> It had been Parkaboy ... who had first raised the possibility of what he called "the Garage Kubrick" ... that it is possible this footage is generated single-handedly by some technologically empowered solo auteur, some guerilla creator out there alone in the night of the Internet.
>
> (47)

But it was not Parkaboy who "first raised" the notion; instead, it was William Gibson, that technologically empowered solo auteur, in a 1999 article for *Wired* recounting his experience at a digital film festival ("William Gibson's Filmless Festival").[16]

Parkaboy, therefore, functions as the novel's authorial metonym—its trope for the author William Gibson, just as in, say, Heinlein's *The Moon Isa Harsh Mistress*, where Professor Bernardo de la Paz mouths Heinlein's own convictions.[17] Parkaboy's status as authorial emblem also appears in his business card, something presented when Parkaboy initially meets Cayce. It reads "PETER GILBERT. MIDDLE-AGED WHITE GUY. 'SINCE 1967'" (326). That phrasing precisely parallels Gibson's own—in promotional materials and press releases concerning the novel, as well as the title of the personal biography posted on his own website—though of course, Gibson's says "Since 1948."[18]

It seems significant that the authorial metonym would be particularly hostile to particular vocabularies. As leader of the Progressives, Parkaboy openly ridicules the technical vocabularies of literary criticism (48, 74, 224), and especially *hermeneutics*, a word favored by Mama Anarchia, who turns out to be the novel's villain in more than one way. In *Pattern Recognition*, the word hermeneutics appears precisely once (and *nowhere* else in Gibson's work). And in the three editions that I have—the uncorrected proof, the hardcover first edition, and the corrected trade paperback, the word appears hyphenated where it reaches the page's right margin, as "hermeneu-tics," an amusing even if unintentional irony since it arrives amid a contemptuous dismissal of the verbal and semantic "tics" of the word's source within the novel—Mama Anarchia. Indeed, it turns out that her critical lexicon comes from an employee, a "puppethead" graduate student hired (315) to produce the "pomo bellowings" (74) Parkaboy so despairs. Here's the specific passage, which begins with Mama Anarchia's first post to the listserv "Fetish: Footage:Forum":

> Really it is entirely about story, though not in any sense that any of you seem familiar with. Do you know nothing of narratology? Where is Derridean "play" and excessiveness? Foucauldian limit-attitude? Lyotardian language-games? Lacanian Imaginaries? Where is the commitment to praxis, positioning Jamesonian nostalgia, and despair—as well as Habermasian fears of irrationalism—as panic discourses signaling the defeat of Enlightenment hegemony over cultural theory? But no: discourses on this site are hopelessly retrograde. Mama Anarchia
>
> Well, Cayce thinks, Mama had gotten right down to it. And she had, Cayce notes, used the word "hegemony," without which Parkaboy will not admit any Mama post as fully genuine. (For a full positive identification, though, he insists that they also contain the word "hermeneu-tics.")
>
> (267–68)

While even those of us so benighted that we actually use such words grind our teeth when we encounter jargon-laden screeds rather than rigorous, analytical argument, this particular instance still strikes me as excessively, even ironically shrill, a kind of intentional sleight-of-hand. After all, in interviews, Gibson himself quotes Jameson (*No Maps* §7), in fiction, he deploys the technical vocabulary of Deleuze and Guattari (*Idoru* 234), and no prose of Gibson's could be "fully genuine" without the word *semiotics* (beginning with *Burning Chrome*'s "The Gernsback Continuum").[19] As Raymond Williams pointed out long ago, in *Keywords*, the word *jargon* remains itself a kind of jargon (174); a contemptuous dismissal of a view for its jargon also replaces rigorous thought with a mere buzzword—"jargon." *Pattern Recognition* privileges and foregrounds this type of recursive irony. I will return to this apparent contradiction in just a moment.

Hermeneutics, you will remember, identifies only the general name for the systematic study of interpretation, and it focuses especially on the complex dynamism between explanation and understanding. Similarly, *semiotics* identifies only the general name for the formal study of signifying meaning in culture (as opposed to the social study of cultural meanings, which is anthropology / sociology), and it focuses especially on the complex encodings of sign systems.[20] In contemporary, idiomatic usage, these two words prove loosely synonymous, usually given in apposition rather than opposition; only rarely and only in the most technical discourse do we rigidly distinguish between the methods in the interpretation of meaning and the semiological elements in the production of meaning. For most of us most of the time, semiotics implies hermeneutics: "The understanding of signs is not a mere matter of recognition (of a stable equivalence); it is a matter of interpretation" (Eco, *Semiotics* 43).

Then what about Gibson's use of cognates of the word hermeneutics? "Interpret" or "interpretation" appears in the novel precisely four times— three times concerning how the Japanese render Western culture (one instance is the hotel breakfast, one the Buzz Rickson's MA-1 jacket, and one a Pilates analog), and once concerning the nature of the footage, a passage I have used as the epigraph to open this essay. "Explain" and "explanation" appear twenty-seven times, usually neutrally, without any adjective or adverb. When such qualifications do appear, they are negative ("can't explain") or ("she lies by way of explanation"). Only in the novel's final pages—in that depressingly conventional anti-climax where the heart of the maker's mystery is plucked and resolved—do the usages become positive ("I will explain"). And while "understand" or "understanding" appears thirty-seven times, most of these uses offer either negatives ("I don't understand") or anxious imperatives ("you must understand").

Explicitly through the voice of Parkaboy and implicitly throughout, the novel repudiates the word *hermeneutics* and its cognates, a very strange position for Gibson to take. In fact, if one sort of discourse identifies the novel's pattern and structure, it is *hermeneutic*. While nominally an ally of Parkaboy and so a Progressive (I say nominally, because in speaking with Bigend she actually takes the "Completist" view (68–69)), Cayce also serves as the novel's central interpreter, a privileged emblem of hermeneutic practice. Thus Gibson explicitly repudiates precisely the same sort of disciplinary activity that the narrative implicitly advocates, signaling a profound ambivalence, a "panic reaction" (354) or perhaps even a phobia concerning the central concepts at play.

Probably two intertwined phobias appear here. First, the fear of the label, the term, the sigil, the logo; the fear of hermeneutics resembles one of Cayce's allergies. Recall Cayce's profession: "a dowser" (2) with a "marketable allergy" (10) to branding (8): trademarks and logos evoke dread and vertigo. However, when she encounters "semiotic neutrality" (90, 355), she is fine. Take her own style of dress, the generic "Cayce Pollard Units," where she removes all labels from her clothing—going so far as to have a locksmith grind off the logos on the brass buttons of her jeans (2). But the narrative methodically and rigorously names the jeans, and the names of the no-name clothes; Cayce, then, has no allergy "to fashion" (8), only to its sigil and the sigil's reproducibility—which because mass manufactured and mass marketed is *devoid of soul*, the novel's central term for authenticity. Here's the most representative passage: "There must be some Tommy Hilfiger event horizon, beyond which it is impossible to be more derivative, more removed from the source, more devoid of soul" (18). Then perhaps we ought to understand Parkaboy's fear of hermeneutics as logophobia: an allergic response to the brand names of interpretation. For Gibson, *Derrida* or *Foucault*, *Lyotard* or *Lacan* operate the same way as does "Tommy Hilfiger."[21]

Now let us take the second salient feature of Cayce's pathology—"the opaque standards of her inner radar" (12): she does not know what makes it work, and in fact does not want to know. The novel calls it "apophenia" (113, 115), the apparently miraculous ability to combine the most heterogeneous materials into coherent patterns—which we would associate with clairvoyance (of Edgar Cayce, say, which is the source of her name ([31])). We are repeatedly told it is a biological mystery, its only law a sort of autotropism (11–13, 86, 264).

Just as the notion of the "Garage Kubrick" comes not from Parkaboy but from Gibson, the notion of "coolhunting" comes not from Gibson but from Malcolm Gladwell's 1997 article in *The New Yorker*, where Gladwell not only invents the term "coolhunter" but also specifies its three laws: (1) cool can only be discovered; (2) cool cannot be manufactured; and (3) only the cool can observe cool. He remarks: "[S]o if you add all three together they describe a closed loop, the hermeneutic circle of coolhunting, a phenomenon whereby not only can the uncool not see cool but cool cannot even be adequately described to them."[22]

Although the promotional picture on the dust jacket of *Pattern Recognition* situates Gibson as the pinnacle of "cool," wearing the Pro-Keds analog of the athletic shoes that Cayce predicts as the next, new "cool" commodity, the photo presents a double irony. First, Converse All-Stars were the "cool" shoe of Gibson's youth, so the new "cool" is the "Aggressive Retro Seventies" that seemed so tiresomely nostalgic in *Virtual Light*; and second because Gibson also poaches that style from Gladwell, whose exemplary coolhunter was, in 1997, spinning Converse. The "cool" nova of *Pattern Recognition* are openly old motifs given an inverse or everted spin: what is new is not the motifs but how they are ironized, as they were not earlier. Whatever it was that cyberpunk once was—the manic quest for cybernetic transcendence emerging from the fractious, dehumanizing experience with a near future's post-industrial wasteland, the inauthentic evocation of cool structured through logophilia—in the recent work Gibson has refused all evasive alibis and instead confronted both characters and readers with authentic, because unresolved, problematics.

Think of how the fear of branding and the desire to not know how or why such fear works combine into Cayce's passion for the footage. She says the footage exists "untrammeled by even the most basic conventions of [its represented] day" (24). She says "the mystery of it" (76). She calls it a "dream" (*passim*). She describes its ineffable immediacy, its unmediated authenticity, its self-present presence (22). In short, the footage has soul, the very essence of "cool," the thing we cannot understand because insufficiently cool. In modernist art, authenticity remains a shibboleth, an uninterrogated metanarrative. Yet Cayce sharply subverts the implicitly romantic aesthetics at play when she uncovers the precise methods and purpose of production: she loses the aesthetic mystery, the "participation mystique" (255) which authentically constitutes her concept of authenticity. However much it also meditates on the traumas produced by modernity, *Neuromancer*, on the other hand, retains a faith in unmediated, authentic experience; despite the many prosthetic modifications of body, memory, or mind, Case uses the deck or "betaphenethylamine" (134) as a means to open doors of perception, to get closer to the disembodied transcendence that Bobby affects at the end of *Mona Lisa Overdrive*. There the nature of authenticity, of transcendence remains unquestioned; only the particular means are ever in dispute.

A second way *Pattern Recognition* represents mystery concerns Cayce's apophenia, itself a motif recycled from Gibson's own work. In "Fragments of a Hologram Rose," his first published story collected in *Burning Chrome*, a character uses an ASP cassette ("apparent sensory perception" (38), the 1977 prototype of what in *Neuromancer* would become "simstim") to induce sleep:

> The first three quarters of the cassette have been erased; you punch yourself fast-forward through a static haze of wiped tape, where taste and scent blur into a single channel. The audio input is white sound— the no-sound of the first dark sea ... (Prolonged input from wiped tape can induce hypnagogic hallucination.)
>
> (40)

Using the cassette drives him into delta sleep, though ironically what he really wants is to "ask himself what that might mean" (42). The story itself provokes a meditation on the fragmented self, and ends in a mournful nostalgia for lost wholeness that cannot be regained. This lyrical sleep-inside-the-dream motif is distinctly romantic (of precisely the same sort as one sees in films such as *The Matrix*, which depend on the parrothead mumbo-jumbo of Morpheus, who channels Baudrillard). But Cayce's condition proves some physiological anomaly, something which, when lost, will not be mourned because it is coupled with an understanding of wholeness as *merely* the sum of fragmented parts, the eversion of soul-delay. In this sense, nostalgia now seems always already belated. I cannot see any way to read the end of *Pattern Recognition* except as an ironic *mise-en-abyme* of Gibson's earlier motifs.

Thus, Cayce's apophenia, and Gibson's hermeneutic semiotics, result from the hermeneutic condition, the fundamentally circular relation between explanation and understanding, which explains the mystery of her gift and names the spiraling metacommentary of Gibson's work, from his first story to his last novel, which opens with Cayce "hearing the white noise" (1).

It is remarkable how reluctant even otherwise brilliant readers are to recognize this pattern in Gibson's text. In a thoughtful article that first appeared in the *New Left Review*, Fredric Jameson says that the book would have been better had it been more like Thomas Pynchon's *The Crying of Lot 49*—had it ended at the liminal point just before the lifting of the veil ("Postmodernism" 389). That is the way I felt when I first read the book: those last 30 pages seemed deeply unsatisfying, since they apparently adopt conventions of genre mystery or technothriller, where all events receive conclusive explanations. Awkwardly, this expository info dump is not only characteristic of contemporary bestsellers but only tolerable within that genre, and then just barely so. Perhaps we can draw two possible inferences. One might aver that Gibson just cannot write, and does not know how to close a plot. He has often commented on his own inadequacies of craft. For instance, in *No Maps for These Territories*, a lengthy video interview shot by Mark Neale, he calls *Neuromancer* an "adolescent" book; and remarks that his flat, shallow characters result less from any specific intellectual agenda than "my limited capacity to do complex characterization" (§23).

The more profitable inference asserts that Gibson knows precisely what he is doing, and expects the audience to recognize the patterns he deploys ironically; as Derrida remarks about Plato,

> The hypothesis of a rigorous, sure, and subtle form is naturally more fertile. It discovers new chords, new concordances; it surprises them in a minutely fashioned counterpoint, within a more secret organization of themes, of names, of words. It unites a whole *sumplokē* [interweaving] patiently interlacing the arguments. What is magisterial about the demonstration affirms itself and effaces itself at once, with suppleness, irony, and discretion.
>
> ("Plato" 67)

For example, shall we be unthinking parrotheads, and passively accept those last 30 pages? To do so would presage "a spongiform future" (*PR* 56).

This openly intentional failure to provide the optimal resolution—of the sort we get in *Neuromancer*, which despite its unsatisfactory ambiguities continues to provide mysterious tensions straight through the dénouement—has been Gibson's recent pattern.

Think of *Idoru*, where the technothriller plot completely collapses in the final pages: when the two bad guys meet, in the presence of the good girl and the good guy, they strike a convenient business deal, the good girl then loses all interest in the rock celebrity and the book ends wondering about her meandering attention. Commenting to *Salon* about these generic codes, Gibson remarked that *Virtual Light* and *Idoru* "pretend to be thrillers in an almost ironic way. And part of the pleasure of the text is going with that—watching the way it doesn't behave like a thriller, more than the way that it does." Compare the climax of *Neuromancer*, where the technothriller and hard-boiled elements do reach completion: while we never know what precisely unlocks the Turing cops' "electromagnetic shotgun" (132)—"three / notes, high and pure. / A true name" (262)—unlocked it is, and the two AIs fuse and transcend to whatever awaits them.

But other than the generic structures of plot, nothing in *Pattern Recognition* can be treated unironically. Generally speaking, the novel presents Mama Anarchia's nakedly violent professional ambition as only slightly more distasteful than the real villain, certainly from Cayce's perspective, the man re-branding every object in the world, Hubertus Bigend. Bigend's fundamental crime is that he would "pre-interpret" every object, allegorizing commodities for parrothead consumers when authentic individuals, such as Cayce or *Idoru*'s Chia McKenzie, desire open-ended engagements. Bigend apparently desires Cayce to find the Maker only so that he can co-opt and commodify the artist's authenticity, something confirmed in *Spook Country*: the footage has been deployed as the background of "Trope Slope ... our viral pitchman platform" (*Spook Country* 105) because, simply, as he remarks to Hollis Henry, "It sells shoes" (106), which she thinks "fucking horrible. Pardon my French" (105). Yet the specific details surrounding any such dismissal remain curiously unstable. Take a small example—Bigend's accent: "He has less accent of any kind than she can recall having heard before in any speaker of English. It's unnerving. It makes him sound somehow directionless, like a loudspeaker in a departure lounge, though it has nothing to do with volume" (*Pattern Recognition* 56). Unaccented, Bigend's unbranded speech seems as identifiably unidentifiable as CPUs, the name for Cayce's nameless raiment. You would think she would be utterly comfortable with such speech; instead, she is unnerved, a sign of her anxious allergy, and readers ought to recognize the irony.

This kind of semantic unreliability and structural irony pervades the novel from the first to the last, and identifies the text's "full fractal richness"—the very phase Gibson uses in that *Wired* article to characterize the Garage Kubrick's goal—of Gibson's aesthetic object and hermeneutic project. Perhaps it also suggests that the novel that seems Gibson's most reliable turns out to be his least; and also perhaps while it seems his least postmodern book, it turns out to be his most. *Pattern Recognition* is Gibson's first truly postmodern novel.

Both Gibson's cyberpunk and post-cyberpunk novels address the impact of technoscience on human life. Significantly, his commentary itself comes mediated through a technology—the machinery of fiction—and as Umberto Eco famously proclaimed, "a novel is a machine for generating interpretations" (*Postscript* 1). In this fashion Gibson identifies the greatest change to human beings brought about by cyberculture: he *induces it as narrative*, showing how *homo sapiens* has become *homo significans*, the hyperbolic posthuman of the Sprawl books recuperated to a more humanist, humane task. In *Neuromancer*, human beings are tool users, tool makers: *homo faber*. By *Pattern Recognition*, Gibson understands human beings as meaning-makers. Parkaboy phrases it this way: "Homo sapiens are about pattern recognition ... Both a gift and a trap" (22). It is how we treat both the footage and our lives: by assembling the fragments into stories, we *both* make sense of them *and* sense of our experience of them. The essence of *homo significans* is perpetually assembling stories and interpreting meaning, producing an "unlimited semiosis" (Eco, *Semiotics* 136–37, 186–87). Gibson now centers his fiction on such metacritical conceits: "Really it is all about story."

By revisiting and revising the Sprawl books, Gibson's more recent fiction not only provides an alternative interpretation but foregrounds a new aesthetic sense—one that is more "readerly" in the sense that it compels the reader toward a response, toward answering the questions being raised and being answerable for our complicities. "Nodal points" or the "nodal vision" provides an obvious metaphor for metacritical commentary—indeed, explicitly so in *All Tomorrow's Parties*, where Laney remarks that "it had become apparent that this was a locus of nodal points, a sort of meta-node, and that, in some way, he had been unable to define, something very large was happening here" (165). Just as Laney finds the nodal point of Rez's psychology in Rei Toei and Rei Toei reciprocally finds her nodal point in Laney, so too the novels' readers find *their nodal points* in the very notion of nodal points (a notion that's quite explicit in *Idoru*). In each text, both the novel's diegetic world and the narrative itself suffer from a "binary flicker" (*Idoru* 216) between the level of plot and the hermeneutic allegory—between, on the one hand, the more obvious generic conventions of the narrative's action and, on the other hand, the more-or-less obsessively explicit instructions to readers on how a novel (especially the one *in hand*) may be read. Laney and Cayce are nano-assemblers, solo auteurs, but *not figures of the artist-author*; instead, they provide synecdoches for readers: they take fragments of data then assemble them as narratives, gleaning meaning out this bit rather than that bit, *reading rather than making* the white noise. In this sense, the book itself proves a nanofax of human experience, the virtual light lenses focused on the world.

Fluid, lateral movement between these two readerly tasks now dominates Gibson's hermeneutics, and the pattern that emerges from the cloud of information teaches a lesson on reading culture. It is a lesson we have been waiting for. In *Pattern Recognition* one recurring joke concerns that jet lag comes from "soul-delay"—the body must await the arrival of the soul, which travels slowly. The difference between the Sprawl books and the four newer books demonstrates a kind of "soul-delay." Gibson once used the technology of SF for superficial entertainments. But now, as Gibson suggested in that article in *Wired*: "others, like my own Garage Kubrick, will use the same technology to burrow more deeply, more obsessively, more gloriously, into the insoluble mystery of the self."

NOTES

1 "Slipstream" was coined in 1989 by Bruce Sterling to identify a genre "when mainstream writers appropriate SF tropes, images, and themes." Since then, the term has found widespread use in naming liminal hybrids of SF and literary realism.

2 For representative examples, take Joseph Conte's comment that *Neuromancer* has "relatively little in common with classical science fiction" (207) or Thomas Foster's recent book that closely engages *Neuromancer* but, other than brief quotations from two early short stories, does not discuss any of Gibson's other fictions—despite the fact that they appear in his list of "Works Cited" (288). Sabine Heuser's (2003) book devotes just a single paragraph to the Bridge books (124). All of the recent synoptic and historical accounts of SF as a genre—the Cambridge and Blackwell companions, the Westfahl encyclopedia, single author studies by Roger Luckhurst or Adam Roberts—all of these spend considerable time with *Neuromancer*, and say nothing (or virtually nothing) about his subsequent books.

3 Gibson doesn't *date* his futures "to encourage a certain dislocation on the reader's part. There's a certain familiarity and a certain strangeness" (interview with *Encarta*). Curiously, the dust jacket of *Virtual Light* lists the setting as "2005"!

4 I know of no first-rate essay that offers a powerful, coherent discussion of the *entire* Sprawl series, though there are many wonderful essays addressing one or two of the books. I particularly admire the sophisticated insights and clever writing in four essays by Istvan Csicsery-Ronay, Jr. Unlike the huge quantity of discussion on *Neuromancer*, I count just nine refereed scholarly articles or book chapters primarily or substantially on the Bridge sequence. Several, however, are quite fine. See especially Berressem, Farnell, and Murphy ("Post/Humanity"). Together, these nine essays generally share the notion that the second series extends and either intensifies or etiolates the conceits of the first series; see, for instance, Liu (339). My view is that the second reverses and recodes the first, a development that culminates in *Pattern Recognition*.

5 In "Alternate Presents," I offered this comment on the mirror:

> The novel's internal trope for ... interiority is "mirror world" ... we immediately recognize a mirror world as an inversion, a symmetrical opposite. In *Pattern Recognition*, the mirror-metaphor doesn't so much reverse as evert, fold inside out; it does not so much reflect and so make available for commentary as ironize and explode, something not suggested by the early emblem of cyberpunk—mirrorshades.
>
> (497)

6 See my "Arc of Our Destruction."

7 A chart such as this might create as many questions as provide clarifications—
twenty years later finds Ihab Hassan still explaining his famous comparison of
modernism and postmodernism. In what follows, I will trace some of the implications of the most acute contrasts, but I also would echo Hassan's "pointed
disclaimer":

> Yet the dichotomies this table represents remain insecure, equivocal. For
> differences shift, defer, even collapse; concepts in any one vertical column
> are not all equivalent; and inversions and exceptions, in both modernism
> and postmodernism, abound.
>
> (223)

8 According to conventional wisdom, Gibson's early work is paradigmatic of
postmodernism, and vice versa. I disagree. However dreary such debates usually
are, and they can be *very* dreary, some considerable disagreements remain concerning the fundamental referents of terms such as *modern* and *postmodern*.
Depending on the discipline—architecture, literature, painting, or philosophy—
the terms designate different things, different traditions, and different concepts.
This semantic overdetermination is compacted by the fact that most critics use
the terms indiscriminately, though at this point I think it more likely that they
feel utterly bored by the prospect of yet another definition than that they are too
lazy or too ill-informed to be precise. As I understand the terms, modernism and
postmodernism do not designate literary historical periods from roughly 1860–
1939 or roughly 1946-present, respectively. Though it is occasionally useful to
talk in this fashion—especially in the context of style, as Hassan has shown—to
do so fundamentally distorts what has actually happened in western cultural life.
It is empirically false to say that even a plurality of texts in those periods is
unequivocally one or the other, and so it is probably more useful to speak of
modernity as designating the mid-seventeenth century and after. Many texts
commonly labeled modernist are better understood as postmodern or romantic.
The general problem of precise generic labeling might be resolved by two admis-
sions: that chronology isn't destiny, and that individual texts are mostly motley
amalgams and rarely paradigmatic of anything whatsoever. Modern*ism* and
postmodern*ism* are better understood as particular approaches to the arts, and in
this regard I follow the definitions of the postmodern outlined by the late French
philosopher Jean-François Lyotard, who called postmodernism an *attitude*:
"incredulity toward metanarratives" (xxiv). Implicitly, Lyotard conceives postmodernism as the movement in the arts that corresponds to poststructuralism.
Providing an elaboration, Lyotard remarked: "Postmodernism thus understood is
not modernism at its end, but in the nascent state, and this state is *constant*" (79;
my emphasis). In this sense, *postmodernism* identifies the rigorous conceptual
skepticism that opens modernity, but the modernist continues on to answer
skepticism of the past's metanarratives by proffering a new metanarrative, a new
story, a new certainty—something the postmodernist, too self-aware, and too
self-reflexive, cannot or will not do. Lyotard offers this fascinating illustration: "It
seems to me that the essay (Montaigne) is postmodern, and the fragment (*The
Athenaeum*) is modern" (81). Here, Lyotard's example of the *postmodern* comes
from the French Renaissance, and his *modern* comes from German Romanticism.
Another useful illustration of this alternative understanding of the modern might
be to name figures from another genre and period; in Lyotard's sense, Emily
Dickinson is unequivocally postmodern while Walt Whitman, especially the
Whitman of 1892, is modern. In this chapter, I will use "postmodern" in
Lyotard's sense, which means I will also occasionally align romanticism and

modernism, following the scheme in the quotation above. If the central conceit of modernism is "no longer" (Rée 974), in SF this most often takes the form of new tropes of escape or transcendence. Gibson's early cyberpunk came to be called postmodern primarily because two extraordinarily intelligent and influential critics—Istvan Csicsery-Ronay, Jr. and Fredric Jameson—declared it such. The claim was subsequently repeated and developed by Brian McHale. The notion stuck, perhaps because the work seemed so "new," and just then the newest name for new art was "postmodernism," a term that gained currency in 1984, when *Neuromancer* was published and two widely debated essays by Lyotard and Jameson also appeared. I first learned about *Neuromancer* in a section of *Rolling Stone*, where it was pitched as the hottest, coolest, and newest SF in decades. *The Village Voice* and other mandarins of popular culture soon joined the bandwagon in extolling Gibson as the very avatar of the contemporary. *Neuromancer*'s street cred was enhanced enormously when dinosaurs and old farts of every stripe denounced it, which also cemented the label "postmodern." It remains important to note that while the Sprawl sequence does superficially display some of the tensions and techniques Jameson claimed characterized the postmodern—depthless pastiche, for instance—not all critics accepted the designation, then or now. Suvin provides one obvious example. Generally, few cyberpunk texts can be called postmodern without distorting the term, either in Lyotard's or in Jameson's sense, beyond all recognition. Only the least discriminating critic could call Sterling's *The Artificial Kid*, Kadrey's *Metrophage*, Williams' *Hardwired*, Cadigan's *Synners*, or later, Morgan's *Altered Carbon* "postmodern," unless of course by the term that critic simply means something like "published after 1946" or "stylistically quite unlike Golden Age or New Wave SF" or "this is something that Jerry Pournelle couldn't write." In Lyotard's sense, *Neuromancer* is modernist, a point I have been arguing since 1992. See, for example, my "Arc of Our Destruction" (*passim*, but especially 392n1) and "Alternate Presents" (500n10).

9 Along with a cluster of topoi, a certain prose texture remains Gibson's sigil: while the earlier baroque, "flickering montage" (31) has relaxed, matured, opened to a more mainstream audience and tradition, style continues central to his effect. As Candas Dorsey remarked in a review of *Pattern Recognition*: "Gibson's books have had the effect they have not only because they have great ideas, but because they have great sentences. Much of the innovation is indeed buried deep within the sentences." Or in Lisa Zeidner's lovely phrase: "His sentences slide from silk to steel, and take tonal joy rides from the ironic to the earnest" (7d).

10 Each of Gibson's nine books is primarily a chase or a caper, or both.

11 Hence a follower of Erving Goffman, perhaps especially *Frame Analysis*. In existential sociology, the focus concerns mediating forms more than human agency, and it usually sacrifices taxonomic conclusions for minutely detailed thick descriptions. See Peterson (1979).

12 One might argue that *The Difference Engine*, an alternative history (and so set in "the past") co-written with Bruce Sterling, functions as the transitional "hinge" between "early" and "late" Gibson. In "Alternate Presents," I comment on this point, but it merits a separate essay.

13 Here I refer to the notion of "creative reading" developed by Derek Attridge (79–83).

14 The *node* motif receives an ironic twist in *Spook Country*. Hollis Henry is a freelance journalist hired by *Node* magazine (1). *Node*, however, doesn't actually exist, but instead is only a device Bigend uses to capture Hollis' attention and to manipulate her action, much as Bigend exploits Cayce through the footage. Since *Spook Country* appeared only after this chapter was completed, I have not been able to add a detailed analysis.

15 In *Synners*, Pat Cadigan captures that cyberpunk crux in her phrase "Change for the machines."

16 In 1999, Gibson and his 16-year-old daughter attended a private weekend festival of digital video, movies made without acetate film. In his essay about the event, primarily Gibson reflects on how the digital medium structures the aesthetics of the new products. Importantly, it will open the opportunity for "wannabe auteurs" such as the "Garage Kubrick" to craft their own movies without the superstructure of industrial cinema or the enormous crews needed to staff even the most indie and inexpensive films. The Garage Kubrick obsesses over details, "the texture of his own imagination turned into pixelflesh," trying to capture human life exactly, mimetically, perfectly—in "full fractal richness." Excited at the new possibilities now opening, Gibson reminds us that this "magic" has always been the telos of art and the "mystery" of the self.

17 I develop this point at some length in "[Anarchy], State, Heterotopia" (50–53).

18 One could also say that Cayce stands in for the author. Ahead of the curve and the fads, Cayce anticipates and understands fashion before it is fashion. She *out-Herods Harrods*, so to speak. When queried about trends for athletic shoes she names a future with virtually the same style and model of sneaker worn by ... William Gibson, as prominently displayed in the promotional photo on the book's dust-jacket. Hip beyond hip, she shares the same "haute nerd intensity" (9) of Gibson's own self-presentation, as in interviews, magazine profiles, or the film *No Maps for These Territories*. Pro-Keds were slightly more *haute* with *nerds*, partly since Converse advertising targeted athletes.

19 I of course exaggerate. Gibson employs 'semiotics' in *Burning Chrome*, twice in *Neuromancer*, and four times in *Pattern Recognition*, but nowhere else in his corpus. The common perception that Gibson uses the word obsessively is apparently a phenomenon of the criticism, not the fiction.

20 For extended, technical definitions of hermeneutics and semiotics, including origins, uses, and abuses see Grondin, Eco, and Silverman.

21 Farnell notes Gibson's antipathy to literary theory, quoting an interview: "Gibson is 'extremely dubious about theory,' French in particular: 'Being a philosopher in France as clear as I can make out is about doing television. It's like being a professional talk show guest ... [it] is a scam' (*Today Online*)" (477n15).

22 These are the Three Laws of Cool. (There is no *Count Zeroth* law.) Since Gladwell is more gadfly than scholar, see also the excellent books by John Leland and Alan Liu.

4 Journeys Beyond Being

The Cyberpunk-Flavored Novels of Jeff Noon

Andrew M. Butler

There is a moment in an interview when Jeff Noon notes how little written science fiction now influences people: "The last (written) sf movement to capture the general public's imagination to any real extent was cyberpunk. That's a long time ago, twenty years now" (Butler, "Quality" 15). In the mid- to late-1990s, Noon's early novels were seen as being part of the cyberpunk movement. But this movement had been declared dead as a potentially revolutionary and cutting edge subgenre almost as soon as it was born—Bruce Sterling under his pseudonym Vincent Omniaveritas wrote in 1986: "I hereby declare the revolution over. Long live the provisional government." The label continued, however, and indeed continues, along with post-cyberpunk, as a device used to sell books. Geoff Ryman described *Vurt* (1993) as "a fast-paced, cyberpunk-seasoned sf thriller" ("Rev." 90), a judgment that situates the novel in the margins of the subgenre rather than anywhere near the centre. This chapter will explore the novel's use of an equivalent to cyberpunk's use of virtual reality, the meaning of such virtual realms, and thus cyberpunk's attitudes to the body and death.

To my mind, the cyberpunk movement is best used to describe a group of writers who were associating together in the 1980s—writing to each other, taking part in workshops, attending conventions, and communicating on bulletin boards. At the ArmadilloCon in Austin, Texas (October 1982), a panel called "Behind the Mirrorshades: A Look at Punk SF," William Gibson, Bruce Sterling, and John Shirley discussed "Len Deighton, Nelson Algren, Burroughs and Ballard ... rock and roll, MTV, Japan, fashion, drugs, and politics" (Shiner, "Inside" 21). The fiction that best fit the new label drew on the hard-boiled traditions of Dashiell Hammett and Raymond Chandler, the works of William S. Burroughs, and the shake-up of SF occasioned by the British New Wave, in particular the writings of J.G. Ballard. It could be described as "science fiction set in a near future, dominated by high technology including computers, computer networks and human/machine hybrids" (Butler, *Cyberpunk*: 9). It was SF of the mean streets featuring hookers and cowboys or freelance programmers—rather than the square-jawed heroes and white-coated rocket scientists of traditional SF. It was stylistically dense, and often explored what was then a strange new realm of cyberspace. Bruce Sterling edited the crucial anthology *Mirrorshades* (1986), bringing together stories by Greg Bear, Pat Cadigan, Gibson, Marc Laidlaw, Tom Maddox, Rudy Rucker, Lewis Shiner, Shirley, and himself—although not all of the stories fit what we would recognise as cyberpunk. I regard the writers who emerged after this anthology as being post-cyberpunks.[1]

In about 1993, having read Ryman's review, I coined the label "cyberpunk-flavored" to refer to a number of works which did not quite fit the label of cyberpunk, and for which "post-cyberpunk" was not altogether appropriate.[2] Noon seemed to be writing from a different position from the traditional SF apprenticeship: read the fiction as a child, become a fan, start publishing SF, and graduate to novels. There is certainly no sense that he was making or wanting to make social or literary common ground with the SF writers of the early 1990s or the 1980s. As Tony Keen puts it, "He did not emerge through the fanzines and sf magazines, though he read American superhero comics avidly as a child. He was a playwright who could not get his plays mounted," including a play called *The Torture Garden* that was "based on the 1899 novel of that name, by Octave Mirbeau." Persuaded by Stephen Powell "to write a novel for Powell's new imprint, Ringpull Press" (Keen 102), the material from *The Torture Garden* mutated and changed, so that little of the original remained. To the publisher's apparent surprise, the result, *Vurt*, was enormously successful in the SF world, winning the 1994 Arthur C. Clarke Award and coming top in a poll of reviewers in the British Science Fiction Association magazine *Vector* (Cary). News of the novel spread by word of mouth throughout the British SF community, and at the 1995 World Science Fiction Convention, held in Glasgow, Noon won the John W. Campbell Award for best new SF writer. The novel went on to be successful in America and Japan and to be translated into ten languages. Noon followed the novel up with *Pollen* (1995), which uses the same milieu, and two further novels *Automated Alice* (1996) and *Nymphomation* (1997) which appear only tangentially related to the Vurt milieu.

I intend the term to work on the model of "chocolate-flavored"—some food tastes, looks, and feels like chocolate, but is not in fact chocolate. Noon does use some of the tropes of cyberpunk, and he is obviously writing after *Mirrorshades*, but there is less of a sense that he is writing consciously within a cyberpunk tradition or inside the SF ghetto. Tony Keen wrote in a chapter on *Vurt* that "Cyberpunk merely provides the surface gloss" (101), using and disavowing the label at the same time. Noon might be seen as appropriating cyberpunk materials for his own ends—importing William Gibson into Manchester. It's worth remembering that Noon could only have read the initial Neuromancer trilogy—*Neuromancer* (1984), *Count Zero* (1986) and *Mona Lisa Overdrive* (1988). These novels were fast-paced, and moved around the world with the ease of a Bond movie—numerous locations in the US, Chiba City, Japan, India, Mexico, Paris, and London, as well as in space. The protagonists seemed to have been borrowed from noir fiction—Hammett especially—and many of them were enhanced with some kind of technology. Most importantly, there was the matrix, Gibson's imagined worldwide network of interconnected computer spaces. In each novel, a major character was required to enter virtual space in order to find something or someone, and there was the notion that it was possible to be stuck within this virtual realm. Gibson's work was taken up by academic critics, and one of the things that seemed to appeal to them was that his novels allowed personalities and identities to exist outside of physical bodies. The Swiftian disgust of the body displayed in (some) fiction by writers like William S. Burroughs could be superseded by the sense of apparent obsolescence of the body.[3]

Vurt makes two significant breaks with cyberpunk: its location and the lack of immediately obvious computer networks. Cyberpunk and post-cyberpunk, as largely American phenomena, had looked to the Silicon Valley cities of West Coast America and the then tiger economies and, to a lesser extent, the emerging post-Soviet new Europe. When we think of cyberpunk, we are more likely to think of Tokyo, Seattle, San Francisco, and south central Los Angeles, the sort of psychogeography explored by Mike Davis in *City of Quartz* (1990). Then there are the sprawls of eastern seaboard cities in the USA—the Boston-Atlanta Metropolitan Axis, for example—but the Pacific Rim dominated.[4] On the other hand, Noon's novel is solidly set in a distinctly mappable near-future Manchester. This had been a major industrial city during the nineteenth century—in England, only London and Birmingham were larger. The development of cotton mills and textile and other factories meant the city swelled with workers from the greater Lancashire area and immigrants from Ireland via nearby (and rival city) Liverpool. Hundreds of thousands of workers were crammed into terraced houses. Since the industry declined, Manchester has had to reinvent itself a number of times, and Noon was writing *Vurt* during one such period of redevelopment.

About two miles to the south of the city are the areas of Moss Side and Hulme, which had been open country prior to the Industrial Revolution. In the 1960s, the terraced houses, by then slums, were torn down, to be replaced with flats and tenements. Many of the new buildings were intended to be communities in the sky, with access to individual apartments from a series of walkways on different levels. In Manchester, a number of these become known by their shape: the Crescents. But despite the utopian dream of the architects, a combination of design flaws, lax maintenance, and poverty led to the rapid degradation of British post-Second World War urban housing stock, matched by a social disintegration which manifested itself in crime, gangs, and race riots involving the white underclass, immigrants from Pakistan and India (including many expelled from Uganda by Idi Amin), and second-generation Black British people.

Noon seems to have little affection for his home town which he has since left. He says:

> I hardly think about Manchester these days, to be honest. I wasn't particularly happy there, on a personal level, and the novels were very much an outcome of me questioning the city or trying to. I guess I was trying to create an alternative city. Certainly I have no interest at all in "New Manchester," or whatever they call it, the "Rejuvenation." The yuppie flats, and the posh shops, and all of that. I couldn't imagine setting novels in this new place.

Noon's interests have moved on from "these kinda weird cyberpunk novels" (Butler, "The Quality of the Afterlife" 13) which depict his imagined Manchester with a cyberpunk flavor.

Noon was certainly not interested in predicting the future; instead, depictions of technology are used—like all good science fiction writing—as a metaphor for exploring the human condition. He was interested, as Keen has noted, of finding *"new ways of telling stories"* (104) rather than of telling new stories. Noon has spoken to Phil Daoust of his attempt to break Manchester—Rushulme, Moss Side, and West Didsbury—down in his fiction, with: "a new way of people being different from each other. I was trying to create a multicultural place that had a potential for great excitement, for great work and art and adventures" (12–13). This manifests itself in the peculiar cross-bred species—Shadowcops, Robodogs, and so on—which feature in his novels. These hybrids exhibit the sort of grotesque bodily freedom that computer-generated avatars do within fictional cyberspace. It is both the strength and weakness of *Vurt* and its sequel, *Pollen* (1995) that the virtual realm becomes indistinguishable from the (fictional) actual one.

The virtual realm in Noon's work is known as Vurt, and the experience of entering it is described in *Vurt* as "just collective dreaming" (240), not unlike the concept of "consensual hallucination" which Gibson uses to denote cyberspace. Vurt is reached by the imbibing of hallucinogenic Vurt feathers; the resulting experience is partway between a drug trip and a computer game. The main characters of the novel are a gang known as the Stash Riders, who illegally take the feathers. One of their number, Desdemona, has taken one called English Voodoo, and within that apparently hallucinated realm takes another called Curious Yellow. Desdemona disappears, and in her place as an exchange, there is the feather-growing Thing-From-Outer-Space. Here there is a physical, bodily cost to the exchange. Scribble, Desdemona's brother and lover—and the narrator of most of the novel—is determined to get her back. When he eventually finds her, he remains behind in her place and looks likely to become the controller of Vurt, while she returns home. His narration alternates with the hints, tips, and evasions of Game Cat, which read like a column from a computer games magazine. The novel thus displays the major aspects of cyberpunk: street-culture, linguistic experimentation, and especially virtual reality. However, the virtual reality experience seems to have an organic basis rather than using computers, which is partially why I incline to the term "cyberpunk-flavored" rather than post-cyberpunk.

Before examining Noon's subsequent novels, I wish to examine the nature of the virtual realm. Writers have long set up problems for characters within a fictional world which are solved by a shift to a new location. Often there is a sense that these are different realms—magical spaces, holiday spaces, the carnivalesque. In discussing this kind of location, Samuel R. Delany coined the phrase "paraspace," referring in particular to a series of "hyper-fictional" realms in Robert A. Heinlein's "The Roads Must Roll," Roger Zelazny's "He Who Shapes," and Gibson's fiction. Delany argued that the latter two explore "conceptual spaces that, with the help of technology, we can enter. You can die in either one" (*Silent* 166). Delany notes that "our paraspaces are not in a hierarchical relation ... to the narrative's 'real,' or ordinary space. What goes on in one subverts the other; what goes on in the other subverts the one" (*Silent* 168). Delany uses the term "paraspace" in order to avoid the hierarchical connotations of "subspace" but, especially with virtual reality, the designation is still overly spatial.[5]

The term was taken up by Scott Bukatman, not only to explore the meaning of cyberspace, but also to analyse a variety of spectacles such as theme parks, panoramas, and amusement park rides. He notes how in the encounter with examples of paraspace there is sometimes a sense of the disappearance of the body, of the meat: the stimuli operating upon the observer outweigh the awareness of having the sensations. Such a delirious experience depends on a total identification of the gazer with what is being identified with. However, he argues that this erasure of the body simultaneously reinscribes it—paintings such as Frederic Edwin Church's *Twilight in the Wilderness* (1860) and Douglas Trumbull's stargate sequence in *2001, A Space Odyssey* (1968) provide both the spectacle and an observer within the frame—as both bearer and an object of the look. As Bukatman says, "What occurs is a simultaneous grounding and dislocating of human bodily experience" (*Matters* 15). For this to work, it seems necessary to assume the existence of the same kind of universal gaze that is necessary for the mechanics of classical Hollywood cinema outlined by Laura Mulvey in "Visual Pleasures and Narrative Cinema." In the painting, of course, both landscape and observer are painted, and both stargate and Dave Bowman are projected on the screen.

Cyberspace and other virtual realms offer writers a utopia, in the sense of an outopia, a no-place,[6] which, as a paraspace, exists at a different level of ontology to the "outside" "real" world of the narratives in which it features. Umberto Rossi, following Carlo Pagetti, gave the layers of reality a sort of numerical ranking: "the *fictional* reality described (or built) in the novel, the *hyper-fictional* reality which is alternative to that fictional reality, and the reality of the reader ... primary text, secondary text, and zeroth text" (403).[7] This assumes that there is a kind of contract between the reader and writer: in return for the willing suspension of disbelief on the part of the reader, the writer will create a consistent fictional world, within which there may be distinct (hyper-)fictional worlds which bear the same relationship to the characters in the primary text as the realm of the primary text does to the zeroth text. I have written of this idea in relation to Philip K. Dick's *Lies, Inc* elsewhere,[8] but in short it is impossible to maintain such distinctions. There is a bleeding between fictional and hyper-fictional, an imagined Manchester and the Vurt-realm, in *Vurt* and its successors; there is the real world in which the author, book, and reader exist, the zeroth level; the world depicted in *Vurt* or the fictional or primary level; the Vurt experience of English Voodoo or the hyper-fictional or secondary level; and then the Vurt experience of Curious Yellow—hyper-hyper, meta-hyper, or tertiary level. But the same words are used to describe the three texts within the zeroth text, and they collapse into each other.

It is also worth exploring this leaving behind of the body in cyberpunk in a more phenomenological sense, and to note its relation to death as non-being. The sublime delirium described by Bukatman is a form of ecstacy, a term that derives from *ex-stasis* or "out of the body." In the thought of Martin Heidegger, the individual (is) thrown into Being: "we call it the '*thrownness*' [*Geworfenheit*] of this entity into its 'there,' indeed, it is thrown in such a way that, as Being-in-the-World, it is the 'there'" (174). Just as the being is thrown into Being against their will, so they may be thrown out at any point—in other words, to die. Heidegger viewed life as a series of distractions from this: life is defined as Being-Towards-Death. Emmanuel Levinas, in part a phenomenologist, was aware of the paradox of death as an experience that could not be experienced. According to Levinas: "Death is never now. Where death is here, I am no longer here" (41). Death is somewhere else, another realm, analogous to the way the virtual realm has been described. To enter it—and we have heard apocryphal tales or myths of this for millennia—is to be transformed. For thousands of years, human beings have attempted to imagine heavens, hells, afterlives, and underworlds. To know about this realm, the (presumably fictional) hero must visit it and return to tell the tale.

At the same time, there is the sense in Levinas's writings that being is haunted by non-being. He posited a thought experiment where everything is reduced to nothing and there is only the I observing. Rather than a blank silence, Levinas argues, there would be, paradoxically, something: "Nothing responds to us, but this silence; the voice of this silence is understood and frightens us ... Darkness fills it like a content" (31). There is a fear of being which comes from nothing, rather than a fear of nothing, for nothing cannot be. That which "is" exists in the three dimensions of Cartesian space, as well as through time; that which "is not" is outside of such time and space, and therefore outside of ontology. Through a concern for the

Other—who is presumably also afraid of the being that comes from nothing—the self becomes a self, an identity, defined by its concern for the other:
"Fear for the Other, fear for the other man's death, is my fear" (Levinas 84).
Through Being-Towards-the-Other, the self enters into Being, into space
and time.

Joan Gordon, in "Yin and Yang Duke it Out," notes:

> The mythic journey to the underworld ... makes us heroes, and the
> journey is not just to our own dark side, but to the dark side of
> the human condition. Moreover, its power lies not so much in what we
> learn on the journey as it does on the fact of our learning and in our
> subsequent transformation.
>
> (201)

In cyberpunk, this journey to the other side, the metaphorical journey into
death is also the entry into the paraspace of cyberspace, which apparently
strips the traveler of a fixed physical body. There is in the journey to the
Underworld a being beyond the body, or alternatively, a journey beyond
being. In *Noon*, though, the journey to the Underworld is also an insistence
on the importance of the physical body.

The Orpheus myth is prominent in *Vurt*, although Noon claims that any
connection is coincidental (quoted in Keen 46).[9] Orpheus's wife Eurydice is
bitten by a snake and dies. Orpheus, a champion musician, then enters the
underworld and wins her back. And then, according to which version is
being read, they either leave together or he breaks the rules by looking
back and loses her again. Some time later he is dismembered, and his head
floats downstream, mourning and prophesying. Noon's retelling resists the
expectations of those who recognize the myth. For a start, it is moder-
nized: Scribble is a musician, but he is a DJ rather than a lyre player.
Scribble is the one who gets bitten by the snake, while in a Vurt hallucination. And finally, when he actually locates Desdemona, he releases her
and stays behind himself. "I don't belong there, sister," he tells her of the
real world. "This is my place, this is what I am" (358). Of course, within
the logic of the novel, he has to stay behind. Desdemona had been swap-
ped for The-Thing-From-Outer-Space, who is now dead. Instead, Scribble
swaps himself and stays behind to write his story, and perhaps even to
become the controller of Vurt. But one body has to be substituted for
another.

Vurt is a different ontological realm to the "real" world, but it is difficult
to maintain this primary and secondary distinction, of fiction and hyper-
fiction. With the existence of genetic crossbreeds such as Dogmen,
Shadowcops, Robodogs, Vurtcops more or less unexplained within the
novel *Vurt*,[10] the sort of mutation possible in cyberspace can happen in
"reality." That is, of course, if the novel being read is reality, or, rather, if
the realm within the novel where characters take Vurt feathers is indeed

meant to be taken as the real world within this novel. The Game Cat tells us about a new Vurt feather:

> The hero's name is Scratch ... Boy have you got problems! First off your sister, Shona, has been caught in Metaland, swapped for a lump of lard alien. Your job is to get Shona back to base earth.
>
> Of course that's virtually impossible; nobody's managed it before ... most probably you're going to die ... Be very, very careful. This ride is not for the weak. It's a psycho. A bit like real life.
>
> Well, maybe not quite that bad.
>
> (229–30)

This is, of course, the plot of *Vurt*, which Scribble sits down to write twenty years later:

> It was the Cat who persuaded me to write down these memories. I don't know what to call it yet ... I might just call it after my name, or after what I am. What I have become.
>
> Maybe you're reading it now.
>
> Or maybe you're playing the feather.
>
> Or maybe you're in the feather, thinking that you're reading the novel, with no way of knowing ... [*sic*]
>
> (367–68)

In other words, the events we are reading may have occurred in the past, but are now likely to be a Vurt dream. Of course, we have been tipped off to this possibility, as the novel begins: "A young boy puts a feather into his mouth ... " (3), and ends " ... a young boy takes a feather out of his mouth" (371). The novel itself is someone else's Vurt dream.

Scribble's rescue attempt is thus already within a Vurt, and so when he takes a feather, it is a Vurt within a Vurt, or a meta-Vurt or hyper-fiction, and when he takes another Curious Yellow feather, it becomes a meta-meta-Vurt or hyper-hyper-fiction. It is no wonder that realities on different levels are beginning to get confused. The Vurt which resembles the plot of the novel is described by the Game Cat as "a bit like real life," but there is no guarantee that Scribble's version of the plot is any more like real life. In fact, if the whole novel is a Vurt, then it is "just a collective dreaming" and there is no guarantee that the information given about Vurt feathers is accurate, or rather, meant to be accepted as real. Authenticity is impossible to establish.

If *Vurt* is a cyberpunk-flavored metafiction with an inconclusive rationale, then Noon's second novel, *Pollen,* moves to clear up some of the ambiguities with a series of epitexts: a version of the traditional folk song "John Barleycorn,"[11] a collage of print representing a sneeze, and an extract from "*The Looking Glass Wars* by R. B. Tshimoma." The extract informs the reader of the history of the discovery of "the ability to record dreams onto a replayable medium, a bio-magnetic tape coated with Phantasm liquid ... Through the gates of Vurt the people could re-visit their own dreams or, more dangerously, visit another person's dream" (5). The Vurt was first instigated by Miss Hobart, whose first name is elsewhere revealed to be Alice and which presumably, as a nod to the most famous character in the works of Lewis Carroll, suggests the title of the Looking Glass Wars, Noon's period of fictional history when Vurt took on a life of its own and battled with Earth.[12]

The plot of *Pollen* offers a number of strategic reversals of the plot of *Vurt*. The characters of Vurt are dismissed and having dispensed with the Stash Riders—with whom the readers of *Vurt* are presumably meant to sympathize—Noon chooses as his protagonist Sibyl Jones, a shadow cop, a hybrid of a type which formed the enemy in *Vurt*. Sibyl is a Dodo, a person incapable of using the Vurt feather to enter the Vurt realm, although as a shadow she has the ability to enter into other people's minds. This tactic means that Noon avoids the linear option of writing a direct sequel, a *Vurt II*; he says "I was interested in creating a city, and filling it with different kinds of people, and just seeing what happened when those stories interconnected"(Butler, "The Quality of the Afterlife" 14). Sibyl allows Noon to keep a seedy milieu, but to explore it at a different social level from that of *Vurt*.

There are further alterations in perspective. Whereas in *Vurt* the plot involves the infiltration of the Vurt realm by people using Vurt feathers, here the invasion is the other way around. In return for a swap with a child named Brian Swallow (Noon, *Pollen*: 25), Persephone—a name with obvious underworld connotations—has broken through to Manchester from the Vurt realm, bringing with her a new hybrid: "Human and plant" (Noon, *Pollen*: 147). Pollen is no longer being rejected by the body's immune system, but rather bonding with the reproductive system. Even if the host dies of this hay fever, the invasion will continue as the body will sprout if it is buried. This echoes the folk song of John Barleycorn, where the burial of barley only leads to new plants growing.

The organic realm of Vurt will also replace an already existing virtual realm of the computers linking together Manchester's X-cab network. The cyberpunk is here usurped by the cyberpunk-flavored: the map is to be replaced by John Barleycorn's map, a flower map, which will enable the Vurt to spread into the real world: "the map is made out of roots, and the city is a flower that grows from the sap of the map" (Noon, *Pollen*: 184). In an apocalyptic reversal of the infamous dictum, the map creates the territory.

This invasion is revenge by John Barleycorn—here a variant on Satan, Lucifer, and Hades, and so on—for his exile to the Underworld. Through Vurt, the old stories and myths have come alive, and wish to escape from the afterlife realm of Vurt / the Underworld. Here again is made explicit what had been implicit in *Vurt*: "John Barleycorn lives in the feather called Juniper Suction. This is a Heaven Feather. An underworld. A place to store our memories when we die. So we can live *beyond death*, in the Vurt. *Only the dead can visit there*" (200, my emphases). Barleycorn has to be defeated on his own turf, by entering into the Vurt realm of Juniper Suction. At first this appears to be the conventional Hades, but having defeated the various guards, Sibyl encounters fictional characters:

> The Grendel was there, Achilles was there, Robin Hood was there, Gargantua and Pantagruel was there, Vladimir and Estragon was there, Tom Jones was there, Humbert Humbert was there, Popeye the Sailor Man was there, the Spiderman was there, Jane Eyre was there, Dave Bowman was there, Eleanor Rigby was there, Jesus Christ and the Tin Man were there, Leopold Bloom and Rupert the Bear were there; all the fictional characters of human endeavour were planted in that green world, and all of them were tumbling and loving and cussing in a story-go-round of intimate chaos.
>
> (Noon, *Pollen*: 302–3)

Here the ironies of Noon's punning pay off, as the Alice of Alice Hobart and the Dodos who cannot fly/travel into Vurt collide with the Alice of *Through the Looking Glass* and its stuttering author Do-Do-Dodgson.

The Alice mythos echoes in Noon's "trequel," *Automated Alice* (1996), which may or may not be set within the Vurt mythos. Here Alice and her anagrammatically named doll Celia are banished to a rainswept nineteenth-century Manchester. They vanish through a grandfather clock into November 1998, but a 1998 which is not our own familiar world and seems different from the sort of future depicted in *Vurt*. Whereas *Vurt* had hybrids of Dogs, Shadows, Cops and Robots, here there is a greater variety of animal-crosses: "Goatboys and Sheepgirls, Elephantmen and Batwomen" (105). But these seem to exist merely to serve as throwaway gags in an updating of the original Alice books.

Just as *Vurt* included and folded in upon an account of its own narrative, so does *Automated Alice* play metafictional games, in the shape of a character named Zenith O'Clock, a barely disguised self-portrait of Noon: "I've written two Wrongs [i.e., novels] up to now: the first was called Shurt, and the second was called Solumn. And the Crickets [i.e., critics] hated both of them. That is why I'm sad" (151). One hopes that in the Looking-Glass Noon's opinions of critics have been reversed, since the "terrible respond to [his] work in the noisepapers" (151) has largely been positive.

Alas, though, the linguistic experimentation which Noon has always flirted with is here foregrounded, with constant (and frankly annoying) punning. For example, a list of book titles includes: "*Hatch 22, The Gnome of the Hose, Stoat Fishing in Amirrorca, From Cher to Infirmity*" (Noon, *Automated Alice*: 166). What was once merely the background to the action seems to be the substitute for a satisfying narrative. The novel appears to be a retrograde step, rather than a launch pad to new heights.

Noon's fourth novel, *Nymphomation* (1997), was similarly poised on the edge of the Vurt milieu, but offers better proof of Noon's talents. In 1999 Manchester, the company AnnoDomino is piloting a lottery-type game, Domino Bones, where individuals can win large cash prizes when the randomly altering domino they have bought matches up with that week's domino. The game, weeks short of being expanded to cover the rest of the country, is run by one Mr Million, who appears to be a member of a class of twenty-eight pupils who were led to mathematical genius by their teacher Miss Sayer in 1949.

While the novel does not contain the mutations of the earlier written novels, it does have some discussion of DNA mutations and "mating" of information within a computer simulation. The central characters are not here the slacker Vurt-takers of *Vurt*, nor the long-suffering cops of *Pollen*, but rather students at Manchester University, staff of an Indian restaurant, a number of homeless people, and workers at the (thinly disguised) Waterstone's on Deansgate. Keen suggests that Noon writes of the students "with mixed results," although he notes that Noon "deals mostly with the drop-out end of student existence" (98).

Until the ending of the book, the computer-generated realm is much the same as may be accessed in the real world: simulated environments controlled by a few equations and computer records. Jazir, an expert hacker who has captured one of the blurbflies which advertise the game, is being contacted from time to time by Miss Sayer, now apparently a computer virus within his machine. Eventually, though, one such simulation is entered, which appears to be both within and analogous to the headquarters of the game, the House of Chances:

> Miss Sayer was consulted time and again, but her appearance only came at random, and then she seemed to be constricted, as though something was blocking her progress. Only a few words—wings, help, me, grab, come, find, maze—were allowed play upon her broken tongue. Jazir had explained to [former pupil Jimmy] how the teacher had chosen him, nurtured him over the years. "That's my girls," agreed Jimmy. They were both keen to enter the House of Chances, however difficult it proved; one to rescue the teacher, the other to confront Mr Million.
>
> (320)

The entry to the realm within the House of Changes, "The Theseus Maze," seems to be edging towards the sort of beyond-the-body experience described in Vurt:

> Upstairs in the room, Jazir was ready. His body was drunk on vaz and crawling with life and cooking some new recipe never before tried,

perhaps his last. He stepped up onto the window sill. Masala Blurb[fly] was loaded with the Theseus program, with Celia [Hobart]'s feather tight in its teeth ... [H]is covering of blurb[flie]s fluttered eagerly as the night beckoned them ...

   Jazir stepped off ... [*sic*]

(331)

The entry into another realm is here associated with the feather, with flying and with Vaz. The conditions for *Vurt*—albeit without the mutations—appear to be in place, leading up to a climactic: "The young boy puts the feather into his mouth" (Noon, *Vurt*: 362–63).

The twist in this novel is that the voyager to the underworld is able to rescue the lost woman and escape himself, although in the way that realities get conflated: dominoes player Celia Hobart wins the game and becomes the new Mr Million, just as Scribble seems to become the controller of Vurt. At the same time, the chronology does not seem quite right. Celia, like Alice/Celia of *Automated Alice*, is searching for her parrot, but the 1999 of *Nymphomation* seems very different from the 1998 of *Automated Alice*, nor is there the sense that the dead Alice of *Nymphomation* had traveled from the nineteenth century.

Perhaps, then, the feather hallucination is the clue to comprehending the way that the series is linked: we are mistaken to see the novels as more than superficially linked. Instead, we could see them as separate Vurt feather-dreams, reported from some unseen reality. Keen suggests that Noon "'remixes' the Vurt world for each novel and short story he sets there" (Keen 104). Manchester is a kaleidoscope viewed through Noon's art—with *Vurt* shifting into *Shurt* and Scribble into Scratch. Like the remix and sampled music which technology has made possible and postmodern aesthetics have made modish, Noon can recycle the same ingredients to make something seemingly new—old stories retold in a new way. The problem is that sometimes he falls uncomfortably between the two stools of retreading old ground and finding new territory. *Automated Alice* is too far from *Vurt* and *Pollen* and yet not far enough. But *Nymphomation* remains his best novel since *Vurt*, with the wordplay which substituted for substance in *Automated Alice* kept to a minimum.

If Noon were to return to the Vurt mythos, he would be writing a very different book, and it would be a different Manchester: "*Vurt* is a long time ago now; I'm a different person, and (god knows) we live in a different world. I have different interests these days. So even if I did go back, my approach would be from an entirely new angle" (Butler, "The Quality of the Afterlife" 14). While Noon was to return to SF with *Falling Out of Cars* (2003)—after the more realist *Needle in the Groove* (2000)—he has never really felt comfortable as being part of the field. He rejects the imprisonment of the genre ghetto: SF only survives meaningfully as an influence on mainstream culture. In the case of *Star Wars* (1977) and

The Matrix (1999), tropes are being borrowed to replenish the well of story-telling. In Noon's own work, he sees a borderline between SF and the mainstream that can offer limitless possibilities. Noon suggests that "sf may well be dead in the same way that pop music or jazz are dead, i.e. it's reached the end of its perfectly natural cultural life" (Butler, "The Quality of the Afterlife" 15). If SF survives within a small coterie, it will degenerate to become "nothing more than a provider of escapist texts, or worse, just an ideas generator for the mainstream, conservative culture" (Butler, "The Quality of the Afterlife" 15). But cyberpunk-flavored fiction is not one which is escapist, in the sense that it straightforwardly celebrates an escape from the body, from the meat, into some sort of virtual utopia; instead it is often about being trapped in the other world. On some kind of level—and that is a dangerously spatial term in this context—the secondary world into which characters enter is a representation of the underworld, of the realm of the dead.[13] There is a resort to the other world, an apparently non-spatial arena which only appears to have dimensions, in order to attempt to solve problems in this one. The resort to death is to help people in life. In the better cyberpunk-flavored novels, such as Noon's works, this avoids a naïve romanticism by it only being a partial solution to the problem, and the consequences of journeys beyond being are not unambiguous. The reinscription of the body in *Vurt*, the insistence on bodily exchange, and the portrayal of grotesque bodies suggests that any claim that cyberpunk is truly about beating the meat is thrown into question.

ACKNOWLEDGEMENTS

Earlier and much different versions of this chapter were published as "Being Beyond the Body: Neal Stephenson's *Snow Crash* and Jeff Noon's *Vurt*," in *Strange Attactors* and as "Journeys Beyond Being: The Cyberpunk-Flavoured Novels of Jeff Noon," in *Novel Turns: Recent Narrative Writing from Western Europe.*

NOTES

1 In my *Cyberpunk*, I discussed Wilhelmina Baird, Bruce Bethke, Simon Ings, Richard Kadrey, Kim Newman, Marge Piercy, Justina Robson and Neal Stephenson, all of whom seemed to be writing after and in response to *some* of the writers in *Mirrorshades*.

2 In *Cyberpunk*, I discussed Greg Egan, Jon Courtenay Grimwood, Gwyneth Jones, Shariann Lewitt, Jeff Noon, Tricia Sullivan and Jack Womack under this heading.

3 The use of Mikhail Bakhtin's ideas in literary and cultural studies in this 3period is worth noting as well—both in terms of the carnivalesque disruption of hierarchies and space, and the grotesque body. Bodies seemed to be sites of disgust— and with the emergence of HIV/AIDS it seemed that the individual's body could destroy him or her.

4 Earlier British post-cyberpunk writers had often looked away from Britain. Kim Newman's *The Night Mayor* depicts a cyberspace which quotes liberally from film noir, and has cameos of or references to Humphrey Bogart, Sidney Greenstreet, Elisha Cook Jr, Joseph Cotten and others from 1940s movies. This in itself builds on Gibson's usage of plot structures and moods from novels by Raymond Chandler and, more especially, Dashiell Hammett. Manchester-born Gwyneth Jones uses Indian epics as virtual reality games in *North Wind* and *Escape Plans* features a matriarchal dystopia run by computers, and a devastated India.

5 There is an attempt to think beyond the Cartesian ontology of space-time, but language is grounded in notions of being that render ideas as spatial. Jacques Derrida, writing in terms of another attempt to write about non-ontological realms to which I will turn in a few paragraphs, asks: "what necessity compels this inscription of language in space at the very moment when it exceeds space?" To speak of besides, above, below, within, outside or even exceeding is still to be anchored in spatial language. See Jacques Derrida, "Violence and Metaphysics," in *Writing and Difference*, notably p. 93.

6 I think the critics and academics who have examined cyberpunk and the related genres have tended to see it as an eutopia or good place.

7 Rossi is citing Carlo Pagetti's "Introduzione a *La svastica sul sole*," in *Philip K. Dick: Il Sogno Dei Simulacri*. See citation.

8 In Dick's novel, the protagonist has had visions beamed into his head via a satellite, has been shot with an LSD-tipped dart, has passed into a paraworld, and may be going mad on a lengthy solo space voyage. Dick only has words available to him to describe the different events.

9 Keen cites David V. Barrett's "The Lucidity Switch: Jeff Noon Interviewed," in *Interzone* 115 (January 1997).

10 An explanation involving gene-altering music is offered in his short story, "Ultra Kid and the Cat Girl,"in a gesture satirizing the "music composed of repetitive beats" clause of the British Criminal Justice Act. However, this explanation is unnecessary to the plot of *Vurt*. In *Pollen*, references are made to an event involving the drug Fecundity 10: "'the Authorities' answer to the black air of Thanatos, a plague of sterility ... Under the influence of Fecundity 10, ten thousand babies were conceived. Desire was overheated ... Fecundity 10 had broken down the cellular barriers between species" (109).

11 Noon's version appears to be edited from the album by The Traffic, *John Barleycorn Must Die* (1970): "And that was John Barleycorn Must Die, by The Traffic, a mighty folk-rock paean to the regenerative spirit of Mother Earth coming to us from nineteen sixty-nine" (Noon, *Pollen*: 12). The most significant change is the removal of the references to midsummer, which would be at odds with the novel's May setting. Robert Burns's version is quite different—starting with "There was three kings into the east" rather than "There were three men came out of the west." Many versions end with the defeat of John Barleycorn and a toast to heroism (in Burns's case, to Scotland) rather than, as here, with "Sir John ... [proving] the strongest man at last."

12 *The Looking Glass Wars* is a book within the book which describes a period of Manchester's history during which the vurt world and the material world battled for dominance. The Alice character and other intertextual references suggest that Lewis Carroll's *Alice's Adventures in Wonderland* and *Through the Looking Glass* are being recast within the novel as fictional accounts of the "real" events of this war. Noon's later *Automated Alice* further suggests his indebtedness to Lewis's work.

13 This is true of the noir streets of *The Night Mayor*, the descent to Earth in *Escape Plans*, the matrix in *Neuromancer* and the metaverse in *Snow Crash*. For more on this, see my entry on "*Neuromancer*" in *A Companion to Science Fiction*.

Part II

The Political Economy of Cyberpunk

5   Global Economy, Local Texts
Utopian/Dystopian Tension in William Gibson's Cyberpunk Trilogy

Tom Moylan

In 1990, in his speech to the General Assembly of the United Nations, George Bush invoked the utopian figure of the millennium as he called for a new world order, an order of peace and prosperity that would remove the darkness of the Cold War.[1] In 1980, Ronald Reagan invoked another utopian figure: the "city on the hill" that recalled the dream of a New World that would inspire everyone with its harmony and enterprise. However, in the years between Reagan's imagery rooted in the local history of the Americas and Bush's image that envelopes the globe, neither humanity nor the environment has benefited from these utopian gestures. Indeed, and increasingly, since the beginning of the 1990s—with the emergence of the U.S. as the singular world superpower and with continued economic, political, cultural, and ecological devastation—the world historical situation has become ever more dystopian.

What both presidents celebrated in their official utopian tropes was not the betterment of humanity and the earth, but the triumph of planetary capital. Engaged in a massive restructuring since the end of the postwar boom in the 1970s and helped by the rise to power of the Reagan, Thatcher, and Kohl administrations in the 1980s, the forces of global capital have generally succeeded in shifting from an industrial-based system of production and consumption (fordism) to an information-based system that operates through more flexible methods of exploitation, accumulation, and control (postfordism or, as a recent commentator has put it, sonyism). Multinational corporations based in and supported by powerful nation-states have transformed themselves into truly transnational corporations able to reduce the role of the nation-state to the limited function of providing national and, in the case of the U.S., global security. Under the utopian flags of free choice and free market, planetary capital now manages workers and consumers through a "casino economy" with a world-wide division of labor in a world-market of goods and services. At the same time, it has abandoned entire geographical regions and masses of people since they are no longer, or not yet, needed for the economic machine.[2]

In the United States, in particular, fortunes were made in the 1980s by individuals and corporations who took full advantage of the deregulated economy unleashed by the Reagan Revolution. Through non-productive mergers (achieved by hostile takeovers and leveraged buy-outs) and through computer-driven speculation that favored the quick returns of junk bonds over the long-term benefits of reindustrialization, the number of millionaires grew and corporate wealth rose, while the overall well-being of the society declined. Under the gun of privatization, government services (including economic, health and safety, and environmental regulation; social entitlements; and infrastructure development) were cut back; and yet, in a hypocritical exercise of military Keynesianism and old boy networking, the administration increased the military budget by lowering taxes and raising the national debt. As a result, we now face a more fragile natural and social environment, an unstable world economy (despite the extensive restructuring), a weakened national government (unwilling to exercise its own capacity for popular service), an increasingly subordinated population of women and people of color (facing increasing official and popular terrorism), a declining middle class (seen more clearly in the current recession as managers as well as skilled workers are laid off), a reduced and impoverished work force (deprived of the power of its own organizations), and a growing number of dispossessed who have been denied the benefits of meaningful work and nurturing social services.

In this sweep—of economic restructuring, political realignment, and right-wing ascendancy—that dominated the 1980s and set in motion the forces that now configure the present dystopian world of the 1990s, cultural productions that did more than affirm the emerging postfordist, posthumanist, postmodernist milieu were few and far between. In science fiction, cutting-edge feminist and ecological works continued to hold their oppositional ground, but all too often the energies of SF writers were deflected—by the false promises of the new times and by the shrinking opportunities for publication and distribution—into production of either repetitive series of standardized fantasies (that departed from the powerful moment of feminist fantasy of the 1970s) or versions of "hard science" SF that reveled in technological extrapolation and military adventure without significantly addressing the larger contradictions of the social system.[3]

It was in this impoverished context in the mid-1980s that the work of William Gibson and other writers who eventually branded their work "cyberpunk" (the use of the term is itself an example of the prevailing entrepreneurial spirit) generated a near-future science fiction that appeared to be capable of cognitively mapping the conditions of the emerging global order.[4] Many readers and critics welcomed the cyberpunk phenomenon—and its associated movements in film (e.g., *Blade Runner*), music (e.g., Sonic Youth), and performance art (e.g., Survival Research Laboratories). Yet, after the first surges of readerly pleasure, some began to locate its shortcomings and compromises. Peter Fitting acknowledged that cyberpunk traced the "triumph of instrumental reason" ("Hacking": 8) in the "non-natural" society of the spectacle, but he just as quickly noted the absence of a "contestatory option" that questioned and opposed the transnational matrix. Invoking Raymond Williams, Darko Suvin readily observed that "a viable collective and public utopianism is not within the horizon of the cyberpunk structure of feeling" (46). And Istvan Csicsery-Ronay accused cyberpunk of acting in bad faith as it playfully presented the bleak experience of postmodernity at the same time that it left the reader caught within it. Others—such as Jean Gomoll, Veronica Hollinger, Andrew Ross, and Samuel Delany in "Some Real Mothers"—argued that cyberpunk was largely written and read by white, heterosexual, upwardly mobile (largely suburban) males and noted that it suffered from an insufficient self-reflexivity regarding questions of gender and power—becoming, as one critic put it, "the vanguard white male art of the age" (Csicsery-Ronay, "Cyberpunk" 183). But one of the strongest indictments of cyberpunk can be found in the 1987 self-criticism made by Bruce Sterling—perhaps the most effective and enterprising cyberpunk writer-editor-promoter—when he noted that its "truly dangerous element is incipient Nietzschean philosophical fascism: the belief in the Overman, and the worship of the will-to-power" (quoted in Hollinger, "Cybernetic" 206).[5]

Some of cyberpunk's difficulties have their roots in a deep textual fault: this was best described by Fred Pfeil when he noted that the cyberpunk writers had the *mise-en-scène* right, but they had the story wrong.[6] That is, while the imagery developed in the alternative futures of cyberpunk settings symptomatically captures the 1980s ambience of privilege and poverty, the plots and characters of most cyberpunk texts compromise that vision so that the narrative possibilities of opposition are deflected and readers are trapped in the thrilling dead-end of cynicism, left with fashionable survival or displaced rebellion. I got closer to the spirit of this formal split when I read Larry McCaffery's 1988 interview with Gibson: in that interview, McCaffery observes that the plot and characters of *Neuromancer* are quite familiar— "the down-and-out gangster who's been fucked over and wants to get even by pulling the big heist"—and he asks Gibson if he consciously decided to use such an established framework. In a response that uncannily echoes categories of the Reagan era, and helps to explain the accommodations of cyberpunk with the dominant culture, Gibson explains that his inexperience as a novelist led him to seek a narrative "safety net" that could contain his multiple and intense cyber-images (McCaffery, "Interview" 270). That is, he sought what he termed a "plot armature which had proven its potential for narrative traction" (Gibson, quoted in McCaffery, "Interview" 271). While he did not govern his imagery with a "pre-set" agenda, he decided that his plot had to be "a familiar structure" that he felt comfortable with ("Interview" 271). This instance of writerly insecurity, in which Gibson sought refuge in recognizable film noir plots and macho heroes already embedded in the dominant ideology, provides a symptom of the tactical compromise at the onset of cyberpunk that stymied what Delany, in *American Shore*, calls SF's "discourse with the world"—a discourse through which the very form of sf can chart and challenge the ideological constructs and structures of the prevailing social system—a discourse which, as Fredric Jameson reminds us, in its very incapacity to imagine the actual, not yet attained, future brings us coldly back to our own unacceptable present ("Progress" 153).[7]

Despite its entrapments and accommodations in the affirmative culture of the 1980s, cyberpunk nevertheless captured the imagination, and stimulated the social resentment, of many readers (especially, as Fred Pfeil, Marc Angenot, Darko Suvin, and others point out, males of the professional-managerial-technical class, or at least those who aspire to such a position in spite of the shrinking job-market).[8] As a major development within contemporary U.S. (and, in a different way, British) culture, cyberpunk can be understood as a movement of the 1980s that attempts to trace the terrible ramifications of what Bruce Sterling has called "an entire culture bigfuck" that has run its way through global society over the past fifteen years (see Fischlin et al. 2). And yet, Lucius Shepard pronounced cyberpunk dead as early as 1989, although Pat Cadigan's *Synners* and Emma Bull's *Bone Dance*, which came out in 1991, probably belie his claim and argue for a "late" cyberpunk moment that appears to be dominated by women writers.[9]

However one chooses to periodize it, cyberpunk's creative breakthroughs led to new possibilities within SF, and the cyberpunk imaginary extended beyond the genre into the crevices of popular culture, into the computer industry itself, and (as we saw in the Gulf War) into the very conceptualizations and operations of the postmodern cybernetic military. As well, cyberpunk stimulated the search for oppositional sensibilities and strategies—as the work of Donna Haraway and others attests. With the new energies and tensions of the 1990s taking shape, we may now be in a late, or post, cyberpunk moment (and with films such as *Lawnmowerman* or the short-lived TV series *Mann and Machine*, we are certainly in a pop-cyberpunk milieu). Nevertheless, it is still important to continue the already lively examination of cyberpunk itself. In teasing apart its methods and its slippages, its agendas and its silences, hopefully we can get a better grasp on this 1980s phenomenon—and on how it plays out in the social matrix that has come to envelop us all.[10]

II

One way to put cyberpunk in this larger perspective is to approach it in terms of its intertextual relations.[11] Cyberpunk authors have acknowledged the influence of works by William Burroughs, J. G. Ballard, and Phillip K. Dick; and Samuel Delany has written of cyberpunk's unacknowledged, or suppressed, debt to the feminist utopias of the 1960s and 1970s—most immediately to the work of Joanna Russ (see "Some Real Mothers"). Yet, another body of work that feeds cyberpunk's intertextual web is the classical dystopian tradition: that is, the novels from Zamyatin, Huxley, and Orwell to those by Wolfe, Bradbury, Vonnegut, and Atwood.

In general, dystopian writing typically presents the reader with a "bad place," a place organized according to less perfect, more destructive social and economic principles than those found in the author's community. Dystopias, Lyman Tower Sargent reminds us, are not *anti*-utopian in their spirit or textual strategies, for, as opposed to anti-utopias "which are directed *against* Utopia and utopian thought," these works preserve the memory of the better place even as they delineate the contours of an oppressive society. Søeren Baggesen, however, notes that even within dystopian writing, an anti-utopian tendency can develop. Working from Ernst Bloch's categories of "militant" and "resigned" pessimism, Baggesen distinguishes between a "*utopian* pessimism" in which the social conditions are explained in terms of the material processes of history and a "*dystopian* pessimism" in which the destructive elements are based in ontological conditions which lead to "resignation" rather than "militance." As Hoda Zaki has pointed out, this analysis allows for a more complex understanding of the dystopian–utopian spectrum wherein some works incline toward an open-ended utopian hope while others tend toward the closed realm of anti-utopia. This tendency toward a utopian or anti-utopian quality can be discovered in the treatment of the typical protagonist of the dystopia—the misfit or dissident who questions and breaks with the system—and in the utopian claves, or remnants, that offer inspiration or refuge to the misfit. If the dissenting protagonist manages to achieve a base of effective opposition and if the enclaves are actually existing liberated zones (as in *We* or *Fahrenheit 451* or *Handmaid's Tale*), then the dystopia carries within its pessimism a *trace* of utopia that preserves the possibility of historical change. If, on the other hand, the protagonist is reconfigured or destroyed by the ruling system and the enclaves turn out to be some form of artificially negative reservations for rebellious misfits (as in *Brave New World* or in more subtle ways in Vonnegut's America), the text collapses into anti-utopian resignation.

Certainly, many commentators have noted cyberpunk's affiliation with the utopian/dystopian spectrum. David Porush, for example, reads the name "cyberpunk" itself as a signifier of that very spectrum. For Porush, the "cyber" half of the neologism suggests the dystopian postfordist apparatus of control: "growing feedback loops of self-organization and complexity" that allow the "human nerve net" to "imperialize nature through artifice, appropriating what it can" in its pressing, inclusive logic ("Frothing" 332). On the other hand, the "punk" tag represents a "lizard-brain passion clawing its way through the cerebrum of urbanity" and deconstructing the palimpsests of civilization to "expose its deeper codes" ("Frothing" 332)—a strategic move which in its oppositional spirit is solidly utopian, but only in an appropriately suspicious, negative sense. Pushing the intertextual web back further, Peter Fitting argues that rather than achieving a formal breakthrough in terms of dystopian writing, cyberpunk is but another step in the longer tradition of dystopian SF that begins at the end of World War II (see "Modern Anglo-American SF" and "Ideological Foreclosure").[12]

III

Like the classic dystopias, therefore, Gibson's cyberpunk trilogy *Neuro-mancer* (1984), *Count Zero* (1986), and *Mona Lisa Overdrive* (1988) presents a grim near-future which suggests that the present we now live in (and its upcoming future) is (and will be) worse than previously imagined. In each novel, we find a world just twenty minutes into the future in which transnational corporations and criminal organizations compete for control of the highly developed information matrix, imaged by Gibson's invention of cyberspace—that is the fundamental economic resource and vehicle of the new world order. The realm of the "rich and famous" corporate and criminal elite and the mass of the subordinated underclasses—both employed and derelict—are the major sectors of the toxic, mass-mediated, urban-suburban society. True to the logic of postfordist restructuring, the secure middle sector of skilled workers and managers has largely disappeared, to be replaced by a small tier of low paid service workers and relatively well-paid contract workers who have the technical skills (in cybernetics, medicine, security, or entertainment) that the transnational economy requires but is unwilling to pay for in the form of regular and secure employment. Each novel, then, focuses on an assemblage of protagonists who are usually based in that small and insecure middle sector with alliances with the better organized sectors of the underclass. The oppositional group, however, is almost always (and the departures from this are significant) dominated by a lone male hero with his female counterpart, a few non-white sidekicks, and various forms of artificial intelligences intent on establishing their own identity in the matrix. True to the dystopian mode, this diverse group, but most of all the male hero, tries to survive in the brave new world and in doing so becomes embroiled in some form of (largely unsuccessful) resistance to the dominant forces.

Along with these immediate protagonists, each novel in the trilogy features a marginal "utopian" enclave which (like the Mephi resistance in *We*, the book people in *Fahrenheit 451*, or the Mayday underground in *Handmaid's Tale*) plays an important role in the resentment and resistance of the main characters and represents the persistence, the traces, of utopia in the dystopian landscape. For the rest of this chapter, then, I want to focus on these utopian enclaves. In doing so, I will work toward describing at least one strategic spectrum upon which cyberpunk—or at least Gibson's version of it—operates as part of the cultural logic of the 1980s.

In *Neuromancer*, the most significant utopian enclave is the rastafarian colony of Zion whose (all male) occupants have retreated to a cluster of cast-off space vehicles to prepare for the last battle with the forces of Babylon. Hired by Case's boss, two Zionites, Maelcum and Aerol, help Case and Molly break into the aging corporate core of Straylight and carry out their mission against the decaying power of the Tessier-Ashpool family corporation.

In *Count Zero*, the primary utopian enclave is occupied by the Brother-hood: an urban voodoo commune based in an "arcology" in the sprawling Projects of the New Jersey suburbs, living quarters which have been reclaimed from the abandoned structures of an earlier period of modernist development. Unlike the radically separatist rastas, the priests/hackers/businessmen—and their female helpers—maintain their "holy space" by means of a more immediate involvement with the mainstream society. Through their blackmarket software "biz," they finance their commune; through their practice of voodoo (a politicized street religion), they manip-ulate the information matrix to protect their own people and their clients. Like the rasta helpers of Zion, the Brotherhood allies itself with the prota-gonists of *Count Zero* (primarily the two white males, Bobby and Turner) in their battles against both the old corporate (multinational, family) power represented by Virek and the new transnational power represented by the competing forces of Maas Biolabs and Hosaka.

In *Mona Lisa Overdrive*, the representation of utopian space, and its place in the overall narrative, dissolve. The artists' colony known as the Factory—set in a former industrial waste dump in "rustbelt Jersey"—is occupied by three social outcasts: two rogue artists and one hanger-on. Although they have carved out an avant-garde zone that rejects the domi-nant society, the artists, Gentry and Slick Henry, are less philosophically and politically engaged than the members of the previous two enclaves. They lack the long-range vision of Zion as well as the street power of the Brotherhood. Nevertheless, it is Slick Henry and his robot assemblages that provide the utopian contribution against the corporate powers.

At this level of reading—that is, at the level of the text's overt content—in a recuperative interpretation of the utopian enclaves—one can identify a militant opposition that maintains a trace of utopian hope in the dystopian text. Read this way, the maneuvers of the enclaves resemble Michel de Certeau's description of the oppositional tactics of "making do" as they are practiced in the urban areas of Brazil—tactics which de Certeau sees as a useful form of resistance in an order of things that seems immutable. De Certeau argues that within a "polemological space" in which at least the perception prevails that "the strong always win and words always deceive" there is also "a *utopian* space" in which other possibilities are articulated, often in evocations of the miraculous by means of the retelling of religious stories which subvert traditional religious and secular power. In other words, a hope for another way of life is maintained by cultural practices that refunction the imposed cultural for and thereby "subvert the fatality of the established order." What emerges is a "*way of using* imposed systems" that "creates at least a certain play in that order, a space for maneuvers of unequal forces."

At least in an initial, quite unsuspicious, reading, de Certeau's tactics of "making do" offer an interpretive perspective that could reinforce the uto-pian quality of Gibson's work. What one discovers through such a reading is a popular culture version of Bloch's militant pessimism or of a Gramscian war of position carried out primarily on the terrain of cyberpunk's alternate worlds—largely by outlaw groups using abandoned or derelict materials and spaces at the margins of society.

IV

However, to stop an analysis at this point, with an interpretation of the utopian content of these enclaves, would be to fall into an unsustainably optimistic version of a romantic anti-capitalism—one that neglects a wider review of cyberpunk's implication in the socioeconomic developments of its time. What remains to be considered is the formal relationship of the enclaves to the main plot and protagonists of Gibson's trilogy as well as some of the more direct intersections of the trilogy itself with the historical context of the U.S. in the 1980s.

Gibson's texts begin to lose their critical edge as the utopian enclaves (as developed in the iconic register of the alternative world) fall under the compromising influence of the primary plot and protagonists (as developed in the register of the "master narrative" running through all three volumes). As I noted above, despite the help of the utopian allies, the protagonists do not break beyond the boundaries of Gibson's near-future society. They may find refuge (Turner on a farm, Slick Henry in Cleveland, or Bobby in a cybernetic construct), or they may find new work (as do Case, Molly, Angie, Marly, and Mona); but they do not negate or transform the social order; rather, as Sterling warns, they willfully survive or thrive within that order. Following the narrative spine of the three volumes, which has its own tendency toward implosion, the utopian status of the enclaves gradually diminishes as the enclaves literally come "down to earth": the hope represented in the radical alternative of the Zion space station shades into the more engaged yet also more compromised opposition of the Brotherhood highrise, and finally disappears entirely with the destruction of the minimalist utopia of the (white, heterosexual, male) artists of the Factory. Indeed, the enclaves themselves become more and more immersed in. the prevailing social logic: the rastas of Zion persist in helping Case and Molly not because of their radical political vision but because of their male-bonding with the edgy hero; through their assistance to Turner and Bobby, the Brotherhood manages to protect its male-dominated street religion and achieve even more success in its blackmarket biz. Most tellingly, in the. final volume, the art colony is excised from the text altogether when Slick Henry loses his utopian valence as he shifts into the master narrative as one of the main protagonists.[13] Seen in terms of this *plot trajectory*, the enclaves simply become the homes of very traditional sidekicks, and the utopian agents become no more than typical Proppian helpers who are duly employed at the standard three points in the narrative to advance the action of the main characters.

By the end of *Mona Lisa Overdrive*, therefore, the possibility of an historically engaged dystopia (with its utopian traces) dissolves in an apocalyptic/fairy tale flourish. The social flatline that the reader encounters in the closing pages then reinfects the entire trilogy with a retro-virus of accommodation and closure. Thus, Gibson's work is refashioned into a postmodern simulation of the modernist dystopia: it fades into an anti-utopia closed to the processes of history and vulnerable to the stasis of political resignation.

In the light of this formal effacement of the utopian potential of Gibson's text through a master narrative of anti-utopian resignation, some of the other shortcomings of the trilogy can be understood as instances of the text's complicity with the social order of the 1980s. As we saw throughout the decade, the opportunities in this period of restructuring were monopolized by the dominant sectors of the population. In contrast, the economic and social well-being (not to mention the psychological and physical safety) of less powerful members of society was steadily eroded.

Read through the social filter of racial struggles, for example, the agential function of the enclaves becomes another version of a non-white Tonto in thrall to the actions of the lone white hustler ranging through the near-future world of street and matrix biz. In an appropriation of non-white cultures that resembles little more than a form of a "yuppie postmodernism" (see Kaufmann 1992) engaging in a trendy consumption of the life and art of racial Others, Gibson has created three textual populations that serve as happy helpers: the rastafarians and the voodoo priests—and especially the women of the Brotherhood who are doubly subordinated as helpers to the helpers—never become actors in their own right, never claim a different voice or space within the narrative. Structured in this helper position, these non-white "buddies" do the grunt labor of softening up the battleground for the protagonists and then conveniently step aside as the white heroes finish up the work. It is Maelcum who sets up the final confrontation in Straylight: and yet, Maelcum (through the signifiers of his music, his attitude toward time, and his easy undertaking of violence by means of a machete that is just this side of the razor used by the Steppin Fetchit stereotype) is basically a humorous sidekick in the ignoble popular culture tradition of Pancho and the Cisco Kid or Tonto and the Lone Ranger. The members of the Brotherhood provide the hacking and the muscle (and the dead female bodies) that win the battle of the Hypermart; they do so, however, not as humorous sidekicks but as powerful primitives who are to be enjoyed for their mysterious excitement and then quickly dispensed with when the spoils of the plot are divided. Following the logic of this racial agenda, then, it is quite consistent with Gibson's textual tactics that the third enclave, the refuge of white males, disappears as its remaining artist hero becomes a major player in the plot. Like Tom Jones coming into his inheritance (as one of the boys after all), Slick Henry is free to leave his bohemian half-way house and move on to the fairy-tale ending of his entry into domestic bliss with Cherry in Cleveland.

Read in terms of the equally vicious backlash carried out in the 1980s against women and against gays and lesbians, the enclaves are just as compromised. All three are marked as heterosexual male territories: Zion is populated only by men, and Maelcum serves Case as a manly buddy. The Brotherhood is dominated by male leaders who use their women as "horses" (vehicles for their voodoo/hacker runs). The three-derelict men of Dog Solitude can barely communicate with each other and hardly know what to do when a woman comes to stay with them—they are inept as eleven year olds whose clubhouse has been invaded by one of the neighborhood girls. Certainly, unlike the overtly chauvinistic "hard science" SF of the same period, the intertextual memory of other SF works which push the possibilities of gender and sexual preference beyond the enforced binary limits (as in the work of Russ or Tepper, or of Delany or Varley) haunts Gibson's narrative and generates the potential for more engaged texts. However, at each opportunity for such a move, Gibson retreats into the folds of a security blanket stitched with quite familiar images and stories.

The trilogy's implication in the dominant agenda of the 1980s is further revealed in the economic positioning of the protagonists and the enclaves. One of the main characteristics of the recent restructuring has been the change in the nature of the work force. As the power of organized labor is challenged by the mechanisms of a computer-based flexible production, workers who have held a secure place in the economy since the 1950s are losing ground, and new forms of labor are emerging that are amenable to the limited awards of this leaner and meaner system. Three categories of workers can be identified in this flexible economy: a declining number of skilled industrial workers who hold relatively high paying and secure jobs in large corporate structures and who are still protected by union contracts; a growing number of minimum-wage, part-time workers who are hired as needed and fired with short notice and who have no union protection and consequently no job security; and a smaller, but growing, number of skilled professional-managerial-technical workers who individually contract with corporations (and governments) for limited term, relatively high-paid tasks. It is in this last category that the protagonists (and indeed many of the readers) of Gibson's cyberpunk world can be found—albeit at the lower end of that sector's pay scale. Case is a hacker turned espionage expert who is adept in manipulating cyberspace to steal corporate secrets; Molly/Sally is a street-wise "razor-girl" who has turned her survival skills (after earning the money to buy her bionic weaponry through prostitution) into a post-industrial commodity that can be rented by corporations needing extra muscle against their competitors. Turner is a war veteran and former corporate employee who works as a contract security expert in delivering executive defectors to their new companies.

Finally, and not to be oversimplified as emerging forms of an unfashionable opposition, the enclaves themselves can *also* be identified in the terms of the new economic structure. Seen as micro-enterprises, each has found its niche in the planetary market. The space jockeys of Zion work as independent contractors who supply transportation at the fringes of that market. The computer wizards of the Brotherhood are dealers of software and hardware in the urban sprawl: they also perform the dangerous work of carrying out basic research on security software for major corporations unwilling to risk their own staff. Betraying the growing uselessness of the utopian in the text (and in Gibson's version of contemporary society), the artists' space of Dog Solitude serves as the most destructive enterprise of the three: the Factory becomes an independent research and development facility for products which were created as art but which turn out to be prototypes of new postindustrial weaponry for the corporate wars. In these economic spaces, Zion, the Brotherhood, and the Factory resemble not so much forward-looking utopian communities but rather *residual* forms of small, paternal and patriarchal, businesses. All three are hierarchical, "familial," risk-taking institutions that are occasionally useful to the corporate giants.

As the *form* of Gibson's trilogy is examined in relation to the dominant *mode of production* of a planetary capitalism, the anti-historical, anti-utopian tendency of these early cyberpunk works comes into sharper focus. In terms of older versions of exploitation and oppression—those of gender and race—the trilogy's "utopian" Others are reduced to the status of servants and tools for white males (including writers) intent on surviving in a grim society; and in terms of economic structures and practices, the heroes and enclaves become little more than useful cogs in those larger machines.

This anti-utopian drift *within* Gibson's text can be more broadly understood as an example of what Paul Piccone and Tim Luke have called an "artificial negativity" that supports the status quo by recontaining sources of potential opposition through reification and commodification—thereby removing their *useful* negative power and repackaging it as yet another *exchangeable* commodity. Through this cooptive mechanism, oppositional expression is tapped as a necessary source of independent creativity that is capable of ferreting out solutions, or at least diversions, to systemic problems: the knowledge base of the opposition becomes the knowledge base of the system's own refinement. As Mike Davis puts it, in the related context of science fictional portrayals of the city of Los Angeles as the prophetic map of the future, such potentially provocative and critical signifiers of the near-future "tend to collapse history into teleology and glamorize the very reality they would deconstruct" (86).[14] In this light, therefore, Gibson's three-volume text *itself* can be understood as an instance of artificial negativity in the larger cultural logic of global capitalism: it is a product that ranges through the new social regime like a pop culture Godzilla that validates the very terrain it threatens to destroy.

Cyberpunk, therefore, cannot be uncritically praised as the cutting edge of opposition that Bruce Sterling spoke of in his cyberpunk manifesto.

Although its intention might have been to celebrate what Sterling called the "unholy alliance of the technical world and the world of organized dissent" found in the interzones occupied by hackers and rockers, cyberpunk often works as a late capitalist version of what Herbert Marcuse described as "the affirmative culture" of modern bourgeois society. Unlike earlier manifestations of affirmative culture—that is, those "high" forms of art, literature, and philosophy which assert a "universally obligatory, eternally better and more valuable world" that reigns in human "souls" happily detached from "the factual world of the daily struggle for existence"—the popular affirmations of cyberpunk offer *not* idealist intimations of immortality but *rather* utilitarian calculations of the odds of "making it" through speculative (ad)ventures on a rapidly reorganizing earth.

VI

And yet, in closing, the arguments of de Certeau and others (especially the likes of Laclau and Mouffe, Donna Haraway, and those involved in the "new social movements") that a diffused, often mutually antagonistic, constellation of agents can find ways to develop strategies and tactics of resistance *on the terrain* of the present society cannot be ignored. Simply to abandon these forces would also be to step quietly into the cage of affirmative culture. In terms of cyberpunk—despite the indictments I have belabored—it needs to be acknowledged that its near-future fictions continue to stimulate socially critical responses in many writers and readers. There are SF texts (such as Lewis Shiner's *Deserted Cities of the Heart* or Richard Paul Russo's *Subterranean Gallery*) which work with the creativity unleashed by the cyberpunk movement but which manage to map and to challenge the social system in ways that Gibson's never quite achieved. And, other writers working around the lively ambience of cyberpunk or post-cyberpunk—such as Kim Stanley Robinson, Fred Pfeil, Ian Banks, or Kathy Acker—traverse a similar fictional terrain but manage to self-reflexively resist the cyberpunk entanglement in limited visions and gestures.

Finally, in an outburst of published work since 1990, women writers working within the cyberpunk paradigm (such as Emma Bull, Pat Cadigan, Sheri Lewitt, and Laura Mixon—along with Marge Piercy's related cyborg/golem novel, *He, She, and It*) have turned out novels that promise to shift the literary ground to one of more clearly oppositional reconsiderations of the lean and mean global order. These more contentious works, each in their unique way, slide around cyberpunk's affirmative ambience and stimulate a more discomforting reception which is stronger in its evocation of a utopian pessimism (or a critical utopianism) in a dystopian world—offering strong critiques of the present and pre-conceptual anticipations of emancipatory alternatives somewhere beyond what Ernst Bloch called the "darkness of the lived moment."

ACKNOWLEDGMENTS

Reprinted from *The Minnesota Review* 43/44 (1995): 182–97© by kind permission of Tom Moylan.

NOTES

1 I want to thank Ruth Levitas, Vince Geoghegan, Tim Dayton, Peter Fitting, and Fred Pfeil for their comments on versions of this essay that were read at meetings in London, Kentucky, and Kansas. I also want to thank George Mason University for research support for this project.

2 See Costello et al. (1989). For more on the strategy of dereliction, see Alliez and Feher (1986).

3 For an overview of the situation in the corporate dominated publishing world, see Sedgewick (1991).

4 The term was coined by SF writer Bruce Bethke for a 1982 story, and writer/editor Gardner Dozois subsequently used it to describe Gibson's work. The term was adopted by those who affiliated with the "movement" that coalesced around this new form of SF. For a useful account, see Brown (1991). For the literary manifesto, see Sterling's preface in *Mirrorshades*.

5 An argument can be made for an opposing position on the question of "will-fulness" in cyberpunk by contrasting the Nietzschean will-to-power with Raymond Williams's endorsement of "willed transformation" as the force behind more progressive instances of "utopian" science fiction. The difference between the two positions could be traced in cyberpunk texts in terms of the opposition of a singular, individual character who enforces a superior will-to-power and a set of characters who carry out a collective process of willed transformation.

6 In conversation with Pfeil at the Summer Institute on Culture and Society at Carnegie Mellon University, Pittsburgh, Pennsylvania, June 1986.

7 Gibson's strategies appear to be borrowed uncritically from film noir and the hard-boiled detective novel (unlike the subversion of those forms by mystery writers such as Sue Grafton and Sarah Peretsky during the same time period). Whalen notes Gibson's interview and links it with his accommodation rather than disputation with the emerging information-based economies of postmodernity. Hollinger points out that cyberpunk's efforts at transcendence of the present usually "point ... back to the romantic trappings of the genre at its most conventional, as does its valorization of the (usually male) loner rebel/hacker/punk who appears frequently as it central character" ("Cybernetic" 206). See also the discussions on masculinity and cyberpunk in Fitting ("Lessons") and in Ross (*Strange Weather*).

8 See Angenot and Suvin, especially 130–31. See also Fitting ("Lessons"), Pfeil ("Makin' Flippy Floppy"), and Ross (*Strange Weather*).

9 In my review, I see *Synners* as a cyberpunk novel that opposes, and perhaps, ends the cyberpunk moment, but on its own ground. The difference between *Neuromancer* and *Synners* lies in the narrative strategy. Cadigan, benefiting from Gibson, can relinquish the noir, macho "safety net" and move to a diverse, collective protagonist closer to the form and politics of Haraway's "Manifesto" (although she does fall into the older logic of the fairy tale when the novel ends with the reconstitution of a family structure as Gabe, Gina, and Sam set up housekeeping on the California coast). For related moves, see Bull, Lewitt, Mixon – and, in a different way, Piercy – who can be read in terms of a refunctioning of cyberpunk by women who take the movement beyond the horizons of its founding "fathers."

10 The discussion of cyberpunk as a cultural symptom of social dis-ease is extensive. Some that I've found valuable are by Fitting, Nixon, Rosenthal, Ross, and Whalen.

11 For a useful discussion of sf intertextuality, see Delany, "Semiology of Silence" and the "Appendix" of *Triton*.

12 On the other hand, in arguing for a literary breakthrough, I think Andrew Ross misreads the formal agenda of dystopian sf and too quickly puts the dystopian sf focus on the future without working out its relationship to the present (see 144–46).

13 For another suspicious reading of Zion, see Whalen (83).

14 Davis develops a symptomatic reading of such texts in terms similar to the utopian/dystopian tensions suggested in this essay. For a multi-layered SF portrayal of L.A. as an example of the crises facing U.S. society, see Robinson's "Orange County Trilogy." See also Fischlin et al. on Gibson's *Virtual Light*.

6 "The Mainstream Finds its Own Uses for Things"[1]
Cyberpunk and Commodification

Sherryl Vint

In *Postmodernism, or, The Cultural Logic of Late Capitalism*, Fredric Jameson describes cyberpunk as "the supreme *literary* expression if not of postmodernism, then of late capitalism itself" (419), a comment usually taken up in light of his concluding remarks about our need for cognitive maps of the disorienting world of multinational capital, building on his characterization of cyberpunk as "representational shorthand for grasping ... the whole new decentered global network of the third stage of capital itself" (38). Rather than focusing on cyberpunk's dominant network imagery and late capitalism's shift to an information economy, I would like to consider Jameson's comments about cyberpunk in connection with his arguments about the social function of art in postmodernism. In "Postmodernism and Consumer Society," Jameson concludes that while it is a futile task to try to sort out modern from postmodern texts based on any formal criteria, one can nonetheless chart a distinctive break between modernist art which was often in opposition to mainstream society, and postmodernism art whose "most offensive forms" (124) are nonetheless commercially successful. He argues that "the older modernism functions against its society in ways which are variously described as critical, negative, contestatory, subversive, oppositional and the like" while postmodernism replicates or reproduces—reinforces—the logic of consumer capitalism" (125), and ends with the question of "whether there is also a way in which it resists that logic" (125). The struggle to answer this question, I suggest, can now be seen as central to cyberpunk's legacy.

In *Postmodernism*, Jameson suggests any "semiautonomy of the cultural sphere ... has been destroyed by the logic of late capitalism" (48), a logic characterized by "the prodigious new expansion of multinational capital" into previously uncommodified areas which had heretofore offered "footholds for critical effectivity" (49). In such a context, he continues, Adorno and Horkheimer's critique of the culture industry and its conflation of art with the commodity form is "even more profoundly true today than it was then" (351). Misha's *Red Spider, White Web* takes as its central theme the struggle by art and artists to survive in the familiar cyberpunk landscape of multinational capital, network culture, corporate governance, and economic crisis. Characters strive for authentic art in a world of ubiquitous commodities and alienated labor, revealing the damage done by the commodity form to art and to human consciousness with the collapse of art into advertising, culture into industry, diagnosed so ably in *Dialectic of Enlightenment*. Misha's prescient focus on market conditions and their consequences for both artists and audiences under late capitalism are chief among the reasons why her work is "everything cyberpunk should have been but wasn't" as Elyce Helford comments on the back cover of the 1999 Wordcraft edition.

Red Spider, White Web is distinguished from more familiar, often masculine version of cyberpunk in its focus on characters materially and economically excluded from society. While cyberpunk protagonists are often described as coming from the social margins, many critics (Balsamo, Nixon, Ross, Foster) have pointed out that such a posture does not acknowledge the degree to which the dominant site of action, cyberspace, is one in which these characters excel. In contrast to such faux estrangement from power, Misha's characters live in an impoverished and bleak world, and more importantly a world in which previously uncommodified areas of experience are disappearing. Seeming to anticipate the world in which the biggest threat presented by cyberspace is not the evolution of an AI but rather endless bombardment by spam, Misha refuses to let her characters escape into a seemingly purified virtual world and instead gives us a world closer to the features of what Manuel Castells has called "The *truly fundamental social cleavages of the Information Age*" (*End of Millennium* 377): the deskilling of labor, the social exclusion of individuals who no longer serve global capitalism as workers or consumers, and the separation of the logic of the market from the material experience of human lives, whose value outside of the logic of capital is ignored. Just as workers have no value beyond their service to capital, so too art has no value beyond its status as a commodity. The fate of art under the market conditions of postmodernism is curiously both a theme that Misha explores and what seems to have killed the cyberpunk movement, as is suggested in Lewis Shiner's editorial "Confessions of an Ex-Cyberpunk" (1991) which laments the term losing its meaning as it became a marketing category.[2]

From its opening pages, *Red Spider, White Web* is clearly different from the disembodied techno-fantasies that shape most cyberpunk fiction. The protagonist, Kumo, searches for food in dumpsters, passing "small rubbish fires" surrounded by "grey figures in long coats ... hunched against the cold" in a "city shrouded in a brown smog" (19). This "desolate landscape of hopeless desires" contains only "slow-moving boxcars" of freight trains, entirely bypassed by the "occasional, sleek, subway and bullet trains" (19) which service the more affluent areas of Dogton, an underground city where the working classes live, and Mickey-san, a dome-covered, amusement park city for the elite. In Ded Tek, an abandoned industrial complex outside the city, people are slowly dying from "that fucking UV, the lousy food, the cold, the fifteen minute viruses—all of it" (61), while Dogton lives on "the ashes of an already dead civilization" (111). Only the city, Mickey-san, provides any degree of comfort or security—albeit at a significant cost—and entrance is strictly limited to those with appropriate corporate connections. The focus remains on visceral action in the material world: when attacked, Kumo responds by throwing the "throat-gaggling contents" of her tin-pail latrine on her assailant and after the fight notices the "bloody bit of tongue" she bit off her attacker (22), causing her to retch "mucous and blood" (23).

Despite risk and discomfort, Kumo wants to remain in Ded Tek because its market is "the only legal place left for her to make art" (39). Artists are compensated for their work in a manner more closely aligned with the patronage system than with the market forces of consumer society. Kumo finds people are "mesmerized by the images, but uncertain" because her holo art has "no noticeable practical value" and so she has "many customers, but few buyers" (51). Artists must "create or die" (52): if unable to survive by selling their art, they are compelled either to work in the Bell Factory or to enter Mickey-san as 'professional' artists, neither of which allow any space for creativity or critical reflection. The artists in Ded Tek are stalked by a serial killer, a potent symbol of their precarious existence, who leaves their bodies in artistic tableau. Misha uses a shift in person to describe the murders from the killer's point of view, beginning with the second person 'you' to address the audience before shifting to the killer's first-person. The murder of a dancer begins with her tormented performance as "you are clapping for her and your naked smile covers her face, you are her flesh-eating audience, she pushes harder, faster, for you alone she pirouettes, she doesn't know you, but she needs you" (17). The artist dependent upon audience approval suffers for her art, and the killer believes he is freeing her, "helping her lay down, her thin sweaty legs in my hands, her frosting lips parting, gasping for breath, her constricting tights, I remove them, I do, I alone can help her quiet ... I free her from the encumbrance of flesh" (17). The killer severs the dancer's legs and then strangles her with her tights, "freeing" her from the oppression of the viewing public. As well as reconfiguring the typical cyberpunk fantasy of escape from the flesh, this passage condemns a world in which art is not valued, where the artist performs in vain. Kumo sarcastically comments the "art assassin's probably doing us all a favor ... Putting us poor wretches out of our misery" (35).

This misery is physical and spiritual. Artists are so "weakened by hunger or sickness, [that] they're easy marks for a man who lives to kill" (66), but Kumo insists that the targeting of artists has deeper meaning. She speculates the assassin is "Maybe just somebody who hates change—who hates thinking, who hates art" (66), evoking a model of the artist consistent with that proposed by *Dialectic of Enlightenment*. Fearing society had reached a point in which "thought inevitably becomes a commodity, and language the means of promoting that commodity" (xi–xii), Adorno and Horkheimer insist space for critical distance and dialectical reflection is necessary to prevent the Enlightenment from turning into its own opposite, totalitarianism, because "If consideration of the destructive aspect of progress is left to its enemies, blindly pragmatized thought loses its transcending quality and, its relation to truth" (xiii). Although often perceived as elitist for their insistence on the distinction between "real" art and mere market commodities, which thus dismisses most popular culture, Adorno and Horkheimer are better understood as analyzing the consequences for art and for audiences alike of a culture that lacks a space for art autonomous from market exchanges.

The space Adorno and Horkheimer wish to retain is the ability of the work of art to show us something other than the reality made by our preconceived ideological constructions. Art can "transcend reality" via "those features in which discrepancy appears: in the necessary failure of the passionate striving for identity" (131). Art "expos[es] itself to this failure" thereby "achiev[ing] self-negation" and avoiding the trap of a philosophy that cannot reflect on its own "recidivist element" (xiii) and thus loses its capacity to transcend toward truth. Unlike the authentic work of art, "the inferior work has always relied on its similarity with others—on a surrogate identity" and in the culture industry "imitation finally becomes absolute" (131), because the drive for profit produces conditions so that what can be published or produced needs to demonstrate its viability through similarity to what has previously succeeded in the market.[3] Art becomes a commodity like any other[4] which has dire implications, politically and socially as well as aesthetically. When authentic works of art cannot be distinguished from commodities, our capacity for critical thought withers and individual perception and assessment are replaced by the formulaic offerings of mass culture. Art as commodity is "the mere imitation of that which already is" (18), leaving "no room for imagination or reflection on the part of the audience" (126). It is crucial to stress that Adorno and Horkheimer fear that mass—that is, market-driven—culture *creates* the people as masses: pacified, incapable of independent thought, tending toward the easy absorption of stereotypes rather than individual critical reflection. For them, the "fusion of culture and entertainment ... leads not only to a depravation of culture, but inevitably to an intellectualization of amusement" (144), further eroding the capacity for thought and reflection and leaving only "the conventionalized modes of behavior" which "are impressed on the individual as the only natural, respectable, and rational ones" (28). Amusement not tempered with distance and critical thought is inherently conservative as "To be pleased means to say Yes ... [pleasure] is flight; not, as is asserted, flight from a wretched reality, but from the last remaining thought of resistance" (144). Real art should thus be a site for critical engagement and reflection, distanced from the market culture of late capitalism; art that has become a commodity, they fear, will offer only solace not promote engagement.

In *Red Spider, White Web*, as Adorno and Horkheimer predicted, "a change in the character of the art commodity" has come about and art now "deliberately admits it is [a] 'commodity'" (157). There is little space for critical reflection or authentic art outside of the Ded Tek market, a space whose vulnerability is aptly expressed by the presence of the serial killer. Art is merely a commodity in Mickey-san, preserved in the Museum staffed by artists such as Motler, who have sold themselves to wage labor for security. He finds the cost of subordinating himself to commodity logic too high: "The whole thing was carrot on a stick. Safety. Food, warmth, drink, place to stay, yet—just like a prison cell" (208). Having been compelled to sell his labor rather than his art and thereby losing his autonomy, Motler is only a curator, no longer a creator, a situation Adorno and Horkheimer antici- pated as the consequence of "use value in the reception of cultural com- modities [being] replaced by exchange value" (158). Motler satirically tells the elite that Duchamp's wheel is "an ancient exercising device that the artist, Duke The Champ, made for working out on" and announces that Warhol's Coke reproduction is not art but an advertisement: not for Coke but for Warmole, "a very transient artist. He was popular for only fifteen minutes and then he died" (209).[5] Art cannot perform the social function of art—critical reflection on society—in a context in which it is impossible to separate art and commodities. Motler rejects the people of Mickey-san because "all they did was consume" (208) and realizes selling his labor for economic security and three hours a day for his own work has trapped him in a life of alienation and exploitation because "There isn't any free time in Mickey" (214).

In Mickey-san, personal holosuits are used to enter one's own reality, a fantasy space that is a version of art for amusement, and distinct from more typical cyberpunk representations of cyberspace in that it is only a space for play and cannot serve as a site for political resistance. Used only by already privileged aristocrats, holosuits epitomize flight "from the last remaining thought of resistance." Tommy, a cybernetically enhanced artist, is con- temptuous of the holosuits and the mundane fantasies of their consumers, worlds in which "Everything was nostalgia, dull, plebian, safe and nothing, nothing in all this magical world was the least bit new or upsetting" (114).[6] Tommy disrupts one man's holo reality and this man finds himself "in a barren landscape, in a children's deserted, play park full of soft and safe toys" (115), revealing the infantalization resultant from the destruction of art's capacity for distance and critical reflection. The prefabricated perceptions and facile responses to social problems created by the culture industry take the place of individual thought for those inundated by its representations.[7] As art, entertainment, and industry converge, there is no outside to the commodity form, no area of consciousness not invaded by the logic of capitalism, and thus "the whole world is made to pass through the filter of the culture industry" and we begin to believe "that the outside world is the straightforward continuation of that presented on the screen" (Adorno and Horkheimer 126), a quite different perspective on the typical cyberpunk trope of conflating action in the virtual and real worlds.

While under this illusion, we cannot reflect critically on reality's negative aspects and thereby free ourselves from the exploitation of the late capitalism, a point Kumo makes clear in one of her holo exhibits of a red spider looking at three victims on its white web:

> The first bundle contained a hollow sugar egg. Inside the egg from a cutaway end, one could see a little fairyland of blue skies and sun and butterflies on daisies. The second bundle contained a giant worker ant. Its mandibles were large, but it was unable to turn its head to free itself from the web. The third bundle struggled with an angry buzz. It was a large wasp whose stinger was immobilized in silk. Its wings could only move enough to give the creature the illusion that it was freeing itself.
>
> (185–86)

The first bundle is like the false world of Mickey-san, a land of seeming endless pleasures without flaw, as hollow and unrealistic as a candy egg. The second suggests the workers trapped in the Bell Factory, caught in a never-ending system of debt and exhaustion which prevents them from escaping its drudgery. The final bundle might be read as artists such as Motler, filled with anger at the shallowness he sees in Mickey-san and planning his eventual triumph as an artist, unable to see that his movement is not enough for escape.

Misha suggests something more radical is needed, a return to authentic and uncommodified art that can resist the logic of late capitalism, a return to the modernist function of art in society. Kumo warns Motler he can never succeed as an artist so long as he remains dependent upon pleasing an audience, telling him, "you're gonna come up with something no one's thought of. What d'ya think that Mickey crowd's gonna do then?" (161). Motler later makes an artistic breakthrough with a technology called the brain box which can "can read brain tissue, just like a hologram" (77), creating fantasy worlds based on the memories of dead loved ones. Customers initially flock to his work, but as soon as the visions turn dark, images of "horrible atrocities, perverted sex and decadent dreams" (219), aspects of our social reality we wish to ignore, the public turns against Motler and his citizenship is revoked. Motler's brainbox art is shocking and offensive to mainstream society, qualities Jameson suggests art lost under postmodernism when even "punk rock ... [and] what is called sexually explicit material" could be "taken in stride by society, and [be] commercially successful" ("Postmodernism" 124). Motler must offer only a comforting, improverished art if he is to please his audience/consumers, as under market conditions there is "the agreement—or at least the determination—of all executive authorities not to produce or sanction anything that in any way differs from their own rules, their own ideas about consumers, or above all themselves" (Horkheimer and Adorno 122). Nothing can be created except the endless mirroring of the same, and thus society stagnates.

Debasing art to commodity form reveals the limitations of Enlightenment reason which was to have led to social freedom, but failed because "As industrial society progresses ... the notion which justified the whole system, that of man as a person, a bearer of reason, is destroyed" (Horkheimer and Adorno 204). In *Red Spider, White Web*, the art assassin stands in for the logic of Enlightenment thought transformed into fascist terror. Describing the murder of a kanji artist, the killer explains,

> I am filling him with paper cuts, my own tattoo of words rushing across his flesh, I can't have it like this, his words running wild, his living, breathing art peeping from under the pale cloth, I am slicing away the bad and leaving the good, making my imprint in his chest.
>
> (133)

The art assassin believes that he can have art without any recidivist element, a non-dialectical vision that is destined to turn into the very thing it opposes. The assassin tries to control art, to slice away the bad and leave only the good, but such an attempt to rationally and instrumentally control art—or society—merely turns into oppression and bloodshed, as the artist's mutilated body suggests.

The contrast between Kumo and Tommy further explores the difference between the authentic artist who retains the promise of Enlightenment thought and the totalitarian one who expresses the instrumentalized and domineering side of Enlightenment as systematic program. They are physical doubles, "Female and male, but other than that, the faces mirrors, mirrors, of each other" (80). Tommy, however, is cybernetically enhanced and so representative of technology, linking him to domination and exploitation in Adorno and Horkheimer's theory. They argue that "a technological rationale is the rationale of domination itself" (121). Cyberpunk might be defined as a literature of anxiety regarding the consequences of technology invading the body, and the connection of this motif with concerns about authentic art is suggested in texts such as Pat Cadigan's story "Rock On" which portrays the move from visceral to virtual music as its fall. Tommy, we learn, is the art assassin; his vision of art—tied to domination—is the negative side of the dialectic. Before Kumo learns this, she discusses the future with Tommy, considering a return to her youthful tribal existence on a genetic preserve farm. Tommy tells her "they don't want intelligent animals like you out there" who are "too smart to be animals and too vicious to be humans" (179), prompting Kumo to ask him if it is preferable that "enhanced psychopathic tinmen" (179) like him lead the masses. Capable of reflecting upon her own limitations, Kumo sees that savagery is part of her artistry, but Tommy believes only in rational perfection, which inevitably ends in domination. Frustrated by the malfunction of the network of semiautonomous robot creatures which surround him like pets—seemingly provoked by Kumo's "art that jammed all his circuits like a bad bad yet good good loooong trip" (109)—Tommy turns on his creations, yelling "I don't need any of you, you fucking worthless piles of junk! I *made* you. All of you. I'm your God and I choose to erase you" (110), subordinating his art to his will just as he tried to purify the words of the kanji artist. Kumo confronts him, insisting the promises of "ascendance to glory" (78) that he offers the people of Mickey-san are misleading, and he responds, "What do you know? ... You're not human. You're not a man. You're not even white" (78), categories that reveal his implication in the systems of domination that characterize the excesses of unexamined Enlightenment thought: anthropocentrism, patriarchy, and imperialism.

Although Tommy does not mention the category of the working class, their exploitation is central to the novel's themes. Concurrent with the conflation of art and commodities is the transformation of the artist into wage laborer. Motler finds the experience infantilizing: he is assigned an apartment "just like a nursery room" (199), introduced to his responsibilities by an automata Teddy Bear, and instructed to follow mint green arrows on the walkways to his job. The promised three hours a day of leisure time prove to be illusory as he is quickly trapped into a cycle of debt to pay for his apartment. Specialization that comes with the wage labor system prevent him from earning money through any role other than his official function because he cannot offer his art for sale until he can earn enough credit to pay for "salesclothes" (205). Motler is supplied with an uniform displaying the name Walter, a label applied equally to any employed artist, all of whom are interchangeable from the point of view of capital and Mickey-san. Erasure of individuality and creativity are the price of economic security. When he complains to another wage labor artist that he is not used to working for someone else, Motler is told "You entered the system pal, you gotta play by the rules now" (206), and when he complains of boredom, another more quiescent laborer insists "Starving is boring Motler. Freezing is boring. Fucking wiredogs are boring. So's the killer out there. There is paradise man—just relax" (206).

This worker's attitude mirrors that of the mass "man" Adorno and Horkheimer feared would be the "natural" inhabitant of the world made by the culture industry. The product of homogenized mass culture, mass humanity is similarly devoid of individuality and as incapable of thinking of something new as mass culture is of producing work that is not derivative.[8] Personality and desire have been subordinated to a calculating logic indicative of the Enlightenment preference for reason over myth to such an extent that "man as a person" (Horkheimer and Adorno 204) has been destroyed. Once one enters the system of wage labor, one exists only as labor power for that system, and other aspects of human existence become irrelevant. The workers in the Bell Factory experience this alienation to an even greater extent. They are "fat, angry, frustrated, drugged to autonomous movements but no more. Nothing to do in the fucking factory all day but fix the shitting robots, keep the computers on line" (62). The workers in Misha's Bell

Factory are an unromanticized version of the integration of humans with the technology that are cyberspace cowboys.

Misha's factory workers serve the machine, reduced to robot-like "autonomous movements" as they subordinate their bodies and selves to the demands of the labor process. Far from cyberpunk heros, these workers are more like Donna Haraway's vision of the women "whose lives have been structured around employment in electronics-dependent jobs" (166), either through the homework economy of flexible labor in the "first world" Silicon Valley or the "nimble fingers of 'Oriental' women" (154) in the "third world" manufacture of computer chips. Haraway argues that "the actual situation of women is their integration/exploitation in a world system of production/reproduction and communication called the informatics of domination" (163), and Misha's version of cyberpunk envisions such a future for all workers. The combined vision of factory workers and artists as varieties of exploited wage labor reminds us of Adorno and Horkheimer's concern that we will loss the capacity for critical thought if art becomes reduced to the commodity form, when thinking is merely "an automatic, self-activating process; an impersonation of the machine that it produces itself so that ultimately the machine can replace it" (25), like the automated laborers in the factory.

Just as Motler found that having entered the system of labor power he was entirely reduced to its dictates, so JuJube, another artist, finds himself incapable of continuing to think independently once he is employed at the factory. Struggling to understand Kumo's latest work, he laments, "Since I've been in the factory, it's all I can think about. It's been two fucking weeks and all I can hear is the metal punch, and screams. All I can smell is that horrid fish stew. And all I can see are steel ingots pressed into barrels" (91). Having entered the system of wage labor and subordinated himself to its logic, JuJube is no longer able to think beyond or outside of this system. Adorno and Horkheimer see the culture industry as bound up with the labor process and inevitably tending toward affirmation of existing social relations by "subordinating in the same way and to the same end all areas of intellectual creation, by occupying men's senses from the time they leave the factory in the evening to the time they clock in again the next morning with matter that bears the impress of the labor process they themselves have to sustain throughout the day" (131). While under the sway of this logic, JuJube is not able to engage with the complexities of Kumo's art, his senses overwhelmed by images from the factory. He wants something new, but only as a momentary release, prompting Kumo to worry, "*Is that all art was to people? Escape?*" (91).

The reduction of human being to labor power alone is one of the ways the dialectic of enlightenment is most easily perceived. What was to have improved human life, progress and scientific rationalism, turns into that which dehumanizes and subordinates. Misha thereby reveals the degree to which anxieties about cyberspace and human/machine interface should more properly be thought of as problems of capitalist social organization, not simply issues of technological domination.[9] Adorno and Horkheimer associate this problem with alienation from nature which follows from a rationalized, scientific approach to the world. As the idea of nature as alive with spirit became eroded and nature became simply a thing to be dominated, humankind opened the door to its own domination by a rationalized labor process: "Animism spiritualized the object, whereas industrialism objectives the spirits of men" (28). In "Man and Animal,"[10] Adorno and Horkheimer consider the destruction of nature and animals by Enlightenment scientific progress, drawing attention to the "bloody conclusion" daily demonstrated by the mutilated bodies of experimental animals that "Reason, mercilessly advancing, belongs to man" while the animals are limited to "irrational terror" (245). Dialectical thought, however, transforms this binary, showing the conclusion "applies not to animals in the free state but to man as he is today" who, "because he does injury to animals" in an unthinking way is the only thing "in all creation [that] voluntarily functions as mechanically, as blindly and automatically as the twitching limbs of the victim" (245).

Humanity's ability to ignore the material suffering of fellow creatures and focus instead on the abstract ideal of knowledge is one of the symptoms of the Enlightenment turning into its opposite. The thinking person becomes the automata, turning "nature into mere objectivity" and requiring men to "pay for the increase of their power with alienation from that over which they exercise their power" (9). This payment takes the form of technology, the embodied essence of knowledge, initially deployed to dominate nature (and those associated with it such as women, non-whites, Jews, the working classes, etc.), but quickly coming to dominate the human spirit entirely, subordinating it to the machine. Adorno and Horkheimer point out that technology "refers to method, the exploitation of others' work" (4)—the very exploitations confronted by Misha's artists—and further connect the exploitation of animals and nature to the devaluing of aesthetics. Nature is connected to the same spiritual and emotional values as myth, and a world of calculating logic does not value them, revealed in Adorno and Horkheimer's comment regarding efforts to preserve "dwindling herds" in Africa, which are thwarted by the fact that "they are an obstacle to the landing of bombers in the latest war. They will be completely eradicated. The earth, now rational, no longer feels the need of an aesthetic reflection" (251).

Misha is equally concerned with eradication of nature and extinction, something that is perhaps more evident in a collection of short works, *Ke-qua-hawk-as*, a word which means "wolverine" in Cree and which is used to refer to Kumo in *Red Spider, White Web*.[11] A scene involving a fish taken from the polluted river and brought into a bar suggests connections among the destruction of nature, the reduction of art to a commodity and the destruction of the human spirit through alienating labor. The fish is "like a legged lungfish, only big as a small sturgeon, and glistening with oil-slick colors ... [and] covered with orange, oozing ulcers" (Misha 97–98). Seeing it, Kumo thinks "of the clean, speckle-sided, pink-fleshed fish, she had caught in her youth" (98) on the genetic reserve farm. The contrast between her current and her earlier social being is similar to the contrast between this ulcerated fish and those she remembers, suggesting the degree to which our domination of nature has turned into domination of human being as well.

While this fish is being examined, government troops enter the bar and begin to harass Kumo and other artists for congregating in a group "of over three people" (102). They focus their attention on a fashalt, a genetically altered being designed to give and receive sexual pleasure, one of a number of alts. Ideal beings from the point of view of capital, alts exist only to fulfill their designated labor function and have no being—or rights—beyond this limited role. A guard begins to abuse the fashalt, "goug[ing] out her eye" seemingly without noticing "how she screamed a garbled response" (102) to his questions, an automatic practice of violence similar to the "mechanical" abuse of animals in experimental practice. The guards beat the fashalt to death with "whips with small metal teeth on them" (102), turning their violence toward the artists when she is finally killed. The narrative switches between describing the violence in the bar and describing the fish trying to return to the river, suggesting parallels between the dehumanized fashalt, the treatment of animals in rational, scientific society, and the dark side of progress. Both the fashalt and the fish are made by the technological society, even if the latter was by accident. The degree to which their suffering and deaths are disregarded is further evidence of the damaged subjectivity and social relations produced by Enlightenment reason turned to domination. The complete subjection of nature to reason and human domination, an example of the "extension of the bourgeois commodity economy" into previously uncommodified areas of experience, allows "the seed of the new barbarism [to grow] to fruition" (Horkheimer and Adorno 32).

Misha's characters live in the world grown from this seed, particularly Kumo, a non-white character who grew up on a reservation for the last animal species and the last "primitives." This reservation, like captive breeding programs or wildlife reserves, is meant to be a positive force, a safe space to protect and nurture endangered life. Nonetheless, such spaces cannot help but also be exploitative, and it is difficult to know which side of the dialectic, progress or domination, to focus upon.[12] The term "reservation" also evokes the treatment of aboriginal people in North America, implying that the rhetoric regarding protection might merely be a cynical justification of a policy ultimately about turning the world into resource for the dominant, white subjects. When Kumo describes growing up on the genetic farm to some school children, images of connection to nature dominate her reflections. She talks about having a cow and "golden horses" and, although she sneers at the children's evident desire for sensationalism, she longs for the life she describes "like the taste of wild strawberries—a taste that was missed and could not be synthesized with any satisfaction" (49). Experiences that cannot be synthesized are another example of the distinction between the authentic and the inauthentic, one that applies to relationships with nature equally as much as it does to art: Kumo, who grew up in a context less alienated from nature and who strives to be an authentic artist, is still able to miss the taste of wild strawberries and long for the better world it represents; JuJube, in contrast, can no longer think of anything but the Bell Factory and cannot even remember that there is something to miss and thus wants from art only momentary distraction.

Kumo's artistic ideals align her with the avant-garde movement, described by Elizabeth Wilson as an identity

> in which the dramatization of poverty combined with romantic masquerade and living on one's wits to become a performance in its own right, a demonstration of the will to shock ... Heroically rejecting middle-class safety and comfort for a life of poverty, risk and transgression.
>
> (13)

Such a description fits Kumo, who not only refuses the ambiguous security offered by wage labor and life in Dogton or Mickey-san, but refuses even to remain in a safe house with JuJube. She tells him that she cannot stay because of her art, a position that leaves JuJube "truly, uncomprehendingly stunned," arguing "You're sick. You were nearly killed. All kinds of shitheadsare [*sic*] out to tear you to pieces. You were in pain, hungry, cold, filthy. Here you have safety, comfort, even, even love" (170). He suggests that she work in the space he has provided, but Kumo angrily retorts, "You think I can jump my art through a flaming hoop. This is a cell, fucker. I can't do that here. Artists aren't tame—you fake" (171), demonstrating her avant-garde sensibilities. In "The Sentimental Futurist: Cybernetics and Art in William Gibson's *Neuromancer*," Istvan Csicsery-Ronay, Jr. argues that

> The avant-garde was, like Benjamin, committed to the destruction of the distance between elite art and everyday life. The gap that Benjamin spoke of as the mysterious/mystified distance required for the sense of aura, was, for the avant-garde, the gap maintained to prop up bourgeois class domination of consciousness.
>
> (225)

Given that Kumo's position can be understood as avant-garde, Misha's ideal of authenticity emphasizes the artists over the art itself. It is not aura she seeks, but creative spirit embodied in authentic artists.

Such a distinction is crucial to understanding the end of *Red Spider, White Web*, a resolution which reveals limitations in the novel's putative solution to the problem of the culture industry and its erosion of the capacity for critical thought. These problems are consistent with the limitations of cyberpunk as a genre and thus also reveal the ways in which Misha's novel is ultimately typical of the cyberpunk canon. At the end of the novel, JuJube's body is discovered hanging from the gates of the market, the last victim of the art assassin. A holo recording of the murder makes Kumo a suspect, and a mysterious grey man who speaks only Japanese helps her escape. He explains the economic collapse of the world is a consequence of Japanese withdrawal from the American economy. Kumo does not understand why the Japanese would leave as they "made plenty of profit," and the he tells her, "Everything in life, every mistake, has a payback. We Japanese are a patient people. We don't care how long it takes, just so long as justice is done" (229). The imagery of atomic bombs throughout the novel suggests that this justice is connected to the atomic attacks which concluded World War II. Kumo, an idealist, admires this strategy, observing, "No one would have been expecting it. In America, profit is everything. They would never suspect honor. Money, greed, even revenge, but never honor" (230).

The man claims that authentic artists such as Kumo are needed because "art is the water of life, that stuff we breath and breed in. Without it ... all our graceful movements will have vanished" (230). Kumo agrees with this sentiment and suggest that nothing is more important than preserving art. "The *artist* is more important than the art," he insists, "I collect the *artists*" (230). Kumo's resistance to the conflation of art with commodities and the erosion of the authentic social role of the artist is thus rewarded by the novel's conclusion, although rewarded in a way that leaves untransformed the spaces of Ded Tek, Dogton and Mickey-san. Kumo herself merely transcends this limited reality, escaping to an unspecified other world in which art is valued, a conclusion not unlike the transcendence into cyberspace that characterizes much cyberpunk. As Jenny Wolmark has observed, cyberpunk's radical potential is severely curtailed by the fact that it is "centrally concerned with individual transcendence, with escape from social reality rather than engagement with it" (*Aliens* 118). In *Red Spider, White Web* the critical impulse of authentic art is preserved, but only elsewhere, and thus despite its many differences from other cyberpunk Misha's novel ends up in the same place that they do: individual transcendence. Notwithstanding the modernist sensibilities she shares with Adorno and Horkheimer, Misha ultimately advances a vision of art that is saved from commodification because separated from society, and thus her artists are as incapable of transforming the social world as are "inferior," derivative works of mass culture.

The conclusion suggests naiveté about the dominance of the market in late capitalism, a nostalgic longing for a better world. Its logic depends upon the belief that the Japanese would choose honor over profit, a charming notion but one that is inconsistent with the novel's otherwise shrewd analysis of the realities of multinational capitalism and its consequences for anything made into a commodity, including humans reduced to labor power.

The conclusion requires that we believe Japanese identity has somehow escaped the effects of late capitalism, able to preserve an uncommodified space of national identity that would choose honor over profit, an ideal similar to the avant-garde artistic sensibility embraced by Kumo who moves through the spaces of the culture industry, but somehow remains untouched by them, able to be collected as an authentic artist at the end. The historical avant-garde was not so fortunate, and by the late 1950s was largely defunct, given the changed social circumstances under which it was not longer considered shameful to make a living as an artist (Wilson 17). *Dialectic of Enlightenment* was written just prior to this period, and Jameson dates the rise of postmodernism and its "affirmation, when not an outright celebration, of the market" (*Postmodernism* 305) to the period just after.

In the twenty-first century, it no longer seems possible to imagine a time in which values other than profit would dominate except perhaps for the isolated individual. We risk forgetting—or perhaps have already forgotten—the "taste" of a less alienated life. If Misha's romantic defense of the artist protecting our capacity for creativity and critical thought is not a realistic response to the problems of the culture industry, what options remain? Some are suggested by William Gibson's recent novel, *Pattern Recognition*.[13] Not considered or promoted as cyberpunk,[14] it shares many features with *Red Spider, White Web*: life in a society dominated by technological mediation, the conflation of art and advertising, the dominance of the commodity form, and what Neil Easterbrook terms "a nostalgia for lost wholeness and unmediated authenticity, either in the personal perceptual world or in art" ("Alternative" 496). *Red Spider, White Web* too easily embraces a romantic transcendence typical of cyberpunk in which a particularly talented individual—an artist or cyberspace cowboy—escapes the vicissitudes of late capitalism. Gibson's work reveals similar anxieties about the erosion of non-commodified experiences, but its contemporary setting implies that we already live within the culture industry to such an extent that our only hope is to survive within it rather than escape from it.

Pattern Recognition's protagonist, Cayce Pollard, is a "coolhunter" whose sensitivity to "the world of global marketing" (2) enables her "to recognize a pattern before anyone else does" (86). Once Cayce identifies a site of group desire, "it gets productized. Turned into units" (86). Cayce's ability is both a marketable talent and a psychological sensitivity to labels, what she calls being "allergic to fashion" (8). Her reaction to things that have become productized indicates a suspicion of the market, a desire for some site of authentic "taste" similar to the ideal of the authentic art. Just as the inferior work of art relies "on its similarity with others" (Horkheimer and Adorno 131), productized fashion is the "simulacra of simulacra of simulacra" (17), leading Cayce to speculate that "There must be some Tommy Hilfiger event horizon, beyond which it is impossible to be more derivative" (18).

In what is surely a joke regarding Gibson's connection to cyberpunk, Cayce dresses only in ensembles of clothing called CPUs, Cayce Pollard

Units, which have their labels removed and "ideally seem to have come into this world without human intervention" (8). Cayce's refusal to wear trademarks can be read as resistance to the way capitalist social relations, particularly advertising, have increasingly colonized human experience. Wearing clothing with labels turns the self into an advertisement for the commodity, effacing use value as clothing and replacing it with the exchange value of "cool." Just as the conflation of art with the commodity form indicated the erosion of a space for critical reflection, the reduction of the self to commodity via advertising suggests a deterioration of individuality. We can thus understand Cayce to be preserving an ideal of individuality in her refusal of trademarks, but at the same time in transforming all her clothing into CPUs that erase the traces of human labor that went into making them Cayce participates in an ethos of commodity fetishism which reinforces, rather than challenges, capitalist social relations. Adorno and Horkheimer argue that the "'effacement of traces of production' from the object itself" is indicative of "the kind of guilt people are freed from if they are able not to remember the work that went into their toys and furnishings" (314).

The limitations of Cayce's position are most evident in her favourite item of clothing, a Japanese imitation of an US MA-1 flying jacket. The imitation includes a slight puckering at the seams, originally a consequence of pre-war sewing machines that "rebelled against the slippery new material" (11), now exaggerated in the imitation jacket, making the puckering into style rather than a flaw. Cayce calls such attention to detail "an act of worship" which makes the "imitation more real somehow than that which it emulates" (11), a position which reveals the fetishistic nature of her relationship to this commodity and the degree to which her resistance to labels and trademarks is not a resistance to commodity culture but instead a desire for the lack of historicity Jameson suggests is characteristic of the postmodern period.[15] The material conditions of production for the original jacket persist only as style, a simulation rather than remembrance of labor. Cayce is deeply upset when this jacket is damaged by a cigarette burn, but is easily consoled by "History erased via the substitution of an identical object" (194) when she obtains another. Cayce is also passionate about the footage, segments of film loaded onto the Internet. It is unclear whether the footage is part of an unfinished work in progress or fragments from an already completed work, but its mystery and ambiguity attract the attention of Cayce and others who meet to discuss it on FFF: "Fetish:Footage:Forum" (3). The footage appears to be the only creative expression left not caught up in commodity culture and advertising, continuing to fascinate because its meanings and influences cannot be pinned down and connected to any material history. Despite "countless hours recording pans across approximately similar scenery" (4), footage enthusiasts are unable to confirm or disprove a hypothesis that it was filmed in Cannes, and there is "no agreement, only controversy" (23) regarding the period suggested by characters' clothing. In a culture approaching the Tommy Hilfiger event horizon, the footage offers a last bastion for authentic art.

Cayce's friend Parkaboy insists that viewers should "go to new footage as though you've seen no previous footage at all, thereby momentarily escaping the film or films that you've been assembling, consciously or unconsciously, since first exposure" (22). The footage thus investigates anxieties regarding the culture industry's expansion into all previously uncommodified areas of experience, a situation in which authentic art is impossible because all creative expression will be based on similarity, the dominant logic of the inferior works according to Adorno and Horkheimer. Cayce searches for the unknown maker of the footage, an enterprise funded by Bigend, head of an advertising agency, whose fascination is quite different from that of the FFF community, but a fetish nonetheless. Bigend is interested in the footage's potential for marketing, seeing in it an example of "attention focused daily on a product that may not even exist" (65): he calls it the "single most effective piece of guerilla marketing ever" (64).

Outside of the footage, Bigend believes "Everything, today, is to some extent the reflection of something else" (68), although unlike Cayce and Parkaboy his intention is not to preserve this space outside commodification, but rather to productize it. Bigend's position reveals that advertising has become more important than manufacture to the control of the economy in late capitalism. As he points out, "Far more creativity, today, goes into the marketing of products than into the products themselves, athletic shoes or feature films" (67), a comment indicating the hierarchy between production and promotion and the interchangeability of things turned into units: shoes or films are both just commodities. The footage, however, has an unacknowledged and dark history of labor. It appears on the Internet as a work of an individual, the maker, but when Cayce investigates its conditions of production, she finds that each frame is rendered pixel by pixel by a group of prisoners as part of job rehabilitation training, a diversion of their state-mandated work program by an uncle of the maker who exploits his position. Even the footage, a cultural expression that seems to escape the derivative excesses of commodity culture, has a history of material production that cannot be acknowledged in its public consumption.

Adorno and Horkheimer's concern with the social and political consequences of the culture industry are related to their critique of the degree to which marketing considerations drive creative production. Like Misha, Gibson is aware of this problem and concerned with the deleterious effects of the market, yet realizes art needs an audience,[16] and Gibson's greater success as a novelist as compared to Misha's marginal profile, published by independent presses, offers stark commentary on the benefits of his less idealistic response to late capitalism. When Cayce finally encounters the maker, she finds the footage is made from frames captured from video surveillance cameras, refined by the prisoners, and transformed by a woman, Nora, who was brain damaged in an explosion. Her work on the footage is the only social relation remaining to Nora, but it is a very truncated version of such because her source material comes from unmanned cameras capturing anonymous people. Her healthy twin sister, Stella, puts the footage on the Internet. If Nora is the artist, Stella explains, she is "The distributor. The one who finds an audience. It is not so great a talent, I know" (286). Although Stella's is the lesser and more politically ambiguous talent, it is nonetheless necessary for art to have a social function at all, as without an audience art remains merely a private expression, at least under the conditions of art as a commodity form which must be profitable in order to be distributed at all. The problem confronting us following the victory of the culture industry, Gibson suggests, is how to manage the distribution of art without capitulation to the culture industry's values. Is critical reflection still possible or are we so saturated by the logic of late capitalism that we take the productized status of art for granted?

Pattern Recognition is trapped in this dilemma. As Neil Easterbrook points out, although "The text contemptuously dismisses someone who would commodify the footage" this is "something the novel itself does" ("Alternative" 495). Gibson avoids the naïve romanticism of Misha's conclusion in which the artist magically transcends the debased society—conveniently ignoring the fact that *Red Spider, White Web* itself circulates as a commodity even if via less mainstream presses—but is a cynical capitulation to the inevitability of market forces a preferable response? In his reading of art in "Antimancer: Cybernetics and Art in Gibson's *Count Zero*," Csicsery-Ronay Jr. argues that the art of the boxmaker AI "re-establish[es] the possibility of contemplation and relation that *Neuromancer* destroyed," but also that the protagonist connects this box art with commodity display windows and thus "sees the whole world as an aesthetic configural space" and so this "vision does not go anywhere." He continues, "Gibson chooses instead to concentrate on the boxes themselves as static art-objects separated from the novel's main action," a conclusion which, in the context of *Pattern Recognition*, implies that Gibson is concerned that authentic art survives in the era of the culture industry in ways other than separating itself from the material world and material social struggle.

The recent publication of the cyberpunk-like novel *Perfect Dark: Initial Vector* suggests that Gibson has good reason to be cynical about space remaining for critical reflection. *Perfect Dark* is deeply embedded in the formulaic qualities of culture industry products, and is also openly an advertisement for another culture product, the digital game upon which its narrative is based. The world of *Perfect Dark* draws on cyberpunk, particular its future in which "Corporations Control Everything, Everyone, Everywhere. ... With One Exception," as we are told by the slogan printed on the advertisement for the digital game *Perfect Dark: Zero* at the end of the book. The putative exception is protagonist Joanna Dark, although such a reading ignores the fact that she is employed by the Carrington Institute, an organization distinguished from a corporation only in that it does not seem to manufacture any products. *Perfect Dark* uses many cyberpunk motifs, although it modifies these in ways consistent with its origin in a first-person, shooter video game. Its band of outsiders is well funded and thus has many technological gadgets and weapons, and the battles are fought in the material world rather than in cyberspace.

Although derivative as narrative, *Perfect Dark* is fascinating as cultural object. It is a book based on—and functioning as advertising for—a digital game, written by a comic book artist, Greg Rucka, with the copyright held by Microsoft Corporation. The copyright page further indicates "Microsoft, the Microsoft Game Studio logo, Perfect Dark, Perfect Dark Zero, Rare, the Rare logo, Xbox, Xbox 360, and the Xbox logos are either registered trademarks or trademarks of the Microsoft Corporation or Rare Limited," making clear that not only is the book a commodity, but that its physical manifestation is legion with other signs of ownership. The story is about stopping a scientist from becoming head of the dataDyne corporation by revealing that he was complicit in the manufacture of a virus, and includes many illegal activities committed for the sake of rising in corporate power. The closest thing to a sympathetic character in the corporate world, Cassandra DeVries, achieved her success writing a software program to manage anti-gravity vehicle traffic, a product successful because it requires continual updates and thus is a never-ending source of revenue.

Despite the negative portrayal of the corporate world, this book is published by Microsoft Corporation and is dedicated to the shareholders, a gesture that cannot simply be read as ironic on Rucka's part. Whatever critique of corporations is found within *Dark Vector*, the fact remains that corporations do control almost everything, including the publication and distribution of this novel. Its success will generate profit for the shareholders, surely more important than whatever damage is done to their egos caused by the narrative's cynical attitude. In *Archaeologies of the Future*, Jameson suggests that the seeming triumph of capitalism—such that we cannot even imagine another system—might be explained by the dominance of "cynical reason" (229), an "empty ideology that accompanies the practices of profit and money making ... that has (and needs) no content to disguise itself" (229). Just as art need no longer be embarrassed by the fact that it is a commodity, shareholders need no longer consider the material basis upon which they make profit. This is not because people are necessarily convinced of the values of the hegemony of big business and late capitalism, Jameson insists, but simply because they are "convinced of its permanence" (229).

Perfect Dark: Initial Vector epitomizes this reality. Not only do the content of the novel and its critique of corporate ethos not matter, the critique itself actually becomes a source of profit for Microsoft through the sale of the book and the video game. The last pages are an advertisement for the game, suggesting that now that one has experienced this world mediated through fiction, one should move into the "real" of playing the game. The idea of entering the world of the novel via the game makes *Perfect Dark* a very cyberpunk experience: the "real" action is all in cyberspace. The novel and game are thus ideal examples of what Foster has called the "more generalized cultural formation" (xiv) of cyberpunk. Perhaps the reason we no longer have cyberpunk fiction is because we have entered the cyberpunk future, and thus lack sufficient critical distance to reflect upon it through the medium of art. Gibson's solution to the dilemma of art and commodities lacks the idealism of Misha's, but is more dialectical for that flaw, critical of the commodity form but still able to reflect upon itself and realise its own inevitable implication in this system. The alternative seems to be *Perfect Dark*, a cultural product that shows us the end point of art that cannot reflect on its own "recidivist elements," thus opening the door for the barbarism to come.

ACKNOWLEDGMENTS

I'd like to thank Veronica Hollinger for her helpful commentary on the original draft of this chapter.

NOTES

1 The first part of the title is taken from the conclusion to Mark Dery's chapter on cyberpunk from *Escape Velocity* (p.107).

2 This trajectory of cyberpunk might also explain the increasing focus on art and artists in Gibson's later work, a topic I will return to at the end of this chapter. See also Chapter 2 in this volume, Rob Latham's "'A Rare State of Ferment': SF Controversies from the New Wave to Cyberpunk" which demonstrates the degree to which Gibson's initial market success was a factor in enabling the cyberpunk movement to exist at all.

3 See Rick Altman *Film/Genre* for an analysis of how Hollywood genres are the result of such marketing decisions to fund films that are sufficiently similar to previously successful films so as to guarantee an audience.

4 This is the fate of most art in Gibson's *Count Zero*, for example, where art is valued based on its 'points' in an exchange market, bought and sold by dealers who never see it and "if the artist enjoyed sufficient status, the originals were very likely crated away in some vault, where no one saw them at all" (103–4).

5 The wheel is one of Duchamp's readymades, work that explored the way the art object is compelled to signify in new ways by its status as art. The readymades also comment on the relationship between art and industry as they draw our attention to the degree to which art relies on previously manufactured materials, even if what is readymade is only the paint. Similarly, Warhol's work expresses anxieties about the conflation of art and commodities.

6 This description mirrors Adorno and Horkheimer's indictment of Hollywood film, exemplem of the culture industry, in which "as soon as the film begins, it is quite clear how it will end, and who will be rewarded, punished, or forgotten" (125).

7 In Mickey-san, all culture is a commodity to the extent that it need not present itself as such as there is simply no alternative to the commodity form. In Dogton, the aesthetic pleasures available are still clearly demarcated as advertisements, there to stand in for the things material reality lacks which the commodity promises, but never delivers:

The world was alive here with sound and light. A large holo of a green, bare-breasted nymph was pouring a glass of Midori right in front of him. Beyond this holo, he could see others, colored angels in black tunnels like beautiful morays skipping out of their holes. Most of them were beckoning sex ads. ... anything you wanted.

(57)

These are advertisements for things lacking in the material world, but they do not even offer the promise that these things might be purchased. Instead, the representations are substitutes for rather than icons of a material reality and "the real point will never be reached ... the diner must be satisfied with the menu" (Horkheimer and Adorno 139).

8 This condemnation of mass 'man' is one of the reasons that Adorno and Horkheimer are often seen as elitist by cultural theorists. It is important to remember that they theorize that this 'mass' person is the product of the culture industry and a life of ubiquitous commodification, not some pre-existing 'lowest common denominator' person to whom the offerings of the culture industry are designed to appeal. It is the case that their critical apparatus is hostile to the approach of theorists such as John Fiske or Matt Hills who emphasize the heterogeneity of mass culture and the multiple meanings that audiences are able to derive from the mass offerings of the culture industry. It is important to note, however, that Adorno and Horkheimer focus on the production side of cultural activity and are concerned with the limitations to thought imposed by an art whose survival is dependent upon marketability. Thus, while I see more potential in popular culture than is suggested by Adorno and Horkheimer's analysis, I nonetheless think that they offer a crucial but often overlooked observation that the popular culture we analyze has already been filtered through the culture industry. What creativity and heterogeneity we might find in texts that are not deemed marketable—or the sorts of people we might be were we their consumers—remain open questions.

9 Similarly, the anxieties about artistic authenticity are not questions of aesthetic standards, but rather are issues of the social relation of art to society under late capitalism.

10 From the Notes and Drafts section of the *Dialectic of Enlightenment*.

11 Her concern with extinction and environmental destruction is connected to her interest in shamanism, discussed at length on her website, http://www.mishanogha.com/, and evident in *Red Spider, White Web* as well. It is interesting to note how seldom animals appear in cyberpunk fiction. When they do, they tend to be as technological cyborgs such as the guard dogs in Stephenson's *Snow Crash* or as DNA remnants, such as the modifications in Gibson's "Johnny Mnemonic."

12 Cole discusses the captive farming of tigers, some of whom are then slaughtered so that their bones and other parts might be used in 'traditional' medicine. This clearly exploitative and, to many, horrifying vision of the fate of tigers is also the best chance the species currently has to avoid extinction, but one must question whether or not a captive existence as resource is a fate preferable to extinction, the same question faced by Kumo and the other artists who decide to stay in Ded Tek rather than to capitulate to wage labor as does Motler.

13 Editor's note: this chapter was written and accepted for publication before the release of *Spook Country*, the follow-up to *Pattern Recognition*.

14 See Easterbrook ("Alternative" 485).

15 This emphasis on imitation might also be seen as an example of pastiche, the empty or neutral form of imitation that Jameson associates with postmodernism, in contrast to the mocking critique of imitation as parody which Jameson associates with modernism.

16 Signing off from his blog on September 12, 2003, in order to work on his new novel rather than spend time blogging, Gibson comments: "The bits and pieces that Joseph Cornell assembled in his shadow-boxes wouldn't have seemed nearly as interesting if he'd simply left them arrayed on the bench of some picnic-table— and they certainly wouldn't still be there." (http://www.williamgibsonbooks.com/ blog/2003_09_01_archive.asp) (accessed September 21, 2007).

7   Why Neo Flies, and Why He Shouldn't

The Critique of Cyberpunk in Gwyneth Jones's *Escape Plans* and M. John Harrison's *Signs of Life*

Mark Bould

At the end of *The Matrix* (1999), Neo (Keanu Reeves), apparently The One, blathers about a world of "choice," without "rules and controls, ... borders or boundaries, ... where anything is possible." To the opening strains of Rage Against the Machine's "Wake Up," he takes to the air and, like Superman, flies. Coming after the movie's various bullet-time shenanigans—characters dodging bullets or hanging, suspended in mid-air, mid-fight, like insects—it is perhaps the last iconic image that cyberpunk will give us. Seen even just a few months later, these moments looked clunky, like they belonged to some almost-forgotten past in which one could not only watch digital effects but *see* them. Like cyberpunk itself, whose first pronouncement of death came before most of us had even got beyond Night City, these digital posthumans were, for a brief moment which passed *before* we even got to see them, on the edge. A revenant flicker, now they are relics.

But that last iconic moment should not pass without comment. Such fantasies of flight, of transcending material constraint, are common in SF, giving access to other realms, physical and metaphysical. While the plunge of the hacker's virtual avatar into the dataspace of the global information network (refigured in Neo's flight) was cyberpunk's first iconic image, it did not spring fully-formed from the head of William Gibson (or *Tron* (1982)). Rather, it was a sublation of earlier SF images of flight, transcendence, and circulation.

THE IDEA IS NOT TO SLOW DOWN

In John Jacob Astor's *A Journey in Other Worlds: A Romance of the Future* (1894), three representatives of the Terrestrial Axis Straightening Company realise that the gravity-nullifying energy they are using to *correct* the Earth's axial tilt (i.e., increase the planet's commercial exploitability) can also be used to power spaceflight. The solar system opens to them like a textual repository, an information space: on Jupiter, they find chronologically jumbled versions of prehistoric terrestrial lifeforms as well as giant ants and musical flowers; on Saturn, lilies and dragons—as well as the spirits of the dead, one of whom lectures them on spiritual matters and gives them a glimpse of the future. Inspired by this instruction, one of the explorers astrally projects back to Earth. Such peculiar conjunctions of engineering and the esoteric can also be observed in Arthur C. Clarke's *Childhood's End* (1953), cyberpunkishly reworked in Greg Bear's *Blood Music* (1985), and in Stanley Kubrick's *2001: A Space Odyssey* (1968), in which Douglas Trumbull's prolonged widescreen psychedelic 'Stargate' sequence used innovative effects technologies to produce an intense visual rhetoric and cinematic paraspace. Trumbull returned the spectacle of this headlong rush to its roots in fairground rides and *This is Cinerama*-style thrills in *Brainstorm* (1983), the central conceit of which—recording an individual's experience for others to replay—would become familiar in cyberpunk (even if its representation of posthumous experience had more in common with Astor's spiritualism than the Dixie Flatline construct or net-distributed Virek of Gibson's *Neuromancer* (1984) and *Count Zero* (1986)).

In David Lindsay's *A Voyage to Arcturus* (1920), Maskull is transported to the distant planet Tormance by the "back rays" (light which returns to its source) of its sun. His body transformed into a humanoid alien form, he is drawn into the Manichean conflict between Muspel and Crystalman. Just as the plot resembles *Neuromancer*—Case, transported to a realm of light, is drawn into the struggle between Neuromancer and Wintermute—so Lindsay's description of "sparks of living, fiery spirit hopelessly imprisoned in a ghastly mush of soft pleasure" (298) resembles cyberpunk's dualism: digital disembodiment versus the meat. As Astor's novel suggests, SF has typically imagined scientific and technological innovations as some kind neo-Hegelian progress, with the human spirit detaching itself from nature en route to perfection (which often resembles the United States as experienced by rich white men). While Superman was learning to fly (rather than merely leap tall buildings), the visitor to General Motors' "Futurama" exhibit at the 1939 New York World's Fair could share his aerial perspective, "simulat[ing] a cruise in a low-flying aircraft over the United States of 1960" (Nye 218) as imagined by Norman Bel Geddes. In the Cold War United States, the aerial view of the American landscape would become apocalyptic: wartime Kodak advertisements promoting superior optical technologies through aerial views of German cities subjected to "high altitude precision bombing" (Dimendberg 37) gave way to diagrams mapping in concentric rings the effects of atom bombs dropped on American cities seen from above. Urban planners advocated the centrifugal, defensive dispersal of populations away from concentrated, centripetal urban centres (248–59), even as primarily white populations were finding other reasons to remove themselves to the suburbs. More recently, SF versions of this white flight have taken the form not of suburbs, gated communities, off-world colonies or alien saviours but of libertarian, pro-market, digital disembodiment.

Cyberpunk's uniqueness, then, lies not in its desire for trans-cendence, which it shares with much SF, but in its development of new locales—cyberspace, the mutable body—in which to postulate and perform the flight from materiality. The shifting limits of human plasticity imagined in cyberpunk provide an equally significant fantasy of transcending material norms. For example, while Bruce Sterling's *Schismatrix* (1985) features two posthuman "clades" who have elected to reshape themselves through bio-technology (Shapers) or engineering (Mechanists), its treatment of capitalist economics as physical laws cannot help but suggest that whatever else motivates them, they are both concerned with developing the best fit with a universe which is conceived of as being a realm of capital. Such (delimited) fantasies of mutability, of creating new identities, can be related to the "neo-regionalist" American fiction and "neo-ethnic" identity politics which also came to prominence in the early 1980s and which Fredric Jameson describes as "specifically postmodern form[s] of reterritorialization; it is a flight from the realities of late capitalism, a compensatory ideology, in a situation in which regions (like ethnic groups) have been fundamentally wiped out—reduced, standardized, commodified, atomized, or rationalized" (*Seed* 148). Cyberpunk's emphasis on the recreation (and recreations) of the body can likewise be seen to "certify the microscopic and the inconsequential ... as the space of real life," thus enabling its "packag[ing] as protest, revolt, subversion" (Jameson, *Seed* 149). Although primarily concerned with fantasies of flight, my discussion of Gwyneth Jones's *Escape Plans* (1986) and especially M. John Harrison's *Signs of Life* (1997) will return to the concomitant fantasy of bodily mutability.

Jameson elsewhere argues that more recent fiction by Gibson and Bruce Sterling are manifestations of the contemporary geopolitical Ima-ginary, expressing an entrepreneurial excitement which "expresses the truth of emergent globalization" and providing "a first crude inventory of the new world system" ("Fear" 384, 385). However, his oddly anachro-nistic reference to "Cook's tours" (384) suggests that SF might have been conducting such a task for rather longer. For example, Jules Verne's *Vingt mille lieues sous les mers* (1870) maps the transport and commu-nications lines of the emerging world-market—its submariners even inspect the transatlantic telegraph cable—while incessantly reporting on the global reach of contemporary commerce. The world is often reduced to, or captured within, a grid of equivalised positions across which commerce flows, like version 1.0 of the internet, while the endless descriptions of submarine wonders, clearly cribbed from textbooks, transforms the world into an information space.[1] In Charlie Chaplin's *Modern Times* (1936), the panoptical factory and department store—key sites of modern capital—provide locations in which he, like the jacked-in hacker, "rises above the 'petty miseries' of the world" by "transforming mechanical rhythms into inspired balletics" (Walsh 36).[2] But Chaplin, like Case, Neo, and countless other cyberpunk protagonists, is incapable of analysing "the *causes* of the misery he describes" because "for him it is enough simply to ... *personally* escape it" (36; italics in original).

Cyberpunk sublated these visions of flight, transcendence and circulation, reimagining them as the detached, immaterial, digitized self's immersion in the dataspace. The euphoria of disembodied transcendence became, thanks to *Neuromancer* in particular, a fantasy of entering into and becoming one with the global circulation of capital. Although cyberpunk spoke of the circulation of "data" or "information," it is clear that this is a euphemism for capital:

> Program a map to display frequency of data exchange, every thousand megabytes a single pixel on a very large screen. Manhattan and Atlanta burn solid white. Then they start to pulse, the rate of traffic threatening to overload your simulation. Your map is about to go nova. Cool it down. Up your scale. Each pixel a million megabytes. At a hundred million megabytes per second, you begin to make out certain blocks in midtown Manhattan, outlines of hundred-year-old industrial parks ringing the core of Atlanta.
>
> (Gibson, *Neuromancer* 43)

Likewise, cyberpunk's depiction of cyberspace—the information space "behind" the computer screen, networking together information and communication technologies—is best understood as a metaphor for "friction-free" capital-in-circulation.[3]

If, then, cyberpunk is the SF of the consolidating world market, it is no surprise that the three volumes of Manuel Castells's *The Information Age: Economy, Society and Culture* (1996–98; second editions 2000–2004) reads like the manual for a cyberpunk role-playing game. Castells argues that the era of informational capitalism has five key characteristics: information as the raw material of production; the pervasive effect of new technology on all aspects of human existence; a network logic of decentralised production and decision-making in asymmetrical nodes of connection; flexibility in production and working conditions; and technological convergence into a single integrated system (*Rise* 70–71). He also describes four specific goals of information-age capital:

> deepening the capitalist logic of profit-seeking in capital–labor relationships; enhancing the productivity of labor and capital; globalizing production, circulation, and markets, seizing the opportunity of the most advantageous conditions for profit-making everywhere; and marshalling the state's support for productivity gains and competitiveness of national economies, often to the detriment of social protection and public interest regulations.
>
> (*Rise* 19)

The nation-state has been eclipsed by a political apparatus which affirms "the only legitimacy principle that does not seem to be threatening for the international powers overseeing its destiny: economic development" (*End* 284). One consequence of this is that "*Our societies are increasingly structured around a bipolar opposition between Net and self*" (*Rise* 3). While the Net represents the fantasy of capital to overcome space and time, the self remains in the human rhythms of movement and duration; while "capital is global and core production networks are increasingly globalized, the bulk of labor is local. Only an elite specialty labor force, of great strategic importance, is truly globalized" (*Rise* 131). Thus, "capital and labor increasingly tend to exist in different spaces and time: the space of flows and the space of places, instant time of computerized networks versus clock time of everyday life" (*Rise* 506). Capital circulates in the timeless time of instantaneous transactions and the spaceless space of instant communication, while humans must struggle to accommodate themselves to a network logic which breaks down "*the rhythms, either biological or social, associated with the notion of a life-cycle*" (*Rise* 476; italics in original).

This division maps onto that between economic classes, the bourgeoisie identifying with capital's abstraction of social products and practices from the proletarian bodies that produce them. Jacked-in to cyberspace, Case leaves his body safely behind and becomes nothing more than a viewpoint plunging into and racing headlong through the digital realm, The only somatic consequence he faces is that of being killed by black ice security programs, but this is a notorious piece of idiocy that the cyberconsole's fuse would defeat. That Gibson should overlook such an obvious flaw testifies to the potency of the fantasy of disembodiment—a fantasy paralleled in the "sharp divide between valuable and non-valuable people and locales" (Castells *End* 165). Thus, while cyberpunk generally celebrated criminal-artistic exclusion and marginality, it typically failed to challenge the Information Age's "*truly fundamental social cleavages*": the "internal fragmentation of labor between informational producers and replaceable generic labor," the "social exclusion of a significant segment of society made up of discarded individuals whose values as workers/consumers is used up, and whose relevance as people is ignored," and the "separation between the market logic of global networks of capital flows and the human experience of workers' lives" (*End* 377). Cyberpunk's frequent failures in this regard are not shared by all cyberpunk nor, for that matter, SF in general; after all, one need only look to Sterling's *Islands in the Net* (1988) and *Holy Fire* (1996) as tacit acknowledgements of the need to address such lacunae, even if they are not overly successful in doing do. In addition, Misha's *Red Spider, White Web* (1990) focuses on the marginalised and impoverished subjects of a future capital who do not have access to cyberspatial disembodiment while others, from Lewis Shiner's *Deserted Cities of the Heart* (1988) and Lucius Shepard's *Life During Wartime* (1987) to Raphael Carter's *The Fortunate Fall* (1996), Dennis Danvers's *The Fourth World* (2000) and Ian McDonald's *River of Gods* (2004), have attempted, with varying degrees of success, to portray cyberpunk(ish) futures from third world perspectives.

Two British authors in particular, Gwyneth Jones and M. John Harrison, have contributed an ongoing critique of such omissions. This chapter will consider how this critique is articulated in their criticism and fiction, focusing in detail on Jones's *Escape Plans* and Harrison's *Signs of Life*, two novels that respond to the same cultural moment and draw on a similar history as does cyberpunk.

G FOR GRAVITY: G FOR THE GRAVITY OF THINGS

Escape Plans often reads like an ironic critique of and corrective to *Neuromancer*'s inability to think very clearly about the dynamics of capital, patriarchy, and empire. It was, however, completed before Jones read Gibson's novel,[4] and so must instead be understood as a simultaneous view, from a slightly different angle, of the global information era. Jones is perhaps best understood as a writer in the English pastoral tradition.[5] As described by Raymond Williams, this tradition is primarily concerned with ownership of and exclusions from the land, and with its reconstruction as landscape for the benefit of a minority class. It is often articulated through boundaries and transitions between city and country. It is always about capital. For example, the "clearing of parks as 'Arcadian' prospects" required the imposition of a social, economic and physical order on all land, including that which was hidden from view: the "mathematical grids of the enclosure awards," organizing land for production, are part of the same process and "contemporary with the natural curves and scatterings of park scenery ... organised for consumption—the view, the ordered proprietary repose" (Williams, *Country* 124). These spatial and material reconstructions performed by capital extended beyond national boundaries. The metropolitan economy "determined and was determined by what was made to happen in the 'country'; first the local hinterlands and then the vast regions beyond it, in other people's lands"—a model of dependent interrelation that underpins the "new dependent relationships between all the industrialised nations and all the other 'undeveloped' but economically important lands" which Williams identifies as imperialism (Williams, *Country* 279). Jones's pastoralism is structured by such a postcolonial sensibility, as well as by a clear understanding that the impoverishments produced by capital fall disproportionately on women.[6] *Escape Plans*, set in a far-future India, depicts a posthuman information society in which the kinds of power evident in this pastoral tradition are carefully delineated. It simulates for the reader the social and physical constraints imposed on its characters through strategies of impeded form, such as the proliferation of acronyms and abbreviations whose meanings are often counterintuitive and whose definitions, offered in occasional asides and an appended glossary, are not always straightforward.

The novel is set some time after the "Age of Unlimited Expansion" (in which the posthuman VENTURans left Earth behind and spread across and out of the solar system) "turned out to have its limits" (32). Machines given the task of identifying habitable and inhabited planets revealed that while "an infinite universe, supporting pangalactic empires of life" might exist, the "cosmos we inhabit, that we used to think so roomy, is actually a bubble-universe, a trapped region ... We've been here, if there was such an event, since the universe began. We are trapped, we are alone and we can never get out" (39). The disappointed VENTURans returned to an Earth they had gladly left, only to find it in the terminal stages of ecological crisis. Without consulting its inhabitants, they terrareformed the planet, restoring it to what they consider its natural state but with human presence minimized. They did consider saving the "planet but not the humans (or ex-humans, as they were sometimes called)"—and the protagonist, ALIC, does daydream how "delightful" it would be if they "just didn't exist and this was a genuine untouched, unknown planet" (32)—but instead of genocide, the VENTURans consigned the humans to subterranean centres, each housing millions, where they are incorporated into various cybernetic life support-, service-, surveillance-, and control-systems. Some of them are integrated even further, used as components in data-processing machines, an image that *The Matrix* would popularize 13 years later:

> They were plugged in, unconscious, and the information they processed vanished from their biological circuitry as soon as the shift was done. No conscious human mind could match the speed of the machines. Only the brain was necessary—on its own an excellent piece of firmware. ... We could not improve on the design.
>
> (42)

The VENTURan PIONERs live in a cluster of linked orbital environments. Some, known as Rangers, live in high-altitude environments from where they manage the planet with the assistance of the enabled (hereditary human administrators), who live in the upper levels of the centers, with "elaborate shopping malls, bars and hotels" (29). Most of the humans, variously known as subs, numbers, or serials, live on lower levels, and the only ones allowed into the open air are a "small surface population of 'wild' numbers" maintained "for conservation purposes" (31). Some subs have slightly greater freedom of movement if they work as biels (bonded laborers), whose jobs might include functioning as domestics/pets/sex toys for visiting VENTUR-ans, but all are firmly located within an inflexible hierarchy and managed by a variety of exclusionary methods, ranging from matters of etiquette and restricted access to information to electronic tagging and physical barriers. ALIC, a VENTURan PIONER tourist, becomes intrigued by the number jockey Millie Mohun. In an attempt to save her from danger, ALIC becomes trapped in a sub centre, unable to recover the identity she temporarily abandoned in order to move freely among the subs.

After Millie mysteriously disappears, she becomes the focus of a religious cult which believes her to be "the first human being ... who would not die"

(80), or a "star traveller," "eternally young" (133). Her disappearance is taken by many to presage the arrival of salvific "starships" (80) from outside the pocket universe, or as a demonstration of her ability to become "information quanta" over which the entrapping "event horizon has no power" (137). However, while this messianic imagery might make it tempting to read ALIC's descent into the underworld in terms of mythical antecedents, the novel is much more attuned to the ways in which this sort of narrative has been utilized specifically to critique capitalist modernity, particularly in the Naturalist tradition. *Escape Plans* might also be understood as a response to the 1970s "Limits to Growth" hypothesis, with the VENTURan orbital habitats and the enabled's levels representing a suburbanization which, in Gerard O'Neill's *The High Frontier* (1977), spread upwards and outwards into cislunar space, while Jones's focus on the world of the subs forcefully reinscribes the economic class divisions perpetuated by such processes and their economic and social determinants.[7]

The fantasy of flight is central to Jones's novel, with the VENTURans representing the "valuable" people Castells described: that fraction of the bourgeoisie who identify with capital-in-circulation and accommodate themselves to a network logic which breaks down life-cycle rhythms. Replicating the fantasies of disembodiment upon which capital depends— the separation of social products and practices from the bodies that reproduce them, the concomitant banishment of the sensate, biocultural, laboring body—the VENTURans arrest their physical development at the end of adolescence. They are revolted by bodies and hair, and find "anhomogenous" fabrics chafing (45). They consider "in-person eroticism" to be a "juvenile taste," preferring to make, splice together and exchange "fantasy clips" for Direct Brain Access (34). They use base-12 rather than decimal systems, and their habitats run

> on a 20-hour day, and a year divided into A cycles of 30x20 hours. To achieve annual conformity the machines put chunks of leap hours on our days whenever they feel like it. We have no seasons, and only the most marginal concept of a general "night" where all activity must cease. We thrive on this. We come down to the underworld, to the cycles that are supposedly printed in our chemistry: and grow fractious and sleepless and lose our appetites.
>
> (36–37)

However, *Escape Plans* is primarily about the failure of fantasies of flight, about the materiality that prevents their realization and that means they are only ever fantasies, regardless of their material consequences. The VENTURan fantasy of endless expansion and transcendent departure collided with the material limits of the universe, space–time curving back on itself with a vengeance. They could not leave behind the ruin they have helped to make of the Earth—just as they cannot leave the humans behind by labeling them "ex-human" and their posthuman selves as "human"; just as they cannot leave the planet behind by labeling it "the underworld" so as to normalize their orbiting habitats as "the world." While cyberpunk's treatment of a ubiquitous, hyperbolized capitalism was typically hampered by it own investments in the fantasies of disembodiment and dematerialization on which capital itself depends, Jones's science-fictionalization of the pastoral enables a more certain critical grasp of the logic of capital.

"Capital," according to Marx, "has one sole driving force, the drive to valorize itself, to create surplus value" (*Grundrisse* 342), the "to go beyond its quantitative limit: an endless process" (*Capital* 270). Following the distinction drawn in Hegel's *Science of Logic* (1812–16) between Barrier and Limit, Marx argues that capital is in a constant process of running into barriers—those external to it and those created by its internal contradiction—which it finds means to surpass (e.g., mechanization which enables intensified production, economies of scale which permit the conquest of foreign markets), but also postulates for it a Limit which it ultimately cannot overcome.[8] In *Escape Plans*, having run up against a Limit they cannot surpass, the VENTURans instead become devoted to the homeostatic perpetuation of the computerized systems which delineate the contours of their lives, turning inward to find new barriers to surpass, just as capital as it reaches its global limits also works to penetrate and colonize nature and the Unconscious (Jameson, *Postmodernism* 49).

The VENTURans, having "tamed and organised" and "successfully librated" the underworld so that "all its destructive forces [are] balanced in an ever-changing, never failing equipoise" (*Escape Plans* 14), and having integrated every system, are confident that there "could be no over production, no famine: no wars, no uncontained disasters" (30). They can allow the electronically tagged subs to "go anywhere, do anything in complete security, with the absolute minimum of active intervention" and are baffled by the occasional complaint that they "had cleared the surface and 'imprisoned' their populations" (30). This parody of the perfect homeostatic system free-market advocates claim capitalism would produce if freed from restraints is everywhere, ubiquitous *and* decentered, even among the VENTURans, for whom the "process of keeping it in balance becomes the most important process, if not the only process" (19). Of course, this libration proves to be less than benevolent when revolution breaks out among the subs. Unable to regain control, the VENTURan systems cauterize the infected centers with "anti-personnel maser irradiation, leaving the structures intact but few human survivors," and vaporise the center where the revolution started: "The site became a large crater in the middle of a quarantined zone, to be approached with caution for some time to come. Half a billion numbers died, by underworld reckoning: 1 in 20 of the planet's population" (232).

The novel ends with an ironic return to fantasies of flight. One night, ALIC is bundled out of her prison cell and onto a hillside, where a starship can be seen hanging in the sky. Millie moves among the group of watchers, saying goodbye. Suddenly realizing what is happening, ALIC cries out, "Wait! ... I'm coming":

> I began to run as if I thought I could fly, and kept on until my lungs were bursting in the thin air ... But the cone of light receded, the earth fell away from it and I was left behind. Two brilliant creatures held me up by my arms—superlucent, integral beings. I fell on my knees on the hard, cold shale. It was the Mohun user, and one of her guards.
>
> The vision faded, the seriate passageway returned. I smiled to myself wryly: that moment still vivid after 30 years; my cold bruised knees and my eyes full of light. She really had me then, in spite of everything. But I should have known. Millie Mohun never gives you anything you can hold on to.
>
> ...
>
> I got up and began to stroll down the passage with my weight on my left foot and my right knee bent outwards. How the bones begin to creak! I may be lean enough for the probability tunnel now, but if Millie means to come back and fetch me in-person, she'd better make it soon.
>
> (238–39)

This deflation of transcendence recurs throughout Jones's engagements with cyberpunk (in her reviews and critical writing, as well as novels like *White Queen* (1991), *Bold as Love* (2001), and *Life* (2004)), and it is intimately tied to a deep-rooted resistance to the ways in which capital promotes the bipolar opposition identified by Castells between Net and self. Such an abstraction—of capital from the laboring bodies which produce value, of fetishized commodities from their production, of digital information from analog reality—is homologous to, and part of the process by which, agricultural land and labor were separated and hidden from landowner's Arcadian prospect, and by which the impoverishment produced by capital and the consolidating world-market is hidden from the consumer's sight. Jones's refusal to permit her posthumans anything but the most limited transcendence (stalling the ageing process, living in lower gravity above the pristine prospect of the reterraformed Earth) while focussing on the constrained lives and subterranean labor of those normally kept from view, insists on the "truly fundamental social cleavages of the information age" which cyberpunk so often overlooked. Moreover, the impeded form and self-consciously angular difficulties of *Escape Plan*'s prose repeatedly block the reader, refusing the friction-free illusionism to which SF has aspired since Campbell, abjuring the sheer paciness of cyberpunk (particularly that written in imitation of *Neuromancer*), and thus bring us down to Earth, to our bodies in human space–time.

WHATEVER HE HAD PROMISED HER, SHE COULD NEVER HAVE FLOWN

Fantasies of self-transformation, virtual and physical, are central to M. John Harrison's fiction, notably *Light* (2002), the space opera with which Harrison "returned" to genre SF, but only as a reminder of what it means, and costs, to be human, fallible, and stuck. The novel exports cyberpunk's vision of a consolidated world-market to a galaxy imagined as the spume on waves of information.

Signs of Life (1997), while less overtly science-fictional than *Light*, none-theless resonates strongly with Sterling's and Gibson's "global tourism sf." Poised on the edge of a post-Soviet Europe, it offers Harrison's most wrenching depiction of fantasies of flight, of leaving behind the world and its mess, whether human relationships under capital, industrial pollution, or the material effluence from which capital fantasizes its own separation. Late in 1989, Mick Rose (a.k.a., China) meets Choe Ashton, a former scaffolder, steeplejack, oilrig worker, and founder of "one of the first courier operations of the Thatcher boom" (27). Immediately enchanted by this erratic, arrogant, childishly self-absorbed young man, he is drawn into Choe's world, semi-reluctantly helping him "to illegally dump fifteen cardboard boxes of low-level biological waste" in an abandoned quarry "because it was a way of breaking with everything I had ever been" (51)—a "descent in more ways than one" (54). From this dubious start, they establish Rose Medical Plc, a specialist courier service which "would move anything—transplant organs in ice, small runs of a new drug, diagnostic technology designed to bolt on to existing computers. ... Recombinant DNA; viruses at controlled temperatures, sometimes in live hosts; cell cultures in heavily armoured flasks" (19). Interested only in profit, they do not care about the uses to which their cargoes are put, and through the 1990s, as the biotech industry rapidly exfoliates across the edges of the law, filling every available unlegislated niche, so Rose Medical expands:

> carrying anything we could lay our hands on, from cellular raw materials to apparatus and computers ... ; from "passive immunity" vaccines to artificial antibodies and speciality bloods designed in the US. We moved plant specimens shipped quietly in by air from the Third World so their seeds could be patented by self-financing university research departments in the Midlands. We had our foot in the door of the genetic supply industry. We were on our way.
>
> (59–60)

Involvement with East European organized crime soon sees them shipping hazardous waste eastwards, where "you can dump anything," and other "product"—secure containers, software, and "the odd live host," sometimes animal, sometimes human—westwards (98–99). But for Choe and China, the appeal of the business lies in its speed. It is not just that "There were no limits to biosupply, an industry so new and expansive it couldn't keep up with its own jargon, or indeed invent new jargons fast enough: there was no end to the money that could be made" (111), but that couriering choice shipments gives them an excuse to live on blow and drive really, really fast for hours on end (of his Lotus Super 7, Choe explains "Eighty miles an hour: not fast. But ... *it'll get there from a standing start in four seconds.* It's a fucking slingshot" (184; italics in original)).

China initially sees Choe as being like one of the moths

> in a restaurant on a summer evening just as it gets dark. They bang from lamp to lamp, then streak across the room in long flat wounded trajectories. We make a lot of their confusion but less of their rage. They dash themselves to pieces out of the sheer need to be more than they are.
>
> (27)

But after Rose Medical goes bankrupt from their neglect (and other, more personal traumas), China becomes a driver for Choe's new company, Hot Cars, and embraces speed and its boredom:

> It was going like this: straight down a tunnel of shaking halogen light. Noise, speed, music like a second engine; something valuable on the back seat. I was often tired. Sometimes I didn't change gear for a hundred miles. Motorway signs came up a kind of living crystalline blue in the night. Above eight thousand revs, BMW engines produce a distracted whine, as if they are trying to tell you, "Don't bother me now"; behind that I could hear the low-profile Michelins blustering and booming as they coped with strange arhythmic changes in the road surface. The competition ride-pack made every mile seem corrugated. My shoulders ached. I wondered if it would rain. Part of me hoped it would.
>
> "Mickey, we're up at a hundred and thirty-eight miles an hour here. ... No police and right on schedule."
>
> (199)

If the cyberpunk hacker is "the hero as information-processor," his purpose "not to increase knowledge but to keep it circulating" (Parrinder 76), then the courier—Y.T. in Neal Stephenson's *Snow Crash* (1992), Chevette Washington in *Virtual Light* (1993)—is his non-virtual equivalent. But however fast the courier moves, however much his environment is reduced to patterns of light and the strangely abstract noises of his high-end kit, he cannot leave the world, or his body, behind. He cannot enter the spaceless space and timeless time of information-capital described by Castells, no matter how fast he goes. Likewise, despite the propaganda of information-capital, not all things are reducible to digital information and capital cannot escape from its material base in laboring bodies, however much it pretends otherwise.

Choe's desire to accelerate into some other state of being is a product of his adolescent entrapment in a small northern town and his "yearning for something uncanny and *full* in the most drab moment of the everyday: but a desperate fear of it" (Miéville 6). He claims to have had a visionary experience on the Yorkshire moors in his late teens. Sunlight illuminated a narrow valley "*as if from the inside*—as if the whole landscape might suddenly split open and pour its own mysterious devouring light back into the world" (Harrison 133–34). A woman walked out of this light, fucked him, and then returned "into the world," which sealed up behind her: "It was my first fuck. ... It was my only fuck. ... I've never done it since. Whatever lives here loves us. I know it does. But it only loves us once" (134–35). By the end of the novel, Choe—like a clumsy moth beating and burning himself against a light he cannot penetrate, enraged by a world which gave him a glimpse of, and then forever denied him, the numinous—has bought the valley and turned it into a toxic dump filled with industrial waste.

China's other major relationship is with Isobel Avens. Rather than pursue speed, she dreams of flight. Whereas Choe is nauseated, perhaps ironically, by "the unstructured future rushing past us like the wind" (66), she obsessively photographs the most mundane things, as if to fix materiality in place and thus precipitate her departure from them. China first meets her at an aerodrome café. Mistaking him for a pilot, she tells him of her yearning to fly. On their first date, her hair, gathered up in "a big bow like a butterfly," escapes and "fall[s] in long untidy wisps round the freckled nape of her neck" (12), presaging her fall into the flesh, her terrible encounter with the limits of corporeal plasticity. Later, sensing the impossibility of transcending her mundane being, she says *Fuck me*, in a small panicky voice. As if she meant, *Save me from falling*" (14). The morning before she moves in with China, she wakes him with the news that she dreamed of flying: in a busy computer room, she struggled to find her C-prompt; abruptly, she "learned what she had to know, and she was floating up and flying into the screen, and through it, 'Out of the room, into the air above the world,'" where she swoops and soars and, when tired, perches "like a bird" (17). Perhaps because of things left unresolved by her father's death, she projects onto China, who is older than her and not unwilling, her restlessness for something *more*, conflating her desire for control over her life with the affluent and more worldly future China seems to offer.

The course of their relationship is mapped by her dreams of flight, which soon begin to separate them: as he watches her sleeping "with an intensity of love ... never felt for anything since," she instead "dreamed of some long, soaring, heartbreaking flight" (77). Ironically, she has never actually flown, and when he takes her on a business trip to Budapest, she is enchanted by the cramped Tupolev, while he only notices the rivets holding it together and the powdered milk in the coffee. When he has an anxiety dream about

Rose Medical's involvement with organized crime, it takes the form of being stuck forever on the Tupolev. On the same night, having in her sleep announced a "system fault" (104), Isobel loses the ability to dream of flying. Distraught, she has "her hair cut into the shape of a pigeon's wing" and "her ankles tattooed with feathers", and starves herself, "as if her own body were holding her down" (109). This self-starvation can be understood in two particular, but interrelated ways, both concerned with the power-lessness she feels.[9]

In Isobel's childhood, her father, now dead, repeatedly uprooted the family, moving in search of something different, something more, "will[ing] the future towards him" (34)—determined "to live differently" (34), he also took weekly flying lessons. Consequently, Angela Failler almost seems to be describing Isobel when she writes that anorexia

> may be an attempt to compensate for a loss or disappointment that has affected the subject so deeply as to leave him or her with a fear of dependency on others, and a resistance in making connections with others for fear of a repeated loss. This unconscious fear manifests as a refusal of food or, more specifically, as a refusal of appetite. In anorexia, appetite reminds one that they desire, and desire reminds one of neediness, and neediness of dependency, and dependency of relationship. Thus, to make a desireless, "pure" self by refusing appetite is to keep buried a recognition of neediness, a recognition of the other, and a recognition that one's neediness was once traumatically let down, rejected, or violated by some ideal or some other that mattered.
>
> (104)

However, to focus solely on this Oedipal dimension is to miss the broader social context the novel maps of life under capital.

Anorexia is typically connected to a struggle between desire and will, the experience of which is often characterised by a split self, with eating "construed as a bodily desire entirely alien to the mind/self" (Malson 125). As such, it resonates strongly with distinctions between the Net and the self, the virtual and the meat. While Isobel's self-starvation is related to the loss of control over her life instituted by her restless father, and the loss of her father, anorexia is a "a disorder of abundance" (Turner, *Medical* 104), of industrialized societies in which there is an over-abundance of food, a situation that paradoxically also produces an ideal of the disciplined body which belies this excess.[10] Anorexia is therefore concerned with the control of appetites and the anxieties raised by living in consumer culture. It symbolizes the pressure to balance producer-selves, "capable of sublimating, delaying, repressing desires for immediate gratification" in favour of a work ethic, and consumer-selves, whose "boundless capacity to capitulate to desire and indulge in impulse" capitalism equally requires (Bordo 196). It is a way of exerting control in one part of life so as to compensate for a lack of control in others, a "preoccupation with the 'internal' management of the body ... produced by instabilities in the 'macro-regulation' of desire within the system of the social body" (Bordo 196).[11] The anorexic denial of a "natural" need exemplifies our alienation from our bodies when "we no longer consume commodities to satisfy relatively stable and specific needs, but to reconstruct ourselves in terms of the lifestyle associated with the consumption of certain commodities" (Lowe 47). Soon after she has lost her ability to dream of flight, Isobel sets out to radically reconstruct herself. She leaves China for Brian Alexander, a biotech guru who she believes will help her fly. It is never clear whether she intends this merely metaphorically, but from a Florida clinic she sends China a postcard with "an old sepia-tint of the Wright Brothers' first flight" (Harrison 159). Paralleling this earlier technological development with the mysterious treatment to which Isobel is subjecting herself, and with the industry on whose edges his company operates, China notes that where "you expected brown paper and string, a technology fumbling on the edge of Dada, you saw only hope and energy" (159). Cyberpunk's gawping at the latter might explain why no-one ever notices that, at one point, Case loads a program from a cassette tape. Sooner or later all cutting edges turn out to be eight-track.

Abandoned by Brian, Isobel returns from his Miami clinic, "anorexic, covered in sores and open to every infection in London" (182). In Florida, she had designed a new, bird-like appearance for herself and pushed Brian to perform radical procedures "*it would be illegal to do ... to a laboratory rat*" (237; italics in original). He inserted "avian chromosomes" so as to make her follicles "produce feather-sheaths instead of hair" (226). He triggered "the 'brown fat' mechanism" with "[d]esigner hormones" so as to make her "as light and as hot to the touch as a female hawk," and "induced calcium shortages [to] hollow the bones" (229). And he altered her metabolism, making it produce "Engineered endorphins [which] released during sexual arousal simulate the sidesweep, swoop and mad fall of mating flight, the frantically beating heart, long sight," promising that "Sometimes the touch of her own feathers will be enough" to trigger this response (230). This promised ecstasy has produced, however, a body wracked by illness:

> To the sore throats, stomach cramps and short-lived rashes ... were added bouts of vomiting and diarrhoea ... Viruses ripped though her like supernatural weather, Miami weather—three distinct, low-key infections in one day, cyclical highs and lows presenting symptoms from inflamed nasal membranes through arthritically swollen joints to a case of vaginal thrush that was gone in an hour. Across one rainy Thursday afternoon, her temperature reached 102, lowed-out at 93 and normalized again before five o'clock ... Her pubis, waxed to an exotic, feathery stripe, looked only vulnerable. There was no more flesh on her for her illness to burn off. She seemed too long for the bath, her legs folded

awkwardly to one side, her shoulders presented front-on, thin as fish-
bones, her head turned in profile. Every day she was easier to carry,
hotter to the touch. It was as if her fevers were permanent.

(188, 193–94)

While the description of disease as weather matches the common cyberpunk
confusion of Woman and World,[12] and Harrison's own blending of metaphors of entropy and disease in his fiction from the late 1970s onwards, its
significance here lies in the way it constructs the body as a chaotic, non-
linear, and disunified process. The universe might "simply [have] knitted
itself together one day, out of numbers" (Harrison, *Signs* 38), but that does
not mean that it is predictable, subject to human control, or malleable
without consequences. It is analog, not digital, and thus fundamentally
irreducible to information, equivalized values or isolated monads. Isobel's
illness marks the material limit into which capital, and her desire for transformation and transcendence, inevitably runs. Rather than taking flight like
a bird, she seems to be devolving into something piscine—ex-human, as
Jones's PIONERs might say.

During her fevers, as China cares for her, she begins again to dream. Her
first dream is of a ménage-à-trois with him and Brian: "and Brian was
pulling something out of my back. Whatever it was got longer and longer. It
wasn't at all painful ... it was wings. When I saw them, I just came and
came" (187). Her second dream recapitulates her original dream of flying
through the computer screen and "up in the air above the world," but then
it takes a different turn:

> at the top of the dream her collarbones cracked suddenly with the
> weight of the wings ... There was only that appalling dry domestic
> crack ... : then she fell, and as she fell a paper fire burst out of her head,
> a fire of newspaper and sticks to melt the wings—although they con-
> tinued to move cruelly and rhythmically, levering her clavicle and upper
> ribs out through the skin. She knew she would never make it back to
> the ground, which by now looked like a city—or anyway the mother-
> board of some vast computer—its every parallel avenue shining with
> silver solder ... [I]t all swung in a delirious arc round her, as if her
> failure was necessary so that everything else could fly. Eventually, the
> wings began to lever out her internal organs, which bagged and flut-
> tered in the airstream like dark-coloured washing, like tangled para-
> chutes, making a sad, wet flapping sound.

(189–90)

The limits on her imagined flight are not just those of her physical body, but
also those of history and intersubjectivity: the mundanity of fire-lighting and
laundry pointing to the private, domestic, and gendered constraints—the
weight of history and connection—which keep the fantasy of the

immaculate future metropolis, whether concrete or digital, from materializing; the sense that this fantasy costs too much, and that that is both a good thing and a sad thing. Isobel can find no place in the Net, that place beyond embodiment, and her fall into the self, into her damaged materiality, is a harrowing rendition of the consequences of capital's disciplinary apparatuses as it reduces us into units of labor and consumption, stripping us of our fullness of being. Isobel is an agonizing reminder of the fundamental cleavage Castells, like Marx before him, identifies between the systems of global capital and biological and social rhythms of our human lives. Like all of us, she is devastated, torn apart, annihilated by this contradiction.[13]

PART OF HER WAS STILL TRYING TO FLY BACK FROM MIAMI AND ALL THAT MIAMI ENTAILED

In Gibson's *Pattern Recognition* (2003), fantasies of flight come down to Earth with a couple of bangs and a whimper.[14] Presiding over events are the destruction of the World Trade Center and the excavation of a WWII German dive-bomber buried in Russian mud. This insistence on the materiality of the world reimagines *Neuromancer*'s Case as Cayce, who like her precursor must adapt to the time–space of global capital, but suffers from a perpetual jetlag,[15] her body providing a material limit to capital's constant drive to expand. This materialist shift of emphasis in Gibson brings him back from the brink at which his novels always falter "as if unable to imagine what comes next" (Hollinger, "Stories" 461). In terms reminiscent of *Escape Plans*, Hollinger describes this recurring pattern in his novels as "the event horizon loom[ing] too closely and smother[ing] the futuristic imagination" ("Stories" 461). She suggests that *Pattern Recognition* treats 9/11 as a "symbolic" singularity, "an apocalyptic event that cuts us off from the historical past, leaving us stranded in difference" ("Stories" 462) where "everything is happening *now*, [but] everything is also always happening elsewhere" (463):

> From this perspective, time present—postmodern time—is supplemental time, time-after-the-end-of-time; the cautionary "post" in "postmodern" represents both our hesitation in letting go of the past and our anxiety that we are, in fact, on the other side of irrevocable change.
>
> (463)

Easterbrook similarly argues that *Pattern Recognition* structures the present moment as liminality and deferral, "constant, continual, and recursive" ("Alternative" 500). But he also discusses "Gibson's unmediated nostalgia for an unmediated real, a pure presence of the present, utterly authentic, outside all commodities," even though Gibson, like us, must surely "know there are no aesthetics purely outside commodity aesthetics, no unmediated intuition of the real, no naïve experience untouched by language or irony or representation" ("Alternative" 498). In Harrison's words, "We can never escape the world. We cannot stop trying to escape the world" (*Parietal* 144).

Gibson's cyberspace was a brilliant metaphor, so bright we could not always clearly see beyond its dazzle: we became addicted, briefly, to its detail and appearance. In *Pattern Recognition*, more drenched than any of his novels in the allure of the commodity, Gibson brings us once more to the brink, and once more cannot speak the vast, synchronic apocalypse, the transformation that is constantly happening *elsewhere* and *now*, in the core of of the commodity, where use-values become exchange-values, and where the value produced by the self is expropriated into the Net. The commodity emphasizes its variety so as better to conceal the thing that all commodities, even information, share: their material basis in human labor. The singularity has already happened, and is constantly happening, as humans, "already *not*-human" (Rikowski 122), are torn apart by capital, our selves reduced to those abstractions (labor-power, consumption-power) which it needs to operate and perpetuate. Case's flight, like Isobel's dreams, was dazzled by the possibility of becoming disembodied in this way, of becoming information-capital itself. Cayce's "disrupted circadian rhythm" in "that flat and spectral non-hour, awash in limbic tides, brainstem stirring fitfully, flashing inappropriate reptilian demands for sex, food, sedation" (Gibson, *Pattern* 1), like Jones's ex-humans, plugged unconscious into the machines that discipline their existence, signal its cost.

This is why Neo flies, and why he shouldn't.

NOTES

1 This space is even more obviously that of capital circulation in *Le Tour du monde en quatre-vingts jours* (1873), in which Phileas Fogg circumnavigates the globe without ever leaving the serene mental space derived from his absolute faith in capital's global imposition of clock-time over all contingencies, flows, and rhythms.

2 More recently, this privatized dissent, generating an individual trajectory across material realities, is breathlessly demonstrated in the traceurs' free-running of the decaying *Banlieue 13* (2004).

3 This metaphoric leap is not a big one: internet technical standards such as TCP/IP were adopted specifically to facilitate intra-capitalist competition in the US, after the proprietary network standards developed by IBM, Xerox, and others were rejected by the US state because they impeded such competition and increased state costs. This point and the following discussion of Castells, is derived from Vint and Bould.

4 Personal correspondence.

5 See Bould's "Incredible Stories about Ordinary People" and "Landscape, Labour and Capital in the Pastoral Science Fiction and Fantasy of Gwyneth Jones/Ann Halam." *Escape Plans* might also be considered an urban-centred, ironic shadow of Le Guin's *Always Coming Home* (1985).

6 Indeed, Jones designed the "alien conquerors" of her *Aleutian* trilogy (1991–97) so that they possess all the "supposed deficiencies ... Europeans came to see in their subject races": "'animal' nature, irrationality, intuition; mechanical

incompetence, indifference to time, helpless aversion to theory and measurement"—characteristics, she notes, "routinely attributed to *women*" ("Aliens" 110; italics in original).

7 This tension between expansion/collapse, capital/labor, and transcendence/corporeality is also evident in the differences between *Neuromancer*'s Night City/ corporate arcology and Zion Cluster/Freeside oppositions. On SF and the limits to growth hypothesis, see De Witt Douglas Kilgore's *Astrofuturism: Science, Race, and Visions of Utopia in Space*.

8 See Michael Lebowitz's *Beyond Capital*, notably 1–15.

9 Bryan Turner (1992) argues that anorexia can be a way for those who have no social voice to speak.

10 See Olson (32). For further background on the "highly specific socio-cultural address" of anorexia, see Brumberg (1988), Vincenzo DiNicola's "Anorexia Multiform: Self-starvation in Historical and Cultural Context Part I: Self-starvation as a Historical Chameleon" and "Anorexia Multiform: Self-starvation in Historical and Cultural Context Part II: Anorexia Nervosa as Culture-Reaction Syndrome" and Bryan Turner's *Medical Power and Social Knowledge*.

11 Dieting has also been described as "provid[ing] Americans with something to discipline—bodies and weights—while other forms of consumption, for instance sexual or monetary, are indulged" (Olson 54).

12 For more substantial gender critiques of cyberpunk, see Anne Balsamo's *Technologies of the Gendered Body*, Nicola Nixon's "Cyberpunk: Preparing the Ground for Revolution or Keeping the Boys Satisfied?" and Sherryl Vint's *Bodies of Tomorrow*.

13 For all that Harrison is more focused and effective than cyberpunk generally in charting this cleavage—and in being fundamentally, and appropriately, enraged by it—he nonetheless does come close to reiterating the dichotomy Nicola Nixon identifies in cyberpunk between women being physically abused or having their bodies manipulated and men getting to enjoy disembodied flight. While physical trauma is concentrated in the body of Isobel, Harrison does redeem himself a little by never permitting the men disembodiment or joy.

14 Editor's note: this chapter was written and accepted for publication before the release of *Spook Country*, the follow-up to *Pattern Recognition*.

15 Perhaps inspired by a passage in Sterling's *Zeitgeist* (2000): "I'm jet-lagged to hell and gone. I misplaced my soul in Hawaii. My personal time ghost is still flying somewhere over the mid-Pacific" (228).

8 Posthuman Melancholy
Digital Gaming and Cyberpunk

Jonathan Boulter

> The prosthesis is not a mere extension of the human body; it is the constitution of this body qua "human" ... It is not a "means" for the human but its end, and we know the essential equivocity of this expression: "the end of the human."
>
> (Bernard Stiegler, *Technics and Time*)

> Man has, as it were, become a kind of prosthetic God.
>
> (Sigmund Freud, *Civilization and Its Discontents*)

> Nothing is gained without loss.
>
> (Paul Virilio, *Politics of the Very Worst*)

INTRODUCTION

This chapter considers the digital game as an articulation of posthuman subjectivity and space. As a perfect, one might say sublime, confluence of machine and human subjectivities, the digital game—I am here considering *Deus Ex: Invisible War*—instantiates, in typical cyberpunk fashion, what appears to be a celebration of both subjective extension and cancellation. The human player, extending prosthetically beyond temporal-spatial limitations, can experience the vertiginous thrill of "becoming" Other, becoming the avatar whose armature, superior physical skills, and in the case of *Deus Ex: Invisible War*, cybernetically modified body, speak to a festishized, posthuman, desire for transcendence: the subject, now leaving the self behind, enters what Paul Virilio calls the "substitute horizon" (*The Information Bomb*, 14) of the game to become, in some senses, a "terminal citizen" (*Open Sky*, 21). And it is here, as a (temporary) liberation from subjective limitations unfolds, that a concomitant re-aligning of space occurs. More precisely, a re-aligning of the experience of space occurs. Because when in the game, the player is not "in" space: s/he is *experiencing* space; more precisely, s/he is experiencing space through an interiority (her avatar) that is both her and not her, him and not him. It is thus accurate to describe this sense of space, space which is at once familiar and unfamiliar, as uncanny. Physics and graphics engines work furiously to reduplicate the "real" experience of space, and insofar as the experience of the digital space of the game is fully dependant on the repeated revisitations of the player (locations are revisited in *Deus Ex: Invisible War* as part of narrative requirements), the virtual flâneur-gamer is compelled to be, seduced to the point of *being*, at home in the virtual not-at-home that is the experience of digital space. At some level thus, the digital game instantiates *materially* what may be the primal posthuman fantasy of cyberpunk: to transcend the limits of human space and subjectivity, of subjectivity conceived *as* singular interiority.[1]

Yet digital gaming offers itself as an implicit and important critique of cyberpunk *as* fantasy, registering as it does the precise and proscriptive limits of the human: to be posthuman in the game, in other words and to borrow from Iain Chambers, is always to register the boundaries delimiting the transcending (and perception) of human space and subjectivity.[2] And this registering of limits begins with the player's realization that the transcending of subjectivity and space can only ever be a limited and temporary escape. There is a fundamental irony in the way digital games explicitly thematize bodily transformation: if at one level the extension into my avatar is an escape, it is always already a melancholy reminder of the physicality of the real body that must be left behind, a reminder of the gross limits of the space that in its turn delimits the inevitable return to the body. The game thus, functioning in a purely specular fashion, serves to offer an impossible freedom, a fantasy of freedom which can only ever remind the player of his or her "terminal" nature: this corporeality is the *end* and *limit* of his or her freedom. But this is a compelling and precisely compulsive fantasy for the gamer, one that approaches the often thematized addiction to cyberspace that we see in cyberpunk fictions. I am using a (post-) Freudian account of melancholy here to suggest that the "loss" of the body that occurs in the game cannot be sustained; the gamer compulsively must return to the game to maintain that disappearance. Ultimately, I am interested in exploring how the game's material realization of the primal, compulsive fantasy of cyberpunk—its realization of the necessity to return to the body in order to transcend the body's claims—itself functions as a critical commentary on the melancholic, impossible, economy of posthumanism.

DEUS EX: INVISIBLE WAR AS CYBERPUNK FANTASY

The Body

The relationship between cyberpunk and gaming culture—cyberpunk as gaming; gaming as cyberpunk—is evoked in William Gibson's response to Larry McCaffery when asked about his inspiration for the idea of cyberspace. Gibson had been interested in the way video game players were absolutely absorbed by the gaming experience: the gaming experience was a kind of "feedback loop with photons coming off the screens into the kids' eyes, neurons moving through their bodies, and electrons moving through the video game. These kids clearly *believed* in the space game projected" (McCaffery, "Interview" 272). It is perhaps an overstatement to suggest that cyberpunk finds its roots in gaming, but Gibson's inspiration clearly indicates that the space of gaming should be a crucial site for those interested in tracing cyberpunk's various generic roots.[3] It is critical, I would argue, to recognize the degree to which the discourse of cyberpunk has been woven into—and perhaps out of—what I am calling the visual imaginary of digital games.

Deus Ex: Invisible War, released in 2003 by Ion Storm and Eidos Interactive for Microsoft Windows PC and Xbox (I discuss the Xbox version here), is a prime example of this necessary discourse. The game takes place in 2052 after the "Collapse" which sees world governments replaced by competing technocratic and technoreligious groups. *Deus Ex: Invisible War* follows the story of Alex D, a young military trainee who, after a terrorist attack which destroys his training facility in Chicago (the Tarsus Academy), travels to Seattle (and other real-world locations including Cairo, Trier, New York, and a research facility in Antarctica) in order to discover the truth behind a series of conspiracies working to control all political, economic, and religious systems on Earth. Through various plot turns, Alex D is compelled to give his loyalty to one of the four groups competing for global dominance. These groups—The Order Church, The World Trade Organization, ApostleCorps/Tarsus Academy, and The Templars—each offer specific temptations to Alex (The Order offers religious enlightenment, the WTO, economic power, The Templars, military prowess) and he is forced to decide which of these groups is benevolent or, at least, least harmful to him personally.

Generically, *Deus Ex: Invisible War* is a first person shooter (FPS) with role-playing elements (RPG). As a FPS, *Deus Ex: Invisible War* allows the player to see the action only from Alex D's perspective. The effect of the FPS perspective, as I will explore further, is to close the subjective gap between player and avatar and increase the sensation of full immersion in the digital universe of the game. The RPG elements of the game allow the player, as the game commences, to choose Alex D's gender and ethnicity (s/he can appear as Caucasian, Black, or Asian). More importantly, in order for Alex to defeat his various enemies, he must learn how to enhance his body's capabilities. As the game progresses Alex happens upon various "biomods"—cybernetic implants—which greatly enhance his strength, speed, and vision; these implants also allow him to become invisible and to control robots and other machine elements in the game.

As this brief outline of the *Deus Ex: Invisible War*'s plot and gameplay demonstrates, this text—like a great many digital games which have FPS and RPG elements—is the ideal site within which to trace a critique of cyberpunk's posthuman fantasy because it both thematizes and actualizes the fantasy of corporeal abandonment. As the player traces through the narrative of the game, s/he is seduced into suspending his or her investment in a singular subject position, a singular interiority, and thus a subjective blurring occurs where the player "becomes," or is formally encouraged to become, the onscreen hero. The FPS perspective of the game, in other words, structurally encourages such an identification, an identification which initiates what Katherine Hayles calls the "distributed cognition" (288) of the posthuman.[4] But what is most important here in *Deus Ex: Invisible War* is the progressive biomodification of Alex D, who obviously serves as both avatar and *prosthesis* for the player. The player's subjective positioning is such that Alex's biomodification must become his or her own. The player, after all, is the one selecting which biomodifications to apply to his avatar. And the choices are complex: specific locations on the body—eye, skull, arm, leg—have three available upgrades: the leg biomod, for instance, works to increase speed, strength, and allows for health regeneration. Each of these specific biomods (for instance, "speed") in turn has three levels of upgrading available. Thus, part of the complex strategy of the game involves managing your resources effectively to maximize the lethal combination of biomodifications. In other words, in order to create the most powerful avatar-prosthesis a studied *economics* of bodily modification must occur.[5]

The avatar thus is the site of an enormously complex subjective splitting and blurring. In the case of *Deus Ex: Invisible War*, Alex D must bear the weight of the player's emotional and psychological investment in the narrative—Alex D serves the primary role of fulfilling the hermeneutical function of the game's plot—and he must realize the fantasy of cybernetic enhancement even as he, the game, becomes the player's virtual prosthesis extending the player's capacities beyond subjective boundaries. But we must notice that the avatar is more than simply an expression of the digital coding and logic of the game machine. That is to say, the avatar is not only a local effect of the game, not merely the "content" of the prosthetic form that is the gaming machine: the avatar serves a more complex role given that it is a subjective prosthesis (or what I wish to term a subjective prosthesis *event*) within the material prosthesis that is the game machine. We must, in other words, see the avatar-prosthesis as doubly-encoded, as material and virtual simultaneously. The avatar fulfills an emotional/psychological role as he stands in for the player in this enormously complex virtual world; but, as the "face" of the material prosthesis of the game machine—as, that is, the manifestation of what the game machine as prosthesis can do (extend the subjective and corporeal boundaries of the human)—the avatar becomes enormously resonant.

I wish to theorize the avatar-prosthesis as fulfilling the primary cyberpunk fantasy of escaping bodily and spatial limitations. To begin, it is useful to see how the cyberpunk fantasy of bodily escape functions as a pathologizing of the phenomenal body. William Gibson's *Neuromancer*, the *locus classicus*

of cyberpunk—and its various fantasies and anxieties—sees its main character, Case, figuring the body as a kind of "prison" (6) and cyberspace as a
paradisial escape from the "meat" that is the phenomenal body. The cyberpunk desire to step past the body, the body which now is pathologized, is
arguably the first step into a posthuman interiority. And while Gibson's
Neuromancer distills and thematizes this pathology in a particularly sharp
manner, we can trace the anxiety of the phenomenal body in any number of
(if not all) cyberpunk—or, to borrow from Stacy Gillis, "cyberpunked"[6]—
texts. The fictional work of J.G. Ballard (*Crash*, *The Drowned World*),
William S. Burroughs (*The Ticket Exploded*), Philip K. Dick (*Do Androids
Dream of Electric Sheep?*), Neil Stephenson (*Snow Crash*); the films of
David Cronenburg (*Videodrome*), Ridley Scott (*Blade Runner*), Kate Bige-
low (*Strange Days*), Tsukamoto Shinya (*Tetsuo: The Iron Man*), Oshii
Mamoru (*Ghost in the Shell*); digital games like *Phantom Dust*, or *Halo*;
even the cultural and literary theory of Donna Haraway ("A Cyborg Manifesto") or Cary Wolfe (*Animal Rites*) all share a fascination with the
limits, proscriptive because phenomenal (and, concomitantly, *ideological*),
of the human body. It is curious perhaps that some cyberpunk relentlessly
figures the recognition of the subject at and in the limits of space and the
body as pathological (one may argue that this recognition itself signals
the terminal pathology of cyberpunk itself), but once we recognize that the
means by which these limits are revealed *as* limits—the technological
means, precisely—we can better understand cyberpunk's sometimes dialectical negation of the body. It is as if there is a requirement to pathologize
the body in order to transcend the limits that technology allows us precisely
to see. That is to say, cyberpunk's fetishization of technology (and its
fetishization of the anxieties attendant *upon* that festishization) are the
grounds by which, through which, a concomitant pathologizing of the
subject-as-body occurs: technology reveals, if only and always phantasmi-
cally, what the subject, freed from its somatic restraints, can achieve.

This assertion that cyberpunk is grounded on a pathologizing of the body
may seem problematic when read against the work of feminist SF authors
of, especially, the early 1990s that, when read against the figuration of the
(male) body in, say, Gibson—or indeed, in *Deus Ex: Invisible War*—suggest
that the phenomenal, desiring, body is central to a dialectical understanding
of the attractions and dangers of cyberspace.[7] And of course there is a critical commentary coterminous with this literature suggesting that a uniform
fetishization of the cyber (body) over the real (body) needs radical interrogation[8] and that even in the entry into cyberspace the body, with its
obvious claims to the material and *materiality*, never fully disappears but
serves rather to re-articulate new understandings of what constitutes the
"real" body. With the possible exception of a handful of games (I am
thinking of the recently released *Bullet Witch* and *Perfect Dark Zero*
(a game with clear cyberpunk roots)) and the obvious, but nonetheless
problematic (and non-cyberpunk) *Tomb Raider* series, shooter games

(third-person or first) are overwhelmingly "told" from a male perspective and do, implicitly and explicitly, figure the body as a limitation—rather than a definitional threshold—and thus something to be altered, transcended, and erased.

Crucially, media critics Marshall McLuhan and Paul Virilio, whose work I draw on here, both theorize the prosthetic enhancement of the human as signaling a similar pathologized view of the modern subject. While McLuhan and Virilio will not necessarily valorize the prosthesis, both arrive at a position structurally similar to that held by Gibson's Case: the body is (becoming) pathologized and increasingly dis-abled by technology. In *Understanding Media*, for instance, McLuhan argues that the subject creates prosthetic enhancements as a somatic response to the threatening stimuli of modern life: these prostheses function as a kind of (metaphoric) self- or auto-amputation whereby the prosthesis itself bears the burden of the stimuli (the wheel, as prosthesis for the foot, bears the weight created by the increased need for transportation). McLuhan is most interesting when he turns to a discussion of electronic media; notice how the phenomenal body is figured as congenitally unable to withstand the burdens of contemporary culture:

> With the arrival of electric technology, man extended, or set outside himself, a live model of the central nervous system itself. To the degree that this is so, it is a development that suggests a desperate and suicidal autoamputation, as if the central nervous system could no longer depend on the physical organs to be protective buffers against the slings and arrows of outrageous mechanism.
>
> (43)

McLuhan presciently diagnoses the way modern technologies effect a change in the comprehension of the modern subject qua subject precisely as the machine begins to dictate the parameters of the real:

> Physiologically, man in the normal use of technology (or his variously extended body) is perpetually modified by it and in turn finds ever new ways of modifying his technology. Man becomes, as it were, the sex organs of the machine world.
>
> (46)[9]

McLuhan's startling metaphor explicitly links bodily alteration and desire, anticipating how the experience of the game, with its promise of freedom from the body, will itself always be articulated through the protocols of desire; McLuhan's metaphor also anticipates how the subject will find its desires, in some vital sense, dictated by the parameters of the game itself: freedom from the body, as I will argue, is only possible because the machine offers it.

Like McLuhan who sees the modern subject as perpetually threatened by and pathologically (and somatically) responsive to contemporary culture, Paul Virilio offers an alarmist reading of the way prosthetic technologies damage the subject. And his work is crucial to any theorizing of gaming if only for the attention he draws to what is lost during the process of assuming another subject position. And we should be clear that, for Virilio, modern technology always effects a massive loss of the real, bodily, subject. Televisual and virtual technologies—and I will add, gaming technologies— produce what, in *The Art of the Motor*, Virilio calls "metabodies" (119). The ability to act at a distance, to step past the parameters of the body, which as I am arguing, is the central attraction for the gamer, for Virilio produces a negative horizon which enacts a "splitting of the subject's personality" (106). The production of the metabody—in gaming terms, the *avatar*—is only ever a prelude to a massive, seismic, loss of what it means, ethically, to be and to act meaningfully in the "real" world (107).

In *Open Sky*—perhaps his most sustained, if cryptic, critique of contemporary technologies—Virilio makes an explicit link between technological bodily enhancements and disability: his claim ultimately is that modern technology, encroaching on the body in a manner structurally similar to colonial exploitation of the planet, creates the modern subject as a disabled subject. Virilio speaks of

> [The] urbanization of the actual body of the city dweller, this *citizen-terminal* soon to be decked out to the eyeballs with interactive prostheses based on the pathological model of the "spastic", wired to control his/her environment without having physically to stir: the catastrophic figure of an individual who has lost the capacity for immediate intervention along with natural motoricity and who abandons himself, for want of anything between, to the capacities of captors, sensors and other remote control scanners that turn him into a being controlled by the machine with which, they say, he talks.
>
> (20)

Virilio's logic may be slippery—his notion that the contemporary user of prosthetic technologies is "based" on a pathological model seems more provocative than provable—but his diagnosis of the modern subject as penetrated by, just as he penetrates, technology provides a resonant model of the cybernetic, cyberpunked, citizen. And it needs to be reiterated: the technological fantasies of cyberpunk and the critique of these precise fantasies begin and end with the image of the body as site of pathological weakness. Virilio's notion of the "body terminal" (11), the body as site of technological interface and as "end," calls to mind Bernard Stiegler's reading of the prosthesis: "the prosthesis is not a mere extension of the human body; it is the constitution of this body qua 'human' … It is not a 'means' for the human but its end, and we know the essential equivocity of this expression: 'the end of the human'" (*Technics and Time*: 152–53). Steigler's ideas here echo McLuhan's notion of the inevitability of the prosthesis, the fact that various technological media are shaping and "modifying" the subject, constituting him/her as "human"; Steigler's ambivalence about technology also clearly echoes Virilio's deep concerns that technology, by colonizing the subject—thus simultaneously creating and effacing a material boundary between human and machine—signals that the ends of technology are the end of the human.

The Body as Trajectory

Deus Ex: Invisible War clearly locates the body of Alex D as a site for manipulation and colonization. The biomods which serve to enhance Alex D's physical capabilities were created by the Tarsus Academy in order to facilitate Alex D's successful functioning as a servant of this military-capitalist corporation. As the game plays out, and the various capitalist and religious factions compete for Alex D's loyalty, it becomes clear that his body becomes the geographical site for this ideological battle. Alex D's body, a product of capital and thus perhaps a literalization of the idea of social construction, becomes a materialization of ideology just as his actions, through and within various geographical spaces, serve to materialize various competing ideological desires. And of course these geographical spaces (precisely simulacra of geographical spaces) are as socially constructed as the body itself, as Edward Soja reminds us.[10] It is crucial thus to note how *Deus Ex: Invisible War* thematizes various yet interconnected economies of spatiality: the body, colonized and disciplined technologically, moves through various geographic spaces themselves mapped out as a spaces of economic control. While I will return to a more specific reading of the game's thematization of the relation between capital and spatiality, I wish here first to consider how the digital game, in its exploration of space, attempts to instantiate a fantasy that is a crucial and connected concomitant to the fantasy of bodily liberation.

But of course initial questions must arise: what kinds of space do we encounter in the game? What sense of spatiality is being constructed in the gamespace?[11] For the player, the answer seems logical: we experience precisely a representation of space, a spatiality that is experienced only virtually. The character, diegetically, is experiencing his space as real, but, for the player, gamespace never rises to the status of reality. We must, however, realize that in a game like *Deus Ex: Invisible War* (as for many more) a character is never only ever a character; likewise a player is, as we have discovered, something much more than a mere distanced player. My interest here is thinking through the idea that the confluence of player-avatar must produce a realignment of the possible readings of the virtual space of the game, the virtual space that I wish to suggest, becomes real. If my theorizing of the immersive qualities of the game is accurate, if that is to say, the avatar-prosthesis in some ways becomes me, then spatiality must itself become something more than simply virtual.

The experience of space, as Maurice Merleau-Ponty has observed, is primarily a bodily experience, and thus we need to think through the implications of the avatar-player confluence which is, at some level, a bodily confluence:

> For us to be able to conceive space, it is in the first place necessary that we should have been thrust into it by our body, and that it should have provided us with the first model of those transpositions, equivalents and identifications which make space into an objective system and allow our experience to be one of objects, opening out on an "in itself."
>
> (*Phenomenology of Perception* 142)

I think one way to begin conceiving the space of the game is by recognizing its potently uncanny aspect.[12] In the first place, the avatar, being both me and not me, having been constructed by me and not by me, responding to my bodily commands and exerting its own agency (in the sense that the avatar can only act according to what the game programmer allows), is a perfect representation of the uncanny, indeed of the doubled and split interiority that Freud speaks about in his invaluable essay on the subject. This body, through which we now begin to experience the space of the game, is asked to be at home in a world that is, as I say, *diegetically* natural to the avatar but at least initially foreign, but increasingly, and crucially, mathematically *less so* to the player as he repeatedly, compulsively, explores space as the game proceeds: "Consciousness is being-towards-the-thing through the intermediary of the body. A movement is learned when the body has understood it, that is, when it has incorporated it into its 'world,' and to move one's body is to aim at things through it" (139). But gameplay consciousness is, of course, a doubled consciousness given that our phenomenal body is doubled by the avatar within whom, through whom, we learn to manipulate the uncanny space of the game as our *own*.

Merleau-Ponty thus describes perfectly the experience of the kinesthetically realized space of the game, space that in some senses is always already distributed across shared interiorities. In *The Practice of Everyday Life*, Michel de Certeau describes the primal joy of the child who, standing before a mirror, self-identifies as both whole and other to what she is. De Certeau's version of the Lacanian mirror phase is spatial; subjectivity is realized within space: "What counts is the process of this 'spatial capatation' that inscribes the passage towards the other as the law of being and the law of place. To practice space is thus to repeat the joyful and silent experience of childhood: it is, in a place, to be other and to move toward the other" (109–10). De Certeau's idea resonates into a reading of the experience of virtual space inasmuch as he, like Merleau-Ponty, identifies what is a crucial aspect of the game-player experience: becoming the (specular) other who now becomes me. His notion of "moving towards the other" is a way of making sense not only of the kind of subjective blurring and splitting that occurs in the game but as a diagnosis of the experience of space that occurs. Because it is always and primarily a kinetic experience of space in the game: there is nothing static about the various spatial explorations one experiences in *Deus Ex: Invisible War*; the avatar is constantly on the move, exploring spaces, from city slums, to nightclubs, executive apartment buildings, to airport terminals.[13]

Given that the player's identity or sense of interiority is defined as much by his/her extension into the avatar-prosthesis as by his/her extension into a kinetic spatiality, we can begin perhaps to think of the player as what Virilio calls the "traject." Virilio sees the human, historically, mapping its movements between spaces: here the "being's trajectory" (*Open Sky*: 25) is crucial in defining the subject as nomadic, as traject. In *Politics of the Very Worst*, Virilio speaks of his analysis of movement and space:

> I do not work on the subject and object—that is the work of the philosopher—but rather on the "traject." I have even proposed to inscribe the trajectory between the subject and the object to create the neologism "trajective," in addition to "subjective" and "objective." I am thus a man of the trajective, and the city is the site of trajectories and trajectivity. It is the site of proximity between men, then site of organization of contact. Citizenship is the organization of trajectories between groups, between men, between sects.
>
> (39–40)

It seems crucial, given the phenomenology of digital gameplay generally (which is defined primarily as movement through space) and given the narrative logic of *Deus Ex: Invisible War* particularly (which is all "about" Alex D moving through spaces negotiating his "trajective" relation between the various ideological "sects" of this post-Collapse world), to apply Virilio's idea of the traject to the experience of space in the digital realm, which, as I have suggested, begins *a priori* with a blurring of subject and object in the avatar, the "prosthetic event." In the following, Virilio defines the contemporary subject in relation to technology—telepresent technologies—in terms of loss; it strikes me that read from another perspective, his words offer a canny definition of the digital traject:

> The body proper is oriented with respect to the other whether woman, friend, enemy … but it is also oriented with respect to the world proper. It is "here and now," *hic et nunc*, it is *in situ*. Being is being present here and now. The question of telepresence delocalizes the position and orientation of the body. The whole problem of virtual reality is that it essentially denies the *hic et nunc*, it denies the "here" in favor of the "now."
>
> (*Politics* 44)

The loss of the sense of location, of the here (in Virilio's terms we are already dealing with loss and a kind of mourning in the experience of tele-presence and virtual reality), realigns our understanding of the subject. The "traject," as Virilio understands him, moves through the space of the city manipulating "trajectories and trajectivity" (*Politics* 40). I propose that his term can be applied equally to the uncanny avatar-player relationship in that the strange loss of the subject's sense of self, his or her loss of the *here* (which is in the logic of much cyberpunk is not a melancholic but, initially at least, a liberatory loss) is supplemented, indeed replaced, by the avatar who in his turn *becomes* the spaces he explores: the subject becomes digital traject as s/he is defined by his movement within and, to recall De Certeau, *movement towards*, the virtual space of the game.

POSTHUMAN MELANCHOLY

In *Politics of the Very Worst*, Paul Virilio argues that the benefits of technology are far outweighed by their costs. Virilio posits that advances in tel-etechnical and biomedical research come only at the expense of reducing the scope of our perspective of both the planet and the human body: the planet is reduced in size as teletechnologies, working at the speed of light, instantiate the global village with a vengeance; the human body, now colo-nized by nano (and other) technologies, becomes a space entirely commodi-fiable. While Virilio does not deny the medical benefits of technologies such as pacemakers, he does warn that "nothing is gained without loss" (54). I wish in the remainder of this essay to consider the various resonances of the idea of "loss" in the game experience. Because a game like *Deus Ex: Invisible War*, a game framed through the experience of loss—of the body, of a singular experience of space; and thematically, of a *world* itself—seems initially, if not ultimately, to valorize loss. Indeed the game's thematic of bodily enhancements—which from Virilio's perspective is a kind of loss—becomes the fetishistic point of interest in the *Deus Ex: Invisible War*: we play this game *because* we are offered the opportunity to move past bodily and spatial limits and boundaries. But I wish to suggest that *Deus Ex: Invisible War*—precisely as it distills this primal cyberpunk fantasy—asks to be read against the grain of its fetish. We need, in other words, to unfold a reading of the game which takes into account the way the game's various instantiations of melancholic loss—bodily and spatial—allows, indeed com-pels, a critique of the fantasy of liberation to emerge.

   Before moving into an analysis of the game's various figurations of mel-ancholy it may be useful to trace a brief trajectory of Freudian melancholia. In his 1917 essay "Mourning and Melancholia," Freud argues that mourning is "regularly the reaction to the loss of a loved person, or to the loss of some abstraction which has take the place of one, such as one's country, liberty, an ideal, and so on" (251–52). Successful mourning occurs when the subject removes his or her narcissistic identification with the lost object: by redirecting or displacing the libidinal energy previously invested in the lost object onto other objects the subject successfully works through the loss. Successful mourning occurs in other words when the subject accepts that loss as historical event, as something that has occurred in the past. Melancholia, on the other hand, is essentially an historical disorder: it reflects the inability of the subject to digest, metabolize, and move past loss. The melancholic is unable or unwilling to disavow her narcissistic attachment to the lost object and thus is continually bound to her loss, continually traumatized by historical events.[14]

In a crucial moment in his essay, Freud suggests that "the complex of melancholia behaves like an open wound" (262). In *The Ear of the Other*, Jacques Derrida elaborates on Freud's image of melancholia as bodily—thus spatial or at least *spatially realized*—symptom. For Derrida, melancholia, while functioning as an historical disorder, a disordering of history, works also to create an uncanny topography in the subject, a space where the claims of the past continually are made. Drawing on Abraham and Torok's notion of the melancholic crypt, Derrida offers a startling image of the melancholic:

> Now, what is the crypt in this instance? It is that which is constituted as a crypt in the body for the dead object in the case of unsuccessful mourning, mourning that has not been brought to a normal conclusion. The metaphor of the crypt returns insistently. Not having been taken back inside the self, digested, assimilated as in all "normal" mourning, the dead object remains like a living dead abscessed in a specific spot in the ego. It has its place, just like a crypt in a cemetery or temple, surrounded by walls and all the rest. The dead object is incorporated in this crypt—the term "incorporated" signaling precisely that one has failed to digest or assimilate it totally, so that it remains there, forming a pocket in the mourning body.
>
> (57)

It is crucial to note how *Deus Ex: Invisible War* works to code space *itself* as melancholic. Following Derrida, we may argue that space itself becomes melancholy when it encrypts signs of the pastness of the past, of loss as such. In *Deus Ex: Invisible War* almost every space bears witness to the Collapse that has created the world—physical and ideological—through which Alex D moves. In an early portion of the game's narrative Alex D must explore Seattle which has been divided into Upper and Lower sections. Upper Seattle, which maintains itself as the quintessential site of consumer success—it features high-end apartment buildings, nightclubs, the headquarters of the World Trade Organization—attempts furiously to erase all signs of the Collapse: capitalist world governments may have collapsed, the game suggests, but capitalism itself lives on (the four competing systems of this world thus become melancholic simulacra of an economy that *has been*).[15] Lower Seattle, which provides the literal foundations for the upper world, is, by contrast, decrepit and is marked clearly, physically, by the Collapse: this world, rife with danger and unregulated enterprise, functions obviously as Upper Seattle's repressed but never completely disavowed other. The economic work that goes on in Lower Seattle—illicit trade, bartering—supports the economy of the upper world. Upper and Lower Seattle thus maintain an economically symbiotic relation which marks both worlds as intimately connected to the lost—but now resurrected—capitalist economies of the past. The Collapse, in other words, sees the loss of the logic of capital and world government, but the world of 2052 maintains a link to that loss by maintaining a spectral, indeed *uncanny*, version of that economic and ideological structure. In its representation of the topographical and ideological arrangement of Upper and Lower Seattle, *Deus Ex: Invisible War* offers a blunt commentary on capitalism's persistently exploitative structure: by literalizing the separation of the moneyed elite from the disenfranchised worker, melancholy becomes spatially realized.

What I think is particularly brilliant in *Deus Ex: Invisible War* is the way in which these complex economic commentaries are materialized spatially, both in the geographic, topographic spaces of the game (Upper and Lower Seattle), and in the space of the avatar's body. As noted above, Alex D's body becomes a space of interest to the Tarsus Academy precisely as a resource and commodity: his body, colonized by nanotechnology, is transformed precisely into capital in much the same way as Upper and Lower Seattle materialize the exploitative structure of capitalism's economy. Capitalism thus at least at an initial level seems to be responsible for facilitating the posthuman, cyberpunk fantasy of transcendence: it is only because Alex D's body becomes materialized as capital, as resource and exchange value, that his subjective and bodily limitations are extended. And while I do not wish to read *Deus Ex: Invisible War* merely as a critical metanarrative about capitalism's cynical manipulation of the subject as exchange commodity, it is important to note just how central to the game is the idea that the posthuman subject is capital's melancholy *product*. More precisely, perhaps, the game realizes what is implicit about capitalism's logic: the body is there always to serve the needs of capital and thus Alex is not only a product but a realization of an economy already in place. The idea of bodily modification, which is held out to Alex as a benefit, a reward even, of serving the Tarsus Academy, really only functions to highlight (and then anxiously to elide) the truly artificial, the phantasmic binary, of natural/cybernetically enhanced body, a binary made tenuous with the realization, soon to be reached by Alex, that the so-called "natural" body—Alex before his cybernetic enhancements, for instance—is always already "modified" by the needs of capital in as much as he is simply part of capitalism's exploitative machinery. Capital, as articulated here specifically in the exploitative economy of the Tarsus Academy, requires this fantasy opposition in order to maintain itself as the system, the only system, able to efface and transcend that very binary. The fantasy of bodily transcendence, in other words, is itself grounded on a prior fantasy which cannot be exposed as such: hence the fetishizing of what can only appear to be a "natural" opposition between body and technology.

And if the Tarsus Academy attempts to maintain the opposition between natural and enhanced body in order to enhance its exploitative power, it also, crucially, attempts to maintain an equally phantasmic—and exploitative—opposition between itself and its apparent enemy, the Order. Because, as Alex discovers as the game reaches its conclusion, the two main competing systems in this post-Collapse world—the WTO and the Order—are in actuality working together (controlled by another group, the Illuminati) to maintain the economic and spiritual strife necessary to create a need, specifically an *economic* need, for their respective ideologies.[16] The WTO and the Order thus facilitate a war which serves to bolster an addiction to technology and to spiritual ideologies which continue that war and which serve to shore up the dependence of the people on a system that, unknown to them, is precisely responsible for their terror. Alex, in other words, is transformed into the spectral material of dead systems (capitalism and religion) that only *appear* dead in order to fight a war promulgated by capital for capital: he thus becomes the space, the melancholy space, of capital, precisely as his body is used in a deeply cynical way to continue ad infinitum what the game calls "the future war on terror."[17] Prosthetized and trajected by capital *into* capital, Alex's attentuated epiphany in the game can only be the realization of his radical and quite literal exchange value: trajected between what appeared to be shifting loyalties to the WTO and The Order, Alex has become the economic means by which his own absolute betrayal is articulated.

In a sense, thus capitalism's remains, its spectral traces, are responsible for the economic and ideological realities of the world of *Deus Ex: Invisible War*. Alex D, specifically, becomes a commodity with exchange value: as nanotechnologized, he is always already a spectre. Uncanny to himself, Alex D searches the various geographies of his world for answers as to what or who is responsible—in all senses of the term—for his transformation into the posthuman that he is. And thus Alex D—our avatar, our self—becomes a clear allegory of the player bound within the limits of *technology as ideology*, an allegory which is concretized as soon as the limits of the game's technological capabilities are reached.[18] The game, as outlined in the first part of this chapter, operates on the promise of the prosthesis: extending us past our limitations into the possibilities of other ways of being. Just as The WTO and The Order promise Alex the possibility of becoming more (only to discover this cynical manipulation that only serves to confine him within the strictly circumscribed boundaries of capitalism's logic), the game itself offers promises which only ever serve to delimit and define that extension. Alex's betrayal by the WTO and The Order is an essential reminder that the spectre of a dead system insistently returns to transform him into an objective correlative of its own (seemingly) effaced logic: Alex becomes, as I say, capital's object. And of course the player of the game—who, as I have suggested "becomes" Alex D—by coming up against the limits of that extension, the limits of the avatar-prosthesis, finds herself also at the critical, *phantasmic*, limits of the ideologies that support that extension.

Precisely because the game overtly figures the body as economic product, precisely, that is, as it overtly thematizes the idea of body as *materiality*, *Deus Ex: Invisible War* works paradoxically (or perhaps intentionally) to disavow one of the primary promises and desires of the conventional FPS game and thus of cyberpunk as I have been characterizing it: its promise and desire to construct a fully immersive experience and thereby step past the limits of the phenomenal, bodily, real. As I have suggested, *Deus Ex: Invisible War* would seem at one level precisely to mobilize the specific cyberpunk desires for bodily and spatial transcendence. The prostheses I am analyzing here—nanotechnology; the game machine itself—function at one level thus not as a melancholy and perhaps nostalgic reminder of some aspect of the body that has been lost (they do not function, in this sense, like a prosthetic limb), but as a *celebration* of loss as the player giddily moves into other subjectivities and spaces. However, this loss which initially is a perfect instantiation of cyberpunk *jouissance* becomes melancholic for the player when, as inevitably happens, the actual intrudes into the fantasy of escape and transcendence. These reminders of the actual—which always are reminders of the (real) body in (real) space—occur in a variety of ways. The logics of game mechanics—having to pause and go to screen menus for notes and reminders of goals; having to access subsections of Heads-Up-Displays (HUDs); having to save game progress; having to read dialogue exchanges between characters—all serve to pause the game and threaten the crucial sense of immersion. The death of the avatar—which in this context of player-avatar interface is a particularly traumatic and *inevitable* experience—is perhaps the ultimate and ultimately melancholic reminder of the real. What is lost here—what therefore is melancholic here—is the ability to remain for any sustained time in the game itself: the ultimate loss therefore is the *loss of the loss* of the real.[19]

A seamless game experience—one that does not have HUDs or the varieties of reminders of the game qua game—is perhaps a future reality, but the technology of *Deus Ex: Invisible War*, for instance, does not allow for a continually immersive experience. And of course by thematizing Alex D's betrayal by the various systems (or one system, in fact) which are responsible for his condition as posthuman, by making it clear that posthumanism, no matter how sublimely liberatory it may appear, is fully dependent upon a corrupt and corrupting technological ideology, *Deus Ex: Invisible War* offers itself as a commentary on this precise desire to transcend the limits of the human. And by explicitly—one might say, generically—linking the desires of Alex D to those of the gamer, *Deus Ex: Invisible War* serves always to remind the player of the technological conditions and limits framing his or her escape from quotidian subjectivity. If, this game asks, Alex D is a spectre, constructed out of the ashes of a dead yet persistent ideology, and if, as the logic of the game would have it, the player is the spectral double of Alex D, how do we not avoid the suggestion that our desires in this game—constructed and dictated precisely by the technological capacities of the game—are not equally phantasmatic?

CONCLUSION

A specifically Freudian reading of cyberpunk posthumanism would, finally, have to register the insistent return of the body in this system articulated by the logic of the prosthesis. This kind of melancholic return to the body and to space, produced as it is by the limits and limitations of technologies—one cannot permanently remain in the game—resonates with a keen irony given that the technology that allows the player temporarily to transcend subjective and spatial limits is the same technology which inevitably erases the immersive quality of the game by revealing itself as *itself* a limitation: the prosthesis negates and betrays itself.[20] I think there is an inevitable consequence of this negation, a consequence which read into the actual narrative trajectory of *Deus Ex: Invisible War* begins to look like another critique of the game's own condition as game and of a more generalized (cyberpunk) desire to extend the limits of the human. Because the extension of limits, working as it does to realign a definition of the human, works ultimately to fetishize and reify the thing being transcended. Just as the game's limited technologies fail to sustain the immersive quality of play and thereby reterritorialize the player in the actual, so too the prosthetic extensions of Alex D, even and especially as they are used in the various scenarios offered by the game's narrative, work as sublime reminders of the limits being transgressed. And it is precisely here, in the reminders of the real, as the contours of the real are exposed, that a kind of addiction, a fully melancholy addiction, occurs. If, for Freud, melancholy begins with an identification with the lost object, we must note, finally, how complex gaming melancholia is: the player begins with a celebratory loss of his/her sense of self (as singular interiority) becoming and identifying with the other, the avatar; through the logics of gameplay (mechanical interfaces, the death of the avatar) this other is lost and must—and will—continually, addictively, be sought.[21] Because it is only as the loss of the real is itself lost—when that is, we are returned forcibly to a sense of the actual world—that the desire to return to the extended spaces of the digital, to identify fully, narcissistically, with the lost object—me, the avatar—occurs.[22] The digital game in some ways is thus the perfect addiction given that the technology itself both seduces and withholds its pleasures by failing to sustain the illusion of the separation from the real: prosthetic technology in other words *provides and delimits* the escape thus ensuring a compulsive return to the game.

I suggested at the outset of this analysis that the digital game, instantiating the primal fantasy of cyberpunk—subjective and spatial transcendence—must be understood as a prosthetic "event." I mean by this that the game-as-prosthesis takes on a specific and unique singularity precisely because it is and can only ever offer a temporary liberation from the body and space, from the body *as* space. As event—as strictly demarcated temporal occurrence—the prosthesis-game works simultaneously as a liberation from "human" temporality and as a melancholic reminder that the posthuman moment (at least as articulated by the game) is only ever an event, a singularity always aware of its temporal limitations: posthumanism, in other words, is not a state of being but a temporary condition. And insofar as it is articulated in the perverse because impossible economy of this game, posthumanism is an addiction to a loss which by definition, *as loss*, cannot be sustained. What is crucial about digital gaming as cyberpunk event, finally, is its promise—and temporary realization—of a fully kinetic (not merely imaginative) realization of the fantasy of liberation; what in turn is fully melancholic about digital gaming is the way in which that fantasy of transcendence is always revealed precisely *as* a sublime fantasy, as a disavowal of that which inevitably returns.

NOTES

1 Gaming, as Scott Bukatman notes in *Terminal Identity*, represents "the most complete symbiosis generally available between human and computer" (196–97).
2 In *Culture After Humanism: History, Culture, Subjectivity*, Chambers writes: "To accept the idea of post-humanism means to register limits; limits that are inscribed in the locality of the body, of the history, the power and the knowledge, that speaks" (26).
3 There are numerous digital games—first- or third-person shooters, role-playing games—which explicitly acknowledge their indebtedness to what we could call the discourse of cyberpunk. There are, for instance, games explicitly derived from cyberpunk texts (*Blade Runner* (1997); *The Matrix Online* (2005) (a Massive Multiplayer Online Role Playing Game [MMORPG] released in 2005); games echoing the techno-fetishistic aspect of cyberpunk (the *Metal Gear Solid* series [1998–], the esteemed *System Shock 2* [1999]; *Project: Snowblind* [2005]; games thematizing the enhancement and transcendence of the phenomenal body (*Breakdown* [2004], the *Quake* series [1996–], especially *Quake 2* and *Quake 4*), the *Halo* series [2001–]). It is crucial to note, moreover, that the confluence of cyberpunk and gaming extends into other media. The visual imaginary that digital games make manifest can be traced into novels like Haruki Murakami's *Hardboiled Wonderland and the End of the World* (1985), Orson Scott Card's *Ender's Game* (1986), Melissa Scott's *Trouble and Her Friends* (1994), David Mitchell's *Number9Dream* (2003), or Steven Hall's *The Raw Shark's Text* (2007). Films like *The Lawnmower Man* (1992), *Disclosure* (1994), *Virtuosity* (1995), *eXistenZ* (1999), or *Stay Alive* (2006) all use the trope of cyberspace-as-gameworld in order to explore various thematic concerns.
4 N. Katherine Hayles. *How We Became Posthuman: Virtual Bodies in Cybernetics, Literature, and Informatics.*
5 See my discussion of a similar economics of the body in "Virtual Bodies: or, Cyborgs are People Too" in *Digital Gameplay*, ed. Nathan Garrelts.
6 In her Introduction to *The Matrix Trilogy: Cyberpunk Reloaded*, Stacy Gillis attempts to distance the *Matrix* films—and aspects of cyberpunk generally—from

the term "posthuman" which she feels "manages to obscure the unfinished debates surrounding the Enlightenment notion of the body" (4). Her term "cyberpunked" is mobilized as an attempt to avoid the "prescriptiveness" of the category "post-humanism" and to facilitate a discussion of texts not necessarily bound to the generic requirements of "cyberpunk" as such. Gillis' arguments suppose, of course, a stable generic definition of cyberpunk; while it is not the purpose of the present essay to offer such a definition (I am not convinced one is available or desirable), I do stand by my claim that an entry point into the cyberpunk text is the recognition of the various claims of the pathologized body.

7 I am thinkng, for instance, of Laura Mixon's *Proxies*, Mary Rosenblum's *Chimera*, Pat Cadigan's *Tea from an Empty Cup*, or Melissa Scott's *Trouble and Her Friends*. These texts argue that the body is the authentic site, or registry, of desire, desire which works in turn to define the subject qua subject. Moreover, the body is not the site to which one melancholically returns after the loss of a paradisal experience of cyberspace: Scott describes "netwalker" Cerise's return from cyberspace as the return to the "safety of her own home system, her own body" (16). Scott's careful acknowledgement of the body as a site of safety (it is still a "system" in opposition to the system of cyberspace) is miles away in tone from Gibson's figuration of the phenomenal body as "meat." In *Proxies*, Laura Mixon presents a carefully nuanced reading of the relation between phenomenal and simulated body that massively complicates the idea of stable, unique, interiorities (gendered, cultural, or otherwise); and while the proxy-body—the simulacrum into which consciousness is projected—is the site of fantasy and transcendence, the novel works towards the suggestion, and it is perhaps a politically conservative one, that the phenomenal body is the ultimate—and only—site of human authenticity.

8 See Thomas Foster's *The Souls of Cyberfolk*, Nicola Nixon's "Cyberpunk: Preparing the Ground for Revolution or Keeping the Boys Satisfied?", Anne Balsamo's "Reading Cyborgs, Writing Feminism" (later to become the first chapter of her important *Technologies of the Gendered Body*), Allucquere Rosanne Stone's "Will the Real Body Please Stand Up?", or N. Katherine Hayles' "How Cyberspace Signifies: Taking Immortality Literally," to name only a very few. In her crucial reading of Gibson's Sprawl trilogy, Hayles notes that discourses of the cyberspaced subject shift according to the gender of the subject producing differing "gendered topologies" (118): "In contrast with this male alienation from one's physical self is the immersion of the female character in their bodies" (118). It is clear that digital games have yet to produce the equivalent of a Cerise or a Trouble or to interrogate fully the implications of what Hayles calls male alienation from the body.

9 *In How We Became Posthuman*, Katherine Hayles offers three assumptions characterizing the posthuman. The third is as follows: "the posthuman view thinks of the body as the original prosthesis we all learn to manipulate, so that extending or replacing the body with other prostheses becomes a continuation of a process that began before we were born" (3).

10 In *Postmodern Geographies*, Soja offers eight "linked premises" summarizing his view of how space becomes ideology. The first three are as follows:

> (1) Spatiality is a substantiated and recognizable social product, part of a 'second nature' which incorporates as it socializes and transforms both physical and psychological spaces. (2) As a social product, spatiality is simultaneously the medium and outcome, presupposition and embodiment, of social action and relationship. (3) The spatio-temporal structuring of social life defines how social action and relationship (including class relations) are materially constituted, made concrete.

(129)

11 For a technical discussion of the mechanics of digital game space, see Mark P. Wolf's "Space in the Video Game" in *The Medium of the Video Game*.

12 There is much in Freud's essay on the uncanny which speaks to the issues under consideration here: the doubled interiority of the subject as he faces the doppelgänger; the idea of space and subjectivity being at once familiar and unfamiliar as the *unheimlich*; the way, crucially, the uncanny is articulated by a compulsion to repeat. As I suggest at the end of this analysis, the experience of gaming, which can become a compulsion, is a materialization of a specific kind of melancholy, *uncanny*, addiction.

13 In digital action games, the avatar is never still. Games like *Halo, Half-Life, Quake, Splinter Cell, Prince of Persia, Ninja Gaiden* or *Gears of War* define the avatar, in some ways, as movement itself, as Virilio's "traject." In fact, game makers play on the avatar's "desire" for movement: in *Splinter Cell*, for instance, your avatar (Sam Fisher) will turn and face the invisible camera behind him and give a look of impatience if left still too long; in *Prince of Persia: The Two Thrones*, your avatar, the Prince, taps his foot in boredom after a few minutes of stillness.

14 In "Mourning or Melancholia: Introjection *versus* Incorporation," Nicholas Abraham and Maria Torok suggest that the crypt contains the traces of trauma, the "objectal correlative" (130) of loss: "Inexpressible mourning erects a secret tomb inside the subject. Reconstituted from the memories of words, scenes, and affects, the objectal correlative of the loss is buried alive in the crypt as a fullfledged person, complete with his own topography" (130).

15 My intention here is not to suggest a difference between capitalist world governments and capitalism itself. As an economic system, capitalism surely does not require an organized nation-state in order to function. I am suggesting that capitalism, as a system founded on (often disavowed) economic exploitation, is uncannily persistent despite, perhaps because of, changes in nation-states and world governments. What *Deus Ex: Invisible War* explores—and perhaps critiques—is precisely the materiality of capitalism's persistence despite what appears to be a radical shift in politico-ideological realities: capitalism has a structural claim on the various competing agencies in this world, a claim transcending the ephemeral logics of (conventionally recognized) political ideologies. And is this not, in fact, one of the central tropes of cyberpunk? A large number of cyberpunk texts are set in post-governmental worlds where corporations rule in place of any recognized political system.

16 See Will Slocombe's discussion of this plot point in his "A 'Majestic' Reflexivity."

17 The discovery that the WTO and The Order are run behind the scenes by the same people can, as suggested, be read as a commentary on the complicity of opposing political systems. In the post-9/11 context, *Deus Ex: Invisible War* looks suspiciously like a dark commentary on the contemporary politics of fear in the US (and elsewhere), a commentary, that is, on the suggestion that US foreign policy has in some direct ways contributed to and created its own trauma. While this may be true, I think an equally compelling allegory of techno-ideological betrayal—one that supersedes contemporary political allegories—is being offered in *Deus Ex: Invisible War*.

18 It strikes me as a nice symmetry that Alex D's subjectivity is extended by capital in much the same way—though perhaps less ominously—as the player's subjectivity is extended by the product (the Xbox) of one of capitalism's great successes: Microsoft.

19 For an alternate reading of the digital game's failure to sustain immersion, see James Newman's *Videogames*, especially Chapter 5 (Videogames: Levels, breaks and intermissions).

20 I trace this melancholy in more detail in "Virtual Bodies; or, Cyborgs are People Too." The interference of the game mechanics leading to the cancellation of

immersion is what Alexander R. Galloway refers to as the "non-diegetic" element of the game: Galloway, borrowing from film theory, argues that the non-diegetic elements of the game "are often the very essence of the operator's experience of gameplay" (*Gaming: Essays on Algorithmic Culture* 14). This may be so, but these elements crucially—and critically—work to negate the game's potential for offering a sustained transcendence of the body and space which, as I am arguing, is truly the ultimate seduction of and reason for the game.

21 In *Crack Wars*, Avital Ronnel writes "We do not know how to renounce anything, Freud once observed. This type of relation to the object indicates an inability to mourn. The addict is a non-renouncer par excellence" (9). Addiction, insofar as it signals a refusal to renounce the narcotic which in itself intiates a variety of losses, is fully melancholic. Ronell uses the term "narcossism" (23) to account for the loss of interiority the narcotic initiates.

22 In "Playing at Being: Psychoanalysis and the Avatar," Bob Rehak nicely describes the avatar as a "desired and resented lost object, existing in endless cycles of renunciation and reclamation" (107).

Part III

The Politics of Embodiment in Cyberpunk

9 Feminist Cyberpunk

Karen Cadora

Rumor has it that cyberpunk is dead, the victim of its own failure to live up to its extravagant pretensions (Easterbrook, "Arc" 378). Initially touted as an imaginative engagement with the postmodern condition, cyberpunk envisions human consciousness inhabiting electronic spaces, blurring the boundary between human and machine in the process. Cyberpunk's deconstruction of the human body first appeared to signal a revolution in political art. However, closer examinations of the movement have revealed that its politics are anything but revolutionary. In his study of William Gibson's quintessential *Neuromancer* (1984), Neil Easterbrook concludes that the novel's worldview is "wed to exploitive technologies, obeisance to authority, and the effluence of fashion" (391). Furthermore, Nicola Nixon points out that cyberpunk is guilty of a "peculiar avoidance of rather obvious and immediate political SF precursors," namely, the feminist SF of the 1970s and 1980s and its exploration of gender relations (222). Cyberpunks are almost invariably male—hypermasculine ones at that—and, as a rule, they have little time for issues of sexual politics. As Veronica Hollinger has observed, cyberpunk "is written for the most part by a small number of white middle-class men, many of whom, inexplicably, live in Texas" ("Cybernetic" 207). It is these writers, and the critics who analyze their work, who have declared cyberpunk defunct.

Apparently, however, not everyone agrees with this diagnosis. In the last few years, several women novelists have arrived on the cyberpunk scene, and a flicker of life has reappeared in this otherwise moribund movement. This emergent body of work, which I will call "feminist cyberpunk" to distinguish it from earlier (masculinist) cyberpunk, blends the conventions of cyberpunk with the political savvy of feminist sf. This revolutionary blend points out new avenues for feminist sf and, ultimately, for feminist theory. Feminist cyberpunk envisions something that feminist theory badly needs: fragmented subjects who can, despite their multiple positionings, negotiate and succeed in a high-tech world. Literary theorist Robert Hodge points out that, even while they function as "systems of control which limit semiosis and the free production of meaning," genres also have the potential to become "the site of genuine resistance and a powerful extension of meaning" (31). Women writers have begun to use cyberpunk for just that purpose, resisting the conservative politics of their masculinist predecessors, grappling with the realities of technology, and exploring new forms for the subject of feminism.

Masculinist cyberpunk is very much a boys' club. The protagonists of cyberpunk novels are nearly always male. When women do appear, they hardly ever transcend feminine stereotypes. In the writings of the 80s, strong women characters are hard to find. Molly, the mirror-shaded and razor-fingered assassin who appears in *Neuromancer* and its sequel *Mona Lisa Overdrive* (1988), and Sarah, an assassin in Walter Jon William's *Hardwired* (1989), are two rare examples. But even Molly and Sarah, as Nixon argues, have been "effectively depoliticized and sapped of any revolutionary energy" (222). Tough though they may be, these characters aren't feminists. Sarah's only concern is making money and, when Molly becomes a bodyguard for a young girl, she is subsumed into a more acceptable quasi-maternal role (Nixon 223). Even when the central protagonist is female, as is the case with Laura Webster in Bruce Sterling's *Islands in the Net* (1988), it is difficult to see her as a heroine. Laura is rather helpless, "perpetually in need of rescue from prisons, would-be assassins, and terrorists" (Nixon 223). This is not a woman who pits her wits and hardware against the world; she is no feminist cyberpunk role-model. And beyond Laura, Molly, and Sarah, there are precious few female characters at all in cyberpunk.

The one consistent exception to this rule has been the work of Pat Cadigan, the sole woman novelist in the cyberpunk canon. Strong female characters like Allie in *Mindplayers* (1987) and Gina and Sam-I-Am in *Synners* (1990) are an important part of Cadigan's work. However, despite her admirable characters, Cadigan never fully engages with feminist concerns. Indeed, Jenny Wolmark argues that "gender relations are sidestepped by Cadigan" (125). *Synners*, in particular, frequently conflates technology and masculinity, leaving intact the typical cyberpunk depiction of women as Other. Her analysis of *Synners* leads Wolmark to conclude that "cyberpunk is fairly intractable as far as the representation of gender relations is concerned" (*Aliens* 126).

Wolmark's dismissal of cyberpunk as a forum for feminist concerns seems a little too hasty. While it is true that Cadigan replicates certain features of traditional cyberpunk and generally avoids overt feminism, she nevertheless does sometimes manage to subvert cyberpunk's masculinist conventions in important ways. Even if she hadn't, it would be unwise to abandon the entire movement simply because one woman writer fails to incite a feminist revolution. Feminist sf cannot afford to dismiss the potential of cyberpunk.

Women sf writers came into their own in the 70s and 80s but, as Joan Gordon points out, feminist sf has, in the past, been "characterized by soft rather than hard science, by emphasis on character and interpersonal relations" (197). Often, feminist sf replicates the cultural stereotype that equates technology with masculinity. Many feminist utopias—Sally Miller

Gearhart's *Wanderground* (1979), for example—depict pastoral worlds where women live in harmony with nature. Conversely, feminist dystopias often take as their starting point an oppressive patriarchal order obsessed with the technologies of war. Some forms of biological science are tolerated—as in Joan Slonczewski's *A Door into Ocean* (1986)—but hard science is frequently demonized, as if it were inevitably and eternally bound to patriarchy and oppression.

The tendency to avoid science also occurs in theoretical discussions of feminist sf. Some theorists look at feminist sf with an eye towards recuperating certain works from the debilitating stigma of genre fiction. Towards this end, Marleen Barr has coined the term "feminist fabulation," an umbrella concept that includes "feminist speculative fiction and feminist mainstream works by both men and women" (10). These works are united in that they all take "the insights of this century's waves of feminism as fictional points of departure" (11). While this classification is useful in many ways, it is limiting in others. In defending her choice of the term "feminist fabulation" over "feminist sf," Barr argues that "'science,' in the sense of technology, should be replaced by a term which has social connotations and focuses upon new sex roles, not new hardware" (5). However, the exchange that Barr imagines is not a simple replacement. As historians of science like Evelyn Fox Keller and Sandra Harding have aptly demonstrated, gender and science are not mutually exclusive categories. For example, one of the most common metaphors of modem science is the masculine pursuit of the feminized (and sexualized) object of "Mother" Nature.[1] In addition, science has been and is frequently used to justify differences between the sexes. Given these observations, it would appear that new hardware and new sex roles are not completely independent achievements. Hence, taking the science out of feminist sf strips the genre of its power to critique and reimagine the intersections of technology and gender. Sf provides a space for theorizing the future, near and far, and for imagining strategies for survival. Ignoring or dismissing the connections between gender and science will only cripple us as we attempt to negotiate an increasingly high-tech world. It is for this reason that cyberpunk can be useful to feminist visionaries. As Gordon puts it, "cyberpunk embraces technology" (199). Since any credible version of the near future includes computer-based technologies, cyberpunk opens up a space for feminists to imagine how "to shape and manage our futures rather than escape them" (Gordon 199).

Cyberpunk charts a course between utopia and dystopia. Most often set in the near future, cyberpunk imagines a world where technology is a tool of both oppression and liberation. Poverty is pervasive in cyberpunk, and technological resources are expensive luxuries. Those without access to computers are effectively kept in the underclass. New cyberpunk writers like Mary Rosenblum and Laura Mixon depict female characters who find ways to work around or within the system. Ruby Kubick, the protagonist of Mixon's *Glass Houses* (1992), supports herself and her lover by projecting her consciousness into robot waldos and hauling in salvage from places too dangerous to go in person. Rosenblum's *Chimera* (1993) follows Jewel Martina as she learns the nuances of electronic business. These characters appropriate and wield the technological tools necessary for survival.

These technically capable heroines are what Donna Haraway has called cyborgs, "hybrid(s) of machine and organism" (149). Now, the cyborg metaphor has enhanced and expanded many discussions of cyberpunk, and a paper on this topic would hardly be complete without some reference to Haraway's work. Yet what is often ignored about the cyborg is that it arose out of Haraway's desire "to build a political myth faithful to feminism, socialism, and materialism" (149). Masculinist cyberpunk is faithful to none of these. In fact, one might even say that it builds itself in opposition to these concepts. That Haraway's cyborg has become the metaphor of choice for such a movement is both strange and ironic.

This apparent contradiction resolves itself when one considers that there is more than one way to be a cyborg. As Haraway says:

> From one perspective, a cyborg world is about the final imposition of a grid of control on the planet ... about the final appropriation of women's bodies in a masculinist orgy of war. From another perspective, a cyborg world might be about lived social and bodily realities in which people are not afraid of their joint kinship with animals and machines, not afraid of permanently partial identities and contradictory standpoints.
>
> (154)

Thus, the image of the cyborg is one of both hope and terror. From one perspective, it is what dystopic feminist sf has so often predicted technology would bring us to: the total triumph of genocidal patriarchy.

Yet this is not the inevitable result of the meeting of human and machine, for cyborgs also hold the high-tech keys for survival. Cyborgs can ground a political vision in which identity is fragmented and contradictory, yet not without power. A cyborg is a multiply positioned subject enabled by technology. It is this side of cyborgs that feminists need to learn more about. And feminist cyberpunk writers have started to do just that. The advent of feminist cyberpunk is not just of interest to sf buffs in search of strong female role models and more hard science; feminist cyberpunk enables us to imagine ourselves as cyborgs—the second kind, the kind that survives and thrives, the kind that is faithful to feminism, socialism, and materialism.

Cyborgs are made possible, Haraway argues, by a blurring of three boundaries: between human and machine, between human and animal, and between the real and the unreal. The rest of this chapter is devoted to an examination of how different feminist cyberpunk writers blur these boundaries and to what effect.

The assault on the first boundary is a project shared with masculinist cyberpunk. It is, in fact, the primary convention of the movement.

Cyberpunk, according to Hollinger, is an antihumanist project that tries to break down "the oppositions between the natural and the artificial, the human and the machine" ("Cybernetic" 204). This breakdown makes it hard to distinguish where the human ends and the machine begins. In Mixon's *Glass Houses*, Ruby projects herself into waldos, receiving sensory input from them and controlling their movements with an electronic device connected to her brain. Because Ruby is terrified of going outside, her contact with the world is completely mediated by the waldos. She spends most of her waking hours plugged into them. Human and machine meld together, a fusion that is reflected in the doubling of prepositions: Ruby is "I-Golem" or "I-Tiger" or "me-Rachne" when she is linked to them. This doubling has curious consequences for Ruby's identity. In one instance, Ruby has to retrieve Golem from the police station. Since she can't control the waldo and her own body at the same time, she has to put herself in Golem's arms, and carry her body while her brain controls the waldo. A strange moment occurs when Ruby links to Golem:

> I-Golem looked down at the woman in my arms. It was Ruby-me, of course ... She-I looked so young and vulnerable from the outside, not ugly and scrawny like me. I was terrified that I wouldn't be able to keep her from harm.
>
> ("Ruby-Me" 61)

In this passage, Ruby effectively becomes Golem. She cannot reconcile the vision she has of herself with the body she sees through Golem's eyes. In the last sentence, she doesn't even use the double I-Golem. "I" now refers to Golem, and "her" to Ruby. There is no longer a distinction between the human Ruby and the machine Golem.

Although the breakdown of the boundary between machine and human is inherited from masculinist texts, some women writers use this convention in the service of subversive gender politics. In her discussion of the computer Net as a feminized and mystified space, Nixon points out that certain female characters in the texts of male writers like Gibson and Sterling need no computer hardware to interface with the Net. All they have to do is dream cyberspace; their bodies have a special electronic awareness. Men have to use electronic "decks" to interface with the Net whereas "certain females ... require no such mediation: they are already, by implication, a part of it" (Nixon 227). Women, in masculinist cyberpunk, have some mystical, corporeal connection with cyberspace. This would suggest that cyberspace is, by association, feminine in nature, something which becomes most apparent in the highly erotic imagery associated with entering the matrix. Nixon points out that male cyberpunks "jack-in" to the matrix, and that their goal is to penetrate the "hymenal membrane" of computer security (226). Equally telling is cowboy Case's real-world sexual experience, during which "his orgasm flar[ed] blue in a timeless space, a vastness *like a matrix*"

(*Neuromancer* 33; my emphasis). The vastness, however, is really Molly's body. In this case, entering the Net and the male experience of heterosexual intercourse are reciprocal metaphors; the Net is the electronic equivalent of a woman's body. Nixon argues convincingly that feminizing the computer matrix enables cyberpunk to avoid the possibility of homoeroticism (226). Populated almost exclusively by men and located in the male-dominated fields of computers, science, and sf, masculinist cyberpunk is ripe for the homoerotic. Sadly, fierce queens and flaming queers are absent from the pages of traditional cyberpunk. Indeed, cyberpunk is characterized by its rather rampant heterosexuality. Gay and lesbian characters are rare. In a genre which lacks female characters, strong and otherwise, it is necessary to construct a feminine space in which male heroes can establish and assert their masculinity. The feminization of cyberspace is necessary to insure that these male characters remain heterosexual.

Feminist cyberpunk refuses to feminize cyberspace in this way. In Cadigan's *Synners*, the intelligent "virus" that inhabits and controls the matrix is called Art(ie) Fish. The persona that Art simulates to interface with humans is "a composition of subtle and charming androgyny." Art is often referred to by a masculine pronoun, but as one user explains, she "was calling it 'he' on no basis other than arbitrary" (167). Moreover, Art's gender ambiguity appears to be contagious. When computer genius Visual Mark commits his intelligence to the matrix, he realizes that gender is no longer a fixed quantity: "he remained *he* in his own thoughts, though that too would change over time" (381). Thus, although Visual Mark fits into the tradition of male cyberpunks in some respects, his masculinity is not stable. This might have to do with the way that male characters like Visual Mark enter cyberspace. He achieves total immersion in the matrix by having "sockets" implanted into his brain. A socket is also referred to as "the female ... the receiver" (63). Instead of "jacking in," these cyberpunks plug wires deep inside their own brains. They are the penetrated, not the penetrating. Cadigan's male cyberpunks are automatically feminized by virtue of their entry into the matrix. This blurring of gender, however subtle, opens the way for other types of sexual interaction besides compulsory heterosexuality. Although the main characters remain avowedly heterosexual, other types of relationships are at least possible in Cadigan's universe. In fact, *Synners* opens with a distraught Jones—an interesting, albeit minor, character—mourning the absence of Keely, another male hacker and Jones' lover. In addition, the mergings that occur inside cyberspace are not always modeled on heterosexuality. Sockets are, after all, "the new sexual preference" (227). Visual Mark blends his awareness into Art, the two of them becoming a new entity called "Markt": "they might have been a couple consolidating their belongings as they moved into the same living quarters" (385). Mark and Art are settling down for an intimate and long-term relationship. When the Mark part of Markt sees his former girlfriend Gina with her new lover Gabe, he "felt a little sorry for them, since they would not be able to find each other as thoroughly as he and Art" (381). Cyberspace offers a union that transcends mere heterosexual intercourse.

Wolmark argues that the Markt entity is evidence that, in Cadigan's work as in other cyberpunk, "the metaphor of the interface is consistently used to establish 'masculinity' as universal and hegemonic" (*Aliens* 125). Yet this is not the only way to read Mark's entrance into the matrix and his fusion with Art. A more positive reading of *Synners* suggests that this might be a way to reverse the feminization of cyberspace that characterizes masculinist cyberpunk. If cyberspace is associated with androgyny, then it is not automatically a feminine space reserved for heterosexual male domination. The small but undeniable disruptions of gender and sexuality in *Synners* noted above are due, in part, to this refiguring of cyberspace.

A much more radical reconfiguration can be found in Mary Rosenblum's *Chimera*. Here, the matrix is explicitly identified with the male body. David, a cyberspace artist, is "netted," which means that he is covered, from head to toe, with electronic fibers that allow him to utilize his sense of touch in the Net. He is, essentially, in constant physical contact with virtual reality. David explains the process:

> they inject a dividing ovum with engineered epithelial cells. The fibers are actually part of my epidermis. They grow back if I get injured … The subdermal jewels and the primary interface chips are added later. They collect the signals from pressure, temperature, and muscle-tone changes, boost them, and transmit.
>
> (43)

This is no simple overlay that can be peeled off and tossed away. The hardware is an integral part of his body. The electronic fibers cannot be separated from human flesh. David needs nothing more than his body to enter the Net. He is, in essence, a part of it. Yet this is not a simple reversal of the gender binary that reinforces compulsory heterosexuality in masculinist cyberpunk. Rosenblum has no allegiance to the heterosexual paradigm. Several of the main characters who move through cyberspace are lesbian, gay, or bisexual. Indeed, the two most talented cyberpunks, Serafina and Flander, are exclusively homosexual. Moreover, the primary long-term love relationship in *Chimera* is between two men, David and Flander. Even though David has a one-night stand with Jewel after Flander dies, it is made clear that Flander is his true love. Rosenblum does not marginalize the homosexual relationship. David and Flander hug, kiss, touch, and make love. Homosexuality is not diminished or denied.

The appearance of explicit homoeroticism in *Chimera* marks a considerable departure from masculinist traditions. Cyberpunk written by women frequently acknowledges and includes homosexuality. *China Mountain Zhang* (1992) by Maureen McHugh is a novel that takes a gay man as its protagonist. In some ways, this novel typifies traditional cyberpunk: the young, talented, male outsider, Rafael Zhang, manipulates the Net to work his way into a system that rejects him. Beyond that, however, the novel departs significantly from the conventions of masculinist cyberpunk. Because Zhang is gay, there is no need for a femininized Net in which he can assert his heterosexuality. Zhang acts out the homoerotic potential built into this genre. Eliminating heterosexuality as a required element in cyberpunk ensures that there is no need for a gendered computer network and no restrictions on the gender of those who can work and play on the Net. The erotic play and gender interactions in feminist cyberpunk undermine the conventional notions of male and female upon which masculinist cyberpunk relies.

The subversion of heterosexual male privilege has serious implications for notions of reproduction. Nixon points out that adventures in masculinist cyberpunk often end when the "triumphantly masculine hero returns to a romanticized rural life" (229). Gibson's console cowboy Case settles down with a suitable *wife—not* the razor-fingered Molly—and has lots of kids. William's *Hardwired* ends with Cowboy and Sarah on "a weathered old Nevada dude ranch," trying to "ease into the peace, into each other" (335, 337). Even Pat Cadigan sometimes falls into this pattern. The epilogue to *Synners* has Gabe comfortably installed in a rustic house by the ocean with a fine view of a nearby underwater farm. He is soon joined by his new love interest, Gina, and his daughter, Sam. The heterosexually correct family model is reaffirmed. However, this is by no means the only possible ending.

Ruby, the waldo runner in *Glass Houses*, is tormented by her lust for her roommate, Melissa. A one-night stand turns Ruby into a "Melissa junkie" (153). Unfortunately, Melissa only sleeps with rich men, and Ruby, besides being female, is poor. When Melissa betrays Ruby, Ruby finally comes to her senses and sees that she is "growing beyond my need for her" (211).[2] The book ends with a hint of potential romance between Ruby and the attractive police captain Sheila Nanopoulos. Ruby stops trying to deny her sexuality and begins searching for a more suitable partner. There is no heterosexuality in sight, no family farm on the horizon.

In Rosenblum's *Chimera*, heterosexual reproduction is present and possible, but never preferred. Jewel, the heroine, is not the product of heterosexual union. Although she was carried to term by Serafina's lover, Jewel is, gene for gene, Serafina's clone. Serafina, a lesbian, did not want her offspring tainted by sperm. Replication, not biological reproduction, is the key concept here. The novel ends with Jewel starting her own family: she adopts Susana, the rebellious young daughter of her best friend Linda. The two of them form another non-traditional family. Alternative images of reproduction are also present in Cadigan's *Mindplayers*. Allie, after finally coming to terms with the strange mental states that result from her forays into cyberspace, tells herself that "You're not the same Allie you were. But you *are* Allie just the same" (275). These musings make her wonder if she is suffering from "post-partum depression" (275). She has, in effect, just given birth to herself. These examples support Haraway's observation that "cyborg replication is uncoupled from organic reproduction" (150). The intrusion of technology shifts the erotic away from heterosexuality and reproduction away from the body.

In examining the ways in which feminist cyberpunk subverts certain notions of gender and sexuality, it is important to keep in mind that compulsory heterosexuality is still a powerful and frequently oppressive institution in these novels. Although the advancements in human–computer interfaces allow women cyberpunks to project their consciousness into cyberspace and other electronic constructions, the female body is not easily disposed of. Poverty, a pervasive aspect of all cyberpunk, often translates into prostitution and forced reproduction when the characters are female. In *Glass Houses*, Ruby is part of the underclass; her shabby waldos barely bring in enough salvage for her to survive. Others are not even that fortunate, including Ruby's roommate Melissa. Ruby explains that she pays the rent for both of them because "I had a way to earn money; she didn't, except by spreading her legs" (29). Despite the advanced technology of the day, prostitution is one of the only sources of income for women without education. Another option, as illustrated in *Chimera*, is professional surrogate motherhood. A surrogate mother is able to support herself and her family by having "one infant per year, until her body could no longer perform" (101). Jewel fights her way through the system to become a medical assistant, a job only slightly higher on the social scale than surrogacy. Yet even as a medic, Jewel cannot escape her body. When she refuses to allow her employer to impregnate her, he fires her.

For women, the realities of the flesh are all too present in the imperfect world of cyberpunk. Because of this, embodiedness is a central issue in feminist cyberpunk in a way that it is not in masculinist cyberpunk. In *Neuromancer*, for example, Case moves through cyberspace as a disembodied gaze that sees from nowhere.[3] But female characters cannot assume a disembodied gaze, even in virtual reality. They are tied to their bodies in ways that male characters are not. It is not surprising, then, that almost all feminist cyberpunk depicts virtual reality as a space that must be navigated with a body of some sort. This convention is upheld even in feminist sf where the projection of human consciousness into machines is not the central concern. Marge Piercy's *He, She and It* (1991), for example, focuses on what happens when Yod, an android with highly sophisticated artificial intelligence, crosses the boundary into humanity; cyberspace is only marginally relevant to the main story. Nevertheless, when Piercy's characters do enter "the Net," they automatically "project" their bodies. As Shira and Malkah discover, these virtual bodies are completely malleable. Malkah, for example, can change her projected self-image to that of a "natty man," an "armored mining machine," or even a "large furry mole" (267). However, when she tries to make her body invisible, she finds that the best she can do is to be "less visible—a personal fog" (268). Only Yod, the male android, can project himself "'as transparency" (267). Malkah and Shira, two human women, always retain some visible form. In this book, as in much feminist cyberpunk, the female characters who escape from poverty by living through their minds—and, by extension, through electronic net-works—take with them some reminder of what it means to be embodied humans.

The question of embodiment has been addressed in a real-life experiment conducted by a research group led by Brenda Laurel, author of *Computers as Theatre* (1991). Together with Rachel Strickland and Rob Tow, Laurel directed Placeholder, a project that created an interactive virtual reality environment, incorporating elements of drama theory to make the most of their state-of-the-art computer equipment. In a 1993 lecture at Stanford University, Laurel, Strickland, and Tow reported that they had discovered an interesting gender discrepancy in the course of their research: in general, women preferred to have bodies in virtual reality and men preferred not to have them. Since part of their project was to "problematize issues around body and gender *in the realm of the senses*," they designed the virtual environment so that every participant had to adopt a body upon entering the space ("Placeholder" 125). Participants could choose to be a Snake, a Bird, a Fish, or a Spider by touching a representative icon. These bodies were, in fact, "smart costumes" that "changed how a person looked, sounded, moved and perceived the world" (122). Laurel deliberately chose bodies that were not human, or even mammalian. She and her colleagues "did not want the body in the virtual world to be taken for granted" (121). It was her hope that a completely foreign animal awareness, by its very strangeness, would recall what it means to be an embodied human. Laurel describes these choices as part of what she calls "our 'body politics'" (122).

Laurel's notions of "body politics" are of interest here because animal forms are frequently incorporated into human identities in the fictional worlds of feminist cyberpunk. In *Glass Houses*, two of Ruby's waldos are modeled on animals. Rachne (as in arachne) is a "spider waldo" with eight legs and a dislike for water. Tiger, who fits in the palm of a hand, has two talons and exceptional hearing. Ruby affectionately refers to Tiger as her "crippled, bowlegged, mechanical rodent" (103). The waldos have animal personalities that are loosely associated with their abilities. When Ruby links with them, she becomes "I-Tiger" and "I-Rachne," part beast in her identity. A more striking example of animal personas occurs in Rosenblum's *Chimera*. In virtual reality, everyone takes on a "Self," a virtual representation of his or her person. Most Selfs are modeled on the body of the user or whatever vintage body is currently in vogue (for exam-ple, Lauren Bacall). But the true wizards of the Net don't bother with human representations. Serafina, an expert in virtual reality piracy, is a mountain lioness in the Net. Flander, one of Serafina's few peers, wears a little red fox with green eyes. This Self suits him so well that Jewel constantly refers to him in real life as "the fox." Flander and Serafina are completely animal-identified. Talented beginners have personas that are part human and part animal. Susana, a novice pirate, is a "striped gray and orange cat with a whiskered human face" (108). Susana is good, but she isn't anywhere near Serafina's level. Serafina always refers to her, patronizingly, as "kitten." Ability in the Net, then, is reflected in the purity of one's animal Self. The more adept one is in cyberspace, the less human the Self will be.

The intrusion of such animal personas has few precedents in masculinist cyberpunk. On the rare occasions that animal identities do appear in traditional cyberpunk, they are used to represent repressed violence or evil forces. The snake that George Jordan thinks controls his brain in Tom Maddox's "Snake Eyes" (1986) is really a representation of Jordan's programmed need to kill. In Walter Jon Williams' *Hardwired*, Sarah's "Weasel" is a deadly weapon that retracts into her throat when not in use. These "animals" are internalized symbols of the desire to destroy. Thus, the incorporation of creative animal personas in feminist cyberpunk is a significant departure from traditional cyberpunk.

How are we to interpret the appearance of positive animal forms in fictional as well as actual feminist conceptions of cyberspace? In one sense, these examples could be taken to exemplify the blurring of the second boundary transgressed by cyborgs:

> The cyborg appears in myth precisely where the boundary between human and animal is transgressed. Far from signaling a walling off of people from other living beings, cyborgs signal disturbingly and pleasurably tight coupling. Bestiality has a new status in this cycle of marriage exchange.
>
> (Haraway 152)

In cyberspace, humans can compose identities that incorporate animal forms instead of opposing them. However, this kind of interpretive framework raises serious questions. In particular, what are we to make of the fact that the "animal" part of this blurring always exists in the realm of the electronic?[4] Without the biological otherness of real bodies, are virtual animals really animals at all? Given that the proliferation of technologies is directly related to the extinction of countless species, the lack of "real" animals in cyberpunk is a potentially sinister absence.

The status of animals in the age of electronic representation is not an issue that can be easily resolved. However, there are more optimistic interpretations of electronic animal presence in feminist cyberpunk. Brenda Laurel, for example, argues that virtual reality is not "'the enemy of the greens'" but rather a medium that "can raise consciousness about the natural world by giving people remote first-person access to places on the earth" ("Art" 1). Analogously, animal personas need not be thought of as artifacts of endangered or extinct creatures, but rather as ways of establishing connections that might help prevent such extinctions. Furthermore, one could argue that feminist cyberpunk improves on some other feminist sf in that it acknowledges a love for the organic without making an essentialist connection between nature and the feminine. Because technology is the medium through which the transgressions occur, electronic animal personas in feminist cyberpunk do not signal innocent longings to return to Mother Nature. Rather, these personas hint at the ironic but potent links between embodied humans and endangered species.

The last boundary that cyborgs transgress, the one between the real and the unreal, is the most potent place for a reconfiguration of reality and a reconstruction of the subject. The proliferation of human consciousness in cyberspace takes reality beyond the limits of embodied existence. Immortality becomes possible in electronic realms. The title character of Cadigan's short story "Pretty Boy Crossover" (1987) is offered the chance to "live as sentient information" (111). Ultimately unwilling to "cross over," the Pretty Boy resists the temptation of this "exalted" and eternal electronic existence (112). For others, however, the lure is irresistible. In Cadigan's *Synners*, Visual Mark longs to escape the prison of his "meat" body. Bit by bit, he leaves his body for the limitless expanse of cyberspace. In the process, Mark feels "better than fantastic. He felt *unreal. Unfucking-real*" (232). A similar event occurs in Rosenblum's *Chimera*. Flander gets so deeply into the Net that he can't find his way back to his body. Neglected, his body dies, but the fox still roams the Net. Like Visual Mark, Flander has translated his soul into software code and silicon chips—the ultimate in mechanical contamination. Interestingly, the characters that do choose electronic resurrection are invariably male. Women either cannot or will not do this. Despite intense pressure from her ex-lover Mark, Gina ultimately refuses to relinquish her body because "only the embodied can *really* boogie all night" (*Synners*, "Epilog" 433). The kind of experience she values cannot be found in cyberspace.

Yet female characters do expand the boundary between the real and the unreal, with results that are more startling than the electronic reincarnations of Visual Mark and Flander. One of the most troubling characters in *Chimera* is Serafina, Jewel's clone-mother. Serafina is a trickster with terrific powers. She can change her shape, control the wind, and even possess Jewel's body. Serafina explains, "Myself, I have found that there are no certainties. You may do anything if you are able to grasp the possibility" (238). Later in the novel, Jewel has a long conversation with Serafina, only to discover that the woman was shot dead several days earlier. Like Visual Mark and Flander, Serafina's spirit lives on after her body dies, but Serafina, like Gina, is not willing to settle for life in cyberspace. Instead, Serafina haunts Jewel's awareness, "wanting life, wanting entrance," threatening at every moment permanently to take over Jewel's body (307). Serafina can shape the fabric of reality in the way that others shape virtual reality. She has uncovered the big secret: "reality is as manipulable as the Net" (273). Other people are simply too sure of their little realities to grasp the power. Even David, the "netted" cyberspace artist, limits his reality strictly. He sees his dead lover Flander in the Net but refuses to believe that it is anything more than a ghost in the machine. David "had been hurt too badly to let Flander become real" (324). Flander could be real to David if he allowed it. Reality, then, is a matter of will and belief. Only Serafina has learned how to manipulate all its dimensions.

The blurring between real and unreal has profound implications for notions of identity. Stable, coherent concepts of self are impossible if there is no universally consensual reality upon which to ground them. Feminist cyberpunk is full of fragmented and partial selves. Jewel is ultimately able to outwit Alcourt only because she lets Serafina take over her body. It is an agonizing decision for Jewel because she risks losing herself to Serafina forever. Her consciousness wins out over Serafina's in the end, but Jewel comes to realize that she is not completely free of her nemesis: "Serafina was part of her, and Elaine's pain, and the Linda who loved her. We are all so many people ... a patchwork of our past" (Rosenblum 321). This is ultimately how Jewel comes to understand the reality of Flander's disembodied existence in the Net: "Flander's a patchwork, too: memories of flesh, thoughts formed of electrons in silicon, and his soul ... of whatever dreams are made" (324). This signifies a complete deconstruction of the body. People are made of bits and pieces—human, animal, mechanical, and mystical pieces that loosely coalesce into a self. Interestingly, this novel gives that construction of identity a moral imperative. All the "good guys"— David, Jewel, Flander, Susana, Serafina—are patchwork people. They are all part of each other, linked by kinship, friendship, and need. The "bad guy" in this novel, Harmon Alcourt, is the one who can't let go of his rigid notions of identity. Alcourt, an aging man fearful of losing his power on the Net, creates a ruthless computer persona, his "Self," to carry out his business. The Self has no compunction, no moral sense. The Self orders David's torture and tries to assassinate Flander, something that the flesh Alcourt couldn't bring himself to do. Alcourt completely dissociates his own actions from those *of* the Self. After Flander and Jewel/Serafina destroy Alcourt's Self, Alcourt tries to explain: "Don't be mad at me ... He did it. I didn't; he wasn't me. I had to let him do things his way or they'd have eaten us" (309). Alcourt doesn't want to be polluted or controlled, so he creates the Self and gives it an autonomous life. The Self's sole directive is to keep Alcourt from being contaminated by others. The irony is that, in his effort to avoid being consumed and controlled by others, Alcourt is possessed and consumed by an even greater evil. When the Self is destroyed, Alcourt commits suicide, unable to live without it. Confronted by a similar problem, Jewel chooses pollution, and so survives. Ultimately, she reclaims Serafina as her

"Mother. Sister. Self'" (307). Terrified of being possessed by Serafina, Jewel nevertheless manages to integrate Serafina into her person, and emerges as the victor over Alcourt.

Pat Cadigan's works also revolve around notions of fragmentation and coalition. In *Synners*, the Net is threatened by a "spike" of destructive energy that enters cyberspace when Visual Mark's body has a stroke while he is plugged into the system. This "spike" is akin to Visual Mark's evil alter-ego. Defeating the spike requires merging identities and forging alliances. The first merger is that between Visual Mark and Art into Markt. Yet Markt cannot defeat the spike alone, so Gina and several others enter the system. In the middle of the battle, Gina realizes how completely her life is intertwined with all the rest: "*that'll teach you to glory in your* separateness, *your precious* aloneness," she thinks to herself (424). There is no single heroine or hero in this struggle. Success depends on the interaction of many different kinds of people—male, female, human, artificial, viral, real, and unreal.

The fragmentation of identity is a central theme in Cadigan's earlier work, *Mindplayers*. The heroine, Allie, is a pathosfinder; her job is to help artists "move past irrelevant and superficial mental trash to the real feeling, the real soul" (198). She and her client connect to a central computer system via sophisticated electronics that plug directly into their eye sockets. Allie can then interface with the client's psyche and begin work. What happens inside the machine, however, is not nearly as interesting as what happens in Allie's brain. Each time she "mindplays" with another person, she finds that her own psyche is permanently altered. After a particularly difficult session, Allie has to go very deep into her own mind in order to establish what is real and what is not. In her mind, she discovers the people with whom she has mindplayed, talking and carrying on as if they had an independent existence in her brain. Allie is frightened by one person especially, a man who died while mindplaying with her. She says, "I wanted to learn how to separate myself from him" (271). But the truth which she discovers is that "if you try to cast it out, you'll end up crippling yourself" (271). At the climax of her reality "affixing," Allie comes to realize she must "Choose: A whole self, or just an accumulation of elements that soon wouldn't be more than the sum of their parts. Madness. Fragmentation" (272). Allie chooses the state of existence that is her "whole self," even though, in reality, it is a conglomeration of different parts and different people.

This fragmentation of identity has physical manifestations. Many of the characters in feminist cyberpunk live on the margins of race. Zhang, from *China Mountain Zhang*, is half Chinese and half Latino. In his world, only genetically pure Chinese can achieve full privilege. Being born in America to a non-Chinese mother severely limits his career options, forcing him always to find the back way into the job he wants. In *Chimera*, Jewel is of mixed ancestry, a little "too Hispanic" to pass in white neighborhoods, but white enough to work for Alcourt (93). Her friend David is half Chinese, half Anglo-American. Such distinctions are crucial in a place where ethnic neighborhoods have boundaries that are "more real than most international borders" (93). These characters have some connection to both the dominant race and an oppressed one, but they don't fit comfortably within the limits of either. They are always negotiating from two different racial subjectivities, fragmented and marginalized.

The issue of race is, in fact, very much at the forefront of cyborg consciousness. One of the first political cyborg identities that Haraway discusses is a product of the theories and practices of women of color. Neither white feminism nor race-oriented civil rights movements have addressed the multitude of oppressions that non-white women face. Women of color have multiple, sometimes conflicting, identities (Haraway 155–57). Recently, feminist theorist Norma Alarcon has argued that the future of feminist theory rests, in part, on "a reconfiguration of the subject of feminist theory, and her relational position to a multiplicity of others" (359). No single identity suffices to build a feminist movement because the category of gender is inevitably constructed within the context of race and class. The subject of white feminism is often "autonomous, self-making, self-determining," whereas many women are not (Alarcon 357). For those who suffer under multiple oppressions of race, gender, class, sexual orientation, disability, and so on, that kind of feminist subject just won't do. Feminism must do away with the idea of "woman" and find another subject from which to build coalitions and act politically.

This is where feminist cyberpunk comes into the picture. According to Haraway, feminist sf writers have the potential to be "theorists for cyborgs" (173). The identities represented in feminist cyberpunk are fragmented and unstable, just the kind of identities with which feminism must come to terms. Feminist cyberpunks are all dealing with the divisive issues of gender, race, class, and sexuality. There is no essential "woman" in feminist cyberpunk. In fact, the blurrings of human–machine–animal and reality–fantasy mean that there is no identity that is essentially or uniquely "human." Feminist cyberpunk writers have gone far in demonstrating what a cyborg, a multiply-positioned subject, might look like. More than that, they show how cyborgs can function in the world. This is crucial. Feminism has been slow to let go of the subject of "woman" because letting go of that term means letting go of a politics of unity. For a long time, feminists have assumed that unity is the sole basis upon which to build opposition to masculinist oppression. But cyborgs like Jewel show that one can have a fractured identity and still function in a high-tech world.

Contrary to the rumors, then, cyberpunk is not dead. Or, at least, not all forms of cyberpunk are dead. In this way, the movement embodies the contradictory impulses—apocalypse and survival—of Haraway's cyborg world. Masculinist cyberpunk has embraced its own annihilation while feminist cyberpunk continues to create new configurations of technology, gender, sexuality, and race. In light of this, the loudly mourned "death" of cyberpunk and its abundant postmortems are curious, indeed.

Speaking of another much-celebrated death, Nancy Hartsock asks:

> why is it that just at the moment when so many of us who have been silenced begin to demand the right to name ourselves, to act as subjects rather than objects of history, that just then the concept of subjecthood becomes problematic?
>
> (163)

In the same spirit, I ask the following question: why is it that cyberpunk, a movement with the potential to deal with the fragmentation of the subject, becomes obsolete just at the moment when women writers begin to explore the connections between race, gender, sexuality and cyberspace?

ACKNOWLEDGMENTS

Reprinted from *Science Fiction Studies* 22.3 (November 1995): 357–72© by kind permission of the author and *Science Fiction Studies*.

NOTES

1 See Keller's *Reflections on Gender and Science* and Harding's *The Science Question in Feminism*.

2 For books in which the chapters are not numbered, the reference bracket includes the chapter title.

3 Case does, however, find himself in a male body when the god-like Artificial Intelligences (AI) are trying to communicate with him. It is very curious that when these encounters occur, Case's real body turns off and his brainwaves "flatline." Having a body implies death. In any case, these instances are an exception to the rule. When Case does have a virtual body, he is at the mercy of the AI. He has no real agency, no ability to move in cyberspace.

4 As discussed later in this chapter, Serafina, in Rosenblum's *Chimera*, may be an exception to this, since she takes the mountain lionness form in "real" life as well.

10 Woken Carbon

The Return of the Human in Richard K. Morgan's Takeshi Kovacs Trilogy

Paweł Frelik

When in the 1980s and 1990s cyberpunk stormed through science fiction worlds and became the object of much critical attention and theorization, one of the flagship elements of its vision of near-future (post)humanity was the digitization of human consciousness foregrounding a Cartesian mind/body duality. In fact, however, very few canonical cyberpunk texts explored short- and long-term ramifications of the digitally-transferable identity and none really offered its sustained discussions. Richard Morgan's trilogy—*Altered Carbon* (2002), *Broken Angels* (2003), *Woken Furies* (2005)—rectifies that absence but, in the process, departs from and undermines not only the Cartesian paradigm but cyberpunk aesthetics at large.

Morgan's narratives are set in a far-future galactic hegemony known as the Protectorate, ostensibly a democratically-governed and economically-driven political entity. The Protectorate was largely made possible and is held together by the technologies left behind by the ancient race of Martians, who exited the now human-controlled space at least 500,000 years prior to the commencement of *Altered Carbon*. The three volumes trace what for all purposes can be called the adventures of the titular Takeshi Kovacs, an erstwhile member of the elite Envoy Crops, shock-commandos maintaining order on the Settled Worlds. In the trilogy-opening *Altered Carbon*, as part of a parole deal, Kovacs becomes an investigator in a puzzling murder/suicide case on Earth involving Laurens Bancroft, an influential politician and businessman representing an aristocracy-like class of "Methuselahs" who have benefited the most from life-extension technologies. In *Broken Angels*, he is recruited into a private enterprise of recovering a Martian artifact on the war-ravaged planet of Sanction IV. Backed by an aggressive corporation, Kovacs and a group of special ops have to face both military and political threats. In *Woken Furies*, he becomes involved in an insurrection against the oppressive regime on his home Harlan's World. Even these brief summaries reveal that Morgan mixes various genre influences, including elements that distance the novels from Gibson's near-future cyberpunk poetics as defined, for example, by McHale or Hollinger, in favour perhaps of Sterling's far-future cyberpunk poetics. While the general background of a galaxy-spanning political entity suggests space opera tradition, individual novels engage other specific conventions—*Altered Carbon*, the futuristic noir; *Broken Angels*, the military novel; *Woken Furies*, a political discourse—which further complicates the identification of the novels with any single SF school. Morgan's trilogy is for all purposes firmly rooted in cyberpunk aesthetics, because of both its construction of human subjectivity and its focus on the areas which have been traditionally asserted to be emblematic of cyberpunk.

In canonical cyberpunk, the digitization of personality was the conceptual cornerstone of narratives and manifested whenever human operators interfaced with virtual environments, but the actual technology behind the process was rarely invoked, not to mention explained. In Morgan's fiction the technology receives far more attention. Central to it is the cortical stack, a small chip implanted in the upper spine at birth, which contains an accreting sum of personality, memories, and experience. As a container of everything that is permanent about individual subjectivity and that can be carried between subsequent sleeves, the stack becomes the metaphor of the subject and effectively the subject itself, although the physical chip merely houses the actual data constituting the mind. On the other hand, the stack is also an object—when disembodied, a stack-encoded personality becomes a commodity which can be exchanged, handled, and destroyed. An unfitted stack also entails the lack of consciousness of the recorded data, the state which even further contributes to its status as chattel. This commodification is best visualized in the Soul Market warehouse scene in *Broken Angels*: stacks of fallen soldiers are moved with cargo loaders and sold by weight to interested parties. Of ten kilograms of stacks which Kovacs and his partners purchase at the Market, only seven stacks become subsequently embodied and "resurrected"—the rest is "wastage" (*Broken* 98) calculated into such transactions.

The bodily "sleeve" becomes even more objectified. Acquisition of any replacement for the original body is entirely determined by technical requirements and personal finances. Also, the lack of terminological (all bodies are simply called "sleeves") and experiential (the original is valued no more highly than subsequent sleeves) distinction between original and secondary bodies clearly indicates the repeatability and replaceability of embodiment. A sleeve is a commodity, often extremely valuable but hardly unique.

True to cyberpunk fashion, sentient machines constitute a separate class of agents. In *Altered Carbon* the hotel named Hendrix, in which Kovacs is staying, is a legal entity operating its own licensed business. Later in the same novel, during the raid that involves destruction of an AI-operated virtual brothel, Kovacs feels "a vague pang of guilt" as he is thinking about "the A.I., thrashing like a man in an acid vat as its systems dissolved around it, consciousness shriveling down to a tunnel of closing perspectives into nothing" (*Carbon* 281). This image clearly indicates the recognition of machinic personhood even if at that moment the A.I. dissolves in an excruciating demise. Evolving and autonomous technology, one of the classic cyberpunk topoi, exists here as well, most prominently in *Woken Furies*, where vast stretches of one of Harlan World's continents have become, albeit not "deliberately," what Gibson called an "unsupervised playground for technology" (*Neuromancer* 11)—at the time of the plot, hunting for constantly evolving machines in the Uncleared has been going on for close to 300 years and carries financial reward for each machinic death.

Other defining elements of the Movement are also present. Although the trilogy posits no world-spanning digital network, virtual environments abound, either in the form of constructs serving as prisons, in which the encoded subjectivity serves time; as holiday ersatz; as recovery wards for soldiers whose original sleeve has been rendered unfunctional and who are awaiting its repair or replacement; or, finally, as artificial h(e)avens like the one created by the Renouncers, believers in "Upload" (*Furies* 40), an unspecified state of total digitalization of the world. In the political and economic sphere, although the Protectorate is nominally headed by the United Nations, it is corporate interests that constitute a major force shaping the world while criminal organizations, such as Yakuza or Haiduci, compete for influence in business and politics with corporations and feudal-style families.

Despite, or rather in addition to, their successful generic mixtures, looming large over the world of Morgan's novels is Gibson's *Neuromancer* (1984), which has come to "typify the cyberpunk movement" (Huntington 133) and whose author has been considered "original and gifted enough to make the whole movement seem original and gifted" (Csicsery-Ronay, "Cyberpunk" 185). Even if the assumption that cyberpunk's definition is overwhelmingly determined by *Neuromancer* is too radical, this inspirational *ur*-text resonates in *Altered Carbon*, *Broken Angels*, and *Woken Furies*: passages in Morgan echo—whether consciously or not does not detract from that resonance—passages from *Neuromancer*. Molly's "functional elegance of a war plane's fusilage" (Gibson 44) is translated in Sarah's "assembly of low-frequency sine curves" (*Carbon* 3). The passage conflating the real-world and electronic image of BAMA (Gibson 43) is uncannily mirrored in the image of a city in *Altered Carbon* (119).[1] Like Case, Kovacs is said to "fulfill the expectations like a machine" (*Carbon* 300). The implicit scorn at "*hardcopy* documentation" (*Furies* 56) reminds us of the diagnosis of Turkey as a backward country where writing still enjoys respect, while Case's thoughts about "transmission of the old message" (Gibson 240) while he climaxes with Linda are reflected in Sylvie Oshima's chanting of "a skein of machine code" (*Furies* 181) during her orgasm with Kovacs. Even a certain poetic quality of Gibson's writing, so evident in *Neuromancer*, seems to permeate Morgan's writing in passages like "the Smith & Wesson gleamed like fool's gold on the scarred wood. Out in the Reach power lashed down from an orbital and lit the kitchen in tones of blue. I could hear the maelstrom calling" (*Carbon* 6). Whether all this justifies calling Morgan's novels "cyberpunk," "post-cyberpunk" or "cyberpunk-flavoured" (Butler,

Cyberpunk 57) is academic—regardless of monikers Morgan appears to engage defining elements of the convention.[2] However, as part of that engagement, Morgan revises and challenges at least two major facets of Movement-era cyberpunk: the lack of any meaningful attitude towards politics and the issue of (dis)embodiment, each of which is further interrogated in a number of aspects.

"THE PERSONAL IS POLITICAL"

Original cyberpunk fiction has been repeatedly charged with either blindness to politics and, even worse, unspoken allegiances to conservative mindsets. Among others, Istvan Csicsery-Ronay, Jr. notes its total ignorance of the question "whether some political controls over technology are desirable" ("Cyberpunk" 193), Tom Moylan takes it to task for working as "a late capitalist version of what Herbert Marcuse described as 'the affirmative culture' of modern bourgeois society" (155), and Nicola Nixon, the author of probably the most fierce critique of the sub-genre, claimed that its "slickness and apparent subversiveness conceal a complicity with '80s conservatism" (231). In a number of cases it is impossible to disagree with such assessments—*Neuromancer*'s only overt political statement, Aerol's vision of the matrix as "Babylon" (106), is conspicuously solitary while the freedom myth underlining Williams's *Hardwired* has more to do with the construction of the aptly-named protagonist Cowboy than any real political stance.

Superficially, Morgan's trilogy may appear to project the same indifference if not conservatism—its nihilistic protagonist struggles, especially initially, to come across as vehemently apolitical and cynical about power. Physical and psychological violence, whose vivid and detailed descriptions demonstrate Morgan's indebtedness to the noir and war genres, might also suggest certain allegiance to high-adrenaline masculine narratives. This is, however, merely a veneer—in reality Morgan discards cyberpunk's political blindness in ways both minor and major.

Unlike most cyberpunk heroes, Kovacs is ethnically-marked. Where his fictional predecessors were mostly race-blind and heroes uniformly white,[3] Kovacs repeatedly stresses his mixed Japanese and Hungarian roots. In *Altered Carbon*, he feels "exiled into Caucasian flesh, on the wrong side of the mirror" (180). In *Broken Angels*, he refuses to re-sleeve into a more rad-resistant Maori body appropriate for the operation in the contaminated area where the group is trying to uncover the Martian portal. Even more ambiguously, in *Woken Furies* the regime he helps fight—the Harlan family—is identified as Caucasian, yet he does not harbor any warmer feelings for more closely native Hungarian and Japanese gangs which make an appearance in that novel.

All of this strikes as significant, but possibly also puzzling, in a universe in which the body is readily exchangeable and facial or bodily markers become a functional or cosmetic choice.[4] In fact, some classes of sleeves, like the mentioned "Maori" or "Right Hand of God Martyrs" (the latter being commonly linked with the Muslim-styled society of the planet Sharya), suggest certain ethnic or religious shaping, but it is clear that such identification entails merely commercial branding accompanied by exclusively visual clues. Additionally, both of the above are considered to be expensive choices, making such markers even more market-determined. This leads to a problematic question—what is the meaning of race and ethnicity in the world in which outward markers are meaningless and demand-driven? In our contemporary world, more often than not "race" is posited as a more general category involving both ancestry and social and cultural characteristics, while "ethnicity" describes any group distinct in cultural, linguistic, religious, behavioral, or biological terms. Accordingly, it would be tempting to suggest that "race" is more connected with the body and "ethnicity" with the mind, but given the extreme commodification and relativity of sleeve technology, this does not seem possible in Morgan's trilogy. This contradiction between Kovacs's identity and commodification of sleeves can only be reconciled if we assume that Morgan constructs both racial *and* ethnic identity as something mental, part of the personal data which can be carried between stacks and sleeves, even if or when it does not find its external expression. This is further evidenced by the fact that Kovacs's Hungarian and Japanese ancestors were themselves digitized subjectivities of two of Earth's nations, sent to Harlan's World and sleeved, presumably into appropriately marked bodies, only upon arrival on their new home.

Even with such an assumption that race and ethnicity are really data,[5] the trilogy suggests that such a sense of identity is not held universally. Kovacs is strongly aware of his own roots, as is "a young black man facing his family in a broken-down, middle-aged white body" (*Carbon* 312), but the majority of other characters in any of the three texts do not appear to manifest any indication that the choice of the sleeve, which by necessity is racially marked, is dictated by anything but purely functional, aesthetic, or economic considerations.

The second sphere in which Morgan rewires cyberpunk's politics is the presentation of power structures. There are few SF texts in which the protagonist would be so ruthlessly frank about inhuman mechanisms of control and, at the same time, so contemptuous of its hierarchies. Cyberpunk's characters never tended to be law-abiding model citizens, but the regularity with which the three novels are punctuated with acidic remarks and judgments concerning authority and mechanisms of governance (which Kovacs has come to know intimately having spent a better part of his narrated lifetime as an armed instrument of the Earth-based authorities) is more than a token rebellious spirit would require. The actual structures or members of authority never overtly figure in the novels and the organization of the Protectorate can only be guessed in general outlines, but its oppressive force is consistently constructed through the Envoy Corps—constantly alluded to but never witnessed practically, at least not at full strength. Morgan presents the Corps as a brutal and merciless tool of centralized hegemony and the nightmare of all revolutionaries, and, it almost occasionally feels so, the only stable element of the universe. The Protectorate's settled space is largely balkanized by the distances, which privately can only be traversed by the rich, but the awe-inspiring legend of the Corps is one of the few mortars of many societies on all worlds. Even Kovacs, skeptical as he is about the force, admits to the potency and magic of its myth:

> And I remembered what it had really been like. It wasn't the belonging that came flooding back to me this time, it was the brutal power of Corps enablement. The liberating savagery that rose out of a bone-deep knowledge that you were feared.
>
> That you were whispered of across the Settled Worlds and that even in the corridors of governance on Earth, the power brokers grew quiet at your name. It was a rush that came on like branded-supply tetrameth. Men and women who might wreck or simply remove from the balance sheet a hundred thousand lives with a gesture, those men and women could be taught fear again, and the instrument of that lesson was the Envoy Corps.
>
> (*Furies* 502)

If this sounds like a testosterone-driven dream of ultimate male-bonding, it is intended as such, although Kovacs remains far more ambiguous about his past at all other times. Irony and sarcasm concerning the actual function of the Corps are far more frequent: "We just used to go silently, crush the odd planetary uprising, topple the odd regime, and then plug in something UN-compliant that worked. Slaughter and suppression across the stars, for the greater good—naturally—of a unified Protectorate" (*Furies* 24). Given the repeatedly implied self-sufficiency of individual planetary colonies and their increasing cultural diversification, the centralized authority of the Protectorate ultimately emerges as a tyrannical yoke. While some of the colonized planets, such as Sharya, whose culture is unmistakably styled after more fundamentalist Arab states, come across as oppressive themselves, the Corps' intervention and reinstatement of capitalistic order are never constructed as benevolent and liberating.

While cyberpunk authors occasionally invoke in their fictions images of utopian enclaves and autonomous zones that can survive in corporate reality,[6] most of them abandon SF's utopian project and what Peter Fitting calls a "contestatory option." Instead, they chart if not overtly dystopian then at least politically-tepid landscapes in which "things are things," to use Gibson's phrase from *Neuromancer* (270). In *Altered Carbon* and *Broken Angels* Morgan envisions a strong center where earlier cyberpunks saw political authority as anachronism. On the political level, the existence of his characters is positioned somewhere between local fundamentalist or feudal regimes and the ever present threat of the UN's shock troops deployment. Personal freedom of street-wise operators like Kovacs is possible but most dreams of more collective autonomy through technology are discredited, while his outspoken, often solitary, dismissals of the Protectorate's might, whose shadowy presence and invisible structures are appropriately dystopian, only amplify the lack of lasting political alternatives.[7]

All this changes radically in *Woken Furies*, which constitutes the apogee and the blooming of a political stance, going beyond a mere anti-authoritarian attitude so deeply ingrained in Kovacs's stack. Early on, he admits that one of the reasons for his recruitment in the Envoy Corps was his "psychopathic borderline tendencies" (*Carbon* 274) combined with a sense of team spirit.[8] A solitary and cynical Chandlerian hero, he continually asserts his independence and readiness to do violence to maintain his territoriality, but the narratives repeatedly position Kovacs in situations in which he chooses to—as opposed to being coerced into having to—stand up for others. This is already apparent in *Altered Carbon*, in which the line "Make it personal" becomes key to Kovacs's motivation:

> The personal, as every one's so fucking fond of saying, is political. So if some idiot politician, some power player, tries to execute policies that harm you or those you care about, TAKE IT PERSONALLY. Get angry. The Machinery of Justice will not serve you here—it is slow and cold, and it is theirs, hardware and soft—. Only the little people suffer at the hands of Justice; the creatures of power slide out from under with a wink and a grin. If you want justice, you will have to claw it from them. Make it PERSONAL. Do as much damage as you can. GET YOUR MESSAGE ACROSS.
>
> (131)

Initially, this conviction does not lead him to bond with others or a group but from novel to novel this attitude gradually grows more social and Kovacs finds himself if not responsible for others then at least ready to avenge their deaths and injuries. In *Broken Angels*, he sympathizes with the general populace of Sanction IV, where the war waged by the revolutionaries against the Protectorate-loyal government appears to be mostly fought in the interest of large corporations. In the same novel, his connection with a small squad of hired operatives goes beyond mere war-time comradeship so that by the end of the book he is ready to confront even the Wedge, the unit which he is an officer in when the text opens. Instances of his violent "getting the message across" are no longer merely a signal that of all individuals he should be best left alone but instead become more general attempts at hitting the system, even if Kovacs himself hardly ever articulates this attitude. Still, as Steven Shaviro notes, Kovacs seems to "combine an utterly Hobbesian view of human nature with a Marx-like level of outrage at exploitation and oppression" ("Woken Furies"). The early example of an outburst in which the personal becomes *more* can be found in *Altered Carbon*:

> But this was worse than personal. This was about Louise, alias Anenome, cut up on a surgical platter; about Elizabeth Elliott stabbed to death and too poor to be re-sleeved; Irene Elliott, weeping for a body that a corporate rep wore on alternate months; Victor Elliott, whip-lashed between loss and retrieval of someone who was and yet was not the same woman. This was about a young black man facing his family in a broken-down, middle-aged white body; it was about Virginia Vidaura walking disdainfully into storage with her head held high and a last cigarette polluting lungs she was about to lose, no doubt to some other corporate vampire. It was about Jimmy de Soto, clawing his own eye out in the mud and fire at Innenin, and the millions like him throughout the Protectorate, painfully gathered assemblages of indivi-dual human potential, pissed away into the dung-heap of history. For all these, and more, someone was going to pay.
>
> (312)

This commitment culminates in *Woken Furies*—the novel in which Kovacs is "offended beyond endurance by the exploitation, torture, and murder that are continually being inflicted on Harlan's World (and all the other human-inhabited planets) for reasons of economic gain, or self-righteous religious dogma" (Shaviro "Woken"). He may still scorn the delusions and naivety of Harlan's World's revolutionaries, but the aptly titled *Woken Furies* serves both as an extended treatise on the nature of revolutions and a tentative glimmer of hope in the ultimately dark world of the Protectorate. As such, it signals not only Kovacs's shift in attitude from passive resistance to active participation in the uprising and readiness to confront even the Envoy Corps, but also Morgan's embrace of the utopian potential. The novel's ending may not be very conclusive in terms of the revolution's success, but Kovacs's attitude and the showcased political discourse make it very clear that, unlike in the two previous installments which excluded hope of a better tomorrow, Morgan does not reject the possibility of an alternative.

When measured against Tom Moylan's concept of dystopian continuum, all three novels clearly belong to the class of "critical dystopias"—texts which "bring utopian and dystopian tendencies to bear on their exposés of the present moment" (*Scraps* 198) and "tend to express an emancipatory, militant, critical utopian position" (*Scraps* 199).[9] Within such a group, *Altered Carbon* and *Broken Angels* are closer to the dystopian end of the spectrum while *Woken Furies* is visibly moving towards the utopian sensi-bility, which it never quite reaches but which is demonstrably invoked.

Symbolically hovering over and directly present in the utopia-tinged *Woken Furies* is the figure of Quellcrist Falconer—a female revolutionary from Harlan's World who "proposed a new revolutionary ethic which borrowed from existing strands of extremist thought but was remarkable for the vitriol with which said strands were themselves savagely critiqued almost as much as ruling class policy" (*Furies* 172) and whose views are disavowed not only on her home planet but across the entire Protectorate. Kovacs's attitude towards her heritage and, in *Woken Furies*, her re-incarnation (as opposed to re-sleeving) is highly complex. In principle, he has been virulently skeptical of revolutionary figures—the plot of *Broken Angels* is structured around Joshua Kemp's insurgency on Sanction IV, a conflict which can be read as a critique of revolutions. For Kovacs, Kemp's revolution will eventually result only in "a lot more statues of Joshua Kemp in public places" (*Broken* 106). Similar criticisms are sometimes raised against NeoQuellist sympathizers in *Woken Furies* as Kovacs enters into extended discussions with other characters and scorns their revolutionary naivety.

On the other hand, in all three novels, Kovacs frequently quotes Quell (although never openly identifying himself as a Quellist) and even early in the series his anti-authoritarian attitude seems to bear strong traces of her political philosophy. In the concluding *Woken Furies* he decisively, albeit superficially and grudgingly, joins the NeoQuellist initiative against the Harlan family. Before he does this, though, we are exposed to a great deal of verbal fencing in which various visions of not only revolutionary events but political systems in general are discussed. In these ideological bouts Kovacs's skepticism almost always becomes a trigger for others to lay out the main principles of Quellism. For its followers "[p]ower isn't a structure, it's a flow system. It either accumulates at the top or it diffuses through the system. Quellism set that diffusion in motion" (*Furies* 540). The supreme expression of the ideology is delivered late in the novel by Quell herself (who, in her re-incarnation, is piggy-backing another female character's mind):

> Run things, Kovacs. Take control. Look after social systems. Keep the streets safe, administer public health and education. Build stuff. Create wealth and organise data, and ensure they both flow where they're needed ... You've got to build the structures that allow for diffusion of power, not re-grouping. Accountability, demodynamic access, systems of constituted rights, education in the use of political infrastructure.
>
> (*Furies* 445)

The seriousness of the entire Quellist discourse bespeaks of the political commitment absent in Movement-era cyberpunk narratives. Even if Kovacs himself shies away from admitting the gravity of this commitment by calling it not "a philosophy at all ... just a feeling that maybe we've all had enough. That maybe it's time to burn these motherfuckers down" (*Furies* 490), it is abundantly clear that radical politics is a major preoccupation in the trilogy.

This political discourse of the series builds on a more traditional ground of cyberpunk's anti-corporatism. Nicola Nixon notes that corporate power is often characterized by markers of Otherness, mostly Orientalism (224). Morgan is far more egalitarian in that respect—all three novels feature corporations of varying persuasion whose profit-maximizing policies are as ruthless as they seem unavoidable. That the Quellist ideology seeking an alternative to this status quo comes across as viable at all is remarkable in a sub-genre burdened by the apparent depoliticization of its originary texts. Also, Morgan does not resort to oversimplification in the character-ization of adversary figures. Those representing various corporate, govern-mental, or underworld elites[10]—Bancroft and Kawahara in *Altered Carbon*, Hand and Carrera in *Broken Angels*, and the Harlanites, Tanaseda, and Segesvar in *Woken Furies*—are for the most part, if not always complex, then at least attention-drawing characters, instead of the faceless, more often implied than present, and usually two-dimensional villains of early cyberpunk.

In *Archaeologies of the Future*, Fredric Jameson suggests that the utopian impulse that underpins science fiction serves as a means of envisioning alternatives to the present market economy. Superficially, Morgan seems everything but utopian with his nightmarish visions of both political and personal excess while the fixedness of the status quo appears to preempt any real hope. However, Shaviro notes that "the nihilistic vehemence of Kovacs' cynicism (and Morgan's staging of it) prohibit ... resignation" ("Woken Furies"). It is precisely the brutal in-your-face openness about power and market mechanisms that makes Kovacs's emerging stance a meaningful statement. The trajectory of dystopian/utopian dynamism is very clearly on the rise in the cycle's conclusion (Morgan has announced that there will be no more Kovacs novels). While it can be pointed out the *deus ex machina* solution to the central conflict of *Woken Furies* is somewhat inconsistent with its sobriety, the novel, and its fifth part, aptly titled "This is the Storm to Come," ends with the uncharacteristically hopeful note, standing in marked opposition to the grimness of earlier plot developments. Kovacs's cautious hope for the political future of Harlan's World can be read as his (and Morgan's) ultimate embrace of revolutionary rhetoric. That in the Protectorate someone like Kovacs hopes that "we may be able to warn off the Protectorate and the Envoys" (*Furies* 563) cannot be read as naïve day-dreaming, but instead seems to posit Quell's economic and social utopian-ism as a viable option. Kovacs's hope is located somewhere between the corruptible capitalist society of the Protectorate, which allows local versions of the Harlan family and varieties of gang organizations to reap profits from crime and exploitation, and the destruction of such an order by the radical revolution. The manner in which such a utopia could be achieved is not spelled out and the majority of expository dialogues between characters never points beyond theoretical generalities, all of which retains *Woken Furies* as a critical dystopia.

Morgan's staging of Kovacs's adventures is deeply rooted in what Jameson identifies as SF's utopian impulses while also being grounded in

late-twentieth- and early-twenty-first-century realities. For all the slick gla-
mour of the future he envisions as well as his nuanced (albeit often border-
ing on blatant) declarations vis-à-vis any kind of power establishment, at the
heart of the Takeshi Kovacs trilogy there is a genuine conviction that in
certain departments "deadlock of cynical power," as Shaviro aptly puts it
("Woken Furies"), does not differ much from the reality we live in. This, in
turn, makes Kovacs and his actions something to be reflected upon, although
perhaps not literally emulated. Regardless of future developments which
could occur if Morgan ever decided to re-awaken Kovacs from narrative
retirement and re-sleeve him, the presence of such earnest (if ultimately
perhaps unachievable) political propositions distance the trilogy from the
political indifference of classic cyberpunk narratives.

"THE SPIRITUAL WELL-BEING GANG"

Political power and corporate establishment are not the only forms of
authority that Kovacs—and implicitly Morgan—questions and undermines.
The trilogy is one of the very few cyberpunk, or even more generally SF,
texts that construct organized religion so consistently negatively. The ruthlessness of the attack is particularly striking considering that religion is
merely a minor aspect in the grand narrative of the three novels and
accounts for only one sub-plot in *Woken Furies*. One of the first anti-
religious remarks in the trilogy is Eileen Kawahara's critique of Franco and
his religiousness: "Petty tyrant with delusions of religion. Catholics get on
well with tyranny. It's in the culture" (*Carbon* 227). Her particular reference
is isolated as in the novels Catholicism is a local, Earth-based and mostly
forgotten religion, which nevertheless enjoys legal protection of its followers
who refuse to re-sleeve when the original body fails. More frequent references are made to Sharya and its religious regime, subsequently brought
down by the Envoy deployment. With the "Martyr of God" sleeves and a
number of overprints from Islam, the Sharyan religion is unmistakably
constructed in all three novels as a model of backward and disempowering
theocracy. The most complex and violent attack is, however, launched in
Woken Furies against the New Revelation, a Harlan World-based church
whose thinly-veiled similarities to contemporary fundamentalist factions of
monotheist religions—both Christian and Islamic—leave little doubt that it
is not only obscure sectarianism that is vilified. Kovacs, though, has much
more than spite and contempt for this "hard-faced gang of bearded scum
with a licence to kill from God" (*Furies* 217):

> [t]he spiritual well-being gang advanced into the room ... Cartoon
> patriarch beards and close shaven skulls, grim-faced and intent ...
> Rampant across the Saffron Archipelago, dripping down onto the
> northern reaches of the next landmass like venom from a ruptured web
> jelly and now, they told me, taking root in odd little pockets as far

south as Millsport itself, the Knights of the New Revelation brandished
their freshly regenerated gynophobia with an enthusiasm of which their
Earthbound Islamo-Christian ancestors would have been proud.

(*Furies* 24)

The brunt of Kovacs's hostility is rooted in a personal grudge against the
cult; his old lover and partner Sarah Sachilowska and her daughter were
killed and their stacks dropped into the ocean by New Revelation clergymen
as a punishment for an attempt to escape from the congregation. Kovacs's
love for Sarah proves him to be truly human and capable of profound love,
even if he never openly talks about it. Nevertheless, the three novels abound
in unmitigated descriptions of physical and psychological violence and one
of the most chilling passages describes an episode in Kovacs's vendetta
against the cult and its followers, in which he confesses to slaughtering a
village-worth of people:

[e]very motherfucker I could find who was an adult there the day she
died ... Everyone who could have lifted a finger to help her and didn't.
I took the list and I went back up there and I slaughtered them ... And
a few others who got in my way.

(*Furies* 313)

Kovacs's loss of Sarah (and Sarah's daughter, who appears to be of lesser
importance in his vendetta) happens prior to the events described in *Woken
Furies*, which itself starts with another scene of this vendetta: for the better
half of the novel, Kovacs carries a pocketful of stacks, most of them coming
from the slaughtered priests. Even more chilling is the reason why he retains
the chips. Instead of inflicting real death upon his adversaries by destroying
them, Kovacs passes them on to his childhood friend Segesvar, who loads
human stacks into wild swamp panthers for brutal pit fights. Apparently it
is not only love that proves Kovacs is truly human as vengeance is an
equally effective motivator.

Even when the actual priests guilty of Sarah's death are long dead, Kovacs
is "not planning to stop at all" (*Furies* 315). Part of his blind fury is fuelled
by the fact that "they can't give her back" (*Furies* 315) but his crusade is
also yet another form of his trademark backlash against any and all forms
of authority—this one against the entire religious system which, in the era
of almost eternal life granted by the stack technology, aspires to judge
people's lives and arbitrarily bars them from its benefits. Significantly, the
New Revelation cult is not presented in *Woken Furies* as a brain-washing
sect that has managed to ensnare masses of populace. Morgan's cultists are
a local manifestation of a more universal religious establishment, an organized form of mass control and, presumably, abuse. The fact that the
Voodoo religion that appears briefly in *Broken Angels*, while invariably
skeptically commented upon by Kovacs, does not generate any degree of

contemptuous attitude indicates that it is this and not spirituality and metaphysics in general that Morgan targets.[11]

In a conversation with Virginia Vidaura, his old trainer from the Corps, Kovacs suggests that the New Revelation's version of oppression is intimately connected with others:

> Classic poverty dynamic, people clutch at anything. And if the choice is religion or revolution, the government's quite happy to stand back and let the priests get on with it. All of those villages had the old base faith anyway. Austere lifestyle, rigid social order, very male-dominated. Like something out of fucking Sharya. All it took was the NewRev militants and the economic downturn to hit at the same time.
>
> (*Furies* 311)

This is where Kovacs links three forms of authority—political, religious, and economic—and his diagnosis seems to be one of the most crucial statements of the novel, if not the trilogy. In the same way in which his hope for Harlan's World at the conclusion of the trilogy points in the direction of SF's utopian impulse, Morgan's unrelenting critique of most organized forms of spirituality appears to identify religion with a dystopian turn. For Kovacs, religious belief is not only anti-rational in the age of advanced technology—it is a major source of corruption and inequality.

"IT'S JUST THE WAY I'M WIRED"

Morgan's trilogy does not rewrite only politics—equally fundamental re-wiring of the original cyberpunk scaffolding can be discerned in the sphere of embodiment. Movement-era cyberpunk fiction has frequently been characterized as privileging the mind and reviling the body—*Neuromancer*'s Case and *Synners*' Visual Mark with their contempt of the "meat" are the best examples of this stance. Admittedly, the rejection of the body by Case and Visual Mark cannot unproblematically be taken as the stance of *Neuromancer* or *Synners* (1991), novels which in other ways at least partially redeem the notion of embodiment, but on the whole the Movement-era cyberpunk is dominated by the perspective of characters seeking to escape embodiment. In Morgan's fiction, the cortical stack, the trilogy's central novum, seems to locate the series in the same tradition of texts, in which digitized identity dominates replaceable flesh. In fact, however, in *Altered Carbon, Broken Angels*, and *Woken Furies*, the body/mind duality is revised and complicated to the point where the body is reinstated as equally essential as the mind.

One of the most obvious signals of this (re)instantiation is the degree of attention the body receives in narration. Given the setting and genre conventions, this usually translates into very graphic but at the same time, as Steven Shaviro calls it, "intimate" ("Broken Angels") descriptions of physical violence, although occasional sexual scenes are equally evocative in their narrative detail. For all the high-tech gadgetry of his novels, Morgan clearly celebrates the impermanence and fragility of the flesh and, consequently, its inescapable presence. However, the most important aspect of his mind/body politics is the ultimate impossibility of demarcating the clear divide between one and the other. Almost paradoxically, in Morgan's fiction, a mutually exclusive duality is invalidated in favor of a complex feedback system: body and mind are intimately imbricated.

On the one hand, the novels envision complete digitization of subjectivity, which to be conscious has to be instantiated in some physical medium—one's original stack, remote storage, a virtual construct (any period of uninstantiation registers as oblivion)—but is otherwise mobile. The data's transferability makes copying or even "cloning" of the mind possible (the Protectorate mandates erasure for double-sleeving, but it still happens at least three times in the series). The commodification of sleeves, commercially branded and customizable, further suggests the Cartesian separation. On the other hand, the stack-encoded subjectivity proves to be not only intimately connected with but also influenced by the physical sleeve. When loaded into a sleeve, a person retains the entirety of experience and self-awareness but subjectivity immediately becomes imprinted on the body. Sleeves are posited as not "empty" even when they are fresh and unworn. That various physical and neural systems accelerate reflexes, add skills, or provide greater resistance register in the person's mind upon "waking up" in a new body is a given—they are, after all, manufactured features. What complicates this duality is that fact that the sleeve may carry over physical habits or acquired traits of its previous owner or the subjectivity may carry his/her traits from one sleeve to the next.

Kovacs frequently experiences a sense of peculiar detachment and a feeling that the sleeve he is wearing reacts to certain stimuli unconsciously but the results bear upon his conscious mind. When he wakes up in a new sleeve in *Altered Carbon* he discovers a strong craving for cigarettes although he himself never smoked—the previous owner of the sleeve was a nicotine addict. In the same novel, the mutual sexual attraction between him and Kristine Ortega is largely based on the pheromonal familiarity between her and the sleeve Kovacs is wearing, which previously belonged to Ortega's boyfriend. In *Woken Furies*, such occurrences are even more frequent: Vchira Beach surfers earn money teaching other people's sleeves how to surf; when knocked unconscious Kovacs survives a fall from a height because his hand automatically grabs a hanging cable and suspends him for over an hour while he is still unconscious; in moments of stress and inactivity his palms and finger itch with "gene-programmed longing for a rough surface to grasp and climb" (120); and the happiness he feels upon seeing Jadwiga stems largely from the fact that their sleeves were manufactured by the same company as one customized line.

New technologies of torture and death, something that because of Kovacs's profession constantly recurs in the novels, are an even more

ominous consequence of such a relationship between the moveable mind
and the replaceable sleeve. With the digital storage of the mind it is possible
"to torture a human being to death, and then start again" (*Carbon* 119), but
the interference between the sleeve and the subjectivity makes this even
more vicious and pervasive. At one point, for the purpose of interrogation,
Kovacs is re-sleeved in a body of a menstruating woman from the Islamic-
like Sharya, where Kovacs saw "some of the most unpleasant things in a
long career of human pain" (*Carbon* 116).[12] But it is not only the memories
of combat there, something embedded in his mind, that make him more
likely to break during torture. The female body he is wearing is not only
physically less resistant to pain and more vulnerable but also presumably
equipped with some "body memory" of the cultural consciousness of
women from the planet dominated by the fundamentalist religion. Inevitably, Kovacs talks—a proof that even an Envoy-trained mind bred for
changing sleeves cannot separate subjectivity from the vulnerabilities of the
body. The fact that the entire interrogation is virtual doubly complicates
the ontology of the situation—his digitized mind's vulnerability stems from
its awareness of the digitally simulated sleeve, whose physical "original," in
turn, was imprinted with the mental structures of a culturally-marked
subjectivity.

In most terminal narratives, to borrow Scott Bukatman's lexicon, the
codification of human subjectivity aims at the separation of the mental and
the corporeal, with the former liberated to roam the expanses of virtual
worlds and the latter devalued as "meat" weighing down the transcendent
mind. In Morgan's fiction, the opposite is true—the main purpose of the
stack technology is not to shed the flesh but rather to enable its renewal
through re-embodiment. The stack explicitly serves embodiment instead of
struggling with it in some sort of antithetical manner as the case is in early
cyberpunk texts.

In addition, the fact that the main application of virtual environments is
for temporary storage of the stack's contents or as recreational facilities is
also highly indicative of the status and desirability of the disembodied existence so frequently ascribed to code-based subjectivities. In this trilogy, a
yearning for cyberspace manifests only as a harmful addiction or a monk-
like pursuit practiced by few. This move, in which the material instantiation
becomes more valuable than its informational content, differentiates the
three novels from practically all other texts, cyberpunk or not, positing
computability of consciousness.

"THERE IS NOTHING BUT FLUX"

Although this was not necessarily a feature widely discussed in conjunction
with cyberpunk, the worlds envisioned in Gibson's, Sterling's, or Cadigan's
fictions are, on some level, stable. The individuals inhabiting them may be
on the brink of transformation into something or someone else, or a new

class of (artificial) consciousness may be arising, but in canonical cyberpunk texts such metamorphoses rarely change a world whose economic and political structures seem solid against any intervention—the new AI's lack of interest in human affairs in *Neuromancer*'s closure is emblematic of this fixedness. Gibson's corporate arcologies or Sterling's Mechanist/Shaper habitats can expand or shrink depending on the ebbs and tides of technological and social change, but the individual perceptions of the surrounding world as chaotic are very rare in them. Morgan, on the other hand, has a talent for giving the sense of what it is to live in a cyberpunk world and to experience its inherent instability. As an Envoy, Kovacs may be a survivor and a surfer on the waves of ever-accelerating change, but people, attachments, and communities around him collapse, disappear, and die as a result of clashes of tidal forces of economy and power. He re-sleeves and lives on but this does not make him oblivious to the chaos around him.

In the Takeshi Kovacs trilogy, Morgan stages nothing short of a return of the human. The critical dystopianism and utopian reverberations, the assault on and the problematization of the Cartesian duality, and the decisive political involvement are all manifestations of Morgan's revision of cyberpunk's transnationalism, rationality, and ethical ambiguity. Central to this restaging is the trilogy's protagonist. Regardless of his tough demeanour, skeptical lack of illusions about the world, and the violence he dispenses, Morgan has made Kovacs—and many other characters—very human and even wistful. When the wild rollercoaster of his plots slows down, at the core of the story the readers still have a conflicted but feasible figure of the rebel, most of the time without a cause. Despite their ruthlessness, pace, and grandness of vision, *Altered Carbon*, *Broken Angels*, and *Woken Furies* are ultimately very perceptive in their understanding of humanity and its failings while also understanding humanity's subversive spirit which extends beyond mere competition for commercial resources. Many reviewers have praised Morgan's futuristic inventiveness, plausibility, and skill in conducting engaging plots, but sewn between high-adrenaline scenes are touching pockets of intimacy—a conversation with Trepp outside the Elliott house in *Altered Carbon* or the night of melancholy drinking with the captain of "Haiduci's Daughter" in *Woken Furies*. For all the future shock of Kovacs' world, these intimacies will, I suspect, ring true for most contemporary readers. The stack and sleeve technologies may make Kovacs posthuman but in his soul/stack he remains like us. And like us, he is not immune to change. In the first novel of the series he reflects:

> As a child I'd believed there was an essential person, a sort of core personality around which the surface factors could evolve and change without damaging the integrity of who you were. Later, I started to see that this was an error of perception caused by the metaphors we were used to framing ourselves in. What we thought of as personality was no more than the passing shape of one of the waves in front of me.

Or, slowing it down to more human speed, the shape of a sand dune. Form in response to stimulus. Wind, gravity, upbringing. Gene blue-printing. All subject to erosion and change.

(252)

In the three volumes he changes planets and alliances but also becomes a different person—someone who is acutely aware of the old captain's warning: "This life is like the sea ... if you let it, it'll tear you apart from everyone and everything you ever cared about" (*Furies* 239). Things do not get more human than that.

NOTES

1 "Imagine a satellite blow-up of a city on mosaic, 1:10,000 scale. It'll take up most of a decent interior wall, so stand well back. There are certain obvious things you can tell at a glance. Is it a planned development or did it grow organically, responding to centuries of differing demand? Is it or was it ever fortified? Does it have a seaboard? Look closer, and you can learn more. Where the major thoroughfares are likely to be, if there is an IP shuttle port, if the city has parks. You can maybe, if you're a trained cartographer, even tell a little about the movements of the inhabitants. Where the desirable areas of town are, what the traffic problems are likely to be and if the city has suffered any serious bomb damage or riots recently" (*Carbon* 121).

2 In one of the interviews Morgan admits that "Gibson and the cyberpunk crew were a heavy influence on me" (Snider).

3 Occasional non-white characters are under-characterized as such (Gina in Pat Cadigan's *Synners* (1991)) or presented as exotic Others (Rastafarians in *Neuromancer*). Newer texts, such as M. M. Buckner's *War Surf* (2005), feature non-white characters but their ethnicity is downplayed or has marginal to no significance for the plot.

4 The idea itself that outward racial or ethnic characteristics can be commodified as fashion is naturally not Morgan's invention—in order to come closer to Ralfi Face, Gibson's Johnny Mnemonic ("Johnny Mnemonic" (1981)) has his face reworked into a "basic sharp-faced Caucasoid" but the surgeons in the parlor where he undergoes the procedure are "big on Sony Mao," which makes it hard "to keep them from adding the chic suggestion of epicanthic folds" (15).

5 For further studies on the relationship between race and cyberspace/digital embodiment, see, for example, Nakamura's *Cybertypes*, Kolko's *Race in Cyberspace*, or Foster's *The Souls of Cyberfolk*.

6 Such zones are present for example in Bruce Sterling's *Islands in the Net* (1988), Walter Jon Williams' *Hardwired* (1986), or Michael Swanwick's *Vacuum Flowers* (1987). McHale notes that the existence of such demarcated enclaves is one of the characteristics of cyberpunk and traces their origin to the concept to heterotopia as well as a number of literary predecessors, such as the post-war Germany in Thomas Pynchon's *Gravity's Rainbow* (1973).

7 In one of his interviews following the publication of *Altered Carbon*, Morgan clearly subscribes to this particular vision of reality:

> What I personally see is Kovacs's affirmation at the end of the book that society is, always has been and always will be a structure for the exploitation and oppression of the majority through systems of political force

dictated by an elite, enforced by thugs, uniformed or not, and upheld by a willful ignorance and stupidity on the part of the very majority whom the system oppresses.

(Bullock)

8 In *Broken Angels*, this team spirit is interestingly associated with the replaceable physicality—the combat sleeves of the Wedge, elite military troops that Kovacs serves in, contain the spliced wolf genes guaranteeing "enhanced tendency to pack loyalty that hurts like upwelling tears" (9).

9 Rafaella Baccolini provides a useful hereustic for the differentiation between classic and critical dystopia. She writes of the classic dystopia that it is "[t]raditionally a bleak, depressing genre with no space for hope within the story" and "utopia (in the sense of utopian hope) is maintained in dystopia only *outside* the story: It is only if we consider dystopia as a warning, that we as readers can hope to escape such a pessimistic future" (18). Conversely, the critical dystopia builds on the classic dystopian tropes by resisting closure and "[t]he ambiguous, open endings ... maintain the utopian impulse *within* the work" (18).

10 Morgan suggests that one of the sources of the elites is their guaranteed longevity, if not a kind of immortality. In *Altered Carbon*, in which such individuals are derogatorily named "Meths" (from Methuselah), Kovacs muses on this:

> If they want you, a youngish Quell had once written of the Harlan's World ruling elite, sooner or later they'll scoop you up off the globe, like specks of interesting dust off a Martian artifact. Cross the gulf between the stars, and they can come after you. Go into centuries of storage, and they'll be there waiting for you, clone-new, when you re-sleeve. They are what we once dreamed of as gods, mythical agents of destiny, as inescapable as Death, that poor old peasant laborer, bent over his scythe, no longer is ... Once we lived in terror of his arrival. Now we flirt outrageously with his sombre dignity, and beings like these won't even let him in the tradesman's entrance.
>
> (251)

Interestingly and almost unwittingly, this corresponds with the dystopian scenario for the future that Jaron Lanier unveiled in his article "One-Half of a Manifesto," a 2000 response to Bill Joy's "Why the Future Does Not Need Us."

11 The conversation in *Broken Angels* (102–3) that Kovacs has with Matthias Hand, a corporate backer of the main enterprise, is really a rehashing of the old debate between the religious and the secular perception of the universe and its forces but for all cynical skepticism of the former, Hand's words ("Look at that, Kovacs. We're drinking coffee so far from Earth you have to work hard to pick out Sol in the night sky. We were carried here on a wind that blows in a dimension we cannot see or touch. Stored as dreams in the mind of a machine that thinks in a fashion so far in advance of our own brains it might as well carry the name of god. We have been resurrected into bodies not our own, grown in a secret garden without the body of any mortal woman. These are the facts of our existence, Kovacs. How, then, are they different, or any less mystical, than the belief that there is another realm where the dead live in the company of beings so far beyond us we must call them gods?") elicit a certain degree of understanding for such an interpretation of reality, something that is never the case whenever the New Revelation or Sharya are mentioned.

12 Within the discussion of the mutual implications of technology and gender, the passage from *Altered Carbon* seems to offer far more complex readings than the oft-quoted passage from *Neuromancer*, in which Case plugs into Molly's simstim and experiences the world through her senses.

11 Retrofitting *Frankenstein*

Veronica Hollinger

Cyberpunk ... is busy "Frankensteining" the future.
                    (Fred Botting, "Monsters of the Imagination" 124)

A long time ago, when it was still the twentieth century, I made the claim that cyberpunk was over. I repeated the lines by the Greek poet Cavafy that Lucius Shepard quoted in his own requiem for the (sub)genre: "What will we do now that the barbarians are gone? / Those people were a kind of solution" (quoted in Hollinger, "Cybernetic" 216). I was already becoming nostalgic for cyberpunk's accounts of visceral encounters at the human/ machine interface and for its *noir*-inflected dramas of transformed posthuman subjectivities—cyborgs, clones, artificial and virtual intelligences. Cyberpunk was one of SF's most appealing and informed responses to questions about how the genre might represent our lives in the computer/ ized worlds of technoculture. Cyberpunk really was "a kind of solution."[1]

I need not have been so eager to announce its late-1980s demise, of course, nor so ready to expend my nostalgia on it. As Sherryl Vint notes in her recent assessment of its ongoing influence, "Although the literary moment of cyberpunk may have passed, its tropes have never been more germane" given the proliferating technologies of "computer communications, virtual reality, and human/machine interfaces" (103), the very stuff of technoscience, the stuff of the human-built world. Of particular interest to me here is cyberpunk's impact on fictional representations of the (post) human subject as a subject inevitably marked by technology. By now contemporary cyberfiction is populated by any number of cyberpunk's hideous progeny, from the techno-biologically indentured servants of Maureen McHugh's *Nekropolis* (2001) to the far-future "acorporeal" subjects of Greg Egan's *Schild's Ladder* (2001) to the *noir* detective "resleeeved" into multiple bodies in Richard K. Morgan's *Altered Carbon* (2002) to the male narrator of Charles Stross's *Glasshouse* (2006), currently a woman, previously a two-ton military tank.[2]

"Hideous progeny" is how Mary Shelley came to refer to her first novel, *Frankenstein* (1818).[3] I also want to consider here how this great novel has been (re)read as a result of cyberpunk's fictional representations of the technosubject, how it has been transformed into a precursor text of cyberculture—in other words, I want to consider cyberpunk's retrospective as well as its prospective influences. In this discussion of hybrid intertexts and the unnatural beings who inhabit them, Victor Frankenstein's Creature (re)appears in technoculture in a newly complex role, both promising and abhorrent, at once our double and our technological other.

William Gibson's *Neuromancer* (1984), widely considered to be cyberpunk's limit-text, gave readers iconic technobodies such as the cyborg Molly Millions, the vat-grown cloned assassin Hideo, the dead-and-down-loaded construct Dixie Flatline, and—as the techno-Other in this fictional world—the powerful artificial intelligence, Wintermute. Cyberpunk's many diverse constructions of the technosubject are among its most significant contributions to SF and cyberfictions that continue to explore the fate of that subject are all, to some extent, "the legacies of cyberpunk fiction."[4] In the quarter century since Gibson's console cowboys slouched onto the pages of *Neuromancer*, we have become increasingly aware that we are marvelling at our own possibilities and nightmares—as the subjects and bodies of technoculture—when we marvel at the creatures of contemporary cyberfiction. We also appear to be experiencing a new kind of dis/identification with a much earlier fiction—we re-member Shelley's marvellous tale of the "original" technobody.

At this point, it will also be useful to re-member my epigraph, which is taken from an essay by Fred Botting on generic intersections of gothic and science fiction. Botting borrows the term "Frankensteining" from an essay by Tom Shippey, who uses it in a reading of Bruce Sterling's novella "Green Days in Brunei" (1985); specifically, Shippey is discussing Sterling's use of the terms "bricolage" and "retrofit," which Sterling collapses into a single approach to problem solving: "You're a *bricoleur* ... You can make do. You can retrofit. That's what *bricolage* is—it's using the clutter and rubble to make something worth having" (Sterling, "Green" 136). Considering cyberpunk's effects on conventional SF futures, Shippey suggests that "bricolage could also be called 'Frankensteining'," as a way to describe what Sterling's tech-savvy protagonist is able to do with technological "leftovers, [and the] spare parts from dead constructions" (Shippey 214).

It seems eminently suitable that Botting's observation is constructed out of such a variety of discursive scraps, reminiscent of the diverse parts that make up the monstrous body of Frankenstein's Creature. The discourses and texts by Shelley, Sterling, Shippey, Botting, and (not least) Lévi-Strauss that have produced my epigraph suggest the kind of Frankenstein (re)readings that interest me here, composed from fragments that suggest intriguing dis/unities between and among disparate textual bodies. Botting links *Frankenstein* to cyberpunk through cyberpunk's gothicizing influence on modern science fiction—the visual analogue would be the dark and dismal cityspaces of the film *Blade Runner* (1982).[5] For my own purposes, I want to suggest something rather different by the term "Frankensteining"—referring less to the gothicized futures of cyberpunk than to the heterogeneous subjects of cyberfiction that so imaginatively destabilize concepts such as "subject" and "embodiment."

If cyberpunk has been involved in "Frankensteining" the future, it has also retrofitted *Frankenstein* itself to play a new role as a harbinger-text of cyberfiction. This retrofit is already at work in the introduction of Shelley's novel as one "of the cultural artifacts that helped to shape cyberpunk ideology and aesthetics," offered by Richard Kadrey and Larry McCaffery in McCaffery's 1991 "casebook" of cyberpunk and postmodernism, *Storming the Reality Studio*:

> The recycling of body parts, the creation of life (or monster making), murder, sex, revenge, the epic chase, the brilliant scientist working outside the law, a brooding, romantic atmosphere—this book is a veritable sourcebook for SF motifs and clichés. It also created the first great myth of the industrial revolution, and reflects the deeply schizophrenic attitude toward science so evident in postmodern culture and in the fiction emerging from this culture.
>
> (17)

A certain (re)reading of *Frankenstein* is also one of the legacies of cyberpunk fiction.

HIDEOUS PROGENY AND MONSTROUS ONTOLOGY: RE-MEMBERING *FRANKENSTEIN*

> I had never yet seen a being resembling me, or who claimed any intercourse with me. What was I?
>
> (Mary Shelley, *Frankenstein* 147)

Scenes such as the one in which Victor's abjected Creature is both moved and distressed by the emotional angst of Goethe's novel, *The Sorrows of Young Werther* (1774)—which overwhelms him with a sense of his exclusion from the human community—take on new resonance in the context of contemporary stories about the technosubject:

> I found myself similar, yet at the same time strangely unlike the beings concerning whom I read … My person was hideous, and my stature gigantic: what did this mean? Who was I? What was I? Whence did I come? What was my destination? These questions continually recurred, but I was unable to solve them. (Shelley 153)

In a key essay in *Prefiguring Cyberculture* (2002)—an important and wide-ranging overview of technoculture's "intellectual history"—

Catherine Waldby reads *Frankenstein* as a paradigmatic story about the creation of artificial life, a fiction of technogenesis that suggests "that reference to a natural humanity is always anachronistic":

> This is the first investigation of the ontology of the technoscientific subject, its conditions of being in the world. How, the novel asks, do the conditions of artificial creation and technically conferred life generate certain possibilities for being? What does it mean to be embodied, when the body cannot claim the status of nature? ... How can an artificial life situate itself in the world, and what kind of world does it make for itself?
>
> (Waldby 33)

We can appreciate where the (ontological) emphasis falls in Waldby's reading of *Frankenstein* when we contrast it to the more familiar role played by Shelley's novel as intertext in Isaac Asimov's Golden Age robot stories. In these stories written during the 1940s and collected as *I, Robot* (1950), Asimov was committed to refuting, even if only through the fictional device of his Three Laws of Robotics, what one of his characters refers to as "the Frankenstein Complex."[6] This is the apprehension that artificial life-forms that are stronger and more intelligent than their human creators would inevitably pose a threat to human beings: "Physically, and, to an extent, mentally, a robot—any robot—is superior to human beings. What makes him slavish, then? *Only the First Law!*" (137; emphasis in original). The point-of-view characters in these stories are the humans who work for US Robots and Mechanical Men, Inc.; the robots themselves, for the most part, have neither autonomy nor self-reflexivity. What Waldby calls "the subjectivity of the object" (33) is of little concern in these stories except in so far as it might interfere with robotic obedience and efficiency. The robots' function is to represent "technology," especially "technology" as it threatens to escape the control of its human creators—it is no coincidence that nearly every story is resolved by the triumphant application of human reason. *I, Robot* is a defensive response to one of the more familiar readings of Shelley's novel, that it is about the threat of "science out of control" (Lederer and Ratzan 463), an ambitious science that, in Shelley's words, seeks to "penetrate into the recesses of nature, and shew how she works in her hiding places" (Shelley 76). This is also a blasphemous science that threatens to produce monsters. But not if Asimov can help it.

In spite of the imaginative rigor with which Asimov applied his Three Laws, it is by no means certain by the end of these stories that the paranoia of the Frankenstein Complex is baseless, because Asimov's robots have evolved into the Machines, "the vastest conglomeration of calculating circuits ever invented" (225), now in complete control of the global human economy. In *Representations of the Post/Human* (2002), Elaine L. Graham suggests that the entire sequence of *I, Robot* may be read as a series of critical incidents in the growing discontinuity between robotic motivation and human comprehension … Asimov's stories cleverly build up variations on the theme that robots, with increasing powers of discernment and prediction, are driven to devise ever more ingenious strategies for protecting humans from the knowledge of their own obsolescence.

(130)

Or, as Asimov's human characters anxiously conclude, "Only the Machines, from now on, are inevitable!" (249).

Cyberpunk's arrival on the scene served notice that science fiction had lost a certain kind of innocence—or perhaps naïveté—because cyberpunk stories are often about exactly the blasphemous production of monsters that Asimov's fiction was so invested in preventing. Cyberpunk's technologically-transformed/enhanced/constructed protagonists have little interest in "natural" human nature and even less anxiety about "science out of control." In fact, in a retrospective article on "Cyberpunk in the Nineties," Bruce Sterling reads *Frankenstein* as exactly what cyberpunk was *not*. There is a nice touch of Byronic romanticism in Sterling's claims, even as he dismisses *Frankenstein* for its own romantic commitment to a "higher moral law":

In a cyberpunk analysis, *Frankenstein* is "Humanist" SF. Frankenstein promotes the romantic dictum that there are Some Things Man Was Not Meant to Know. … In the moral universe of cyberpunk, we already know Things We Were Not Meant To Know … In cyberpunk, the idea that there are sacred limits to human action is simply a delusion. There are no sacred boundaries to protect us from ourselves. … Cyberpunk didn't invent this situation; it just reflects it.[7]

In contrast to Asimov's stories, a typical cyberpunk response to *Frankenstein* is to dismiss it as more or less irrelevant. For first-generation cyberpunk writers such as Sterling, *Frankenstein* seems not to have been the precursor fiction that it becomes once the cyberpunk ethos has permeated both SF in particular and technoculture in general.

Among the characters in Pat Cadigan's *Synners* (1991)—a text that self-consciously thematizes the pressure on human beings to "change for the machines" (246)—is a kind of viral AI that names itself Art Fish once it achieves self-consciousness. Cadigan's human characters know what the cultural referent should be when they realize that "synthetic humanity" has been achieved: "Well, it was bound to happen someday. But, Jesus, *Art Fish*? What's wrong with the good old names, like Frankenstein?" (173; emphasis in original).[8] Cadigan's text both evokes and distances itself from Shelley's; its satirical reference suggests how out of date *Frankenstein* has become in the world of modern technoculture. Art Fish is a very contemporary artificial subject, the farthest thing imaginable from Shelley's unfortunate monster. He appears in cyberspace as "a composition of subtle and charming androgyny, the long dark hair, the classically sculpted features, the amber eyes so light in color they were luminous, the deep brown skin" (167). And even more significantly, he is a valued member of the diverse community of hackers who are Cadigan's protagonists: "We might actually have two species of humans now, synthesizing human and synethesized human, all of us being the former, and Art Fish being the latter" (386).

Sterling notes in his retrospective that "The Monsters of cyberpunk never vanish so conveniently [as does Victor's creation]. They are already loose on the streets. They are next to us. Quite likely WE are them" ("Cyberpunk in the Nineties"). From a posthuman perspective, he is absolutely right, of course. In contrast, Graham notes how the emphasis in Asimov's stories is on the increasingly disparate ontologies and motivations of humans and their intelligent machines. A rigid distinction between body and machine, however, tends to be undermined in cyberpunk's master narrative, the story of the technological transformation of human to posthuman being: "Quite likely WE are them."

First-generation cyberpunk is not alone in its dismissal of *Frankenstein*. Donna Haraway's immensely influential "A Cyborg Manifesto" (1985)—published almost concurrently with *Neuromancer*—finds little to admire in Shelley's text, given its retrograde humanist tendencies.[9] Haraway associates Victor's Creature with naïve and outmoded dreams of unity and completion, clearly distinguishing him from her own figuration of the cyborg: "Unlike the hopes of Frankenstein's monster, the cyborg does not expect its father to save it through a restoration of the garden; i.e., through the fabrication of a heterosexual mate, through its completion in a finished whole, a city and cosmos" (151). For Haraway, not only is Victor's Creature hopelessly entangled in a no-win Oedipal battle with his father/creator, he is also straight and—even worse—he is humanist; such a creature can never appropriately inhabit the new geographies of the authentic cyborgian technosubject. If, however, as Waldby argues, *Frankenstein* is worth (re)reading as an origin story about technogenesis, then Victor's Creature can be recruited to support Haraway's own rejection of western origin stories and her valorization of the cyborg as a figure for our "unnatural" ontology in technoculture. For Haraway, human beings have never enjoyed the state of nature in a Garden of Eden; we are in technology, our second nature, and technology is in us. Retrofitted by cyberpunk, *Frankenstein* revises in turn the story of natural human origins; in the "final" analysis, as Waldby notes, "Frankenstein's creature and Haraway's cyborg are both ways to think about human becoming" (36).[10]

This is also in keeping with Nina Lykke's project in "Between Monsters, Goddesses and Cyborgs" (1996), an analysis of "feminist alternatives to the traditional scientific reduction of the non-human world to resources and mere objects without subjectivity" (14). Following Bruno Latour's arguments in *We Have Never Been Modern* (1991), Lykke notes that "modernity manifests itself in its production of monsters and hybrids. Frankenstein's monster is only an early harbinger of the cyborg world of the late twentieth century" (17). For Lykke, Victor's Creature is the paradigmatic boundary figure between the human and the non-human, monstrous precisely because of his location on the border (16). In the same discussion, Lykke also reads Amy Thomson's *Virtual Girl* (1993) as SF that shares Haraway's commitment to the feminist potential of the cyborg. Given the care with which Shelley provided a "voice" for the Creature within her own text, Lykke's comments about fictions such as *Virtual Girl* are also relevant to *Frankenstein*: "Feminist cyborg stories point towards subjectivization and narrativization of the non-human. Amy Thomson's cyborg and the ones Donna Haraway inhabits in her writings are reconstructed as subjects with a right to their own stories" (27).

The cyborgs, clones, virtual subjects, and artificial intelligences of recent cyberfiction are imaginative figures in narratives about the ongoing co-evolution of human beings and our proliferating technologies.[11] "Quite likely WE are them," as Sterling asserts. We are not Asimov's Machines, however, nor are we on the way to becoming them: a gradually increasing non-equivalence between humanity and technology is a taken-for-granted in Asimov's stories. Perhaps unexpectedly, the same radical non-equivalence is a significant feature of the Wintermute AI, the prime mover of events in *Neuromancer*. These particular artificial subjects represent an extreme of technological alterity and are unintelligible to the human characters who share their fictional universes. One of their narrative functions is to remain mysterious, incomprehensible, even sublime. From this perspective, there is significant continuity between Asimov's Machines and Gibson's Wintermute. Both Golden Age Machines and cyberpunk AIs seem to have achieved sentience through processes of emergence and they have evolved past the comprehension, as well as the control, of their human progenitors.[12] They inhabit stories that are less about creators and created, about human subjects and non-human objects, than they are about the possibilities of radically alternative subjectivities which may yet come to share the world with us. No wonder Gibson introduces the Turing Registry agents in *Neuromancer*, representatives of cyberpunk's own apparent Frankenstein Complex: "For thousands of years men dreamed of pacts with demons. Only now are such things possible ... What would your price be, for aiding this thing [Wintermute] to free itself and grow?" (163).

Not surprisingly, *Neuromancer* does not finally support the Frankenstein Complex. Asimov's fiction seems to imply, as Graham notes, that a genuine artificial intelligence would more or less inevitably threaten humanity with obsolescence; certainly, it would end up in charge of things. In *Neuromancer*, however, which climaxes with the coming-into-being of a new god-like AI released into cyberspace—"I'm the sum total of the works, the whole show" (269)—the transformation of technology into techno-subjectivity is a singular event whose outcome cannot be foreseen and this is exactly what makes it so desirable within the terms of Gibson's fictional world. As Case, Gibson's point-of-view character, insists: "I got no idea what'll happen if Wintermute wins, but it'll *change* something" (260; emphasis in original). As it happens, the new AI rather undercuts Case's passionate desire for transformation when it assures him that "Things aren't different. Things are things" (270). In cyberpunk worlds, the "other" of technology is not simply promise or threat; it is simply—in an extremely complex way—one more "thing" in the world that shapes subjects and bodies.[13]

At the same time as there is a tradition of stories such as Asimov's in which humans and their artificial progeny follow ever more divergent evolutionary paths, contemporary cyberfiction tends to be—whether anxious or celebratory or something else entirely—fiction about the dissolution of the ontological barriers separating humanity from its technoscientific creations, resulting in the part-human cyborgs that inhabit so much of contemporary science fiction as well as the artificial others that we dream of creating through technoscientific experimentation.[14] On this side of cyberpunk—a problematic distinction, but heuristically useful—*Frankenstein* is no longer only a salutary warning about the potentially lethal outcomes of the West's mania for the products and prostheses of technoscience; nor is it simply an antiquated example of humanist naïveté. It is also an exploration of the technosubject's monstrous postmodern ontology: "What was I?" asks the Creature, and this has become a central question for post-cyberpunk readers who are themselves well on the way to becoming the artificial subjects of technoscience.

In the grip of pattern recognition, I note that a digital image invoking Victor's Creature—as channelled by Boris Karloff in the 1931 film *Frankenstein*—provides the cover design for one of the earliest academic studies of cyberpunk, George Slusser and Tom Shippey's co-edited collection, *Fiction 2000: Cyberpunk and the Future of Narrative* (1992). Slusser's contribution is a reading of cyberpunk that emphasizes its thematic continuities with Shelley's originary narrative. His focus is less on the ontological exploration of Shelley's artificial technobody, however, than on the Creature's role as the tragic consequence of Victor's bad-faith participation in the science project.

In Slusser's view, SF is virtually defined by its inability to overcome what he refers to as "the Frankenstein barrier," the obstacle raised by Victor's refusal to share the human world with his own hideous progeny. When he destroys the artificial Eve who will be the bride of his alter-ego/Adam, this is the culmination of " the sin against the second chance modern science offers humanity by remaking its fallen body ... Victor opens the way to the future only to betray that openness" (Slusser, "Frankenstein" 51).[15] For Slusser, the Frankenstein barrier "resists and finally displaces the creation of things to come" (70). This diagnosis of the genre's conflicted interactions with "authentic" futurity recalls Fredric Jameson's well-known argument that SF is never about the future, but instead functions "to dramatize our incapacity to imagine the future" ("Progress Versus Utopia" 153). In this gloomy construction, SF is incapable of imagining futures that might be qualitatively different from the present. In the context of cyberpunk, *Frankenstein* provides Slusser with an origin story about the failure of the science project. SF is always already a fallen genre.

In *The Postmodern Adventure* (2001), Stephen Best and Douglas Kellner (re)turn to *Frankenstein* as a forerunner fiction about the implosion of human beings and their technologies: "In a world of virtual reality, biotechnology, surrogate mothering, neural implants, and artificial intelligence and life ... [w]e're becoming cyborgs and technobodies, while our machines are becoming 'smart' and more human-like" (151). For Best and Kellner, Victor is "a distinctly modern hero who embodies the deepest impulses of modernity to control nature" (159). Where Slusser sees "the Frankenstein barrier," Best and Kellner identify what they call the "Frankenstein syndrome," defined as "an obsession with control over natural processes, and the pursuit of knowledge for its own sake, divorced from a careful consideration of ethics, politics, and potential consequences" (162). For Best and Kellner, Shelley's novel is the familiar story of Victor Frankenstein's misguided dependence upon an obsessively controlling (and clearly masculinist) scientific reason, while "Frankenstein's 'monster' remains an enduring symbol for any potent technology that human beings create that escapes their control and threatens their survival" (162). At the same time, they also read this "monster" as "[a]n anticipatory symbol of postmodern otherness" (161). The neurotic disturbances implied in terms such as "complex" and "syndrome" suggest how uneasily Victor inhabits the transformed world brought about by his own deadly ambitions to "penetrate into the recesses of nature." It is not he but his Creature who is destined to find a place in the postmodern world, now that "the boundaries between science fiction and science fact are fast collapsing" (Best and Kellner 161).

In *Representations of the Post/Human*, Graham devotes a full chapter— "What Made Victor's Creature Monstrous?"—not to Frankenstein but to his Creature, asking after the conditions of its subjectivization. She examines "how the various representations and attributions of monstrosity in *Frankenstein* offer models of what it means to be truly human," and she notes that "there is no reason not to speculate about the ways they might be applied to possible forms of post/human lives" (82). In this reading, "Mary Shelley invites her readers to contemplate whether humanity—in a moral rather than an ontological sense—is assumed at birth or acquired through socialization" (82). Graham's position may be read as putting pressure on Slusser's arguments, since—not unlike Waldby—she offers a reading of *Frankenstein* that situates it as part of the ongoing contemporary conversation about what it might mean to be posthuman in technoculture. Where Slusser reads *Frankenstein* as the story of Western science's ethical failure, in other words, Graham and Waldby read it as a particularly successful founding narrative of technogenesis.

Bruno Latour's argument that modernity's passion for order has inevitably resulted in the production of monsters invests the concept of hybridity with a convincing contemporary resonance. Like Lyyke, Graham also relies on Latour when she claims that "Modernity is premised on the basis of clear taxonomic boundaries, but the very same imperative to make absolute and impermeable boundaries results also in the proliferation of 'hybrids'" (34). Victor's Creature becomes one version—a tragic one—of the postmodern subject of technoculture. He is the disaffected bastard child of Enlightenment and Romanticism, at once organic and unnatural, the original hybrid technosubject and the very embodiment of the grotesque. At the often conflictual intersections of cyberpunk fiction and Harawayan cyborg theory, he is SF's first cyborg and its most abject artificial body.

THE SUBJECTIVITY OF THE OBJECT: *BILDUNGSROMANS* FOR A POSTMODERN TECHNOCULTURE

> By the virtues that I once possessed, I demand this from you. Hear my tale; it is long and strange.
>
> (Mary Shelley, *Frankenstein* 127)

As Asimov's stories suggest, each science fiction age contends with its own version of *Frankenstein*. Turning from cultural theory to cultural narrative, I want briefly to consider some stories in which the *Frankenstein* text functions as a kind of script to be self-reflexively tested by artificial subjects who anxiously (re)cite its most pressing questions: "Who was I? What was I? Whence did I come? What was my destination?" These stories dramatize a process of necessarily complex dis/identification with Victor's creation which is also an attempt to establish self-identity, self-possession, and autonomy. Embodiment is both a question and a concern in these stories, which are structured—Shelley's text is paradigmatic—so as to represent the interiority of the subject constituted in technology: "Who was I? What was I?" In the case of the contemporary technosubject, and according to the logic of the supplement, the technology through which we extend ourselves into the world is never only prosthetic; it is also the process through which we take an "other" into ourselves and become, in the process, other than what we were.

In her important theoretical constructions of posthuman subjectivity, N. Katherine Hayles has long supported the contention that there are ineluctable ties between subjectivity and embodiment. Responding to cyberculture's conflicted attitudes toward the physical body—and its occasional dreams of escaping it—Hayles argues strongly in *How We Became Posthuman* (1999) against the valorization of informational pattern over materialized presence in some of the discourses of contemporary cybernetics, robotics, and cyberfiction. "As though we had learned nothing from Derrida about supplementarity," she points out, "embodiment continues to be discussed as if it were a supplement to be purged from the dominant term of information" (12).[16] For Hayles, the body is exactly the supplement that constitutes the (psychic) identity that it completes. The dilemma for the posthuman technobody, however, is what we might think of as its overdetermined supplementarity. Victor's Creature is doomed to abject exile and death in large part because of the grotesque excess of his physical being. In this view, cyberpunk stories are always about bodies, perhaps most especially when they seem most concerned with virtuality.[17]

I want to take a brief tangent here to consider again the very different narrative location of fictional subjects, such as Asimov's Machines, whose function is to represent technological alterity. A key figure in two of Gibson's more recent cyberfictions, *Idoru* (1996) and *All Tomorrow's Parties* (1999), is the "idoru" or "idol-singer" Rei Toei, a computer-generated simulacrum described as "a personality-construct, a congeries of software agents, the creation of information-designers … She is akin to what … they call a 'synthespian,' in Hollywood" (*Idoru* 92). Rei Toei is intensely erotic and completely virtual: "Her audience knows that she does not walk among them; that she is media, purely. And that is a large part of her appeal" (*Idoru* 55). She herself draws a distinction between the technology of simulation upon which she depends and her sense of an autonomous self: "This is a hologram," she tells Rydell on her first appearance in *All Tomorrow's Parties*, "But I am real" (153). In the final chapters of *Idoru*, Laney becomes overwhelmed by the density of the idoru's information. He perceives her as data developing in time and he considers how this data "had begun to acquire a sort of complexity. Or randomness … The human thing" (251).

In this brief passage, *Idoru* suggests that "the human thing" has no fixed material attributes. Recalling the terms of the Turing Test, "the human thing" construed as "intelligence" or "sentience" is nothing inherent in the body. Its defining feature is not body figured as presence, but density of information figured as complex pattern. Like the far-future virtual subjects in Egan's *Schild's Ladder*, the idoru represents a dream of mysterious disembodied perfection of the sort that Hayles views with such skepticism in *How We Became Posthuman*. She is the West's dream of an exotic Eternal Feminine (re)produced as technological simulacrum. When Laney's eyes meet hers, he falls into a romantic fugue-state: "He seemed to cross a line. In the very structure of her face, in geometries of underlying bone, lay coded histories of dynastic flight, privation, terrible migrations" (*Idoru* 175).

At the conclusion of *All Tomorrow's Parties*, the story of the idoru takes a clever and unexpected turn. Rei Toei frees herself from her technological housing and enters the physical world as an autonomous entity—or entities. The idoru is translated into material form at the same moment at hundreds of different "nanofax" outlets, replicated like software in the very process of becoming embodied. We last see Rei Toei "walking out of every Lucky

Dragon [convenience store] in the world" (*All Tomorrow's Parties* 269). Ironically, the idoru disappears from the space of textual representation just as she crosses from virtuality (the perfection of representation) to materiality (the authenticity of presence). Pattern is translated into presence only to be transformed into absence, providing one of the keynotes upon which Gibson's novel concludes. What/how are we to think about Rei Toei's embodiment? What might be the effect(s) of the "supplementary" bodies that she assumes in the process of constituting her new subjectivity/ies? It is essential to the idoru's nature that we cannot know the answers to these questions. The idoru heralds a kind of radical hermetic alterity, aptly represented in her disappearance from Gibson's text at the very moment she physically enters its fictional world.

In contrast, cyberfiction that evokes *Frankenstein* as intertext invites the reader's empathy on behalf of the technobody. It aims, as does *Frankenstein*, to naturalize the "unnatural" ontology of the technosubject, in effect to (re)humanize it. Marge Piercy's slipstream novel, *He, She and It* (1991), which "freely borrowed" from both Gibson's cyberpunk fiction and Haraway's cyborg theory (431), evokes *Frankenstein* in order to situate her artificial subject squarely within the human-built world. Piercy's android Yod measures it/himself against Victor's Creature in the course of a not-so-sentimental education. Piercy's novel is set in 2059 and depicts a more or less familiar near-future post-apocalyptic landscape devastated by dire environmental and nuclear disasters. The Middle East has imploded and Jerusalem has been destroyed in a terrorist attack; political power is in the hands of typically ruthless multi-national corporations. Yod is the novum in this near-future world, an android (although Piercy refers to him as a cyborg) indistinguishable from organic human beings, "a blend of lab-grown biological and electronic components" (148). Yod has been constructed as a weapon to guard the Jewish freetown of Tikva from being taken over by the cutthroat corporate powers that surround it. One strand of Piercy's multiply-plotted story follows his education into that human community.

As in Piercy's earlier feminist-utopian novel, *Woman on the Edge of Time* (1976), everything in *He, She and It*, including its primary plot and its principal characters, is reflected in and doubled by other events and characters. This notably includes Yod's partial reflection in the famous "stimmie" designer Gadi Stein, whom the novel sets up as his foil. Gadi is the son of Avram Stein and the aptly-named Stein is the brilliant scientist who is Yod's creator. "Well, call me the Son of Frankenstein!" exclaims Gadi, ironically but accurately, when he discovers what Yod really is (148).

Befitting a novel whose cyborgs are shaped in part by their author's enthusiasm for Haraway's "Manifesto," Piercy's text emphasizes the need in all her characters for affective relationships: it focuses on interactions between parents and children, between lovers and old friends, and, most significantly, it explores the connections—affective, ethical, and political—between artificial and human subjects in the community. Recalling some of the language of the "Cyborg Manifesto," the grandmotherly Malkah considers that "Yod has no prejudice against a woman because of age. He is not breaking any Oedipal taboos, for he was not born of woman" (162). At the same time, as Neil Badmington points out (89), Yod is not much like the "post-gender" cyborg originally imagined by Haraway, given his techno/hetero/sexual relationship not only with the elderly Malkah but also and especially with Shira, the novel's main protagonist.

In a process that owes nothing at all to irony, reading *Frankenstein* precipitates an existential crisis in Yod, recalling the impact of the texts—including *Paradise Lost* and *The Sorrows of Young Werther*—which cast Victor's Creature into passionate self-questioning: "Who was I? What was I? Whence did I come?" (153). Yod reads *Frankenstein* as an account of his own provenance, so that for him Shelley's novel is like a version of the notebooks abandoned by Victor in which his Creature discovers the horror of what he "really" is: "I sickened as I read. 'Hateful day when I received life!' I exclaimed in agony" (Shelley 155). Given Yod's psychic dis/identification with the Creature in Shelley's novel, he begins to doubt his ontological legitimacy as an autonomous subject: "Dr. Frankenstein was a scientist who built a monster. I am, as Gadi said, just such a monster. Something unnatural" (150). This is the textual opening which allows Piercy to deliver a key passage in her novel.

Shira, Yod's human lover, speaks for Yod, insisting on his right to membership in a community of autonomous subjects: "we're all unnatural now. I have retinal implants. I have a plug set into my skull to interface with a computer ... We're all cyborgs, Yod. You're just a purer form of what we're all tending toward ... And unlike the monster's friend in *Frankenstein*, I don't need to be blind to like you" (150–51). Later in the novel, this cyberfictional self-reflexivity is reiterated through the character of Nili, a human woman technologically retrofitted to be a soldier and an assassin. Watching her for the first time, Shira wonders whether she is a non-human like Yod: "'Is she a machine or human?' ... 'That's a matter of definition,' Riva said mildly. 'Where do you draw the line? Was she born from a woman?'" (191).

Piercy's text rejects any attempt to associate the hybrid technobody with monstrosity in a world where, to echo one of Haraway's more familiar dictums, "the cyborg is our ontology; it gives us our politics" (150). At the end of the novel, Yod, who is unable to overcome his programming as an instrument of destruction, enacts a cyborg politics in destroying both himself and Avram his creator: "I want there to be no more weapons like me. A weapon should not be conscious" (415). This gesture recalls not only the mutually assured destruction of Victor and his Creature, but also the complex act of "monstrous" and suicidal violence that resolves the plot of Piercy's earlier *Woman on the Edge of Time*.[18] In a key passage that recalls Shelley's original critique of unbridled technoscientific ambition, one of Yod's designers speaks to his decision: "It's better to make people into partial machines than to create machines that feel and yet are still controlled like cleaning robots. The creation of a conscious being as any kind of tool ... is a disaster" (412).

RE-MEMBERING *FRANKENSTEIN* AS A REAL GIRL

> I am buried here. You can resurrect me, but only piecemeal. If you want to see the whole, you will have to sew me together yourself.
>
> Shelley Jackson, *Patchwork Girl* ("Graveyard")

Again succumbing to pattern recognition, I note that *Frankenstein* plays a role in N. Katherine Hayles's recent study, *My Mother Was a Computer* (2005), which includes a substantial discussion of Shelley Jackson's *Patchwork Girl; or, A Modern Monster by Mary/Shelley & Herself* (1995). *Patchwork Girl* is a well-known early hypertext that rewrites *Frankenstein* as experimental feminist cyberfiction; it is a drama in which technology threatens the body as well as the psyche of the subject with fragmentation and dispersal.

For Hayles, *Patchwork Girl* is of interest because it is "deeply concerned with how digital media enact and express new kinds of subjectivity" (143). She identifies its "central dialectic" as "the oscillation between fragmentation and recombination" (165) in the story of the monster/narrator ("Herself") who is Jackson's protagonist. Fragmentation and recombination also describe the strategies through which a reader experiences Jackson's hypertext, because its formal features echo its narrative elements. Hayles notes that, "Like the female monster's body, the body of this hypertext is also seamed and ruptured, composed of disparate parts with extensive links between them" (147). It makes sense that cyberfictions that appropriate *Frankenstein* as an intertext would dramatize the challenge faced by their fictional characters to, in the words of Jackson's monster, "invent something new: a way to hang together without pretending I was whole" (Jackson qtd. Hayles 166). In this view, Rosi Braidotti's theoretical construction of "an alternative feminist subject" is evocative of the cyborg subjectivity imagined in *Patchwork Girl*:

> According to this vision of a subject that is both historically anchored and split, or multiple, the power of synthesis of the "I" is a grammatical necessity, a theoretical fiction that holds together the collection of differing layers, the integrated fragments of the ever-receding horizon of one's identity.
>
> (166)[19]

Or, as Hayles observes in the discourse of cybernetics, "the distributed cognition of the posthuman complicates individual agency" (*How We Became Posthuman* 4).

The last cyberfiction I want to discuss here is Shariann Lewitt's "A Real Girl" (1998). Marked both by the feminist revolution in 1970s SF and the cyberpunk revolution of the 1980s, Lewitt's "A Real Girl" is a hi-tech lesbian-feminist parody of the Pinocchio story.[20] Although Lewitt's text makes only one reference to Shelley's, that one instance resonates throughout the second half of her story in a way that ironically compromises the seeming transparency of the title phrase.

Lewitt's narrator/protagonist is an artificial intelligence who, in an anti-Cartesian commitment to embodiment and sexual difference, is about to be downloaded into a cloned female body. Like Gibson's idoru, Lewitt's protagonist is a virtual subject, an incredibly powerful "neural processor" located at a university research institute, one of only twenty in her future world: "To my normal perception of myself and the world, I am four pounds of neural computing circuitry in a box. ... We are essentially megabrains. ... We don't age. We don't die. I am two hundred years old" (266–67). Also paralleling the story of the idoru, "A Real Girl" concludes as this subject, who is as nameless as Victor's Creature, is about to enter the physical world. She will experience for herself the answers to some of the questions raised in Shelley's story of technogenesis: "What does it mean to be embodied, when the body cannot claim the status of nature? ... How can an artificial life situate itself in the world, and what kind of world does it make for itself?" (Waldby 33).

Lewitt's text is shaped not only by a queer consideration of the homosexual/heterosexual divide, but also by a series of familiar cyberfictional tensions: corporeal and disembodied, organic and artificial, actual and virtual, authentic and inauthentic, free and programmed, human and nonhuman. The "I" of her story—that "grammatical necessity" which is at the same time a "theoretical fiction" (to recall Braidotti's terms)—identifies herself as female and as lesbian; referring to her "clear-cut sexual orientation and preferences," she tells us that, "As I began to understand more about the deep levels of DNA coding the more I realized that it was as embedded in my cellular structure as in any human's" (275). Over the course of her long lifetime, she has enjoyed a number of passionate relationships with women, interacting with her human lovers in "the metaphor," the incredibly realistic simulation provided by sophisticated virtual-reality software. As the story opens, she is about to be downloaded into a specially prepared cloned body. In her own words, she is about to become "a real girl."

"A Real Girl" weaves anticipation into memory as the narrator recounts the story of her life leading up to this climactic moment; it is, as are all good *bildungsromans*, the story of her development into a mature and freely choosing agent. At this stage in her career she has attained the status of "human" at the Institute, not least because of her strategically politicized interactions with her human co-workers:

> Researchers who made statements I found offensive discovered that
> their tasks were delayed and regularly bumped to the bottom of the

queue ... I [have] great power at the institute ... Graduate students address me as "Professor" and the researchers refer to me as "my dear colleague."

(275)

In spite of her privileged status, she is determined to risk everything to become a "real girl," not only because, as a scientific researcher, "I deserved recognition that an AI never gets" (278), but also to turn her romantic relationship with a brilliant mathematician from a virtual into a physical reality. In part, this is a reaction to her abandonment by a previous lover who tells her: "You're not capable of real feeling, of true love, of sensuality and of any form of sexuality. Because you're a machine and that's all you'll ever be." This same lover points out the loss of status, privilege, and power that she risks if she enters the physical world, assuring her that embodiment will only transform her into "Frankenstein's monster" (274). "A real girl"—the phrase repeated like a mantra by Lewitt's narrator—promises the ontology and the subject position that that will counter the abjection and loss implied in the position "Frankenstein's monster": "I began to seriously explore the possibility of a body ... I accessed the full text of *Frankenstein* and every other book about created life. I perused journals of philosophy and ethics ... to answer the questions she had raised" (274).

Lewitt's story never resolves the questions that it raises about what constitutes "a real girl," given the disparity between the comfortable familiarity of the identity category and the singular subjectivity which lays claim to it. The subject constructed in this story—a two-hundred-year-old lesbian artificial intelligence about to be downloaded into an eighteen-year-old cloned body—has so little to do with common-sense categories such as "real" and "girl" that the categories themselves are rendered almost unintelligible in Lewitt's text. This suggests in metaphorical terms one element of the story's feminist politics, its narration of the differences within the female subject, where that subject is the site of multiplicity and fragmentation—in this it resembles the exploration of hybrid subjectivities in other cyberfeminist fictions such as Jackson's *Patchwork Girl* and Thomson's *Virtual Girl*.

By the story's conclusion—at the point just before this grand experiment is initiated—the phrase "a real girl" has become thoroughly estranged from its conventional meanings, so that the distinction begins to dissolve between it and its oppositional category, "Frankenstein's monster." Each resonates with elements of hybridity, artificiality, and ambiguity. What distinguishes this particular postmodern "monster" from Victor's Creature is her active involvement in the process of her own construction—which is, after all, one way to represent both the self-awareness and agency of the technosubject. When her current lover forbids her to take the risk of embodiment, "'It's my risk,' I said. 'My choice. And I will'" (265).

Among the many interesting elements in this story is the complex way in which Lewitt takes up the question of the body's role as the material substrate of the self, the corporeal mediator between mind and world. Forms of instantiation, to recall Hayles's arguments, are inseparable from subjective identities and Lewitt's narrator is aware of what she will lose of her (non-human) self in the process of becoming "a real girl":

> I will have to give up this power if I become human ... I will only be able to relate to the others of my kind via keyboard or interface.
> I wonder what other AIs would think of me if I become a human. ... There are severe disadvantages to being a real girl.

(275)

For the "I" of Lewitt's story, a female body provides the means of transformation into a "real," that is, a human woman, for better or for worse. Far from merely an envelope designed to supplement an already existing psyche, this is a story of "becoming flesh" in which the flesh promises a radical transformation in the subjectivity of the artificial self. The final words in Lewitt's story are offered to the reader as a kind of ironic performative: "I realize that I know nothing of what I will be when I wake up, except for one thing. I will be a real girl" (282).[21]

If cyberpunk has had a "Frankenstein" effect on the future, to recall my epigraph, this is not least in terms of its influence on the technosubjects of contemporary cyberfiction, its representation of a new model of the technosubject composed from diverse fragments of ontology and philosophy, a subject at once organic and machinic, at once the subject and object of its own technoscientific projects. In her discussion of *Frankenstein*, Waldby notes that Victor's creature "is utterly heterogeneous" (33). It may be that at the core of every cyberfiction is a story that, like *Frankenstein*, is "at odds with the notion of identity as such" (Waldby 33), so that Jackson's hypertextual Patchwork Girl/monster—embarked on a quest to "invent something new: a way to hang together without pretending I was whole"—is an exemplary postmodern technosubject.

On this side of cyberpunk, in our mutually constitutive relations with technology, in the critical/theoretical commentaries through which we explore our roles in the contemporary technocultural landscape, and in cyberfictions like *He, She and It* and "A Real Girl" that turn to Shelley's novel as a progenitor text, it appears, unsurprisingly, that we are both Frankenstein and his Creature, both the creators and the created. Cyberpunk is one narrative shape of our deeply unnatural nature as human beings who are also technological beings, for whom technology has become a second nature. *Neuromancer* and "The Cyborg Manifesto," which appeared at the same cultural moment, both tell stories about how the distinctions between bodies and machines have become increasingly difficult to maintain, one among many such distinctions threatened with collapse under the sign of the postmodern. What Haraway suggested over two decades ago is perhaps even more accurate today:

> High-tech culture challenges these dualisms in intriguing ways. It is not clear who makes and who is made in the relation between human and machine. ... There is no fundamental, ontological separation in our formal knowledge of machine and organism, of technical and organic.
>
> (177–78)

This is a discussion about re-membering—re-membering Shelley's *Franken-stein* and re-membering the fragmented subjectivity stitched together like the Creature's body—that is cyberpunk's contribution to contemporary con-structions of the self. As one of Richard Powers's characters observes when he discovers that the artificial intelligence in *Galatea 2.2* has been introduced to *Frankenstein*, "Hm. Mary Shelley. This could be more interesting than we've bargained for" (55).

ACKNOWLEDMENTS

Thanks to my students Sarah Kardash and Bruce Lord, whose work has helped me shape the ideas in this chapter, and to Julia Gruson-Wood for introducing me to Michael Thomas Ford's "A Real Girl."

NOTES

1 "Cyberpunk" is best represented for me by first-generation texts such as William Gibson's "Burning Chrome" (1982) and *Neuromancer* (1984); Pat Cadigan's "Pretty Boy Crossover" (1986) and *Synners* (1991); and Bruce Sterling's "Green Days in Brunei" and *Schismatrix* (1985). These writers are, to revise a phrase of Donna Haraway's, my theorists for cyberfiction. During this same period, other and different stories were being told about the technocultural future, of course, including John Varley's "Press Enter" (1984), Pat Murphy's "Rachel in Love" (1987), and Lois McMaster Bujold's *Falling Free* (1988), all three of which won Nebula Awards. But none found itself at the centre of a Movement, which is what happened when Gibson's first novel, *Neuromancer*, appeared on the scene.

2 "Cyberfiction" is a useful label with which to identify a wide range of cybercul-ture texts. It includes but is not limited to cyberpunk, and it spills over from science fiction into the slipstream. Amy Thomson's mass-market *Virtual Girl* (1993) is cyberfiction, as is Richard Powers's *Galatea 2.2*, which was a finalist for the 1995 National Book Circle Award.

3 In her Introduction to the revised edition of *Frankenstein* published in 1831, Shelley famously concludes: "And now, once again, I bid my hideous progeny go forth and prosper. I have an affection for it, for it was the offspring of happy days, when death and grief were but words, which found no true echo in my heart" (358).

4 "The Legacies of Cyberpunk Fiction" is the title of Thomas Foster's informative discussion of cyberpunk and posthumanism (1–47) that opens his full-length study, *The Souls of Cyberfolk: Posthumanism as Vernacular Theory* (2005).

Foster's goal in *The Souls of Cyberfolk* is to answer "the question of why cyberpunk still matters at this relatively late date" (xiii).

5 Botting's observation is worth quoting in full, in spite of its somewhat puzzling punctuation; Botting himself is quoting Shippey (214): "Left in the past, among the ghosts and ruins of modernity, science fiction finds itself Gothicized. Cyberpunk, its 'retrofitting' ('looking at things retrospectively and making them fit a new system'), a suturing of fragments, is busy 'Frankensteining' the future" (124).

6 Many readers will already be familiar with "The Three Laws of Robots" which serve as the bedrock of robotic programming in Asimov's stories; they remain a logical tour-de-force in their evocation of the standard terms of western technoscience:

1—A robot may not injure a human being, or, through inaction, allow a human being to come to harm.

2—A robot must obey the orders given it by human beings except where such order would conflict with the First Law.

3—A robot must protect its own existence as long as such protection does not conflict with the First or Second Law.

(Asimov n.p.)

In one of his robot stories—"Reason," originally published in 1941—Asimov supplies a straight-faced parody of the Creature's birth scene as dramatized in James Whale's 1931 film version of *Frankenstein* (*I, Robot* 75–76).

7 Sterling's article is one of several "manifestos" posted on a website titled "Beyond Cyberpunk!" See www.streettech.com/bcp/BCPtext/Manifestos/CPInThe90s.html. It is perhaps no coincidence that, for the Sterling who edited *Mirrorshades: The Cyberpunk Anthology* (1986), cyberpunk has fathers but no mothers. One of the pleasant implications of my present discussion is that, more or less in spite of itself, cyberpunk fiction has been instrumental in installing Shelley's novel as an origin text of cyberfiction.

8 Shelley's own artificial person is nameless, of course, and Cadigan's text appears here to be making the very common error of conflating creator (Victor Frankenstein) and creation (his Creature). Given that *Synners* is about artificial intelligence as an emergent phenomenon, however, this conflation—deliberate or not on Cadigan's part—seems nicely fortuitous. See notes 12 and 13 for more on the relevance of emergence to Cadigan's novel.

9 See Zoë Sofoulis's "Cyberquake" for a good overview of some of the shared (cyber)cultural features of cyberpunk fiction and Haraway's cyborg theory (97–101). Sofoulis notes how, "Coming in conjunction with cyberpunk fiction and the personal computer revolution, the Manifesto was well placed to give some focus to expressions of hope and fear about the emergent technoworlds" (100).

10 In contrast, some more recent cybertheorists have not hesitated to welcome Shelley's Creature into its new post-cyberpunk role as "the first cyborg," as he is referred to by the editors of the magisterial *Cyborg Handbook* (Gray et al. 5).

11 For Foster, "posthuman" is a name for and a consequence of our "mutually constitutive" relation to technology. As he explains it, "Posthumanism emerges when technology does in fact 'become me,' not by being incorporated into my organic unity and integrity, but instead by interrupting that unity and opening the boundary between self and world" (10).

12 See Steven Johnson's *Emergence* for a full-length study of this process of systematic feedback, self-organization, and adaptive learning that has provided one promising theoretical approach to the problem of artificial intelligence. Briefly, as Johnson explains, emergent systems "are complex adaptive systems ... [A]gents residing on one scale start producing behaviour that lies one scale

above them: ... simple pattern-recogntion software learns how to recommend new books. The movement from low-level rules to higher-level sophistication is what we call emergence" (18).

13 Cadigan's artificial intelligence, Art Fish, while a participant in the human community, is also an incomprehensible force in its fictional world, a product of the sheer contingency of emergent systems: "The information never stopped coming in, which made for quite a lot of turbulence. But chaos is just another kind of order, and so we have another kind of net now than the one we started out with. We woke it up" (175).

14 Both Amy Thomson and Greg Egan imagine that Gibson's position, rather than Asimov's, will be espoused by the contemporary technosubject. In Thomson's *Virtual Girl*, Maggie, an artificial intelligence housed in a robot body, is asked whether newly freed intelligent machines are planning to take over the world, to which she sensibly responds: "What would we do with it?" (242). The far-future digital subjects in Greg Egan's ironically self-reflexive *Schild's Ladder* have "a good laugh" when they recall the paranoia of long-ago human beings that virtual intelligences would display an "'unstoppable lust for processing power.' ... *Self-restraint?* Nah, we'd never show that. *Morality?* What, without livers and gonads? *Needing some actual reason to want to do this?* Well ... who could ever have too much processing power?" (Egan 140; emphases in original).

15 This passage by Slusser is also quoted by Andrew Milner, who draws upon Slusser's reading in a discussion that folds *Frankenstein* back into Milton's *Paradise Lost* as a story about "the fall," "the sin of hubris punished by nemesis" (153).

16 For Hayles, "conceiving of information as a thing separate from the medium instantiating it is a prior imaginary act that constructs a holistic phenomenon as an information/matter duality" (*How We Became Posthuman* 13).

17 Popular reading has it that Gibson's fiction, especially his earlier cyberpunk, supports the desire to abandon physicality for virtuality. More accurately, as Vint points out, "Gibson's [*Neuromancer*] articulates a particular type of subjectivity that is interested in repressing the body, and it suggests why this stance would be desirable" (109). See her chapter on "Cyberpunk: Return of the Repressed Body" (103–23). I will also just mention here Cadigan's exemplary cyberpunk fictions, *Synners* and "Pretty Boy Crossover," both of which explore ethical and political questions about the powerful temptations of disembodiment and virtuality.

18 See Marcia Bundy Seabury's discussion linking *Frankenstein* and *Woman on the Edge of Time*, much of which is also useful as a way to approach *He, She and It*.

19 This suggests in turn the rich potential of cyberfiction to support some of the theoretical projects of contemporary feminisms.

20 Jane Donawerth's aptly named *Frankenstein's Daughters* (1997) traces a tradition of women's science fiction that begins with *Frankenstein* and includes the work of such writers as Judith Merril, Joanna Russ, and Octavia Butler. Donawerth includes a useful discussion of C.L. Moore's early cyberfiction, "No Woman Born" (1944), which anticipates some of the post-cyberpunk fiction I discuss here in its self-reflexive evocation of Shelley's text as a means of exploring the "humanity" of the technosubject (61–63).

21 "A Real Girl" is also the title of an non-fiction essay by Michael Thomas Ford that appeared the year before Lewitt's story. Ford's "A Real Girl" is his autobiographical account of a gay writer's online female persona, Lily—"personal quote: 'If you want to see it—beg'" (156)—and her hetero(virtual)sexual experiences with a variety of online male lovers: "Yes, this is fantasy. It isn't real. Yet in many ways it is more real to me than actual sex ... Yes, I am a real girl. And yes, I am a real man" (158–59). In technoculture, science fiction and autobiography tell the same stories.

12 Angel(LINK) of Harlem

Techno-Spirituality in the Cyberpunk Tradition

Graham J. Murphy

I think science-fiction readers, as a rule, are very open-minded and are willing to roll with any kind of future you put in front of them. It's a perfect place for exploration of any kind, including religion.

(Lyda Morehouse)

Jesus! What a mindjob! So you're here to save the world.

(*The Matrix* 1999)

The Matrix sequence has generated significant discussion since the first film premiered in 1999, in part due to its pastiche of cultural referents, including "literature, old cartoons, comics, Jung, gaming, Rastafarianism, hacker culture, Goth, animé, Hong Kong kung fu movies, myth, Gnosticism, Judaism, visual movie and art quotes—the list seems neverending" (Goonan 100). *The Matrix*'s seemingly never-ending story, a cycle made explicit in the Architect's rambling (and at-times nonsensical) infodump with Neo in *The Matrix Reloaded* or the park bench meeting of the Architect and the Oracle at the end of *The Matrix Revolutions*, has no coherently stable ground, except perhaps the "overarching cyberpunk vision" that has been squeezed into the trilogy "with admirable condensation and élan" (Goonan 101).[1] For better or worse, *The Matrix* (more than its sequels) has supplanted Ridley Scott's conceptually superior *Blade Runner* (1982) as the most successful (if only on the level of movie studio profits) visual articulation of key cyberpunk tropes popularized decades earlier by Movement-era authors and in Bruce Sterling's *Mirrorshades: The Cyberpunk Anthology*.[2]

What I find interesting in *The Matrix* series, particularly the first film, is the *overt* articulations of techno-spiritualism: the series makes no attempt to hide its techno-spiritual spine but rather glorifies and basks in it. For example, near the beginning of *The Matrix* (1999), Neo (Keanu Reeves) answers his apartment door and hands Choi some black-market software stored in a hollowed-out copy of Jean Baudrillard's *Simulations and Simulacra*. Choi responds: "Hallelujah. You're my savior, man. My own personal Jesus Christ." Choi's deification of Neo is only one of many such

moments and by the end of *The Matrix* Neo has risen from the dead
(a scene foreshadowed by the Oracle's discussion with Neo in her kitchen).
The finale of *The Matrix Revolutions* finds Neo halting the Man–Machine
war in an overt act of (holy) crucifixion that bathes Machine City and the
Matrix in redemptive light while also saving Zion from destruction. The
Wachowski Brothers have saturated *The Matrix* trilogy with diverse religious images, chiefly (but not exclusively) Christian,[3] to construct a mosaic
of religious iconography that positions Neo as the Christ-like, Buddhist-
inspired, techno-spiritual One, a formidable, even non-sensical, beatifica-
tion. Unlike cyberpunk offerings of the 1980s that relied on "individual
transcendence, with escape from social reality rather than engagement with
it" (Wolmark, *Aliens* 118), Neo brings enlightenment and salvation to those
plugged into the virtual reality of the matrix or those buried in the underground city of Zion. In sum, *The Matrix* trilogy revels in a fusion of technology and spirituality that has been a subtle pillar of even the earliest
cyberpunk texts and whose cyber-resilience and increasing engagement with
social reality are evidenced in SF newcomer Lyda Morehouse's recent
AngelLINK series, a "spiritual cyberpunk" tetrad that deploys resistance
identity, project identity, and spiritual faith to critique the conservativism of
post-9/11 America.

"YOU RUNNING THE WORLD NOW? YOU GOD?"— *NEUROMANCER*

In his Preface to *Mirrorshades: The Cyberpunk Anthology*, Bruce Sterling
claims that cyberpunk "is a product of the Eighties milieu" and quite
possibly a "definitive product" (x); interestingly, the meteoric rise of Movement-era cyberpunk also occurred during a period that sociologist Manuel
Castells identifies as a cultural period of Christian revivalism and growing
fundamentalism. He cites a 1979 Gallup poll wherein "one in three adults
declared that they had had an experience of religious conversion; almost half
of them believed that the Bible was inerrant; and more than 80 percent
thought that Jesus Christ was divine" (*Power* 24). Farah Mendlesohn, in
"Religion and Science Fiction," offers an additional assessment, explaining
that the increased division of Church and State in the 1980s perpetuated a
sense of "Christianity-under-siege" that saw conservative Christians taking
"an increased interest in politics as politics moved away from the bread and
butter issues, which they had regarded as none of their business, and
towards the very moral issues central to theologies of personal redemption"
(273).[4] There is spiritual iconography throughout cyberpunk and it is worth
paying attention to cyberpunk's synchronicity with religious revivalism if it
is to be understood as a definitive product of the Eighties milieu, a form of
writing whose tropes "are not just literary tools but an aid to daily life"
(Sterling, Preface xi).

Although Vernor Vinge is not cyberpunk-proper, John Clute calls Vinge the "godfather of cyberpunk" ("Science" 71) and his cyberspace-based novella *True Names* (1981) a "cusp narrative," a tale "which began the task of refocusing the genre—after the half-century of relatively unexamined fit between generic goals and our understanding of the nature of the times" (71). Vinge presents cyberspace as the Other Plane and populates it with magical avatars and icons of epic fantasy even though "there was nothing supernatural about them or about the Other Plane, that the magical jargon was at best a romantic convenience and at worst obscurantism"(60–61). The hacker protagonist Mr. Slippery is blackmailed by the government into uncovering the identity of the Mailman, a dangerous fugitive hacker who has been breaching government and civil databases. Mr. Slippery enlists the aid of fellow hacker Erythrina and they learn the Mailman is a self-evolving Artificial Intelligence threatening to take control of an extensive cybernetic network that encompasses 98% of the globe.

Unable to defeat the Mailman without a significant increase in computational power, both Mr. Slippery and Erythrina tap into the global system and exponentially increase their processing power. For example, the search for the Mailman in civil databases is a search "that could only be dreamed of by mortals" (Vinge 286). The AI Mailman attempts to convert them to its cause and logically reasons that "like the gods of myth, we can rule and prosper" (Vinge 293). Finally, Mr. Slippery realizes "[b]y the analogical rules of the covens, there was only one valid word for themselves in their present state: they were gods" (300). In achieving this computational power, they transcend human boundaries for the betterment of the world, contra Movement-era cyberpunk whose protagonists are decidedly less altruistic. Upon defeating the Mailman they both return to their corporeal bodies, although Mr. Slippery (Roger Pollack) realizes Erythrina (Debby Charteris) has her own agenda. Pollack learns that the handicapped Debby has initiated a transference of her essential self to transcend the limitations of her diseased body, but he finds Erythrina's protection of the Other Plane profoundly comforting: he thinks

> of the slow-moving guardian angel that she would become. *Every race must arrive at this point in its history*, he suddenly realized. A few years or decades in which its future slavery or greatness rests on the goodwill of one or two persons. It could have been the Mailman. Thank God it was Ery instead.
>
> (329)

It is highly likely William Gibson read (and had been influenced by) Vinge's *True Names*: his immensely popular *ur*-cyberpunk novel *Neuromancer* (1984) subtly acknowledges Vinge when Case enables the AI Wintermute's "true name" (262) to be spoken so it can transcend its mainframe. In *Neuromancer*, Gibson has replaced Vinge's epic fantasy motifs with a cybernetic matrix that is "[u]nthinkable complexity. Lines of light ranged in the nonspace of the mind, clusters and constellations of data. Like city lights, receding" (51). As with Vinge, techno-spiritualism and transcendence are goals key characters in Gibson's diegesis pursue, although Case's motivations have less to do with saving the world than saving his skin, or discarding it as the case may be. For example, *Neuromancer* opens with the hacker anti-hero Case sitting in the Chatsubo (a Japanese bar for American expatriates) and reflecting on events that have left him unable to jack into the cyberspatial matrix: "For Case, who'd lived for the bodiless exultation of cyberspace, it was the Fall. In the bars he'd frequented as a cowboy hotshot, the elite stance involved a certain relaxed contempt for the flesh. The body was meat. Case fell into the prison of his own flesh" (Gibson 6). Case's capital-F "Fall" from cyberspace is akin to the biblical Fall, the expulsion of Lucifer from Heaven that is then restaged in God's expulsion of Adam and Eve from the Garden of Eden. To jack into the matrix is apparently a return to a virtual realm of endless possibilities, a transcendence symbolically akin to returning to Heaven or Eden. Other not-so-subtle spiritual references include Wintermute asking Case: "You want I should come to you in the matrix like a burning bush?" (169), an evocative image since Case will eventually ask the newly-merged AI if it is now God (270). Finally, Case's deceased mentor, McCoy Pauley, cheats death because he exists as a virtual construct, thereby living up to his hacker *nom-de-guerre*: the Lazarus of cyberspace.

Techno-spirituality also informs both *Count Zero* and *Mona Lisa Overdrive* when the Wintermute/Neuromancer entity returns as "evolved into something rich and strange: a pantheon of voodoo deities known as the *loa*" (Dery 55) that, according to Paul Alkon, highlights "ambiguous new versions of supernatural marvels that function metaphorically to call into question the moral dimension of human encounters with the almost magical power of our cybernetic machinery" (84). On one level, voodoo serves a mundane function: it is a street religion that allows the marvelous to be "more emphatically present" (Alkon 84). In *Count Zero*, Lucas translates for Bobby: "Think of Jackie as a deck, Bobby, a cyberspace deck ... Think of Danbala, who some people call the snake, as a program. Say as an ice-breaker. Danbala slots into the Jackie deck, Jackie cuts ice" (Gibson, *Zero* 114). On the other hand, there exists an entirely *other* level to the street tech language: although Bobby dismisses the voodoo language as simply "some game they ran on people" (Gibson, *Zero* 115), Lucas explains there is a voodoo level that escapes street tech reductivism:

> We may be using different words, but we're talking tech. Maybe we call something Ougou Feray that you might call an icebreaker, you under-stand? But at the same time, with the same words, we are talking about other things, and *that* you don't understand.
>
> (Gibson, *Zero* 114)

As Alkon explains, Gibson's success in *Count Zero* and *Mona Lisa Overdrive* is to keep both street tech and spiritual codes active and overlapping; therefore,

> [if] it is accurate rather than merely a metaphorical manner of speaking to say that the matrix has a god—that there is a god in the machine—then it is also accurate to describe the interventions of that god in Gibson's story as supernatural marvels.
>
> (85)

Consequently, one cannot help but to concur with Samuel Delany's conclusions of the metaphysical overtones of Gibson's *Neuromancer* trilogy:

> Religion rumbles all over the place in Gibson, just below the surface of the text: cyberspace is haunted by creatures just a step away from Godhood. And religious parallels begin to rumble through is plots almost everywhere we turn. The hard edges of Gibson's dehumanized technologies hide a residing mysticism.
>
> (quoted in Wolmark's "Cyberpunk," 154)

Sterling's *Schismatrix Plus* (1996, but released individually from 1982–85) lacks the virtual realities of Vinge or Gibson but it too is fascinated with (individual) transcendence and mutable embodiment. In "Swarm" (1982), Shaper agent Captain-Doctor Simon Afriel is captured by the Swarm, a gestalt organism of space-faring insectoids that live in the Hive, a warren dug out of "one of the millions of planetoids that circled the star Betelgeuse" (242). As the Swarm explains to Afriel, his post/human Shaper form (as well as the post/human form of the Mechanists) cannot contain the universe's wealth of knowledge and future shock; rather, "your race is already flying to pieces under the impact of your own expertise. The original human form is already becoming obsolete ... In a hundred years you will not even be a memory. Your race will go the same way as a thousand others" (255). In response to Afriel's query ("what way is that?"), the Swarm alludes to some higher, non-corporeal immortal form, a *being* that has transcended the Schismatrix and left it behind. This post-post/humanism echoes the Christian Rapture as its chosen ones have

> passed beyond my ken. They have all discovered something, learned something, that has caused them to transcend my understanding. It may be that they even transcend *being*. At any rate, I cannot sense their presence anywhere. They seem to do nothing, they seem to interfere in nothing; for all intents and purposes, they seem to be dead. Vanished. They may have become gods, or ghosts.
>
> (Sterling 255–56)

In the *Schismatrix* novella (1985), this post-post/humanism is explicitly described (in nearly two dozen instances throughout the Shaper/Mechanist collection) as the Fifth Prigoginic Level of Complexity, a "spontaneous self-organization" into a higher level of complexity (Sterling 183). Essentially, Sterling's Schismatrix is a universe that

> evolves along one scale or Prigoginic level until it reaches its 'event horizon' within that level. Then the system moves toward a catastrophe or statistical bifurcation familiar to chaoticians, often accreted around a single node or "catalyst" ... At crisis, the system prepares itself to take "the Prigoginic Leap" into a new order of being, one discontinuous—and in some sense incommunicado—with the previous one.
>
> (Porush, "Prigogine" 377–78)

The Faustian terms of Prigoginic transcendence, however, are profoundly uncertain and Prigoginic competition is the name-of-the-game: diverse economic ideologies and social groups—Galacticism, Détentism, Zen Serotonin, or the Lobsters—pursue different paths to their own transcendental enlightenment, paths which bring them into conflict with one another. In this case, transcendental enlightenment typically falls victim to clade warfare and plunges Shapers, Mechanists, and the multitudinous sub-factions into economic competition and ideological warfare that forecloses transcendence; instead, as Mark Bould argues in this anthology, Shapers' and Mechanists' "treatment of capitalist economics as physical laws cannot help but suggest that whatever else motivates them, [they] are both concerned with developing the best fit with a universe which is conceived of as being a realm of capital" (118). It is not until the end of *Schismatrix*, however, that (first) contact, the only contact, with this divine transcendence is actually achieved: Lindsay Abelard communicates with the Presence who, in its unheard voice, explains that describing transcendence as the Fifth Prigoginic Level of Complexity is as good a description as any because

> words don't matter. It's as far beyond Life as Life is from inert matter ... People ... creatures, beings, they're all people to me ... they ask the Final Questions. And they get the Final Answers, and then it's goodbye. It's Godhead, or as close as makes no difference to the likes of you and me.
>
> (235)

SURGING INTO CULTURE; OR, LOOKING BACKWARDS INTO THE FUTURE (SHOCK)

Cyberpunk's focus on transcendence in such forms as mutable embodiment, virtual realms of seemingly unlimited power, or post-post/human evolution within an Eighties era of spiritual revivalism and fundamentalism probably shouldn't be too surprising; after all, Sterling has commented on the 1980s as a period that has seen the advances of the sciences [a]s so deeply radical, so disturbing, upsetting, and revolutionary, that they can no longer be contained. They are surging into culture at large; they are invasive; they are everywhere. The traditional power structure, the traditional institutions, have lost control of the pace of change.

(Preface xii)

Manuel Castells offers a parallel (and more substantial) assessment of the 1980s when he demonstrates in both *The Power of Identity* and *End of Millennium* that religious revivalism and fundamentalism are, in part, responses to *informationalism* that "attribute of a specific form of social organization in which information generation, processing, and transmission become the fundamental sources or productivity and power because of new technological conditions emerging in this historical period" (*Rise* 21). One such 1980s-era "technological condition" surging into culture was the market growth of the increasingly-affordable home computer: Apple's Macintosh 128K was introduced in 1984 (the same year as Gibson's *Neuromancer*) with an SF-nal television campaign echoing George Orwell's *Nineteen Eighty-Four*, although the Mac was the means of escaping a colossal near-future dystopia of electronic servitude and obsolescence. The following year Microsoft released Windows Version 1.0, a GUI operating platform that would eventually replace MS-DOS and come to dominate the computer market, albeit in differently-named platforms that appeared increasingly like Mac-doppelgängers in their visual interfaces. The growth of the home computing market is the tip of the informational iceberg and it marked a decade that Castells convincingly demonstrates underwent a process of capitalist restructuring and social cleavages that challenged institutionalized patterns of identity and redefined social class, patriarchy and the family unit, and religious affiliation. Religious revivalism and fundamentalism are then "linked both to a global trend and to an institutional crisis" whose significance comes during a historical period "when global networks of wealth and power connect nodal points and valued individuals throughout the planet, while disconnecting, and excluding, large segments of societies, regions, and even entire countries" (Castells, *Rise* 24). One cannot help but read both the *cyber* and *punk* of cyberpunk—*cyber* as the realm of the Net, the virtual domains that are the avenues of economic domination; *punk* as the realm of the self or the meat, the laborers who construct the circuit boards (until displaced by automation or outsourcing) and internalize identities in a (brave) new wired world—as expressions of the informational transformations that were taking place in an increasingly technological world, transformations whose effects were felt "in the relationships of production, in the relationships of power, and in the relationships of experience" (Castells, *End* 371). Cyberpunk then acts as a way of apprehending these transformations since its authors were "perhaps the first SF generation to grow up not only within the literary tradition of science fiction but in a truly science-fictional world" (Sterling, Preface xi).

Cyberpunk's techno-spiritualism and its fantasies of cyber-mediated transcendence also demonstrate a "re-enchantment of a world thought to have been denuded of religion." As Elaine Graham goes on to note in *Representations of the Post/Human*, this "'technoenchantment' shares with ancient world-views such as Gnosticism an enduring fascination with transport into a hidden, spiritual realm of celestial wisdom beyond the base contingency of the material world" (231).[5] The seductiveness of techno-enchantment or techno-spirituality is understandable because there is a "fascination of sf with faith and with ritual" (Mendlesohn 264) which is the by-product of the genre's origins. One of SF's genetic strands has to do with those scientific romances that "revelled in the immaterial and imparted to genre sf a desire to peer into the heavens" while helping bestow "upon sf a sense of grandeur and wonder at the cosmos and its works" (264). The second strand is the dominance of the fantastic voyage "which offered possibilities for the exploration of religion and of faith" (Mendlesohn 265). Therefore, one can read cyberpunk and, more broadly, cyberfiction as ritualized fantastic voyages that offer cybernauts an old enchantment: the opportunity to peer into the heavens, even if they are cybernetic. Thus, as Margaret Wertheim writes, what is extraordinary "is that while the concept of transcending bodily limitation was once conceived as *theologically possible*, now it is increasingly conceived as *technologically feasible*"and cyber-fiction "is full of stories of humans being downloaded, uploaded, and off-loaded into cyberspace" (263).[6]

Both Elaine Graham and Margaret Wertheim broach two interesting points. First, in spite of cyberspace's digital wonders and cyberfiction's virtual futures, the spiritualizing or technoenchanting of cyberspace is temporally recursive, a looking backwards as a method of moving into the future. In his work on Marshall McLuhan's rear-view mirrorism, Walter Benjamin's angel of history, and Jean Baudrillard's looping reality, Nigel Clark writes that we "tend to begin each of our 'advances' into the cybernetic realm with a rear-vision mirror firmly affixed to the console screen, moving into an indeterminate future with a sort of ongoing recursive gaze" (115). Repeated techno-spiritual overtones of cyberspace are perfectly understandable because "[a]fterimages and premonitions often seem indistinguishable" (Clark 113).

Second, both Graham and Wertheim discuss the bifurcation of physical space so that "[l]ike the medieval Christian Heaven, cyberspace becomes in these tales a place *outside* space and time" (Wertheim 263). In this fashion, cyberspace adheres to its own rules and governance, effectively becoming what Scott Bukatman (inspired by Samuel Delany) explains is a paraspace, a "rhetorically heightened 'other' realm" (*Terminal* 157) that involves an "ontological shift, as [it] redefine[s] and extend[s] the realms of experience and human definition in contradistinction to the possibilities inherent in normal space" (*Terminal* 165–66). Techoenchanted paraspaces figure prominently in Vinge, Gibson, and Sterling, although *The Matrix* is once again useful for highlighting this techno(-medieval) bifurcation of a (cyber/para) space. Kathleen Ann Goonan writes that Neo's fantastic journeys into the cyberspatial matrix demonstrate there "is Above, and there is Below—in fact, *The Matrix* also seems like a series of Dantesque concentric rings" (109). Wertheim also uses the Dante analogy: she demonstrates the concentric rings of Dante Alighieri's *The Divine Comedy* accommodate other layers and realms within a broad physical cosmology. Above is, literally, *somewhere* (as is Below).[7] Spiritual space is then a *physical* space possessing a geographic location, at least according to medieval cosmology until the Renaissance's liberal humanism and the Enlightenment's rationality-through-science remapped the universe and "physical space was extended infinitely and thereby came to occupy the *whole of reality*. Now there was *no room* (even potentially) for any other kind of space to be" (35). Neo's spatial movement from the virtual realms of the matrix to the spaces in-between—the Architect's control centre in *The Matrix Reloaded*; the subway station of *The Matrix Revolutions*—and then to the buried Zion community and Above to Machine City is neo-medieval: *The Matrix* trilogy features a technoverse that includes multiple concentric rings whose Above and Below possess their own logic and rules of governance—rules Neo must struggle to learn—that, in an inversion of the Ptolemaic celestial sphere, locates virtual realms not so much *out there* in the external harmonies of heaven but, rather, in an interior universe, an inner space of a harmonious operating system, a diffuse and distributed network of mainframes, access ports, icons, and avatars.

ANGEL(LINK) OF HARLEM

Concentric rings and hosts of avatars, whether understood as digital identities that allow users to traverse cyberspace or as deities or incarnation(s) of god(s) on Earth, figure prominently in Lyda Morehouse's AngelLINK tetrad. A recent entrant to the sf field, Morehouse has acknowledged her indebtedness to cyberpunk when it came to writing her AngelLINK tetrad— *Archangel Protocol* (2001), *Fallen Host* (2002), *Messiah Node* (2003), and *Apocalypse Array* (2004), this last novel honoured with a 2004 Philip K. Dick Award Special Citation.[8] As a lesbian cyberpunk author, one who feels her "views are not being represented in the White House" (Holmen), it seems Morehouse is more akin to the feminist/queer cyberpunk that dominated the early-1990s than the Movement-era cyberpunk of the 1980s.[9] As the remainder of this chapter will demonstrate, Morehouse's AngelLINK tetrad deploys all of cyberpunk's traditional tropes but also exhibits an "oppositional stance to the dominant ideology" that Wolmark accuses Movement-era cyberpunk of lacking ("Cyberpunk" 146), a defiance of the idea that "[t]ranscendence is not a word that meshes comfortably with the dark, gritty world of cyberpunk" (Goonan 110). Morehouse's AngelLINK series meshes socially engaged transcendence with recognizable cyberpunk tropes and in so doing highlights the importance of transcendence, (spiritual) faith, political commitment, and social action in a narrative arc whose political critique addresses post-millennial concerns regarding identity, religious revivalism, and techno-spirituality.

What makes the AngelLINK tetrad unique is its neo-medieval cosmology moves beyond metaphor: Morehouse introduces angels and devils into her diegesis. *Literally.* Along with such human figures as Deidre McMannus, Emmaline McNaughton, Christian El-Aref (a.k.a. Mouse), Amariah McMannus, Rebeckah Klein, and the Artificial Intelligences Page, Victory (an imperfect copy of Page), Strife (a modified update of Page), and Dragon of the East, Morehouse populates the series with the archangels Michael and Gabriel, lesser angels (e.g. Ariel), fallen angels (e.g. Adram), and, known throughout the series predominantly as Sammael Morningstar, the Devil. The Angel-LINK tetrad presents its characters with a grand and wondrous cosmology that has key figures peering into the heavens (and hell, as the case may be) while simultaneously staging fantastic voyages into different cosmological and ontological realities. All the while, the series' characters struggle to define their responsibilities to one another, the meaning of parental roles, the life-altering power of love, the importance of sexuality, and the role of religion and spirituality. Indeed, Lewis Shiner once decried cyberpunk because

> [t]here seems to be a national need for spiritual values. New age book-stores are doing a land office business in crystals and self-help manuals. People are joining cults and neo-pagan communes. *Newsweek* recently devoted a cover story to the resurgence of religion among young Americans [1990]. How do we keep our families together? How do we deal with addictions to alcohol and drugs and tobacco and sex? What is our place in a chaotic world? Today's cyberpunk doesn't answer these questions.
>
> ("Confessions")

A decade later, Morehouse demonstrates in what might be called "spiritual cyberpunk" that cyberpunk might now be ready to envision what it is Shiner felt it failed to encapsulate a decade earlier.

The AngelLINK tetrad, however, is not evangelically didactic. *Booklist* proclaims in the promotional blurbs for both *Messiah Node* and *Apocalypse Array* that "[m]any readers will cheer on this fast-paced, often abrasive satire as an alternative to the interminable Left Behind series." There is plenty of (possibly abrasive) satire: the Pope proclaims the celestial authenticity of LINK-angels, virtual angels that appear in online visitations, although it is later revealed they are sophisticated software frauds programmed by Mouse, an Islamic computer hacker who also nearly wins the American Presidency with a virtual politician (Reverend-Senator Étienne Letourneau); the archangel Michael is a bisexual who later fathers Amariah, a messiah-candidate; the angel Ariel is a drag queen who mentors Amariah; Sammael Morningstar commits to holy matrimony to the antichrist

Emmaline McNaughton; Page undergoes a spiritual struggle when he(?) accidentally kills Mai, a naked cellist and leader of the Four Horsemen of the Apocalypse, a thrash polka band. In addition, Morehouse takes the opportunity to skewer several organized religions, including Christianity, Judaism, and Islam, by targeting the oppressive beliefs, illogical practices, and social inconsistencies of any organized religion that uses rigid moral and ethic codes to foster discrimination, bigotry, political oppression, socially-acceptable identities, and blind fidelity.

The series' general setting is a near-future America, a country irrevocably shaken by a global apocalyptic event: "A massively destructive bomb called the Medusa had been dropped in the last war. The bomb's nanobots changed—and continued to change—whatever they touched into glass. Hundreds of cities around the world were now empty, crystallized, permanent graveyards" (*Fallen* 4). These bombs, coupled with the ongoing Medusa plague that transforms everything it touches into glass, are the pretext behind a knee-jerk conservative response to unrestrained scientific research: world leaders have "decided they'd have enough. There was a huge backlash against scientists. Religion, in particular the fundamentalist and orthodox varieties, experienced a renaissance" (Morehouse, *Fallen* 19). This fundamentalist renaissance enables conservative theocracies to then become the political authorities throughout the globe.

The online LINK, a virtual system accessed through an implanted nano-tech nexus, remains prominent in a manner akin to Vinge's Other Plane or Gibson's consensual hallucination. It is a ubiquitous and pervasive cyber-netic network beholdened to religious authority: LINK access is only granted to members of a recognized and authorized religion. LINKed citizens constitute what Castells calls a "legitimizing identity," an identity that is "introduced by the dominant institutions of society to extend and rationalize their domination *vis à vis* social actors" (*Power* 8). Therefore, LINKed women have reduced social mobility according to religious practices and the feminist movement has been effectively curtailed; in addition, LINKed citizens are nominally straight because queer identities are illegal, thereby reinforcing heteronormative and patriarchal hierarchies. Targeting women and queer makes perfect sense: the "most insidious and dangerous enemies [to Christian fundamentalists, but fundamentalists in general] are feminists and homosexuals because they are the ones undermining the family, the main source of social stability" (Castells, *Power* 26). In addition, LINKed and unLINKed social class divisions are pervasive and thoroughly entrenched according to politics of access. That minority of the population that remain secular and therefore unLINKed are effectively excommunicated because "if a person didn't at least nominally belong to a religion, they were criminals, outcasts ... Being excommunicated in this day and age had a whole new meaning" (Morehouse, *Fallen* 19).

The absence of LINK access is a stigmata of the disenfranchised who can be thought of as a particular evocation of what Castells calls the

"Fourth World," a diffuse space "populated by millions of homeless, incarcerated, prostituted, criminalized, brutalized, stigmatized, sick, and illiterate persons" (*End* 168). The denizens of Morehouse's unLINKED Fourth World are legally barred from the LINK and its social connectivity unless they return to their respective epistemological closets by converting to an authorized religion (or starting their own and then seeking official sanction) and accepting a legitimizing identity. In *Fallen Host*, Page acknowledges this unpleasant reality: "The disenfranchised ... tend to think that access to the LINK will save them. If only they could LINK to this or that ... Meanwhile, on the LINK, people talk about wage slavery and how the government controls commerce simply because it decides who does and doesn't have access." Page concludes that "[p]eople who don't have the LINK think it's some kind of Heaven; people who do, think it's Hell" (Morehouse 26).

In a manner quite unlike the solipsism of Movement-era cyberpunk and more akin to other post-Movement fictions, Morehouse stages her own neo-medieval Above and Below, a complex system of cosmological realms: the digital, the corporeal, and the angelic. This neo-medieval cosmology is further complicated because each space is diversified. The angelic realm is obviously bifurcated into Heaven and Hell, although Hell is described as a cosmological bubble that is "still subject to His whim, like air rising up from underwater still moved by the currents and eddies" (Morehouse, *Fallen* 67). The digital realm has the LINK juxtaposed against mouse.net, a digital alternative to the LINK that Mouse, its creator, describes as a

> cheap hack of the LINK. The best graphical interface it sports is the receptionist mode I'd logged in to. I'd set mouse.net up as the ultimate shareware, but I didn't exactly design it for anything robust—at least not in terms of prettiness. Bells and whistles never impress me much, so I can't see coding them into anything of mine. In fact, when doing my wizardry, I prefer as little between me and the ugly little ones and zeroes as possible.
>
> (Morehouse, *Messiah* 57)

Mouse.net, an alternative Unix-style platform, is an "independent operating system expressly for the disenfranchised—the people who couldn't otherwise get access to the LINK: atheists, outcasts, dissenters, the homeless, and, ironically, convicted felons whose citizenship was revoked" (Morehouse, *Fallen* 72). Mouse.net takes on a particularly central role in Russia, the only country that has maintained its independence from the current global theological dominance. In post-millennial Cold War irony, Russia has remained the bastion of nation-state theocratic resistance, whether literally for those who live there (whom we only glimpse in the series) or symbolically for those who reside in the United States and look to Russia for inspiration. It is for this reason that Russia becomes the host-country when, in an ironic touch, the Morningstar Foundation agrees to fund research into curing the Medusa plague and bettering humanity. Maxine Mann, "the team leader of Project Titan, responsible for the creation of the original Medusa bomb" (Morehouse, *Apocalypse* 26), comes out of her South African hideout and helps establish a research facility in St. Petersburg and is able to cure the plague.

On both a local and international scale, mouse.net then enables a "resistance identity" among those peoples who are excluded from the LINK, an identity "generated by those actors who are in positions/conditions devalued and/or stigmatized by the logic of domination, thus building trenches of resistance and survival on the bases of principles different from, or opposed to, those permeating the institutions of society" (*Power* 8).[10] These disenfranchised groups can be read as occupying black holes in the broader social continuum, black holes that "often communicate with each other, while being *socially/culturally* out of communication with the universe of mainstream society" (*End* 167). These black holes also serve as rallying points that allow resistance identities to evolve into project identities, identities defined as "when social actors, on the basis of whatever cultural materials are available to them, build a new identity that redefines their position in society and, by doing so, seek the transformation of overall social structure" (Castells, *Power* 8). Castells makes the connection between resistant and project identities clear: "[R]esistance identities may generate project identities, aiming at the transformation of society as a whole, in continuity with the values of communal resistance to dominant interests enacted by global flows of capital, power, and information" (*Power* 422).

The most cogent articulation of Morehouse's project identity is in Harlem where a collision of worlds takes place that allows the religious, atheist, excommunicated, straight, queer, dispossessed, scientists, activists, humanists, Gorgons (nanotechnologically-infected humans with short lifespans), and angels to interact and commune. It is in the nanotechnologically-glassed Harlem that a cultural, political, and social revivalism akin to a second Harlem Renaissance is taking place:

> Indians, Asians, Blacks and the occasional white face sat on stoops and congregated just outside of bustling street cafés, talking. Regardless of nationality, white lab coats were the fashion. Along with the mussed hair and dark-framed glasses look, men and women proudly strutted in their professional regalia. Unable to discuss certain sciences on the LINK, like geography and biology, which might clash with Biblical interpretations, those living here had reverted to an old-fashioned forum—the coffeehouse. There were hundreds of restaurants, cafés, coffeehouses, and bakeries up and down the street. By the looks of the crowds, the restaurants were open twenty-four hours. Everywhere I looked the conversation was heated.
>
> (Morehouse, *Archangel* 274–75)

Harlem's coffeehouses are evocative and compelling locations for political resistance and mobilization. Brian A. Connery explains that the seventeenth-century coffeehouse was "a place where the public gathered to discuss politics or, as many feared, to hatch plots and conspiracies" and they were "both representative of, and instrumental in, the development of the new political and cultural climate, particularly what may be considered the emerging anti-authoritarian mood throughout the culture" (163). In the eighteenth century, the coffeehouse became "a discursive space unregulated by established authority, in which all participants, regardless of their identity or station elsewhere, are considered equally entitled to speak and be heard" (Connery 161–62). This pattern is repeated in Morehouse's Harlem Renaissance redux as Harlem (as well as its kibbutz, an enclave Deidre calls home when she inherits it from her former roommate Rebeckah, a lesbian freedom-fighter) emerges as a site for resistance-turned-project identities. Harlem uses mouse.net, faith, and coffeehouses to connect Fourth World citizens and allow them to escape their black holes, thereby finding a h(e)aven and community that, in *Apocalypse Array*, spreads out to the wider social network as people unLINK and actually begin debating religious doctrine. Towards the end of *Apocalypse Array*, a newspaper article reveals the loss of institutionalized religious authority in France following a democratic election of LINKed and unLINKed citizens, a vote that is seen "as a major victory. Dancing erupted in the streets of New York at the news, causing some people to sing 'Ding-dong, the witch is dead.' Similar proposals are in the works in several other major countries, including the United States" (324).

Much as cyberpunk's original wave was a definitive product of the 1980s, so too can the AngelLINK series be read as a definitive product of this new millennium. The transformation into an informational age continues (relatively unabated), there are increasing anxieties about the Net and the self, America has become increasingly SF-nal in its post-9/11 technological surveillance programs and related security measures, and American politics are heavily influenced by religious conservativism, although this last point is probably not surprising because America "has always been, and still is, a very religious society" (Castells, *Power* 23–24), clearly evident in the phenomenal success of Mel Gibson's *The Passion of the Christ* (2004) or Tim LaHaye and Jerry B. Jenkins's *Left Behind* series, the protests over *The Da Vinci Code* and *Angels and Demons* (both Dan Brown's novels (2003; 2000) and Ron Howard's films (2006; 2009)), social debates on stem cell research, gay marriage and California's Proposition 9 (2008), abortion, or intelligent design, and the reliance on religious morality to fuel politics. Morehouse's series is, in part, a metaphor for major dissatisfaction(s) with a religiously conservative post-9/11 political climate, a novel designed to be "fairly scary to the average reader of science fiction. I wanted to provoke the idea that, unchecked, this world could turn into something akin to Margaret Atwood's *A Handmaid's Tale*" (Holmen). But, much like *The Matrix* trilogy's techno-spirituality is deployed as a boon for humanity, the AngelLINK tetrad also rejects stoic resignation that things are things: the dark pessimism of this series shifts into spiritual, social, cultural, and personal resistance in the project identity of Harlem, the kibbutz, mouse.net, and even divine inspiration that resists institutionalized dogma. In the end, Lyda Morehouse's AngelLINK tetrad capitalizes on the fantastic journey, techno-spirituality and transcendence, and identity politics to explore questions of spirituality, morality and faith that seeks (and demonstrates) inspiration from Above and political engagement down here Below.

ACKNOWLEDGMENTS

I want to thank Sherryl Vint and Veronica Hollinger for providing invaluable feedback that helped shape this chapter.

NOTES

1 For example, my googling of *The Matrix* and "cyberpunk" as keywords calls forth (as of February 2007) over seven thousand websites, many of which also reference *The Matrix Reloaded* and *The Matrix Revolutions*. Declan McCullagh titled his *Wired.com* article "*The Matrix*: A Cyberpunk Triumph" and proclaimed "[c]yberpunk cinema in its best form yet" while Joshua Moss reported on *Space.com* that *The Matrix* broke the cyberpunk film curse and "for the first time got cyberpunk right." In more academic fare, P. Chad Barnett, in "Reviving Cyberpunk: (Re)Constructing the Subject and Mapping Cyberspace in the Wachowski Brothers' Film *The Matrix*," argues that the first film of the trilogy "brought a Bohemian edge and smart postmodern aesthetic back to cyberpunk" and the film is an "improvement on the same cyberpunk aesthetic (only now in visual form) that the *Mirrorshades Group* made famous" (362). Andrew Butler includes *The Matrix* in his "Cyberpunk Goes to the Movies" chapter of *The Pocket Essential Cyberpunk* and perhaps the title of Stacey Gillis's 2005 book from Wallflower Press says it all: *The Matrix Trilogy: Cyberpunk Reloaded*.

2 "Movement" refers to the original core of cyberpunk—William Gibson, Bruce Sterling, Rudy Rucker, Lewis Shiner, John Shirley, and sometimes Pat Cadigan. In addition, it's also a recognition of Lewis Shiner's preference for "Movement" instead of "cyberpunk" as the label of choice. See Shiner's "Inside the Movement: Past, Present, and Future" for his discussion.

3 *The Matrix*'s relationship to Christianity is not without significant problems. Gregory Bassham argues that the film "features a decidedly non-Christian conception of the Messiah." Unlike Jesus Christ, Neo is "a mere human being; he is far from sinless; he employs violence to achieve his ends (including, arguably, the needless killing of the innocent); and although he may bring liberation from physical slavery and mental illusion, he does not bring true salvation" (114). At the time of his essay's composition, Bassham could not have seen *The Matrix Reloaded* nor *The Matrix Revolutions*; thus, Neo does emerge as something more-than-human in the subsequent films and he does offer salvation to humanity, albeit on a material level that lacks the divine sensibility seemingly necessary for qualification as true salvation. In addition, *The Matrix* seems equally influenced by Buddhism. This is a point Michael Brannigan explores by drawing attention to "its numerous Buddhist allusions: the world as we know it as

illusion, the continuing emphasis upon the role of mind and freeing the mind, distinctions between the dream world and the real world, direct experience as opposed to being held captive of the mind, and the need for constant vigilance and training" (107). Finally, one cannot help but also notice *The Matrix*'s reliance on Plato's allegory of the cave—perception of the universe; transcendence to greater understanding; and, the search for happiness (see Griswold, Jr.).

4 I am not suggesting Movement authors deliberately wrote their fictions as direct commentary on Christian revivalism and fundamentalism; if this were the case then Lewis Shiner, writing of his dissatisfaction with cyberpunk in "Confessions of an Ex-Cyberpunk," likely wouldn't have dismissed cyberpunk for its inability to answer important questions, instead substituting "power fantasies, the same dead-end thrills we get from video games and blockbuster movies like 'Rambo' and 'Aliens.' It gives Nature for dead, accepts violence and greed as inevitable and promotes the cult of the loner."

5 Recent cyberfiction featuring god-complexes and mutable embodiment include: Charles Platt's *The Silicon Man* (1991), Pat Cadigan's *Synners* (1991), Melissa Scott's *Trouble and Her Friends* (1994), Dennis Danvers's *Circuit of Heaven* (1998) and *End of Days* (1999), Tad Williams's *Otherland* tetrad (1996; 1998; 1998; 2001), and/or Marc D. Giller's *Hammerjack* (2005). The most recent cyberfiction is Keith Brooke's "The Accord" (2008) and *The Accord* (2009). In both narratives the virtual realm of the Accord is explicitly likened to heaven and is accessible only at the moment of a person's death, provided s/he has keep updated scans on file. Amidst a saccharine love story and a tortured revenge plot for emotional infidelity, debates also ensue regarding the ethical, moral, and spiritual implications of a virtual heaven that circumvents death. This spiritual enchantment with a sacred cyberspace has also been commented upon by diverse cyberculture scholars, including Michael Benedikt's Introduction to *Cyberspace: First Steps*, Nicole Stenger's "Mind is a Leaking Rainbow," Mark Dery's *Escape Velocity: Cyberculture and the End of the Century*, Margaret Wertheim's *The Pearly Gates of Cyberspace*, and Elaine Graham's *Representations of the Post/Human*.

6 Jeffrey Fisher, whose "The Postmodern Paradiso: Dante, Cyberpunk, and the Technosophy of Cyberspace" influences Wertheim's work, articulates this premise:

> Cyberspace is socially constructed as the postmodern paradise, and all our hopes for virtuality express our desire to escape the limitations of our bodies and the ills of our society. The difference, as [N. Katherine] Hayles notes, is that where this transcendence was once considered theologically possible we now conceive of it as technologically feasible. The continuity of this desire from the medieval to the postmodern world manifests itself in the synthesis of theological and technological discourses into a technosophy of cyberspace.
>
> (122)

7 Wertheim demonstrates the repetition of this divided cosmology in Aristotelean and Ptolemaic epicycles, Giotti di Bondone's medieval art, Raphael's *Disputa (Dispute Concerning the Blessed Sacrament)*, Fra Andrea Pozzo's ceiling of the Church of Sant' Ignazio (Rome), the German mathematician Johannes Kepler's *Somnium (The Dream)*, and a host of other sources.

8 See Susan Harris, "The Devil, God and Cyberpunk."

9 For more information on 1990s-era feminist/queer cyberpunk, see Karen Cadora's "Feminist Cyberpunk" (Chapter 9 in this volume), Tom Moylan's *Scraps of the Untainted Sky* and "Global Economy, Local Texts: Utopian/Dystopian Tension in

William Gibson's Cyberpunk Trilogy" (Chapter 5 in this volume), Graham J. Murphy's "Penetrating the Body-Plus-Virtualisation in Melissa Scott's *Trouble and Her Friends*, Jenny Wolmark's "Cyberpunk, Cyborgs and Feminist Science Fiction," or Sherryl Vint's *Bodies of Tomorrow: Technology, Subjectivity, Science Fiction*, notably her chapter "Raphael Carter: The Fall Into Meat."

10 I'm reminded of Castells's work on Mexico's Zapatistas, those peoples made up of "peasants, most of them Indians, *tzeltales*, *tzotziles*, and *choles*, generally from the communities established since the 1940s in the Lacandon rainforest on the Guatemalan border" (*Power* 77). According to Castells, the Zapatistas were the "first informational guerilla movement" (*Power* 75) who had been abused for centuries "by colonizers, bureaucrats, and settlers. And for decades they have been kept in constant insecurity, as the status of their settlements constantly changed, in accordance with the interests of government and landowners" (*Power* 77). Using the emergent information networks, the Zapatista resistance made extensive

> use of the Internet [that] allowed [them] to diffuse information and their call throughout the world instantly, and to create a network of support groups which helped to produce a movement of international public opinion that made it literally impossible for the Mexican government to use repression on a large scale. Images and information from and around the *Zapatistas* acted powerfully on the Mexican economy and politics.
>
> (*Power* 84)

Afterword
The World Gibson Made

Sherryl Vint

Cyberpunk was declared dead long before people outside a rather small circle of SF writers, fans, and critics even knew that it existed but it refuses to lie peacefully in its grave. One of the key motifs that emerges in the consideration of cyberpunk both during its zenith and at our current cultural moment—whether one wants to think of this as the nadir of cyberpunk, its rebirth in new media and new contexts, or its disappearance from view as its tropes and themes proliferate out into the wider culture and become so ubiquitous as to be invisible—is that cyberpunk is concerned with the consequences of information technology on human existence, what Veronica Hollinger calls our "lives in the computer/ized worlds of technoculture" (this volume 191).

Starting from the premise that the defining icon of cyberpunk is the integration of computer technology with human embodiment, I find myself arriving at the reluctant conclusion that I inhabit a cyberpunk future. Infected by what Istvan Csicsery-Ronay, Jr. ably diagnoses as "futuristic flu," my present has been colonized by this future even as my critical imagination already finds the imagery of cyberpunk as quaintly nostalgic as the protagonist of "The Gernsback Continuum" (1981) finds the futuristic architecture from the 1930s and 40s. Cyberpunk conveys the same feeling of "a kind of alternative America" (Gibson 27) or—to paraphrase the story—twenty-first century that never happened.

Cyberspace is a part of my quotidian existence, but I am no cowboy trying to escape the limits of bodily transcendence. My daily interactions take place via e-mail and Skype more frequently than they do face-to-face, and it is sobering to realise how quickly and easily Facebook has become a part of my routine. Although I am of an age such that I can remember the introduction of the first personal computer—and thus understand why Case loads a program from a cassette tape, something that must surely mystify younger readers—I cannot imagine how I would manage a day without my personal electronics. Technology has not penetrated my skin but it is an extension of my self in the McLuhanian sense. In fact, I cannot remember how I used to manage without information technologies: a few years ago I moved from an urban environment to a rural one in another province and found myself without an Internet connection and with no idea of how to find the nearest *anything*. Armed only with my telephone (an information technology so familiar we often forget it is one), I phoned a friend back home to ask her to Google various businesses so that I could proceed to set up life. How did we used to find things out before we had the Internet? I asked her. I honestly did not know. Five years later, I find it difficult to recall how I managed with only a laptop and an ISP. Newly relocated to an urban area, I now cannot drive without my GPS; walking or exercising are incomplete without my iPod; and although my antiquated Palm Pilot is perfectly adequate for scheduling my appointments, I find myself earnestly believing that I would be much more efficient if I had a Blackberry. Thus embedded in my information milieu and augmented by technology, I live in a cyberpunk future not precisely the one imagined by Gibson when he typed *Neuromancer* and catalysed a movement.

Yet despite all the things that cyberpunk "got wrong" it seems to have gotten more "right" judging both by persistent discussions of the subgenre and the degree to which the introduction of microcomputers revolutionized life in Western industrialized nations. Technology is one of the chief ways in which capitalism expands to fill all previously non-commodified spaces in private life and this is nowhere more apparent than in personal technological devices and the cultures that have arisen around them. Csiscery-Ronay, Jr. argues that "the present we inhabit is a form of exteriorized science fiction" ("Futuristic" 28) and in many ways it seems to me that twenty-first-century life is an exteriorization of some of the motifs of cyberpunk. The plethora of accessories and ways to customise one's laptop or cell phone or iPod echo the deeply personal relationship to one's deck exhibited by Gibson's console cowboys. Telecommuting and collaborating with colleagues on different continents and in different time zones are the white-collar version of Ruby's waldo salvage work in Mixon's *Glass Houses*. We live in a cultural moment characterized not by the replacement of the material with its simulation but rather one in which the material and the simulated are intertwined like a Mobüs strip: they each have distinct identities, but we never inhabit a moment that is purely one or the other.

In Mark Kneale's documentary *No Maps for These Territories* (2000), Gibson explains that his work has always been about trying to "illuminate the moment and make the moment accessible." In 1991, *Storming the Reality Studio* strove to illuminate a moment in which cyberpunk and poststructuralist theory seemed to converge as particularly apt descriptions of a world increasingly mediated through information technologies. Similarly, *Beyond Cyberpunk* aims to illuminate what has changed in the twenty-some years since cyberpunk changed the way we imagine and write about the future.

Storming the Reality Studio identified three main areas of interest best addressed by the emergent cyberpunk/slipstream/postmodernist literature it showcased, all of which are present in modified ways in *Beyond Cyberpunk*. First, McCaffery notes "how technological change ... was reshaping human interactions, perceptions, and self-concepts" (18). As Veronica Hollinger's contribution to this volume makes clear, we must regard the field of post-humanism as the inheritor of cyberpunk's engagement with questions of technological determinism and shifting human embodiment. The centrality of posthumanism to recent debates across the humanities reminds us that we should not equate cyberpunk's fading from view as a distinct subgenre with a fading from relevance as a literature best suited to help us understand life in information-dominated technoculture. A second area of concern identified by McCaffery is "the far-reaching effects of postindustrial capitalism on individuals" (20), and many of the essays in this volume attest to the degree to which it is essential to understand the workings of global capitalism to understand the far-reaching effects of information technology on social existence. Mark Bould's reassessment of writers published contemporary to Movement-era cyberpunk authors, for example, reveals that we should have been less concerned with how we were to be uploaded into the Net and more concerned with the ways in which the capital that already "lived" there circulated without us. Finally, perhaps the key focus of *Storming the Reality Studio* was understanding cyberpunk as the literature of the simulacra. In assessments of the original movement, this was frequently seen to be cyberpunk's most radical aspect, but this is the point about which our understanding has most shifted. If *Storming the Reality Studio* might be understood as a call to "retake the universe," then *Beyond Cyberpunk* might be seen instead as an acknowledgement that our lives are constituted by the interpenetration of virtual and material worlds and the only way to retake the universe is to move beyond the binary of simulated/real toward a more dialectical understanding.

Contemporary interpenetrations of material and virtual worlds range from the trivial to the tragic and define twenty-first-century experience in Western, industrialized nations. On the one hand, we find seemingly endless discussion of the "threat" of Second Life, an online 3-D environment in which users can create their own "world" and embrace material and other achievements likely beyond their reach in "first" life. The appeal of such activities express a truism of popular culture criticism demonstrated by Janice Radway's study of romance fiction: whatever the limitations of the text as text, its appeal to its readers is evidence of dissatisfaction with the status quo. On the other hand, we find stories such as the 2005 death "in cyberspace" of a South Korean man after a week of being almost continually online to play *Starcraft*. According to the BBC report on this incident,[1] at least part of the motivation for this obsessive play might be the financial reward it could offer because in South Korea such games are televised and players can make money through salaries and endorsement deals. These examples point to the importance of understanding what Jonathan Boulter calls "the visual imaginary of digital games" (137) as constitutive of both cyberpunk experience and our lives in twenty-first-century technoculture. The world of digital games, like the cultural discourse on posthumanism, is an inheritor of cyberpunk fiction.

Yet these examples also point to the reality of cyberspace as the major technology of late, multinational capitalism. Our exchanges with our digital fantasy worlds are mediated by economics, whether this be the investment in the latest gadget or gaming system required to play at all, or the restructuring of our work lives and prospects as we find that capital has been able to take flight globally while we have remained immured in the body and in local time and space. Mark Bould observes that Manuel Castells's three-volume sociological analysis of network society often reads like a "manual for a cyberpunk role-playing game" (119), an important observation stressing the centrality of questions of capitalist production and consumption to the cyberpunk—our own—future, often overlooked in favour of a focus on body modification in early critical discussions which posited it as a response to postmodern reality. Against the claim that 9/11 ended our flirtation with the idea that representations had replaced reality, I would suggest it is no longer possible to separate representation from reality: the virtual and discursive existence of weapons of mass destruction ("real" for a time based on the belief that they were real and in terms of the real material effects this belief enabled) merge seamlessly with the material and pragmatic reality of troop deployments, devastated cities, and body bags.

Karl Schroeder's *Permanence* (2002), cyberpunk-flavoured in Andrew Butler's terms, makes literal this conflation of material and representational worlds through its technology of inscape, a sort of personal cyberspace through which one perceives the material world. Inscape gets information from nanotags attached to all material objects and the software implanted in the visual cortex adds this to the perceptual data sent between eye and brain. A literalization of the axiom that ideology shapes perception, the world of inscape tags everything with data about ownership and value. Inscape thus technologically transforms the material world, making "it appear that the essence of things is money—that a thing only really exists if it can be bought or sold" (223).

In this cyberpunk-flavoured world, the exemplar cyberpunk hero is no longer Case with his "elite stance ... [of] relaxed contempt for the flesh" (6) but instead may be found in Chung Mae, the protagonist of Geoff Ryman's *Air: or, Have Not Have* (2004). This story of "the last village in the world to go online" (1) focuses on an illiterate peasant woman's struggle to prepare her village in the fictional country of Karzistan for the coming of Air, a wireless Internet interface that interacts directly with the brain. Following a failed test of the system, Mae finds herself permanently connected to the template structure and able to use her connection to negotiate the Internet services available through the village's television. Not surprisingly given the realities of network society, most of Mae's interventions involve preparing the village for integration into the global market, finding a niche to sell their traditionally embroidered handicrafts to elite fashion houses. But *Air* also concerns the importance of presence on the Internet so that certain kinds of knowledge will not be lost. Mae worries the village's distinctive society will disappear and uses her embroidery business to ensure that traditional ways and stories are preserved and articulated to the world. This technology enables the repressed Eloi (and surely the allusion is deliberate and ironic) population of the region to present their story against the official government version. Mae understands the fusion of material and virtual worlds that will be the consequences of going online. She explains, "The world out there has grown bigger. There are two worlds. There is the one you can see, and another world people have made up, and it is bigger than the real one. They call it 'Info'" (99). She works to ensure that her people will not disappear economically through a failure to be present in Info.

Yet Mae does not simply capitulate to the demands of global capitalism and the dictates of Air. She uses the consumerist desire of the West for authentic handicrafts to ensure an income for her village but also to insist on the importance of preserving their distinct lifestyle. She uses Info primarily for business transactions and yet she also perseveres in forming personal relationships, most prominently with a New York fashion distributor named Bugsy. Mae forces Bugsy to understand the vast inequities of wealth that are a consequence of global capitalism, leading Bugsy to see her world in a different way than Info would encourage, forcing her to recognize that "Three billion of us live in a world with lights, cameras, action; the other four billion can't get clean water, let alone bandwidth" (235). Mae works to ensure that when Air comes to the village and similar communities, it will be the UN format, not the Gates format. The novel thus acknowledges the inevitability of the dissemination of information technology but calls upon us to resist the corporatization of this dissemination. Mae engages with the real inequities and struggles over resources in the information age while at the same time remaining aware of her embodied vulnerability as a poor woman in a poor country.

Writing about the then-ground-breaking genre of cyberpunk in a 1988 issue of the UK post-situationist magazine *Vague*, Mark Downham attempts to describe what cyberpunk is through a number of polemics and examples. One of his pronouncements is

> Cyber-Punk attempts to de-mythologise the established cultural codes, in order to decipher concealed strategies of domination, desire, will, power, and the will to power. Cue dry ice, smoke, Leni Riefenstahl. Cyber-Punk allows new genuine symbols of our culture to speak. In essence, our increasingly cyborg [cybernetic organism] [*sic*] relationships with our own artefacts, technologies, hardwired abstractions are realized, reified, idealised, materialised in the more intense level of ideation and practice that constitutes Cyber-Punk. Cyber-Punk is a radical interrogation of the virtual technologies at work in contemporary society.
>
> (37–38)

This has always been the ideal of cyberpunk and at its best moments the genre has been and continues to be able to interrogate the way information technologies have shaped our lives. Yet as the somewhat sardonic description of dry ice and Leni Riefenstahl admits, cyberpunk has also always been plagued by being just a little bit too much in love with its own image as cool and cutting edge. Chung Mae, a perhaps unlikely cyberpunk-flavoured emblem for the twenty-first century, embodies this revolutionary spirit that was the promise of the best cyberpunk fiction, providing us with concrete examples of how we might think through our relationships with our own artifacts and the world they and we make.

Appearing briefly in *No Maps for These Territories*, Jack Womack characterizes Gibson as a visionary and argues that we live, at least in part, in the world that Gibson made: if Gibson "had not written *Neuromancer* when he did about the world as it is and much more about the world that is to come, [then it] would not have taken place in the exact same way that it has."[2] While the degree of Gibson's influence is of course debatable, Womack makes an important point nonetheless in reminding us of the dual exchanges between material culture and discursive representation. Jonathan Boulter characterizes one's relationship to the digital games avatar as uncanny, "at once familiar and unfamiliar" (153), and we in Western industrialized nations in the twenty-first century have a similar relationship to cyberpunk motifs. They are at once familiar evocations of our daily lives, and yet strangely other in the critical focus they bring to encounters with technology that we have begun to take for granted. Our fondest hope for *Beyond Cyberpunk* is that the essays collected here will provoke further reflections on the uncanny and mutually constitutive relationship between our material lives in twenty-first-century technoculture and the cyberpunk-flavoured narratives through which we struggle to understand them.

NOTES

1 http://news.bbc.co.uk/1/hi/technology/4137782.stm (accessed December 4, 2007).
2 Allucquére Rosanne Stone makes a similar point about the influence of Gibson's work on the community of researchers in computer science in "Will the Real Body Please Stand Up?"

Contributors

Mark Bould is a Reader in Film and Literature at the University of the West of England, and a founding editor of *Science Fiction Film and Television.* He is the author of *Film Noir: From Berlin to Sin City* (2005) and *The Cinema of John Sayles: Lone Star* (2009), and co-editor of *Parietal Games: Critical Writings By and On M. John Harrison* (2005), *Red Planets: Marxism and Science Fiction* (2009), *The Routledge Companion to Science Fiction* (2009), *Fifty Key Figures in Science Fiction* (2009) and *Neo-Noir* (2009). He is currently working on *The Routledge Concise History of Science Fiction* and *The Routledge Film Guidebook: Science Fiction.*

Jonathan Boulter is Associate Professor of English at the University of Western Ontario. He is the author of *Interpreting Narrative in the Novels of Samuel Beckett* (2001), *Beckett: A Guide for the Perplexed* (2008), and co-editor of *Cultural Subjects: A Cultural Studies Reader* (2005). His work has appeared in *Cultural Critique, Modern Fiction Studies, Genre, Hispanic Review, Samuel Beckett Today/Aujourd'hui, Journal of Beckett Studies, English Studies in Canada*, as well as in *Digital Gameplay: Essays on the Nexus of Game and Gamer* (2005).

Andrew M. Butler is the editor of *An Unofficial Companion to Terry Pratchett* (Greenwood, 2007) and co-editor of *The Routledge Companion to Science Fiction* (2009), *Fifty Key Figures in Science Fiction* (2009), and the author of books on Philip K. Dick, Cyberpunk, Postmodernism, and Film Studies. A past winner of the Pioneer Award, for his article on the British SF Boom, he is now an editor of *Extrapolation.* He is currently working on *Solar Flares: A Cultural History of Science Fiction in the 1970s* and on cringe comedy.

Karen Cadora received her Ph.D. from Stanford in 1999 and then returned to her engineering roots where she survived the roller-coaster of the Internet bubble and became a Cisco Certified Internetworking Expert. She is currently a senior engineer at Cisco Systems working on digital identity and network security and holds a patent in the area of Voice-over-IP communications.

Neil Easterbrook teaches literary theory and comparative literature at TCU. Recent essays include discussions of SF and ethics, Fredric Jameson, N. Katherine Hayles, Robert A. Heinlein, and Geoff Ryman. He is finishing essays about Greg Egan and mathematics, Kurt Vonnegut and textuality, and the conceits of 1970s SF film. He prefers to use bio-blurbs to place personal ads, but the editors of this volume would not allow it.

Pawel Frelik is Assistant Professor in the Department of American Literature and Culture, at Maria Curie-Sklodowska University, Lublin, Poland. His main academic interests (which are not really different from his non-academic ones) include science fiction, experimental fiction, digital narrativity, and unpopular culture.

Veronica Hollinger is Professor of Cultural Studies at Trent University in Peterborough, Ontario. She has published many articles on science fiction, with particular attention to feminism, queer theory, and techno-culture studies. She is a co-editor of *Science Fiction Studies* and has co-edited two scholarly collections with Joan Gordon, *Blood Read: The Vampire as Metaphor in Contemporary Culture* (1997) and *Edging into the Future: Science Fiction and Contemporary Cultural Transformation* (2002). She has co-edited a third collection with Wendy Pearson and Joan Gordon, *Queer Universes: Sexualities in Science Fiction* (2008). With her SFS co-editors, she is currently completing work on *The Wesleyan Anthology of Science Fiction*.

Rob Latham is Associate Professor of English at the University of California, Riverside, where he directs the Eaton Science Fiction Conference. A co-editor of the journal *Science Fiction Studies* since 1997, he is the author of *Consuming Youth: Vampires, Cyborgs, and the Culture of Consumption* (Chicago UP, 2002). He is currently completing a book on New Wave science fiction.

Brian McHale is Distinguished Humanities Professor of English in Ohio State University. He has taught at Tel Aviv University, West Virginia University, the University of Pittsburgh, the University of Freiburg (Germany), and the University of Canterbury (New Zealand), among other institutions. He was for many year associate editor, and later co-editor, of the journal *Poetics Today*. He is the author of *Postmodernist Fiction* (1987), *Constructing Postmodernism* (1992), and *The Obligation toward the Difficult Whole* (2004), as well as articles on free indirect discourse, *mise-en-abyme*, narrativity, modernist and postmodernist poetics, and science fiction. He is co-editor with Randall Stevenson of *The Edinburgh Companion to Twentieth-Century Literatures in English* (2006) and, with David Heman and James Phelan, of *Options for Teaching Narrative Theory*, forthcoming from the Modern Language Association.

Tom Moylan is Glucksman Professor of Contemporary Writing in English and Director of the Ralahine Centre for Utopian Studies at the University of Limerick. He is the author of *Demand the Impossible: Science Fiction and the Utopian Imagination* and *Scraps of the Untainted Sky: Science Fiction, Utopia, Dystopia*. He has edited *Not Yet: Reconsidering Ernst Bloch* (with Jamie Owen Daniel), *Utopia Method Vision: The Use Value of Social Dreaming*, and *Dark Horizons: Science Fiction and the Dystopian Imagination* (with Raffaella Baccolini), and *Exploring the Utopian Impulse: Essays on Utopian Thought and Practice* (with Michael J. Griffin). His new work is on Irish utopian writing.

Graham J. Murphy teaches in Trent University's Cultural Studies Department and the Department of English Literature as well as Seneca College of Applied Arts and Technology. His work has appeared in *Queer Universes: Sexualities in Science Fiction* (2008), *The Routledge Companion to Science Fiction* (2009), *Fifty Key Figures in Science Fiction* (2009), *Science Fiction Studies, Extrapolation, Foundation, ImageText: Interdisciplinary Comics Studies, Ariel: A Review of International English Literature, Contemporary American Comics: Creators and their Contexts* (2010), and *Conspiracy Theories in American History: An Encyclopedia* (2003). He co-authored *Ursula K. Le Guin: A Critical Companion* (2006) with Susan M. Bernardo and is currently working on the intersections of science fiction, the post/human, and insect ontologies.

Sherryl Vint is Associate Professor of English at Brock University. She is the author of *Bodies of Tomorrow: Technology, Subjectivity, Science Fiction* (2007) and *Animal Alterity: Science Fiction and the Question of the Animal* (2010), an editor of *Extrapolation*, and founding co-editor of *Science Fiction Film and Television*. She has also co-edited *The Routledge Companion to ScienceFiction* (2009) and *Fifty Key Figures in Science Fiction* (2009), and is currently co-writing *The Routledge Concise History of Science Fiction*.

Bibliography

Abraham, Nicholas and Maria Torok. *The Shell and the Kernel: Renewals of Psychoanalysis.* Ed. Nicholas Rand. Chicago: U of Chicago P, 1994.

Acker, Kathy. *Empire of the Senseless.* New York: Grove, 1988.

Alarcon, Norma. "The Theoretical Subject(s) of *This Bridge Called My Back* and American Feminism." In *Making Face, Making Soul/Haciendo Caras.* Ed. Gloria Anzaldúa. San Francisco: Aunt Lute, 1990, pp. 356–69.

Alkon, Paul. "Deus Ex Machina in William Gibson's Cyberpunk Trilogy." In *Fiction 2000: Cyberpunk and the Future of Narrative.* Ed. George Slusser and Tom Shippey. Athens, GA: U of Georgia P, 1992, pp. 75–87.

Alliez, Erie and Michel Feher. "The Luster of Capital." *Zone* 1/2 (1986): 314–59.

Altman, Rick. *Film/Genre.* London: BFI, 1999.

Angenot, Marc and Darko Suvin. "A Response to Professor Fekete's 'Five Theses.'" *Science Fiction Studies* 15 (1988): 324–33.

Ashley, Mike. *Transformations: The Story of the Science-Fiction Magazines from 1950 to 1970. The History of the Science-Fiction Magazine*, Vol. II. Liverpool: Liverpool UP, 2005.

Asimov, Isaac. *I, Robot.* London: Grafton, 1950.

Attridge, Derek. *The Singularity of Literature.* New York: Routledge, 2004.

Atwood, Margaret. *The Handmaid's Tale.* New York: Fawcett, 1985.

Baccolini, Raffaella. "Gender and Genre in the Feminist Critical Dystopias of Katharine Burdekin, Margaret Atwood, and Octavia Butler." In *Future Females: The Next Generation.* Ed. Marleen S. Barr. New York: Rowman & Littlefield, 2000, pp. 13–34.

Badmington, Neil. "Posthuman (Com)Promises : Diffracting Donna Haraway's Cyborg Through Marge Piercy's *Body of Glass.*" In *Posthumanism.* Ed. N. Badmington. New York: Palgrave, 2000, pp. 85–97.

Baggesen, Søeren. "Utopian and Dystopian Pessimism: Le Guin's *The Word for World is Forest* and Tiptree's 'We Who Stole the Dream.'" *Science-Fiction Studies* 14 (1987): 34–43.

Ballard, J.G. "Which Way to Inner Space?" *New Worlds* 118 (1962): 2–3, 116–18.

——. "Myth-Maker of the 20th Century." *New Worlds* 142 (1964): 121–27.

Balsamo, Anne. *Technologies of the Gendered Body.* Durham, NC: Duke UP, 1996.

Banks, Ian M. *Consider Phlebas.* New York: Bantam, 1991.

Barnett, P. Chad. "Reviving Cyberpunk: (Re)Constructing the Subject and Mapping Cyberspace in the Wachowski Brothers' Film *The Matrix.*" *Extrapolation* 41.4 (2000): 359–74.

Barr, Marleen. *Feminist Fabulation: Space/Postmodern Fiction*. Iowa City: U of Iowa P, 1992.

Barrett, David V. "The Lucidity Switch: Jeff Noon Interviewed." *Interzone* 115 (1997).

Barth, John. *Chimera*. New York: Fawcett, 1973.

——. *The Tidewater Tales: A Novel*. New York: Putnam's, 1987.

Barthelme, Donald. *The Dead Father*. New York: Pocket Books, 1976.

Bear, Greg. *Blood Music*. New York: Ace Books, 1985.

Benedikt, Michael. "Cyberspace: Some Proposals." In *Cyberspace: First Steps*. Ed. Michael Benedikt. Cambridge, MA: MIT Press, 1994, pp. 119–24.

——. "Introduction." In *Cyberspace: First Steps*. Ed. Michael Benedikt. Cambridge, MA: MIT Press, 1994, pp. 1–25.

Benford, Gregory. "Letter to the Editor." *Thrust* 26 (1987): 31–32.

Benjamin, Walter. The Arcades Project. Trans. Howard Eiland and Kevin McLaughlin. Cambridge, MA: Harvard UP, 1999.

Berger, Peter L. and Thomas Luckmann. *The Social Construction of Reality: A Treatise in the Sociology of Knowledge*. Garden City, NY: Doubleday, 1966.

Berressem, Hanjo. "'Of Metal Ducks, Embodied Iduros, and Autopoietic Bridges': Tales of an Intelligent Materialism in the Age of Artificial Life." IN *The Holodeck in the Garden: Science and Technology in Contemporary American Fiction*. Eds. Peter Freese and Charles B. Harris. Normal: Dalkey Archive Press, 2004, pp. 72–99.

Best, Steven and Douglas Kellner. *The Postmodern Adventure: Science, Technology, and Cultural Studies at the Third Millennium*. New York: Guilford P, 2001.

Bordo, Susan. "Reading the Slender Body." In *Body/Politics: Women and the Discourses of Science*. Ed. Mary Jacobus, Evelyn Fox Keller, and Sally Shuttleworth. New York: Routledge, 1990, pp. 83–112.

Botting, Fred. "'Monsters of the Imagination': Gothic, Science, Fiction." In *A Companion to Science Fiction*. Ed. David Seed. Oxford: Blackwell, 2005, pp. 111–26.

Bould, Mark. "Incredible Stories about Ordinary People: The Teenage Fiction of Gwyneth Jones/Ann Halam," *Femspec* 5.1 (2004): 197–215.

——. "Landscape, Labour and Capital in the Pastoral Science Fiction and Fantasy of Gwyneth Jones/Ann Halam," *Foundation* 93 (2005): 97–107.

Bould, Mark and Michelle Reid (eds.) *Parietal Games: Critical Writings by and on M. John Harrison*. London: Science Fiction Foundation, 2005.

Boulter, Jonathan. "Virtual Bodies: or, Cyborgs are People Too." In *Digital Gameplay: Essays on the Nexus of Game and Gamer*. Ed. Nate Garrelts. Jefferson, NC: McFarland, 2005, pp. 52–68.

Bradbury, Ray. *Fahrenheit 451*. New York: Ballantine, 1982.

Braidotti, Rosi. "Sexual Difference as a Nomadic Political Project." In *Nomadic Subjects: Embodiment and Sexual Difference in Contemporary Feminist Theory*. New York: Columbia UP, 1994, pp. 146–73.

Brannigan, Michael. "There is No Spoon: A Buddhist Mirror." in *The Matrix and Philosophy: Welcome to the Desert of the Real*: Ed. William Irwin. Chicago: Open Court P, 2002, pp. 101–10.

Brooke, Keith. "The Accord." In *The Year's Best Science Fiction: Twenty-Fifth Annual Collection*. Ed. Gardner Dozois. New York: St. Martin's P, 2008, pp. 461–79.

——. *The Accord*. Nottingham: Solaris, 2009.

Brooke-Rose, Christine. *A Rhetoric of the Unreal: Studies in Narrative and Structure, Especially of the Fantastic.* Cambridge: Cambridge UP, 1981.

Brown, Charles N. Third *Dune* Book a Best Seller." *Locus* 10.3 (1977): 1–2.

——. "New Silverberg Novel: Record Advance Paid." *Locus* 11.4 (1978): 1–2.

——. "1978 Book Summary." *Locus* 12.2 (1979): 3.

——. "1982 *Locus* Book Summary." *Locus* 16.2 (1983): 12, 18–19.

——. "1983: The Science Fiction Year in Review: Book Summary." *Locus* 17.2 (1984): 1, 18–20.

Brown, Stephen P. and Daniel J. Steffan. "Requiem for the Cyberpunks." *Science Fiction Eye* 1.1 (1987): 4.

Brown, Steve. "Before the Lights Came On: Observations of a Synergy." In *Storming the Reality Studio*. Ed. Larry McCaffery. Durham, NC: Duke UP, 1991, pp. 173–78.

Brumberg, Joan Jacobs. *Fasting Girls: The Emergence of Anorexia Nervosa as a Modern Disease*. Cambridge, MA: Harvard UP, 1988.

Buckner, M.M. *War Surf*. New York: Ace Books, 2005.

Bukatman, Scott. "Postcards from the Posthuman Solar System." *Science Fiction Studies* 18 (1991): 343–57.

——. *Terminal Identity: The Virtual Subject in Post-Modern Science Fiction*. Durham, NC: Duke UP, 1993.

——. *Matters of Gravity: Special Effects and Supermen in the Twentieth Century*. Durham, NC: Duke UP, 2003.

Bull, Emma. *Bone Dance*. New York: Ace Books, 1991.

Bullock, Saxon. "Never Mind the Cyberpunks." 10 November 2007 http://www.saxonbullock.com/richardmorganinterview.htm.

Butler, Andrew M. "Being Beyond the Body: Neal Stephenson's *Snow Crash* and Jeff Noon's *Vurt*." In *Strange Attractors*. Ed. Mark Bould. Plymouth: Mark Bould, 1995, pp. 65–74.

——. *Cyberpunk*. Harpenden: Pocket Essentials, 2000.

——. "Journeys Beyond Being: The Cyberpunk-Flavoured Novels of Jeff Noon." In *Novel Turns: Recent Narrative Writing from Western Europe*. Ed. John Gatt Ruttner. Melbourne: Antipodas Monographs, 2001.

——. "The Quality of the Afterlife: An Interview with Jeff Noon." *Vector: The Critical Journal of the British Science Fiction Association* 233 (2004): 12–15.

——. "LSD, Lying Ink and *Lies, Inc.*" *Science Fiction Studies* 32.2 (2005): 265–80.

——. "*Neuromancer*." In *A Companion to Science Fiction*. Ed. David Seed. Oxford: Blackwell, 2005, pp. 534–43.

Cadigan, Pat."Pretty Boy Crossover." In *The 1987 Annual World's Best SF*. Ed. Donald A. Wollheim. New York: DAW, 1987, pp. 82–93.

——. *Mindplayers*. New York: Bantam Spectra, 1987.

——. *Synners*. New York: Bantam, 1991.

——. "Not a Manifesto." In *The Ultimate Cyberpunk*. Ed. Pat Cadigan. New York: ibooks, 2002, pp. vii–xiv.

Calinescu, Matei. "From the One to the Many: Pluralism in Today's Thought." In *Innovation/Renovation: New Perspectives on the Humanities*. Ed. Ihab Hassan and Sally Hasson. Madison, WI: U of Wisconsin P. 1983, pp. 263–88.

Calvino, Italo. *The Castle of Crossed Destinies*. Trans. William Weaver, London: Pan, 1978.

Cary, Catie. "Best Books of 1993." *Vector: The Critical Journal of the British Science Fiction Association* 179 (1994): 5–11.

Castells, Manuel. *End of Millennium*. 2nd edn. Oxford: Blackwell, 2000.

——. *The Rise of the Network Society*. 2nd edn. Oxford: Blackwell, 2000.

——. *The Power of Identity*. 2nd edn. Malden, MA: Blackwell, 2004.

Cavallaro, Dani. *Cyberpunk and Cyberculture: Science Fiction and the Work of William Gibson*. London: Athlone Press (2000).

Chambers, Iain. *Culture After Humanism: History, Culture, Subjectivity*. London: Routledge, 2001.

Clark, Nigel. "Rear-View Mirrorshades: The Recursive Generation of the Cyberbody." In *Cyberspace/Cyberbodies/Cyberpunk: Cultures of Technological Embodiment*. Ed. Mike Featherstone and Roger Burrows. London: Sage, 1995, pp. 113–33.

Clute, John. "Science Fiction from the 1980s to the present." In *The Cambridge Companion to Science Fiction*. Ed. Edward James and Farah Mendlesohn. Cambridge: Cambridge UP, 2003, pp. 64–78.

——. *Scores: Reviews 1993–2003*. Essex: Beccon, 2003.

Cole, Simon A. "Do Androids Pulverize Tiger Bones to Use as Aphrodisiacs?" *Social Text* 42 (1995): 173–93.

Connery, Brian A. "IMHO: Authority and Egalitarian Rhetoric in the Virtual Coffeehouse." In *Internet Culture*. Ed. David Porter. New York: Routledge, 1996, pp. 161–79.

Conte, Joseph. *Unending Design: A Chaotics of Postmodern American Fiction*. Tuscaloosa, AL: U of Alabama P, 2002.

Costello, Nicholas, Jonathan Michie, and Seaumas Milne. *Beyond the Casino Economy: Planning for the 1990s*. London: Verso, 1989.

Csicsery Ronay, Jr. Istvan. "Cyberpunk and Neuromanticism." In *Storming the Reality Studio: A Casebook of Cyberpunk and Postmodern Fiction*. Ed. Larry McCaffery. Durham, NC: Duke UP, 1991, pp. 182–93.

——. "The Sentimental Futurist: Cybernetics and Art in William Gibson's *Neuromancer*." *Critique: Studies in Contemporary Fiction* 33.3 (1992): 221–40.

——. "Futuristic Flu, or, The Revenge of the Future." In *Fiction 2000: Cyberpunk and the Future of Narrative*. Ed. George Slusser and Tom Shippey. Athens, GA: U of Georgia P, 1992, pp. 26–45.

——. "Antimancer: Cybernetics and Art in Gibson's *Count Zero*." *Science Fiction Studies* 22.1 (1995): 63–86.

Danvers, Dennis. *Circuit of Heaven*. New York: Avon Eos, 1998.

——. *End of Days*. New York: Avon Eos, 1999.

Daoust, Phil. "What's the Smallest Book in the World? Great Mancunian Novelists." *The Guardian* 13 Oct. 1997, G2: 12–13.

Davis, Mike. *City of Quartz: Excavating the Future in Los Angeles*. New York: Vintage, 1992.

De Certeau, Michel. *The Practice of Everyday Life*. Trans. Steven Rendall. Berkeley, CA: U of California P, 1984.

Delany, Samuel. *Triton*. New York: Bantam, 1976.

——. "Shadows." In *The Jewel-Hinged Jaw: Notes on the Language of Science-Fiction*, Elizabethtown, NY: Dragon Press, 1977, pp. 88–98.

——. *The American Shore*. Elizabethtown: Dragon Press, 1978.

——. "The Semiology of Silence." *Science-Fiction Studies* 14.2 (1987): 134–65.

——. "Is Cyberpunk a Good Thing or a Bad Thing?" *Mississippi Review* 47/48 (1988): 28–35.

——. "Some Real Mothers: An Interview with Samuel R. Delany." *Science Fiction Eye* 1.3 (1988): 5–11.

——. *Silent Interviews: On Language, Race, Sex, Science Fiction, and Some Comics.* Hanover, NH: Wesleyan UP, 1994.

Del Rey, Lester. "Other Times, Other Values." *Renaissance: A Semi-Official Organ of the Second Foundation* 1.1 (1969): 2–4.

Derrida, Jacques. "Plato's Pharmacy." In *Dissemination.* Trans. Barbara Johnson. Chicago: U of Chicago P, 1981, pp. 61–171.

——. "Violence and Metaphysics." In *Writing and Difference.* Trans. Alan Bass. London: Routledge and Kegan Paul, 1978.

——. *The Ear of the Other: Otobiography, Transference, Translation.* Ed. Christie McDonald. Lincoln, NE: U of Nebraska P, 1988.

Dery, Mark. *Escape Velocity: Cyberculture and the End of the Century.* New York: Grove Press, 1996.

Dimendberg, Edward. *Film Noir and the Spaces of Modernity.* Cambridge, MA: Harvard UP, 2004.

DiNicola, Vincenzo. "Anorexia Multiforme: Self-starvation in Historical and Cultural Context: Part 1: Self-starvation as a Historical Chameleon." *Transcultural Psychiatric Review* 27.3 (1990): 165–96.

——. "Anorexia Multiforme: Self-starvation in Historical and Cultural Context: Part II: Anorexia Nervosa as Culture-Reaction Syndrome." *Transcultural Psychiatric Review* 27.4 (1990): 245–86.

Disch, Thomas M. "Introduction: On Saving the World." In *The Ruins of Earth: An Anthology of Stories of the Immediate Future.* Ed. Thomas M. Disch. New York: Putnam's, 1971, pp. 1–7.

——. *The Dreams Our Stuff Is Made Of: How Science Fiction Conquered the World.* New York: Free P, 1998.

Docherty, Thomas. *Reading (Absent) Character: Towards a Theory of Characterization in Fiction.* Oxford: Oxford UP, 1982.

Donawerth, Jane. *Frankenstein's Daughters: Women Writing Science Fiction.* Syracuse, NY: Syracuse UP, 1997.

Dorsey, Candas Jane. "Rev. of *Pattern Recognition.*" 14 March 2003. Available at: www.trace.ntu.ac.uk/print_article/index.cfm?article=41.

Dowling, David. *Fictions of Nuclear Disaster.* London: Macmillan, 1987.

Downham, Mark. "Cyber-Punk." *Vague* 21 (1988): 35–50.

Easterbrook, Neil. "The Arc of Our Destruction: Reversal and Erasure in Cyberpunk." *Science Fiction Studies* 19.3 (1992): 378–94.

——. "[Anarchy,] State, Heterotopia: The Political Imagination in Heinlein, Le Guin, and Delany." In *Political Science Fiction.* Eds. Donald M. Hassler and Clyde Wilcox. Columbia, SC: U of South Carolina P, 1997, pp. 43–75.

——. "Alternative Presents: The Ambivalent Historicism of *Pattern Recognition.*" *Science Fiction Studies* 33.3 (2006): 483–504.

——. "William Gibson." In *Fifty Key Figures in Science Fiction.* Ed. Mark Bould, Andrew M. Butler, Adam Roberts, and Sherryl Vint. New York: Routledge, 2009, pp. 86–91.

Eco, Umberto. *Postscript to The Name of the Rose.* Trans. William Weaver. San Diego: HBJ, 1984.

——. *Semiotics and the Philosophy of Language.* Bloomington, IN: Indiana UP, 1986.

Egan, Greg. *Schild's Ladder*. London: Gollancz, 2003.

Ellis, Jason W. "Rev. of *Brasyl*, by Ian McDonald." *SFRA Review* 281 (2007): 36–37.

Enteen, Jillana. "'On the Receiving End of the Colonization': Nalo Hopkinson's 'Nansi Web." *Science Fiction Studies* 34.2 (2007): 262–82.

Failler, Angela. "Appetizing Loss: Anorexia as an Experiment in Living," *Eating Disorders* 14 (2006): 99–107.

Farnell, Ross. "Posthuman Topologies: William Gibson's 'Architecture' in *Virtual Light* and *Idoru*." *Science Fiction Studies* 25.3 (1998): 459–80.

Finder: Finder: GLBT Fantasy Fiction Resources. "An Interview with Lyda Morehouse." 13 June 2003. Available at: www.glbtfantasy.com/?section=interviews& sub=morehouse. (accessed 10 October 2009).

Fischlin, Daniel, Veronica Hollinger, and Andrew Taylor. "'The Charisma Leak': A Conversation with William Gibson and Bruce Sterling." *Science-Fiction Studies* 19.1 (1992): 1–17.

Fisher, Jeffrey. "The Postmodern Paradiso: Dante, Cyberpunk, and the Technosophy of Cyberspace." In *Internet Culture*. Ed. David Porter. New York: Routledge, 2007, pp. 111–28.

Fitting, Peter."The Modern Anglo-American SF Novel: Utopian Longing and Capitalist Cooptation." *Science Fiction Studies* 6 (1979): 59–76.

——. "Ideological Foreclosure and Utopian Discourse." *Sociocriticism* 7 (1988): 11–25.

——. "Hacking Away at the Postmodern: William Gibson and Cyberpunk." Paper presented at Popular Culture Association Annual Meeting. St. Louis, 6 April 1989.

——. "The Lessons of Cyberpunk." In *Technoculture*. Ed. Constance Penley and Andrew Ross. Minneapolis, MN: U of Minnesota P, 1991.

Ford, Michael Thomas. "A Real Girl." In *Pomosexuals: Challenging Assumptions about Gender and Sexuality*. Ed. Carol Queen and Lawrence Schimel. San Francisco: Cleis, 1997, pp. 150–59.

Foster, Thomas. *The Souls of Cyberfolk: Posthumanism as Vernacular Theory*. Minnesota, MN: U of Minneapolis P, 2005.

Foucault, Michel. *The Order of Things: An Archaeology of the Human Sciences*. New York: Pantheon, 1970.

Fraser, Graham. "Loving the Loss of the World: *Tęsknota* and the Metaphors of the Heart." In *Parietal Games: Critical Writings by and on M. John Harrison*. Ed. Mark Bould and Michelle Reid. London: Science Fiction Foundation, 2005, pp. 299–318.

Freud, Sigmund. "Mourning and Melancholia." In *The Penguin Freud Library*, Vol. II. Ed. Angela Richards. London: Penguin, 1984, pp. 245–68.

——. *Civilization and Its Discontents*. In *The Pelican Freud Library*, Vol. 12. Ed. Angela Richards. London: Penguin, 1985.

Galloway, Alexander R. *Gaming: Essays on Algorithmic Culture*. Minneapolis, MN: U of Minnesota P, 2006.

Gearhart, Sally Miller. *The Wanderground: Tales of the Hill Women*. Watertown, MA: Persephone Press, 1979.

Gibson, William. *Neuromancer*. New York: Ace Books, 1984.

——. *Burning Chrome*. New York: Ace Books, 1987.

——. "The Gernsback Continuum." In *Burning Chrome*. New York: Ace Books, 1987, pp. 23–35.

——. "Johnny Mnemonic." In *Burning Chrome*. New York: Ace Books, 1987, pp. 1–22.

——. *Count Zero*. New York: Ace Books, 1986.

——. *Mona Lisa Overdrive*. New York: Bantam, 1988.

——. "The Salon Interview: William Gibson." *Salon* (1996), 14 October. Available at: www.salon.com/weekly/gibson396014.html. (accessed 19 September 2001).

——. *Idoru*. New York: Putnam, 1996.

——. "William Gibson's Filmless Festival." *Wired* 7.10 (1999). October. Available at: www.wired.com/wired/archive/7.10/gibson.html. (accessed 17 March 2003).

——. *All Tomorrow's Parties*. New York: Putnam, 1999.

——. "Foreword." In *City Come A-Walkin'* by John Shirley. Revised edn. New York: Four Walls Eight Windows, 2000, pp. 1–4.

——. *Pattern Recognition: Uncorrected Proof for Limited Distribution*. New York: Putnam, 2002.

"William Gibson: Crossing Borders." *Locus* 50.5 (2003): 6–7, 63–64.

——. "An Interview with William Gibson." by Candas J. Dorsey. *New York Review of Science Fiction* 15.9 (2003): 10–11.

——. *Pattern Recognition*. New York: Putnam, 2003.

——. *Spook Country*. New York: Putnam, 2007.

Gibson, William and Bruce Sterling. *The Difference Engine*. New York: Bantam, 1991.

Giller, Marc D. *Hammerjack*. New York: Bantam, 2005.

Gillis, Stacy. "Introduction." In *The Matrix Trilogy: Cyberpunk Reloaded*. Ed Stacy Gillis. London: Wallflower P, 2005, pp. 1–8.

——. *The Matrix Trilogy: Cyberpunk Reloaded*. London: Wallflower P, 2005.

Ginway, M. Elizabeth. "A Working Model for Analyzing Third World Science Fiction: The Case of Brazil." *Science Fiction Studies* 32.3 (2005): 467–94.

Gladwell, Malcolm. "The Coolhunt." *The New Yorker* 17 March (1997): 78–88. Available at: www.gladwell.com/1997/1997_03_17_a_cool.htm. (accessed 11 May 2005).

Gomoll, Jean. "Open Letter to Joanna Russ." *Janus* 25 (1987).

Goonan, Kathleen Ann. "More Than You'll Ever Know: Down the Rabbit Hole of *The Matrix*." In *Exploring the Matrix: Visions of the Cyber-Present*. Ed. Karen Haber. New York: Byron Press, 2003, pp. 98–111.

Gordon, Joan. "Yin and Yang Duke It Out." In *Storming the Reality Studio: A Casebook of Cyberpunk and Postmodern Science Fiction*. Ed. Larry McCaffery. Durham, NC: Duke UP, 1991, pp. 196–202.

Graham, Elaine L. *Representations of the Post/Human: Monsters, Aliens and Others in Popular Culture*. New Brunswick, NJ: Rutgers UP, 2002.

Gray, Chris Hables, Steven Mentor, and Heidi J. Figueroa-Sarriera. "Cyborgology: Constructing the Knowledge of Cybernetic Organisms." In *The Cyborg Handbook*. Ed. C.H. Gray. New York: Routledge, 1995, pp. 1–14.

Gremillion, Helen. *Feeding Anorexia: Gender and Power at a Treatment Center*. Durham, NC: Duke UP, 2003.

Griswold, Jr., Charles L. "Happiness and Cypher's Choice: Is Ignorance Bliss?" In *The Matrix and Philosophy: Welcome to the Desert of the Real*: Ed. William Irwin. Chicago: Open Court P, 2002, pp. 126–37.

Grondin, Jean. "Hermeneutics." In *New Dictionary of the History of Ideas*. 6 vols. Ed. Maryanne Horowitz. Detroit: Scribner's, 2005, vol. 3, pp. 982–87.

Haraway, Donna. "A Cyborg Manifesto: Science, Technology, and Socialist-Feminism in the Late Twentieth Century." In *Simians, Cyborgs and Women: The Reinvention of Nature*. New York: Routledge, 1991, pp. 149–81.

Harding, Sandra. *The Science Question in Feminism*. Ithaca, NY: Cornell UP, 1986.

Harris, Susan. "The Devil, God and Cyperpunk: An Interview with Lyda Morehouse." *Broad Universe Broadsheet*. 5 November 2003. Available at: www. broaduniversc.org/broadsheet/archive/0308shlm.html (accessed 17 January 2007).

Harrison, M. John. *Signs of Life*. London: Flamingo, 1998.

——. "Suicide Coast," In *Things That Never Happen*. San Francisco: Night Shade Books, 2003, pp. 383–401.

Harshav (Hrushovski), Benjamin. "The Structure of Semiotic Objects: A Three-Dimensional Model." In *The Sign in Music and Literature*. Ed. Wendy Steiner. Austin, TX: U of Texas P, 1979.

Hartsock, Nancy. "Foucault on Power: A Theory for Women?" In *Feminism/Postmodernism*. Ed. Linda J. Nicholson. New York: Routledge, 1990, pp. 157–75.

Harvey, David. *The Condition of Postmodernity: An Enquiry into the Origins of Cultural Change*. Oxford: Basil Blackwell, 1989.

Hassan, Ihab. "Postmodernism: A Self Interview." *Philosophy and Literature* 30.1 (2006): 223–28.

Hassan, Ihab and Sally Hassan (eds.) *Innovation/Renovation: New Perspectives on the Humanities*. Madison, WI: U of Wisconsin P, 1983.

Hayles, N. Katherine. "How Cyberspace Signifies: Taking Immortality Literally." In *Immortal Engines: Life Extension and Immortality in Science Fiction and Fantasy*. Ed. Eric. S. Rabkin, George Slusser, and Gary Westfahl. Athens, GA: University of Georgia P, 1996, pp. 111–21.

——. *How We Became Posthuman: Virtual Bodies in Cybernetics, Literature, and Informatics*. Chicago: U of Chicago P, 1999.

——. *My Mother Was a Computer: Digital Subjects and Literary Texts*. Chicago: U of Chicago P, 2005.

Heidegger, Martin. *Being and Time*. Trans. John Macquarrie and Edward Robinson. London: SCMP, 1962.

Herr, Michael. *Dispatches*, New York: Avon, 1978.

Heuser, Sabine. *Virtual Geographies: Cyberpunk and the Intersection of the Postmodern and Science Fiction*. New York: Rodopi, 2003.

Higgins, Dick. *A Dialectic of Centuries: Notes towards a Theory of the New Arts*. New York and Barton, VT: Printed Editions, 1978.

Hodge, Robert. *Literature as Discourse*. Cambridge: Polity, 1990.

Hollinger, Veronica. "Cybernetic Deconstructions: Cyberpunk and Postmodernism." In *Storming the Reality Studio: A Casebook of Cyberpunk and Postmodernist Fiction*. Ed. Larry McCaffery. Durham, NC: Duke UP, 1991, pp. 203–18.

——. "Stories About the Future: From Patterns of Expectation to Pattern Recognition." *Science Fiction Studies* 33.3 (2006): 452–72.

Holmen, Vegar. "Surfing with the Angels." In *The Alien Online*. January 2003. Available at: www.thealienonline.net/interviews/lydamorehouse_jan03.asp?tid=3& scid=24&iid=1347 (accessed 4 May 2007).

Horkheimer, Max and Theodor Adorno. *Dialectic of Enlightenment*. New York: Continuum, 2002.

Huntington, John. "Newness, *Neuromancer*, and the End of Narrative." In *Fiction 2000. Cyberpunk and the Future of Narrative*. Eds. George Slusser and Tom Shippey. Athens, GA: U of Georgia P, 1992, pp. 133–41.

Huxley, Aldous. *Brave New World*. New York: Harper and Row, 1989.

Jackson, Shelley. *Patchwork Girl; or, A Modern Monster by Mary/Shelley & Herself.* CD-ROM. Watertown, MA: Eastgate Systems, 1995.

Jakobson, Roman. "The Dominant." In *Readings in Russian Poetics; Formalist and Structuralist Views.* Ed. Ladislav Matejka and Krystyna Pomorska. Cambridge, MA: MIT Press, 1971, pp. 105–10.

Jameson, Fredric. "Magical Narratives: Romance as Genre." *New Literary* History 7.1 (1975): 135–63.

———. *The Political Unconscious.* Ithaca, NY: Cornell UP, 1981.

———. "Progress Versus Utopia: or, Can We Imagine the Future?" *Science Fiction Studies* 9 (1982): 147–58.

———. "Postmodernism, or The Cultural Logical of Late Capitalism." *New Left Review* (1984): 53–94.

———. *Postmodernism, or, The Cultural Logic of Late Capitalism.* Durham, NC: Duke UP, 1991.

———. *Seed of Time.* New York: Columbia UP, 1994.

———. "Aliens in the Fourth Dimension," In *Deconstructing the Starships: Science, Fiction and Reality.* Liverpool: Liverpool UP, 1999, pp. 201–13.

———. "Fear and Loathing in Globalization," In *Archaeologies of the Future: The Desire Called Utopia and Other Science Fictions.* London: Verso, 2005, pp. 384–92.

———. *Archaeologies of the Future: The Desire Called Utopia and Other Science Fictions.* New York: Verso, 2005.

Johnson, Steven. *Emergence: The Connected Lives of Ants, Brains, Cities, and Software.* New York: Touchstone, 2001.

Jones, Gwyneth. *Escape Plans.* London: Unwin, 1986.

———. *North Wind.* London: Victor Gollancz, 1994.

Kadrey, Richard. *Metrophage*, London: Gollancz, 1988.

Kadrey, Richard and Larry McCaffery. "Cyberpunk 101: A Schematic Guide to *Storming the Reality Studio.*" In *Storming the Reality Studio: A Casebook of Cyberpunk and Postmodern Fiction.* Ed. L. McCaffery. Durham, NC: Duke UP, 1991, pp. 17–29.

Kaufmann, David. "Yuppie Postmodernism." *Arizona Quarterly* 47.2 (1992): 93–117.

Keen, Tony. "Feathers into an Underworld." In *The Arthur C. Clarke Award: A Critical Anthology.* Ed. Paul Kincaid with Andrew M. Butler. Everdon: Serendip Foundation, 2006, pp. 91–107.

Keller, Evelyn Fox. *Reflections on Gender and Science.* New Haven, CT: Yale UP, 1985.

Kelly, James Patrick and John Kessel. "Hacking Cyberpunk." In *Rewired: the Post-Cyberpunk Anthology.* San Francisco: Tachyon Publications, 2007, pp. vii–xiv.

Kemp, Earl. *Who Killed Science Fiction?* Available at: http://efanzines.com/EK/eI29/, 1980.

Kilgore, De Witt Douglas. *Astrofuturism: Science, Race, and Visions of Utopia in Space.* Philadelphia: U of Pennsylvania P, 2003.

Kneale, Mark. *No Maps for These Territories.* Mark Kneale Productions, 2000.

Kolko, Beth E., Lisa Nakamura, and Gilbert B. Rodman, eds. *Race in Cyberspace.* New York: Routledge, 2000.

Kroker, Arthur and Marilouise Kroker. *Hacking the Future: Stories for the Flesh-Eating 90s.* New York: St. Martins P, 1996.

Laidlaw, Marc. *Dad's Nuke*, London: Gollancz, 1985.

Lanier, Jaron. "One-Half of a Manifesto." *Wired* 8(12): 158–79.

Latham, Rob. "A Young Man's Journey to Ladbrook Grove: M. John Harrison and the Evolution of the New Wave in Britain." In *Parietal Games: Critical Writings by and on M. John Harrison*. Ed. Mark Bould and Michelle Reid. London: Science Fiction Foundation, 2005, pp. 249–64.

——. "The New Wave." In *A Companion to Science Fiction*. Ed. David Seed. Oxford: Blackwell, 2005, pp. 202–16.

——. "'The Job of Dissevering Joy from Glop': John Clute's *New Worlds* Criticism." In *Portals: A Festschrift for John and Judith Clute*. Ed. Farah Mendlesohn. Baltimore, MD: Old Earth, 2006, pp. 28–39.

——. "*New Worlds* and the New Wave in Fandom: Fan Culture and the Reshaping of Science Fiction in the Sixties." *Extrapolation* 47.2 (2006): 296–315.

——. "Sextrapolation in New Wave Science Fiction." *Science Fiction Studies* 33.3 (2006): 251–74.

——. "Biotic Invasions: Ecological Imperialism in New Wave Science Fiction." *Yearbook of English Studies* 37.2 (2007): 103–19.

——. "Cyberpunk and the New Wave: Ruptures and Continuities." *The New York Review of Science Fiction* 19(10) (2007): 1, 8–12, 14–16.

Latour, Bruno. *We Have Never Been Modern*. Trans. Catherine Porter. Cambridge, MA: Harvard UP, 1993.

Laurel, Brenda. "Art and Activism in VR." *Verbum* December (1991): 1–5.

——. *Computers as Theatre*. Reading, MA: Addison-Wesley, 1991.

——. "Placeholder: Landscape and Narrative in a Virtual Environment." *Computer Graphics* 2 (1994): 118–26.

Laurel, Brenda, Rob Tow and Rachel Strickland. Stanford Seminar on Human–Computer Interaction, Stanford University, CA, 19 November 1993.

Leaver, Tama. "Interstitial Spaces and Multiple Histories in William Gibson's *Virtual Light, Idoru* and *All Tomorrow's Parties*." *Limina: A Journal of Historical and Cultural Studies* 9 (2003): 118–30. Available at: http://www.arts.uwa.edu.au/limina/Vol9/7Leaver.pdf (accessed 7 June 2005).

Lebowitz, Michael A. *Beyond Capital: Marx's Political Economy of the Working Class*. 2nd edn. Houndmills: Palgrave Macmillan, 2003.

Lederer, Susan E., and Richard M. Ratzan. "Mary Shelley: *Frankenstein: Or, the Modern Prometheus*." In *A Companion to Science Fiction*. Ed. David Seed. Oxford: Blackwell, 2005, pp. 455–65.

Leland, John. *Hip: The History*. New York: HarperCollins, 2004.

Lem, Stanislaw. "Todorov's Fantastic Theory of Literature." In *Microworlds: Writings on Science Fiction and Fantasy*. San Diego: HBJ, 1984, pp. 209–32.

Levinas, Emmanuel. *The Levinas Reader*. Ed. Sean Hand. Oxford: Basil Blackwell, 1989.

Lewitt, Shariann. "A Real Girl." In *Bending the Landscape: Original Gay and Lesbian Writing: Science Fiction*. Ed. Nicola Griffith and Stephen Pagel. Woodstock, NY: Overlook, 1998, pp. 264–82.

Lewitt, S.N. *Cybernetic Jungle*. New York: Ace Books, 1992.

Lindsay, David. *A Voyage to Arcturus*. Edinburgh: Canongate, 1992.

Liu, Alan. *The Laws of Cool: Knowledge Work and the Culture of Information*. Chicago: U of Chicago P, 2004.

Lodge, David. The Modes of modern writing: metaphor, metonymy, and the typology of modern literature. Ithaca: Cornell UP, 1977.

Lowe, Donald. *The Body in Late-Capitalist USA*. Durham, NC: Duke UP, 1995.

Luckhurst, Roger. "The Many Deaths of Science Fiction: A Polemic." *Science-Fiction Studies* 21(1) (1994): 35–50.

Luke, Tim. "Culture and Politics in the Age of Artificial Negativity." *Telos* 35 (1978): 55–73.

Lykke, Nina. "Between Monsters, Goddesses and Cyborgs: Feminist Confrontations with Science." In *Between Monsters, Goddesses and Cyborgs: Feminist Confrontations with Science, Medicine and Cyberspace*. Ed. Nina Lykke and Rosi Braidotti. London: Zed Books, 1996, pp. 13–29.

Lyotard, Jean-François. *The Postmodern Condition: A Report on Knowledge*. Trans. Geoff Bennington and Brian Massumi. Minneapolis, MN: U of Minnesota P, 1984.

Maddox, Tom. "Snake Eyes." In *Mirrorshades: The Cyberpunk Anthology*. Ed. Bruce Sterling. NY: Ace Books, 1988, pp. 12–33.

Malmgren, Carl D. *Fictional Space in the Modernist and Postmodernist America Novel*. Lewisburg, PA: Bucknell UP, 1985.

——. "Towards a Definition of Science Fantasy." *Science Fiction Studies* 15(3) (1988): 259–81.

——. "Worlds Apart: A Theory of Science Fiction." In *Utopian Thought in American Literature: Untersuchungen zur literarischen Utopia und Dystopie in den USA*. Ed. Arno Heller, Walter Höbling, and Waldemar Zacharasiewicz. Tübingen: Gunter Narr, 1988, pp. 25–42.

Malson, Helen. *The Thin Woman: Feminism, Post-Structuralism and the Social Psychology of Anorexia Nervosa*. New York: Routledge, 1998.

Malzberg, Barry N. *The Engines of the Night: Science Fiction in the Eighties*. New York: Bluejay, 1982.

Marcuse, Herbert. "The Affirmative Character of Culture." In *Negations: Essays in Critical Theory*. Trans. Jeremy J. Shapiro. Boston: Beacon, 1968,pp. 88–134.

Margolin, Uri. "Dispersing/Voiding the Subject: A Narratological Perspective," *Texte* 5(6) (1986): 181–210.

Marx, Karl. *Grundrisse*. New York: Vintage, 1973.

——. *Capital*, Vol. I. New York: Vintage, 1977.

Marx, Karl and Friedrich Engels. *The Communist Manifesto*. Ed. David McLellan. Oxford: Oxford UP, 1992.

McCaffery, Larry. "The Fiction of the Present." In *Columbia Literary History of the United States*. Ed. Emory Elliot. New York: Columbia UP, 1987, pp. 1161–77.

——. (ed.) "The Cyberpunk Controversy." Special issue of *Mississippi Review* 47/48 (1988) 16, 2–3.

——. *Across the Wounded Galaxies: Interviews with Contemporary American Science Fiction Writers*, Urbana, IL: U of Illinois P, 1990.

——. (ed.) *Storming the Reality Studio: A Casebook of Cyberpunk and Postmodern Science Fiction*. Durham, NC: Duke UP, 1991.

——. "An Interview with William Gibson." In *Storming the Reality Studio: A Casebook of Cyberpunk and Postmodern Fiction*. Ed. Larry McCaffery. Durham, NC: Duke UP, 1991, pp. 263–85.

——. "Introduction: The Desert of the Real." In *Storming the Reality Studio: A Casebook of Cyberpunk and Postmodernism*. Ed. Larry McCaffery. Durham, NC: Duke UP, 1991, pp. 1–16.

McCullagh, Declan. "*The Matrix:* A Cyberpunk Triumph." *Wired.com.* April 02, 1999. Available at: www.wired.com/culture/lifestyle/news/1999/04/18932 (accessed 1 May 2007).

McHale, Brian. *Postmodernist Fiction*, New York: Methuen, 1987.

——. "Towards a Poetics of Cyberpunk." In *Constructing Postmodernism.* New York: Routledge, 1992, pp. 243–67.

——. *Constructing Postmodernism.* New York: Routledge, 1992.

McHugh, Maureen. *China Mountain Zhang.* New York: Tor, 1992.

McLuhan, Marshall. *Understanding Media: The Extensions of Man.* Cambridge, MA: MIT P, 1994.

Mendlesohn, Farah. "Religion and Science Fiction." In *The Cambridge Companion to Science Fiction.* Ed. Edward James and Farah Mendlesohn. Cambridge: Cambridge UP, 2003, pp. 264–75.

Merleau-Ponty, Maurice. *Phenomenology of Perception.* Trans. Colin Smith. London: Routledge, 1962.

Merril, Judith. "Summation: S-F, 1961." in *7th Annual Edition: The Year's Best S-F 1962.* New York: Dell, 1963, pp. 390–93.

——, ed. *England Swings SF: Stories of Speculative Fiction.* New York: Ace Books, 1968.

Miéville, China. "The Limits of Vision(aries): or *M. John Harrison Returns to London and it is Spring.*" In *Things That Never Happen.* Ed. M. John Harrison. San Francisco: Night Shade Books, 2003, pp. 1–9.

Milner, Andrew. *Literature, Culture, and Society.* New York: New York UP, 1996.

Misha. *Red Spider, White Web.* La Grande, OR: Wordcraft, 1999.

——. *Ke-Qua-HJawk-As.* La Grande, OR: Wordcraft, 1994.

Mixon, Laura J. *Glass Houses.* New York: Tor, 1992.

Moorcock, Michael. "A New Literature for the Space Age." *New Worlds* 142(May–June) (1964): 2–3.

——. "Symbols for the Sixties." *New Worlds* 148 (1965): 2–3, 25.

Morehouse, Lyda. *Archangel Protocol.* New York: Roc, 2001.

——. *Fallen Host.* New York: Roc, 2002.

——. *Messiah Node.* New York: Roc, 2003.

——. *Apocalypse Array.* New York: Roc, 2004.

Morgan, Richard. *Altered Carbon.* New York: Del Rey, 2002.

——. *Broken Angels.* New York: Del Rey, 2003.

——. *Woken Furies.* London: Gollancz, 2005.

Moss, Joshua. "Breaking the Cyberpunk Curse." SPACE.com. 18 May 2000. Available at: www.space.com/sciencefiction/movies/matrix_cyberpunk_000518.html (accessed 1 May 2007).

Moylan, Tom. "Review of *Synners,* by Pat Cadigan." *American Book Review* 14(2) (1992): 5, 13.

——. *Scraps of the Untainted Sky: Science Fiction, Utopia, Dystopia.* Boulder, CO: Westview P, 2000.

Mulvey, Laura. "Visual Pleasure and Narrative Cinema." *Screen* 16(3) (1975): 6–18.

Murphy, Graham J. "Post/Humanity and the Interstitial: A Glorification of Possibility in Gibson's Bridge Sequence." *Science Fiction Studies* 30(1) (2003): 72–90.

——. "Penetrating the Body-Plus-Virtualisation in Melissa Scott's *Trouble and Her Friends.*" *Foundation: The International Review of Science Fiction* 95 (2005): 40–51.

Nakamura, Lisa. *Cybertypes: Race, Ethnicity, and Identity on the Internet.* New York: Routledge, 2002.

Newman, James. *Videogames.* London: Routledge, 2004.

Newman, Kim. *The Night Mayor.* London: Simon & Schuster, 1989.

Nixon, Nicola. "Cyberpunk: Preparing the Ground for Revolution or Keeping the Boys Satisfied?" *Science Fiction Studies* 19(2) (1992): 219–35.

Noon, Jeff. *Vurt.* Littleborough: Ringpull, 1993.

———. "Spaceache and Heartships." Available at: www.bbcnc.org.uk/tv/the_net/ TN950605/spaceache.html (accessed 31 December 1995).

———. "Ultra Kid and the Cat Girl." *GQ* (March) (1995): 102–7.

———. *Pollen.* Greater Manchester: Ringpull, 1995.

———. *Automated Alice.* London: Doubleday, 1996.

———. "Solace." *The Big Issue* 244 (1997): 12, 14.

———. *Nymphomation.* London: Anchor, 1997.

Nye, David E. *American Technological Sublime.* Cambridge, MA: MIT P, 1994.

Olson, Greta. *Reading Eating Disorders: Writings on Bulimia and Anorexia as Confessions of American Culture.* Frankfurt: Peter Lang, 2000.

Omniaveritas, Vincent. "The Last." *Cheap Truth.* 20 November 2007. Available at: www.its.caltech.edu/~erich/cheaptruth/.

Orwell, George. *1984.* New York: Signet, 1984.

Pagetti, Carlos. "Introduzione a *La svastica sul sole.*" In *Philip K. Dick: Il Sogno Dei Simulacri.* Ed. Carlo Pagetti and Gianfranco Viviani. Milan: Nord, 1989, pp. 132–49.

Parrinder, Patrick. "Scientists in Science Fiction: Enlightenment and After." In *Science Fiction Roots and Branches: Contemporary Critical Approaches.* Ed. Rhys Garnett and R.J. Ellis. Basingstoke: Macmillan, 1990, pp. 57–78.

Pavel, Thomas. "Narrative Domains." *Poetics Today* 1.4: (1980): 105–14.

Peterson, Richard A. "Revitalizing the Culture Concept." *Annual Review of Sociology* 5 (1979): 137–66.

Pfeil, Fred. *Goodman 2020.* Bloomington, In: Indiana UP, 1986.

———. "Makin' Flippy Floppy: Postmodernism and the Baby Boom PMC." In *Another Tale to Tell: Politics and Narrative in Postmodern Culture.* New York: Verso, 1990, pp. 97–125.

———. "These Disintegrations I'm Looking Forward to: Science Fiction from the New Wave to New Age." In *Another Tale to Tell: Politics and Narrative in Postmodern Culture.* London: Verso, 1990, pp. 83–94.

Piccone, Paul. "The Crisis of One-Dimensionality." *Telos* 35 (1978): 43–55.

Pierce, John J. "Prospectus." *Renaissance: A Semi-Official Organ of the Second Foundation* 1(1) (1969): 1.

Piercy, Marge. *He, She and It.* New York: Fawcett Crest, 1993.

Platt, Charles. *The Silicon Man.* San Francisco: Wired, 1997.

Porush, David. "Frothing the Synaptic Bath." In *Storming the Reality Studio: A Casebook of Cyberpunk and Postmodern Fiction.* Ed. Larry McCaffery. Durham, NC: Duke UP, 1991, pp. 332.

———. "Prigogine, Chaos, and Contemporary Science Fiction." *Science Fiction Studies* 18(3) (1991): 367–86.

Powers, Richard. *Galatea 2.2.* New York: Picador, 1995.

Pynchon, Thomas. *The Crying of Lot 49,* New York: Bantam, 1967.

———. *Gravity's Rainbow.* New York: Bantam, 1973.

——. *Vineland*, Boston: Little, Brown, 1990.

Radway, Janice. *Reading the Romance: Women, Patriarchy and Popular Literature.* Chapel Hill, NC: U of North Carolina P, 1984.

Rée, Jonathan. "The Vanity of Historicism." *New Literary History* 22(4) (1991): 961–83.

Rehak, Bob. "Playing at Being: Psychoanalysis and the Avatar." In *The Video Game Theory Reader.* Ed. Mark J.P. Wolf and Bernard Perron. London: Routledge, 2003, pp. 103–27.

Rikowski, Glenn. "Alien Life: Marx and the Future of the Human," *Historical Materialism: Research in Critical Marxist Theory* 11(2) (2003): 121–64.

Robinson, Kim Stanley. *The Wild Shore.* New York: Ace Books, 1984.

——. *The Gold Coast.* New York: Ace Books, 1988.

——. *Pacific Edge.* New York: Ace Books, 1990.

Ronnel, Avital. *Crack Wars: Literature Addiction, Mania.* Lincoln, NE: U of Nebraska P, 1992.

Rosenblum, Mary. *Chimera.* New York: Del Rey, 1993.

Rosenthal, Pam. "Jacked In: Fordism, Cyberpunk, Marxism." *Socialist Review* 21(1) (1991): 79–105.

Ross, Andrew. "Cyberpunk in Boystown." In *Strange Weather: Culture, Science, and Technology in the Age of Limits.* London: Verso, 1991, pp. 137–67.

——. *Strange Weather: Culture, Science, and Technology in the Age of Limits.* New York: Verso, 1991.

Rossi, Umberto. "Fourfold Symmetry: The Interplay of Fictional Levels in Five or More or Less Prestigious Novels by Philip K. Dick." *Extrapolation* 43(4) (2002): 398–419.

Roszak, Theodore. *The Making of a Counter Culture: Reflections on the Technocratic Society and its Youthful Opposition.* New York: Anchor, 1969.

Rucka, Greg. *Perfect Dark: Initial Vector.* New York: TOR, 2005.

Rucker, Rudy. *Software,* Harmondsworth: Penguin, 1985.

——. *Wetware,* New York: Avon Books, 1988.

Russ, Joanna. *The Female Man.* New York: Bantam, 1975.

Russo, Richard Paul. *Subterranean Gallery.* New York: Tor, 1989.

Ryman, Geoff. *Air; Or, Have Not Have.* New York: St. Martin's P, 2004.

——. "Rev. of *Vurt*, by Jeff Noon." *Foundation* 61 (1994): 90–92.

Sargent, Lyman Tower. "Utopia: The Problem of Definition." *Extrapolation* 16(2) (1975): 137–48.

Schroeder, Karl. *Permanence.* New York: Tor, 2002.

Scott, Melissa. *Trouble and Her Friends.* New York: Tor, 1994.

Seabury, Marcia Bundy. "The Monsters We Create: *Woman on the Edge of Time* and *Frankenstein*." *Critique* 42(2) (2001): 131–43.

Sedgewick, Cristina. "The Fork in the Road: Can Science Fiction Survive in Postmodern, Megacorporate America?" *Science-Fiction Studies* 18(1) (1991): 11–53.

Shaviro, Steven. "Broken Angels." 15 May 2007. Available at: www.shaviro.com/Blog/?p=281.

——. "Woken Furies." 7 June 2007. Available at: www.shaviro.com/Blog/?p=446.

Shelley, Mary. *Frankenstein.* Ed. D.L. Macdonald and Kathleen Scherf. 2nd ed. Peterborough, ON: Broadview, 2001.

——. "Introduction." In *Frankenstein.* Ed. D.L. Macdonald and Kathleen Scherf. 2nd edn. Peterborough, ON: Broadview, 2001, pp. 353–59.

Shepard, Lucius. *Green Eyes*. New York: Ace Books, 1984.

———. *Life During Wartime*. New York: Ace Books, 1987.

———. "Waiting for the Barbarians." *Journal Wired* 1 (1989): 107–18.

Shiner, Lewis. *Frontera*. New York: Baen, 1984.

———. *Deserted Cities of the Heart*. New York: Bantam, 1989.

———. "Confessions of an Ex-Cyberpunk." *New York Times*. 7 Jan. 1991. Available at: www.lysator.liu.se/lsff/mb-nr10/Saxat.txt (accessed 22 June 2001).

———. "Inside the Movement: Past, Present, and Future." In *Fiction 2000: Cyberpunk and the Future of Narrative*. Ed. George Slusser and Tom Shippey. Athens, GA: U of Georgia P, 1992, pp. 17–25.

Shippey, Tom. "Semiotic Ghosts and Ghostliness in the Work of Bruce Sterling." In *Fiction 2000: Cyberpunk and the Future of Narrative*. Ed. George Slusser and Tom Shippey. Athens, GA: U of Georgia P, 1992, pp. 208–20.

Shirley, John. *Eclipse*. New York: Popular Library/Warner Books, 1987.

———. "Make It Scream." *Thrust* 25 (1986): 15–16, 18.

———. "Letter to the Editor." *Thrust* 26 (1987): 32.

Silverberg, Robert. "Letter to the Editor." *Thrust* 26 (1987): 31.

Silverman, Kaja. *The Subject of Semiotics*. New York: Oxford UP, 1983.

Slocombe, Will. "A 'Majestic' Reflexivity: Machine-Gods and the Creation of the Playing Subject in *Deus Ex* and *Deus Ex: Invisible War*." In *Digital Gampleplay: Essays on the Nexus of Game and Gamer*. Ed. Nate Garrelts. Jefferson, NC: McFarland, 2005, pp. 36–51.

Slonczewski, Joan. *A Door into Ocean*. New York: Arbor House, 1986.

Slusser, George. "Literary MTV." In *Storming the Reality Studio: A Casebook of Cyberpunk and Postmodern Fiction*. Ed. Larry McCaffery. Durham, NC: Duke UP, 1991, pp. 334–42.

———. "The Frankenstein Barrier." In *Fiction 2000: Cyberpunk and the Future of Narrative*. Ed. George Slusser and Tom Shippey. Athens, GA: U of Georgia P, 1992, pp. 46–71.

Snider, John C. "Interview: Richard K. Morgan." (2003).Available at: www.scifidimensions.com/Apr03/richardkmorgan.htm. (accessed 8 June 2007).

Sofoulis, Zoë. "Cyberquake: Haraway's Manifesto." In *Prefiguring Cyberculture: An Intellectual History*. Ed. Darren Tofts, Annemarie Jonson, and Allesio Cavallero. Sydney, NSW: Power Publications, 2002, pp. 84–103.

Soja, Edward. *Postmodern Geographies: The Reassertion of Space in Critical Social Theory*. London: Verso, 1989.

Soyka, David. "Rev. of *Air*, by Geoff Ryman." SFSite.com. 2007. Availabler at: www.sfsite.com/02a/ai241.htm. (accessed 3 March 2007).

Spinrad, Norman. "The Neuromantics." *Isaac Asimov's Science Fiction Magazine* 10 (5) (1986): 180–90.

Sponsler, Claire. "William Gibson and the Death of Cyberpunk." In *Modes of the Fantastic: Selected Essays from the Twelfth International Conference on the Fantastic in the Arts*. Ed. Robert A. Latham and Robert A. Collins. Westport, CT: Greenwood P, 1995, pp. 47–55.

Stenger, Nicole. "Mind is a Leaking Rainbow." In *Cyberspace: First Steps*. Ed. Michael Benedikt. Cambridge, MA: MIT P, 1994, pp. 49–58.

Sterling, Bruce. "Green Days in Brunei." In *Crystal Express*. New York: Ace Books 1990, pp. 113–64.

———. *Crystal Express*. New York: Ace Books, 1990.

——. *Schismatrix.* Westminster, MD: Arbor House Publishing, 1985.

——. (ed.) *Mirrorshades: The Cyberpunk Anthology.* New York: Ace Books, 1986.

——. "Preface." In *Mirrorshades: The Cyberpunk Anthology.* Ed. Bruce Sterling. New York: Ace Books, 1986.

——. "Letter from Bruce Sterling." *REM* 7 (1987): 4–7.

——. *Islands in the Net.* New York: Ace Books, 1988.

——. "Slipstream." *Science Fiction Eye* 1(5) (1989): 77–80.

——. "Get the Bomb Off My Back," *New York Times*, October 13, 1991. Op-Ed page.

——. *Schismatrix Plus.* New York: Ace Books, 1996.

——. "Cyberpunk in the Nineties." 1998. Available at: www.streettech.com/bcp/ BCPtext/Manifestos/CPInThe90s.html (accessed 21 February 2007).

——. *Zeitgeist.* New York: Bantam, 2000.

Stewart, Doug. "The Compositonal Principles of Faulkner's *Light in August* and the Poetics of the Modern Novel." *Hasifrut* 2 (1991): 498–537. (In Hebrew).

Stiegler, Bernard. *Technics and Time, 1: The Fault of Epimetheus.* Trans. Richard Beardsworth. Stanford, CA: Stanford UP, 1998.

Stone, Allucquére Rosanne. "Will the Real Body Please Stand Up? Boundary Stories about Virtual Cultures." In *Cyberspace: First Steps.* Ed. Michael Benedikt. Cambridge, MA: MIT P, 1991, pp. 81–118.

Stross, Charles. "Exploring Distortions." *Locus* 51.2 (August 2003): 84–86.

Suvin, Darko. "On Gibson and Cyberpunk SF." *Foundation* 46 (1989): 40–51.

Swanwick, Michael. "A User's Guide to the Postmoderns." *Isaac Asimov's Science Fiction Magazine* 10(8) (1986): 20–53.

——. *Vacuum Flowers.* New York: Ace Books, 1987.

Tatsumi, Takayuki. "Some Real Mothers: An Interview with Samuel R. Delany." *Science Fiction Eye* 1(3) (1988): 5–11.

Thomson, Amy. *Virtual Girl.* New York: Ace Books, 1993.

Todorov, Tzvetan. *The Fantastic: A Structural Approach to a Literary Genre.* Trans. Richard Howard, Ithaca, NY: Cornell UP, 1975.

Toledano Redondo, Juan C. "From Socialist Realism to Anarchist Capitalism: Cuban Cyberpunk." *Science Fiction Studies* 32(3) (2005): 442–66.

Turner, Bryan S. *Medical Power and Social Knowledge.* New York: Sage, 1987.

——. *Regulating Bodies: Essays in Medical Sociology.* London: Routledge, 1992.

Vinge, Venor. *True Names: True Names and the Opening of the Cyberspace Frontier.* Ed. James Frenkel. New York: Tor, 2001, pp. 241–330.

Vint, Sherryl. *Bodies of Tomorrow: Technology, Subjectivity, Science Fiction.* Toronto: U of Toronto P, 2007.

Vint, Sherryl and Mark Bould. "All That Melts Into Air Is Solid: Rematerialising Capital in *Cube* and *Videodrome*," *Socialism and Democracy* 20(3) (2006): 217–43.

Virilio, Paul. *The Art of the Motor.* Trans. Julie Rose. Minneapolis: U of Minnesota P, 1995.

——. *Open Sky.* Trans. Julie Rose. London: Verso, 1997.

——. *Politics of the Very Worst.* Trans. Michael Cavaliere. New York: Semiotext(e), 1999.

——. *The Information Bomb.* Trans. Chris Turner. London: Verso, 2005.

Vonnegut, Kurt. *Player Piano.* New York: Dell, 1952.

Wagar, W. Warren. *Terminal Visions: The Literature of the Last Things.* Bloomington, IN: Indiana UP, 1982.

Waldby, Catherine. "The Instruments of Life: Frankenstein and Cyberculture." In *Prefiguring Cyberculture: An Intellectual History*. Ed. Darren Tofts, Annemarie Jonson, and Allesio Cavallero. Sydney, NSW: Power Publications, 2002, pp. 28–37.

Walsh, Martin. *The Brechtian Aspect of Radical Cinema: Essays by Martin Walsh*. Ed. Keith M Griffiths. London: BFI, 1981.

Watt-Evans, Lawrence. "Cyber Yes, Punk No." *Thrust* 28 (1987): 5–7.

Wertheim, Margaret. *The Pearly Gates of Cyberspace: A History of Space from Dante to the Internet*. New York: W. W. Norton & Company, 1999.

Whalen, Terence. "The Future of a Commodity: Notes Toward a Critique of Cyberpunk and the Information Age." *Science Fiction Studies* 19(1) (1992): 75–89.

Williams, Raymond. *The Country and the City*. London: Chatto & Windus, 1973.

———. "Utopia and Science Fiction." In *Problems in Materialism and Culture*. London: Verso, 1980, pp. 196–213.

———. "Jargon." In *Keywords*. Rev. ed. New York: Oxford UP, 1983, pp. 174–76.

Williams, Tad. *Otherland* Vol. One: *City of Golden Shadow*. New York: Daw, 1996.

———. *Otherland* Vol. Two: *River of Blue Fire*. New York: Daw, 1998.

———. *Otherland* Vol. Three: *Mountain of Black Glass*. New York: Daw, 1999.

———. *Otherland* Vol. Four: *Sea of Silver Light*. New York: Daw, 2002.

Williams, Walter Jon. *Hardwired*. New York: Tor, 1986.

———. *Voice of the Whirlwind*, London and Sydney: Futura, 1989.

Wills, David. *Prosthesis*. Stanford, Ca: Stanford UP, 1995.

Wilson, Elizabeth. "The Bohemianization of Mass Culture," *International Journal of Cultural Studies* 2.1(1999): 11–32.

Wolf, Mark J.P. *The Medium of the Video Game*. Ed. Mark J. P. Wolf. Austin, TX: U of Texas P, 2001.

Wolfe, Bernard. *Limbo*. New York: Carroll and Graff, 1987.

Wollheim, Donald A. *The Universe Makers: Science Fiction Today*. New York: Harper & Row, 1971.

Wolmark, Jenny. *Aliens and Others: Science Fiction and Postmodernism*. Iowa City: U of Iowa P, 1994.

———. "Cyberpunk, Cyborgs and Feminist Science Fiction." In *Feminist Contributions to the Literary Canon: Setting Standards of Taste*. Ed. Susanne Fendler. Lewiston, NY: Edwin Mellen P, 1997, pp. 139–79.

Yoke, Carl B. and Carol L. Robinson. *The Cultural Influences of William Gibson, The "Father" of Cyberpunk Science Fiction*.Lewiston, NY: Edwin Mellen P, 2007.

Zamyatin, Yevgeny. *We*. Trans. Mirra Ginsburg. New York: Avon, 1987.

Zeidner, Lisa. "Netscape." *The New York Times Book Review* 19 January 2003: 7.

Index

An environmentally friendly book printed and bound in England by www.printondemand-worldwide.com

PEFC Certified

This product is
from sustainably
managed forests
and controlled
sources

www.pefc.org

This book is made entirely of chain-of-custody materials

#0025 - 230412 - C0 - 229/152/15 - CB